The Philosophical Writings of Descartes

VOLUME III

Volumes I and II provide a completely new translation of the philosophical works of Descartes, based on the best available Latin and French texts. Volume III contains 207 of Descartes' letters, over half of which have not been translated into English. It also incorporates, in its entirety, Anthony Kenny's celebrated translation of selected philosophical letters, first published in 1970. In conjunction with Volumes I and II it is designed to meet the widespread demand for a comprehensive, accurate and authoritative edition of Descartes' philosophical writings in clear and readable modern English.

Contents

D0840135

The Philosophical Writings of
DESCARTES

VOLUME III
The Correspondence

translated by
JOHN COTTINGHAM
ROBERT STOOTHOFF
DUGALD MURDOCH
ANTHONY KENNY

CAMBRIDGE
UNIVERSITY PRESS

Published by the Press Syndicate of the University of Cambridge
The Pitt Building, Trumpington Street, Cambridge CB2 1RP
40 West 20th Street, New York, NY 10011-4211 USA
10 Stamford Road, Oakleigh, Melbourne 3166, Australia

© in this edition Cambridge University Press 1991

This edition first published 1991
Reprinted 1995

Printed in Great Britain by Athenæum Press Ltd, Gateshead, Tyne & Wear

British Library cataloguing in publication data
Descartes, René, *1596–1650*
The philosophical writings of Descartes.
Vol. III, The correspondence.
1. French philosophy
I. Title   II. Cottingham, John
194

Library of Congress cataloguing in publication data
Descartes, René, 1596–1650.
The philosophical writings of Descartes.
Vol. 3 also translated by Anthony Kenny.
Includes bibliographical references and index.
1. Philosophy.   I. Title.
B1837.C67P481325   1984   194   84–9399
ISBN 0–521–24594 X (v. 1)
ISBN 0–521–28807 X (pbk:v. 1)
ISBN 0–521–24595 8 (v. 2)
ISBN 0–521–28808 8 (pbk:v. 2)
ISBN 0–521–40323 5 (v. 3)

ISBN 0–521–40323 5 hardback
ISBN 0–521–42350 3 paperback

Contents

Introduction

This volume completes the project, begun in the 1980s, to provide an authoritative and comprehensive new English translation of the philosophical writings of Descartes, based on the original Latin and French texts. The first two volumes of the translation, which appeared in 1985 (known as 'CSM'),[1] contained the *Early Writings*, *Rules for the Direction of our Native Intelligence*, *The World* and *Treatise on Man*, *Discourse and Essays*, *Principles of Philosophy*, *Comments on a Certain Broadsheet*, *Description of the Human Body* and *The Passions of the Soul* (Volume One); and the *Meditations*, *Objections and Replies* and *The Search for Truth* (Volume Two). But for scholars and students of Descartes there is, in addition to the large corpus of his published works, another formidable body of source material which is indispensable for a proper understanding of his philosophy: the correspondence. This third and final volume of *The Philosophical Writings of Descartes* is devoted to Descartes' letters.

Descartes himself attached great importance to his letters – an extraordinarily rich and wide-ranging body of detailed commentary and analysis covering every aspect of his philosophical system. Apart from a handful of letters, most of this material was not available to English readers until the publication in 1970 of Anthony Kenny's *Descartes: Philosophical Letters* (known as 'K').[2] This valuable anthology, which has gained wide currency among Anglophone Cartesian scholars, is now out of print; but we are extremely fortunate in that it has been possible to incorporate it in its entirety into the present volume. To serve the more comprehensive aims of the present edition, however, we have sifted through the whole of Descartes' extant correspondence with the purpose of extracting all the material of significant philosophical interest. The result is a greatly augmented collection ('CSM–K'), built round the nucleus of K but more than

1 *The Philosophical Writings of Descartes*, tr. J. Cottingham, R. Stoothoff and D. Murdoch (2 vols., Cambridge: Cambridge University Press, 1985).
2 *Descartes: Philosophical Letters*, tr. A. Kenny (Oxford: Oxford University Press, 1970; repr. Oxford: Blackwell, 1980). Material from this edition is reproduced below by arrangement with Oxford University Press, Basil Blackwell Ltd and the University of Minnesota Press.

double the size of the original anthology. In addition to the 100 items appearing in K, we have translated a further 106 letters not previously available in English. As with CSM Volumes One and Two, we have construed the term 'philosophical' in the broad sense in which Descartes himself understood it; our aim has thus been to include not just writings of an epistemological and metaphysical nature, but the widest possible selection of material on physics, cosmology, theology, mechanics, physiology, psychology and ethics which is likely to be of interest to students of philosophy and allied disciplines.

Descartes' love of solitude, and his self-imposed exile from France for much of his life, led him to depend heavily on correspondents for information about developments in the learned world, and for critical discussion of his own ideas. He preserved drafts of his letters, and his biographer Adrien Baillet aptly comments that 'the most important of his posthumous works is the inestimable treasure of letters' which were found in a chest after the philosopher's death in Stockholm in 1650.[1] The treasure was almost lost when a vessel carrying it to France sank in the Seine,[2] but the manuscripts were recovered and published in Paris by Descartes' disciple Claude Clerselier in three volumes (*Lettres de M. Descartes* (1657, 1659, 1667)). The subtitle to the first volume of 119 letters announces that they deal with the 'most important questions of morals, physics, medicine and mathematics'; the subsequent volumes were chiefly devoted to scientific topics. Clerselier's edition, though it remains the prime source for Descartes' correspondence, was far from a complete collection of the surviving letters, and the work of revising and augmenting it (which has occupied Cartesian scholars ever since) began soon after Clerselier's death, when there was a fruitful collaboration between his literary executor, Jean-Baptiste Le Grand, and Adrien Baillet.[3] In the nineteenth century a considerable number of hitherto unpublished letters appeared, notably in the eleven-volume edition of the *Oeuvres de Descartes* by Victor Cousin (1824–6), and the *Oeuvres inédites de Descartes* published by Foucher de Careil (1860). The monumental edition of Descartes' works by Charles Adam and Paul Tannery (Paris, 1887–1913) devoted its first five volumes to the correspondence; a further batch of 141 letters between Descartes and Constantijn Huygens was discovered and edited by Leon Roth at Oxford in 1926. An eight-volume edition of the complete correspondence was published by C. Adam and G. Milhaud between 1936 and 1963; though it contains a wealth of informa-

1 A. Baillet, *La Vie de M. Des-Cartes* (Paris: Horthemels, 1691; photographic reprint, Hildesheim: Olms, 1972), vol. II, p. 400.
2 Baillet, vol. II, p. 428.
3 Described in the preface to Baillet's biography, vol. I, pp. xxiiff.

tive annotation, this edition is unsatisfactory in many respects (some of which are noted in the introduction to K), and as the standard text of Descartes' letters it has now been superseded by the first five volumes of the definitive new edition of Adam and Tannery published by the Centre National de la Recherche Scientifique.[1] Our own translations are based on this revised edition of 'AT', and running marginal references to the appropriate volume and page numbers are provided throughout. (The marginal references are placed in parentheses where they do not mark the beginning of a page in AT.) The new edition of AT provides a detailed apparatus criticus for each letter, together with introductions and notes giving the manuscript sources, and discussing the attribution of dates and addressees, which often depends on indirect evidence. Considerations of space have prevented us from including this type of supplementary information here (to do so would have at least doubled the size of the volume); but where important question marks remain over the dates or addressees of particular letters, we have briefly indicated as much in footnotes, sometimes drawing on the information noted in F. Alquié's invaluable three-volume edition of Descartes' philosophical works.[2] We have followed the convention in AT of placing the names of addressees within square brackets, where they are conjectural or based on indirect evidence.

The editorial and translating work for the present volume has been divided as follows. The preparation of the text for the press and the overall selection of material have been jointly undertaken by John Cottingham, Robert Stoothoff and Dugald Murdoch. Anthony Kenny's translation has been followed throughout for the letters which appear in his selection of 1970; these are designated by 'K' in our table of letters translated, followed by the page numbers of his edition. The opportunity has been taken, however, to provide a number of emendations (mostly of a minor nature) to the translation, and to make some other revisions, mainly to ensure consistency and conformity of style with CSM Volumes One and Two. In the case of some of the letters which were abridged by Kenny, a certain amount of additional material has been newly translated. With respect both to this material, and to the letters which appear for the first time in this volume, Dugald Murdoch has been responsible for translating all the texts from the years 1631–9, John Cottingham for those dating from 1640–2, and Robert Stoothoff for those dating from 1643–50. All three of us have, however, scrutinized each other's work, and made corrections and numerous suggestions for improvement, many of which

---

1 *Oeuvres de Descartes* publiées par C. Adam & P. Tannery. Nouvelle présentation (12 vols., Paris: Vrin, 1964–76).
2 F. Alquié (ed.), *Oeuvres philosophiques de Descartes* (3 vols., Paris: Garnier, 1963–73).

have found their way into the final version. In addition to the letters, we have taken the opportunity to include substantial extracts from an important exchange between Descartes and Frans Burman based on the notes taken by Burman when he visited the philosopher at his home at Egmond Binnen near Alkmaar in 1648. The translation of this material, known as the 'Conversation with Burman', is by John Cottingham, and follows the Latin text in AT v.[1]

Descartes wrote with equal fluency in Latin and French; over half his letters are in French, but he used Latin in more formal letters and when writing to non-Francophone correspondents. For each letter, the original language is indicated by the symbol (L) or (F) in the table of letters translated. Quite frequently, in the course of a letter written in French, Descartes lapses into Latin, particularly when quoting from his own Latin works, or when discussing how his own philosophical terminology relates to that of his scholastic predecessors or opponents. Such occurrences of Latin within a French context are indicated by daggers, thus † ... †. For reasons of space it has been necessary to abridge some of the letters, and omitted material is indicated by three dots, thus ... Our aim throughout has been to make the translations as accurate as possible while at the same time attempting to produce clear and readable modern English.

Quite apart from their philosophical richness, Descartes' letters provide a wealth of information about his personal outlook on life and his attitudes to the scientific and religious issues which dominated the first half of the seventeenth century. We have supplied brief footnotes explicating any historical or personal references which may be obscure to the modern reader. A table at the end of the volume gives brief biographical details of Descartes' correspondents. We have also included, at the start of the volume, a short chronological table of Descartes' life and works, and, at the end, a table of passages from Descartes' published works which are commented on or discussed in the letters. Finally, we have included a comprehensive index covering both persons and topics; we hope that this, in conjunction with the indexes in CSM Volumes One and Two, will be of assistance to scholars and students working in particular areas of Descartes' philosophy.

Descartes himself described his philosophical ambitions in superhuman terms: *infinitum opus, nec unius* (AT x 157). The infinitely lesser task of interpreting his writings accurately for an English-speaking audience is none the less a daunting one, and we are indebted to the many editors and

---

1 The translation is taken (with minor corrections) from the English version provided in *Descartes' Conversation with Burman*, ed. J. Cottingham (Oxford: Clarendon, 1976), and is reproduced below by permission of Oxford University Press.

commentators (especially those mentioned above) who have established the Cartesian texts and enriched our understanding of them. Following the publication of CSM Volumes One and Two, we were grateful to readers for their suggestions for improvement and the many other points of philosophical and historical interest which were drawn to our notice, and it is our hope that the present volume will in due course benefit from similar attention. As for the shortcomings that remain in the mean time, we can only once again plead that weakness which the author of the Sixth Meditation declared to be inseparable from the human condition: *natura hominis non potest non esse fallax.*

J.C.

Chronological table of Descartes' life and works

1596 born at La Haye near Tours on 31 March

1606–14 attends Jesuit college of La Flèche in Anjou[1]

1616 takes law degree at University of Poitiers

1618 goes to Holland; joins army of Prince Maurice of Nassau; meets Isaac Beeckman; composes a short treatise on music, the *Compendium Musicae*

1619 travels in Germany; 10 November: has vision of new mathematical and scientific system

1622 returns to France; during next few years spends time in Paris, but also travels in Europe

1628 composes *Rules for the Direction of our Native Intelligence*; leaves for Holland, which is to be his home until 1649, though with frequent changes of address

1629 begins working on *The World*

1633 condemnation of Galileo; abandons plans to publish *The World*

1635 birth of Descartes' natural daughter Francine, baptized 7 August (died 1640)

1637 publishes *Discourse on the Method*, with *Optics*, *Meteorology* and *Geometry*

1641 *Meditations on First Philosophy* published, together with *Objections and Replies* (first six sets)

1642 second edition of *Meditations* published, with all seven sets of *Objections and Replies* and *Letter to Dinet*

1643 Cartesian philosophy condemned at the University of Utrecht; Descartes' long correspondence with Princess Elizabeth of Bohemia begins

1644 visits France; *Principles of Philosophy* published

1647 awarded a pension by King of France; publishes *Comments on*

---

1 Descartes is known to have stayed at La Flèche for eight or nine years, but the exact dates of his arrival and departure are uncertain. Baillet places Descartes' admission in 1604, the year of the College's foundation (A. Baillet, *La Vie de M. Des-Cartes* (Paris: Horthemels, 1691; photographic reprint Hildesheim: Olms, 1972), vol. II, p. 18).

Letters translated

Letters

TO BEECKMAN, 24 JANUARY 1619

I have received your letter, which I was expecting. On first glancing over   151
it, I was delighted to see your notes on music. What clearer evidence could
there be that you had not forgotten me? But there was something else I was
looking for, and that the most important, namely news about what you
have been doing, what you are doing, and how you are. You ought not to
think that all I care about is science, I care about you, and not just your
intellect – even if that is the greatest part of you – but the whole man.

As for me, in my usual state of indolence I have hardly put a title to the
books which, on your advice, I am going to write. But you should not think
me so lazy as to fritter away all my time. On the contrary, I have never been
more usefully employed – but on matters which your intellect, occupied   152
with more elevated subjects, would no doubt despise, looking down on
them from the lofty heights of science, namely painting, military architecture and above all, Flemish. You will soon see what progress I have made
in this language, for I am coming to Middelburg, God willing, at the
beginning of Lent . . .

If you look carefully at what I wrote on discords and the rest of my   (153)
treatise on music,[1] you will find that all the points I made on the intervals
of harmonies, scales and discords were demonstrated mathematically; but
the account I gave is too brief, confused, and not properly worked out. But
enough on these matters; I shall say more some other time. In the mean
time you can be sure that I shall not forget you, any more than I shall forget
the Muses who have bound me to you with an unbreakable bond of
affection.

TO BEECKMAN, 26 MARCH 1619

You will allow me, I trust, to bid you farewell by letter, since I was not   154
able to do so in person when I left. I returned here[2] six days ago; since then

---

1 Descartes' early work *Compendium Musicae*, written at the request of Beeckman towards
  the end of 1618, was first published in 1650, the year of Descartes' death. See AT x 89.
2 Breda, Holland.

I have been cultivating my Muse more diligently than ever before. In that short time, with the aid of my compass, I have discovered four remarkable and completely new demonstrations.[1]

155   The first has to do with the famous problem of dividing an angle into any number of equal parts. The other three have to do with three sorts of cubic equations: the first sort are equations between a whole number, a root number and a cube root; the second between a whole number, a square root, and a cube root; and the third between a whole number, a root number, a square root and a cube root.[2] I have found three sorts of demonstrations for these three sorts of equations, each of which has to be applied to different terms owing to the difference between the signs + and −. My account of this is not yet complete, but what I have found to apply in one case can easily be extended to others. It will thus be possible to solve four times as many problems, and much more difficult ones, than was possible by means of ordinary algebra. I reckon there are thirteen different kinds of cubic equations, as there are only three kinds of common equa-

156   tions: $1J$ & $oK + oN$, $oK - oN$, and $oN - oK$.[3] Another thing I am investigating at present is the extraction of roots consisting of many different terms. If I find out how to do this, as I hope I shall, I shall really put this science in order, if only I can overcome my innate indolence and fate gives me the freedom to live as I choose.

Let me be quite open with you about my project. What I want to produce is not something like Lull's *Ars Brevis*,[4] but rather a completely

157   new science, which would provide a general solution of all possible equations involving any sort of quantity, whether continuous or discrete, each according to its nature. In arithmetic, for example, certain problems can be solved by means of rational numbers, while others require irrational numbers, and others again we can only imagine how to solve, but not actually solve. So I hope I shall be able to demonstrate that certain problems involving continuous quantities can be solved only by means of straight lines or circles, while others can be solved only by means of curves produced by a single motion, such as the curves that can be drawn with the new compasses (in my view these are just as exact and geometrical as those

1 Cf. Descartes' *Geometry*: AT VI 391, 442f.
2 I.e. equations of the following sort: $\pm a \pm bx = x^3$, $\pm a \pm bx^2 = x^3$, $\pm a \pm bx \pm cx^2 = x^3$
3 'Common equations' are equations of the second degree. Descartes is employing Clavius' notation here: N denotes a whole number, J denotes a square number, K a root number, and o the unknown quantity. In modern notation the three kinds of equation mentioned here are: $x^2 = x + b$, $x^2 = ax - b$, and $x^2 = b - ax$. The fourth kind, $x^2 = -ax - b$, is excluded, since equations with negative roots were regarded as impossible at the beginning of the seventeenth century.
4 The *Compendium on Method* (*Ars Brevis*) of Raymond Lull (1232–1315), written in 1308 and printed in 1481, purports to provide a universal method of solving problems.

drawn with ordinary compasses), and others still can be solved only by means of curves generated by distinct independent motions which are surely only imaginary, such as the notorious quadratic curve.[1] There is, I think, no imaginable problem which cannot be solved, at any rate by such lines as these. I am hoping to demonstrate what sorts of problems can be solved exclusively in this or that way, so that almost nothing in geometry will remain to be discovered. This is of course a gigantic task, and one hardly suitable for one person; indeed it is an incredibly ambitious project. But through the confusing darkness of this science I have caught a glimpse   158 of some sort of light, and with the aid of this I think I shall be able to dispel even the thickest obscurities . . .

After I left Middelburg I reflected also on your art of navigation, and in   (159) fact discovered a method that would enable me to work out, simply by observing the stars, how many degrees east or west I had travelled from some place I knew, no matter where on earth it might be or whether I had been asleep during the journey and had no idea how long it lasted. It is hardly a subtle discovery, and I find it hard to believe that no one has made it before now. I rather think it has been neglected because of the difficulty   160 of applying it; for in order to make the measurement we would need an instrument in which the interval of one degree would be no bigger than that of two minutes on the instruments currently used to work out the height of the pole star; so the measurement could not be very exact – although astronomers measure minutes and seconds, and even much smaller intervals, with existing instruments. But if that is the only draw-back with it, I would be very surprised if sailors thought it such a useless discovery. So I would like to know for sure whether or not a similar discovery has been made before. If you know of any such, write and tell me about it.[2] It is still a confused speculation in my head, but I would work it out more exactly if I suspected it was as novel as it was certain . . .

TO BEECKMAN, 23 APRIL 1619   AT X

I received your letter almost the same day you sent it. I did not want to   162 leave here[3] without writing to you once more, to keep up what will surely be a lasting friendship between us. But do not expect anything from my Muse at the moment, for while I am preparing for the journey about to begin tomorrow, my mind has already set out on the voyage. I am still

1 A curved line discovered by Hippias (fl. 50 B.C.), who may have used it to trisect an angle, and so called because it was used in attempts to square the circle.
2 The method in question had already been proposed by Gemma Frisius (1508–55) and Johannes Kepler (1571–1630).
3 Breda, Holland.

uncertain 'where fate may take me, where my foot may rest'.¹ The
preparations for war have not yet led to my being summoned to Germany,
but I suspect that many men will be called to arms, though there will be no
outright fighting. If that should happen, I shall travel about in Denmark,
Poland and Hungary until such time as I can find a safer route, one not
occupied by marauding soldiers, or until I have definitely heard that war is
likely to be waged. If I should stop somewhere, as I hope I shall, I promise
to see that my *Mechanics* or *Geometry*² is put in order, and I will salute you
as the promoter and prime author of my studies.

163   For it was you alone who roused me from my state of indolence, and
reawakened the learning which by then had almost disappeared from my
memory; and when my mind strayed from serious pursuits, it was you who
led it back to worthier things. Thus, if perhaps I should produce something
not wholly to be despised, you can rightly claim it all as your own; and I for
my part shall send it to you without fail, so that you may have the benefit of
it, and correct it into the bargain. I did as much the other day, when I sent
you something on nautical matters, which (as if you had read my thoughts)
is identical with what you sent me, for your discovery about the moon is
the same as mine.³ I thought, however, that the method could be made
easier with the aid of certain instruments; but I was mistaken.

As for the other things which in my previous letter I prided myself with
having discovered, I really did discover these with the aid of the new
compasses; there I am not mistaken. But I shall not send these to you in
instalments, for I am thinking of writing a complete work on the subject
some time which, I believe, will be novel and of some merit. For the last
month I have laid aside my studies, because my mind was so worn out by
164   these discoveries that I had not the strength to discover the other things in
this area which I had planned to investigate. But I have the strength to keep
my memory of you ever fresh.

AT X   TO BEECKMAN, 29 APRIL 1619

164   I do not want to miss any opportunity of writing to you, and of
demonstrating my affection for you and my remembrance of you, which
the cares of travel have in no way dulled.

Three days ago I had a conversation about Lull's *Ars Parva*⁴ with a
learned man whom I met in an inn at Dordrecht. He boasted that he was
able to apply Lull's method, and to do this so skilfully that he could talk for

---

1 An allusion to Virgil's *Aeneid*, III, 7.
2 The projected *Geometry*, published in 1637.
3 I.e. the discovery that the position of the moon can be used to determine one's location.
4 See footnote 4, p. 2 above.

a whole hour on any subject you cared to mention; and if he was required   165
to talk for a further hour on the same topic, he would find fresh things to
say, and could even continue for twenty-four hours at a stretch. Whether
you believe him, you will see for yourself. He was a somewhat loquacious
old fellow, whose rather bookish learning dwelt not so much in his brain as
on the tip of his tongue.

I questioned him with some care, to see whether this method consists in
arranging dialectical headings in a certain way and deriving arguments
from them. He said that it did, but he added that in their writings neither
Lull nor Agrippa[1] had supplied certain keys which are, as he put it,
essential for revealing the secrets of the method. I suspect that his motive
for saying this was more to impress someone with little learning than to
speak the truth.

I would gladly go into this question if I had the book; but since you have
it, please look into it if you have the time, and let me know whether you
think there is anything of intellectual substance in the said method. I have
such confidence in your intelligence that I am sure you will easily see what
the omitted points are, if any, that are essential for an understanding of the
rest – the 'keys', as he calls them. I wanted to write to you about this so as
to miss no opportunity of discussing some learned question with you, just
as you asked. If I make the same demand on you, please do not go to too
much trouble.

Today I am setting out on a voyage to Denmark. I shall spend some time
in Copenhagen, where I shall await a letter from you. Ships leave here for   166
that city every day. Though you do not know what inn I shall be staying at,
I shall make a point of inquiring among the sailors whether they have a
letter for me; so it is not likely to go astray. . .

TO GIBIEUF, 18 JULY 1629   AT I

. . . M. Ferrier[2] will give me some news, and I do not expect you to go to   (17)
the trouble of sending me any; but I expect to put you to some trouble
when I complete a little treatise that I am starting.[3] I would not have told
you it was under way unless I feared that the length of time it needs would
make you forget your promise to correct it and give it the finishing touches;
for I do not expect to complete it within two or three years, and perhaps in

1 Henricus Cornelius Agrippa of Nettesheim (1486–1535), author of *De Incertitudine et*
  Vanitate Scientiarum (1527).
2 Jean Ferrier, an instrument maker with whom Descartes had hoped to co-operate in the
  construction of telescopes.
3 Perhaps the short treatise on metaphysics mentioned in the letter to Mersenne of 25
  November 1630; see p. 29 below.

the end I shall decide to burn it, or at least not let it out of my hands or those of my friends without giving it careful scrutiny. If I am not clever enough to produce something worth while, I shall at any rate try to be astute enough not to publish my shortcomings.

TO MERSENNE, 8 OCTOBER 1629

22   I do not think I was so uncivil as to ask you not to put any more questions to me; your kindly taking the trouble to send them to me does me too much honour, and I learn more from them than I do from any other sort of study. But no doubt I should have asked you not to take it unkindly if I do not make the effort to reply as precisely as I would try to do if I were not wholly taken up with other thoughts; for my mind is not so strong that I can devote it to many tasks at once, and as I never make any discoveries except through a long train of diverse considerations, I must devote myself

23   wholly to a subject when I wish to investigate some particular aspect of it. I had experience of this recently when I was investigating the cause of the phenomenon[1] which you write about in your letter. Just over two months ago one of my friends showed me a very full description of the phenomenon and asked me what I thought of it. Before I could give him my answer I had to interrupt my current work in order to make a systematic study of the whole of meteorology. But I think I can now give some explanation of the phenomenon. I have decided to write a little treatise[2] on the topic; this will give the explanation of the colours of the rainbow (a topic which has given me more trouble than any other) and for all sublunary phenomena in general. That is why I asked you for a description of the phenomenon at Rome in particular; I wanted to know whether it agreed with the description I had seen. There was this difference: you say that the phenomenon had been seen at Tivoli, whereas the other account says that it was seen at Frascati, which is called *Tusculum* in Latin. Please tell me whether you know for sure that it did appear at Tivoli, and what that place is called in Latin. I have plenty of time to await your letters, for I have not yet begun to write and I am in no hurry.

     Moreover, please do not speak to anyone about this, for I have decided to publish this treatise as a specimen of my philosophy and to hide behind

24   the picture[3] in order to hear what people will say about it. It is one of the most beautiful subjects I could choose, and I shall try to expound it in such

---

1 Parhelia, bright spots of light on the ring of a solar halo.
2 The future *Meteorology*, published with the *Discourse on the Method* in 1637.
3 I.e. to publish the work anonymously; the allusion is to a story about the Greek painter Apelles.

a way that those who understand only Latin[1] will find it a pleasure to read. I would prefer it if it were printed in Paris rather than here;[2] and if it would not be asking too much, I should like to send it to you when it is finished, so that you could correct it and place it with a publisher . . .

As for the other question, I needed a long time to think about this, for (27) there are many different forces to take into account. Firstly, if the weight in question was in a vacuum where the air would not impede it, and we

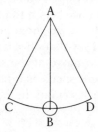

supposed that when pushed by a force twice as great it could travel the same path in half the time, the calculation I made earlier is as follows. If the cord is 1 foot long and it takes the weight 1 second to go from C to B, it will take $\frac{4}{3}$ seconds when the cord is 2 feet long; if the cord is 4 feet long, it will   28 take $\frac{16}{9}$ seconds; if 8 feet long, $\frac{64}{27}$ seconds; if 16 feet long, $\frac{256}{81}$ seconds (which is not much more than 3 seconds), and so on in due order . . .

TO MERSENNE, 13 NOVEMBER 1629   AT I

I am very sorry about the trouble which you have been put to in sending   69 me your description of the phenomenon,[3] for it is just like the one I had   70 seen. I am greatly indebted to you for this all the same, and even more indebted for your offer to see to the printing of the little treatise[4] I am planning to write. But I should tell you that it will not be ready for over a year. For since I wrote to you a month ago, I have done nothing more than sketch an outline of the contents. Rather than explaining just one phenomenon I have decided to explain all the phenomena of nature, that is to say, the whole of physics.[5] I like my present plan much better than any other I have ever had, for I think I have found a way of unfolding all my thoughts

---

1 Descartes later decided to write in French; cf. AT VI 77; CSM I 151.
2 This letter was probably written in Amsterdam.
3 Parhelia; see footnote 1, p. 6 above.
4 The future *Meteorology*.
5 This projected larger work was to become *The World or Treatise on Light*, which Descartes familiarly refers to as his 'Physics' (later on his familiar title for the *Principles of Philosophy*).

which some will find satisfying and with which others will have no cause to disagree . . .

(71)   As for your question concerning the basis of my calculation of the time it takes the weight to fall when it is attached to a cord 2, 4, 8 and 16 feet long as the case may be, I shall have to include this in my *Physics*. But you should not have to wait for that; so I shall try to explain it. Firstly, I make the assumption that the motion impressed on a body at one time remains in it for all time unless it is taken away by some other cause;[1] in other words,[2]

72   in a vacuum that which has once begun to move keeps on moving at the same speed. Thus suppose that a weight at point A is impelled by its own heaviness towards point C: I say that once it begins to move, if it loses its heaviness, it will continue to move at the same speed till it reaches C, falling from A to B at the same speed as it falls from B to C. Of course it does not lose its heaviness; it retains its heaviness, and this pushes it

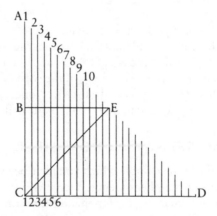

downwards, giving it at each moment a new force which makes it fall. Consequently it covers the distance BC much more quickly than the distance AB, since in the former case it retains all the impetus it had when it covered the distance AB, and acquires an additional impetus on account of its heaviness, which impels it afresh at each moment. The rate at which its speed increases is shown in triangle ABCDE. Line 1 signifies the force of the speed impressed at moment 1, the second line signifying the force impressed at moment 2, the third the force at moment 3, and so on in due

---

1 The law of inertia. The law may have been suggested to Descartes by Beeckman; see AT x 58. It was put forward by Galileo in his *Dialogue Concerning the Two Chief World Systems* (1632), though he had thought of it at least fifteen years before.

2 The following passage, which is in Latin, dates probably from 1617–19; see AT x 75–7,

order. Thus we get the triangle ACD, which represents the increase in the speed of the weight as it falls from A to C, the triangle ABE representing the increase in the speed over the first half of the distance covered, and the trapezium BCDE representing the increase in the speed over the second half of the distance covered, namely BC. Since the trapezium is three times the size of triangle ABE (as is obvious), it follows that the speed of the weight as it falls from B to C is three times as great as what it was from A to B. If, for example, it takes 3 seconds to fall from A to B, it will take 1 second to fall from B to C. Again, in 4 seconds it will cover twice the distance it covers in 3, and hence in 12 seconds it will cover twice the distance it covers in 9, and in 16 seconds four times the distance it covers in 9, and so on in due order.

73

As for the motion of a weight attached to a cord, exactly the same applies as was demonstrated in the case of a weight falling in a straight line. So far as the force which moves the weight is concerned, it is not necessary to consider the arc GH through which it moves, but only the sine KH which is the proportional distance through which it falls. So it is just as if the weight fell in a straight line from K to H, so far as the motion due to heaviness is concerned. But if you take the resistance of the air into account, this resistance is much greater and of a different sort when the motion is along the curved line GH than when along the straight line KH.[1]

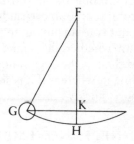

As for the cause of the air resistance which you asked me about, in my view it is impossible to answer this question since †it does not come under the heading of knowledge.† For the air resistance varies, depending on

---

1 The text resumes in French. In the diagram Descartes wrongly takes line ABC to represent time, instead of the distance travelled; this leads him to take the distance travelled as being proportional, not to the square of the time ($d = \frac{1}{2}gt^2$), but to a power of the time, the exponent of which is $\dfrac{\log 2}{\log \frac{4}{3}}$.

whether it is hot or cold, dry or wet, clear or cloudy, and numerous other
factors. Moreover, the same can be said in general about all the questions
you raise about air resistance: the degree of resistance varies depending on
74 whether the weight is made of lead or iron or wood, on whether it is round
or square or some other shape, and numerous other factors.

As for the to and fro motions of a cord which is plucked by the thumb
away from its straight-line position, I say that in a vacuum these motions
decrease in geometrical proportion. That is to say, if CD is 4 at the first

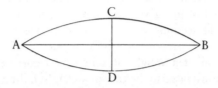

motion and 2 at the second motion, it will be only 1 at the third motion;
and if it is 9 at the first motion and 6 at the second, it will be 4 at the third,
and so on in due order. Now as a consequence of this, the speed of the
motion always decreases in the same proportion, provided the last to and
fro motions take as much time as the first ones. I say 'in a vacuum', for in
air I believe that the motions will be a little slower towards the end than
they were at the beginning, because the motion will have less force then,
and hence will not so easily overcome the air resistance. Yet I am not sure
about this; perhaps on the contrary the air even aids the motion at the end,
since the motion is circular. But you can put this to the test with your ear, if
you investigate the question whether the sound of a plucked cord is
sharper or flatter at the end than at the beginning; for if it is flatter, that
means that the air is retarding it, whereas if it is sharper, that means that
the air is making it move more quickly . . .

TO MERSENNE, 20 NOVEMBER 1629

76   This project for a new language seems more remarkable at first than I
find it to be upon close examination. There are only two things to learn in
any language: the meaning of the words and the grammar. As for the
meaning of the words, your man does not promise anything special; for in
his fourth proposition he says 'the language is to be translated with the aid
of a dictionary', and any linguist can do as much in all common languages
without his aid. I am sure that if you gave M. Hardy[1] a good dictionary of

---

1 Probably Descartes' friend Claude Hardy (1605–78), a mathematician who is reported to
  have known thirty-six oriental languages.

Chinese or any other language, and a book in the same language, he would 77
guarantee to work out its meaning.

The reason why not everyone could do the same is the difficulty of the
grammar. That, I imagine, is your man's whole secret; but there is no
difficulty in it. If you make a language with only one pattern of conjuga-
tion, declension and construction, and with no defective or irregular verbs
introduced by corrupt usage, and if the nouns and verbs are inflected and
the sentences constructed by prefixes or suffixes attached to the primitive
words, and all the prefixes and suffixes are listed in the dictionary, it is no
wonder if ordinary people learn to write the language with the aid of a
dictionary in less than six hours, which is the gist of his first proposition.

The second says 'once this language has been learnt, the others can be
learnt as dialects of it'. This is just sales talk. He does not say how long it
would take to learn them, but only that they could be regarded as dialects
of his language, which he takes as primitive because it does not have the
grammatical irregularities of the others. Notice that in his dictionary, for
the primitive words, he could use the words of every language as synonyms
of each other. For instance, to signify *love*, he could use *aimer, amare,*
φιλεῖν, and so on; a Frenchman, adding to *aimer* the affix for a noun, will
form the noun corresponding to *amour*, a Greek will add the same affix to
φιλεῖν, and so on. Consequently his sixth proposition, about 'inventing a 78
script', is very easy to understand. For if he put into his dictionary a single
symbol corresponding to *aimer, amare,* φιλεῖν and each of the synonyms,
a book written in such symbols could be translated by all who possessed
the dictionary.

The fifth proposition, too, it seems to me, is simply self-advertisement.
As soon as I see the word *arcanum* [mystery] in any proposition I begin to
suspect it. I think he merely means that he can teach the languages he
names more easily than the average instructor, because he has reflected
much about their grammars in order to simplify his own.

There remains the third proposition, which *is* altogether a mystery to
me. He says that he will expound the thoughts of the writers of antiquity
from the words they used, by taking each word as expressing the true
definition of the thing spoken of. Strictly this means that he will expound
the thoughts of these writers by giving their words a sense they never gave
them themselves; which is absurd. But perhaps he means it differently.

Now this plan of reforming our grammar, or rather inventing a new one,
to be learnt in five or six hours, and applicable to all languages, would be of
general utility if everyone agreed to adopt it. But I see two difficulties
which stand in the way.

The first is discordant combinations of letters which would often make 79
the sounds unpleasant and intolerable to the ear. It is to remedy this defect

that all the differences in inflexion of words have been introduced by usage; and it is impossible for your author to have avoided the difficulty while making his grammar universal among different nations; for what is easy and pleasant in our language is coarse and intolerable to Germans, and so on. The most that he can have done is to have avoided discordant combinations of syllables in one or two languages; and so his universal language would do only for a single country. But we do not need to learn a new language to talk only to Frenchmen.

The second difficulty is in learning the words of the language. It is true that if each person uses as primitive words the words of his own language, he will not have much difficulty; but in that case he will be understood only by the people of his own country unless he writes down what he wants to say and the person who wants to understand him takes the trouble to look up all the words in the dictionary; and this is too burdensome to become a regular practice. If your man wants people to learn primitive words common to every language, he will not find anyone willing to take the trouble. It would be easier to get everyone to agree to learn Latin or some other language in current use than one where there are as yet neither books for practice in reading nor speakers for practice in conversation. So the only possible benefit that I see from his invention would be in the case of the written word. Suppose he had a big dictionary printed of all the languages in which he wanted to make himself understood, and put for each primitive word a symbol corresponding to the meaning and not to the syllables, a single symbol, for instance, for *aimer, amare* and φιλεῖν: then those who had the dictionary and knew his grammar could translate what was written into their own language by looking up each symbol in turn. But this would be no good except for reading mysteries and revelations; in other cases no one who had anything better to do would take the trouble to look up all these words in a dictionary. So I do not see that all this has much use. Perhaps I am wrong; I just wanted to write to you all I could conjecture on the basis of the six propositions which you sent me. When you have seen the system, you will be able to say if I worked it out correctly.

I believe, however, that it would be possible to devise a further system to enable one to make up the primitive words and their symbols in such a language so that it could be taught very quickly. Order is what is needed: all the thoughts which can come into the human mind must be arranged in an order like the natural order of the numbers. In a single day one can learn to name every one of the infinite series of numbers, and thus to write infinitely many different words in an unknown language. The same could be done for all the other words necessary to express all the other things which fall within the purview of the human mind. If this secret were discovered I am sure that the language would soon spread throughout the world. Many people would willingly spend five or six days in learning how to make themselves understood by the whole human race.

But I do not think that your author has thought of this. There is nothing in all his propositions to suggest it, and in any case the discovery of such a language depends upon the true philosophy. For without that philosophy it is impossible to number and order all the thoughts of men or even to separate them out into clear and simple thoughts, which in my opinion is the great secret for acquiring sound knowledge.[1] If someone were to explain correctly what are the simple ideas in the human imagination out of which all human thoughts are compounded, and if his explanation were generally received, I would dare to hope for a universal language very easy to learn, to speak and to write. The greatest advantage of such a language would be the assistance it would give to men's judgement, representing matters so clearly that it would be almost impossible to go wrong. As it is, almost all our words have confused meanings, and men's minds are so accustomed to them that there is hardly anything which they can perfectly understand.

I maintain that such a language is possible and that the knowledge on which it depends can be discovered, thus enabling peasants to be better judges of the truth of things than philosophers are now. But I do not hope   82
ever to see such a language in use. For that, the order of nature would have to change so that the world turned into a terrestrial paradise; and that is too much to suggest outside of fairyland.

TO MERSENNE, 18 DECEMBER 1629   AT I

I was astonished to hear that you have often seen a corona around a   83
candle, apparently just as you describe it, and that you have a device which enables you to see it at will. I rubbed and rolled my eyes in all sorts of ways to try to see something similar, but with no success.[2] I am willing to believe, however, that the cause of this must have to do with the liquid of the eye, and this is something that could easily be confirmed if not everyone saw the coronas at the same time. I would like to know at what time you see the coronas: whether it is at night, when your eyes are laden with the vapours of sleep, or after having read for a good while, or whether you have been awake for some time or have gone without food; whether it is during a dry or rainy spell, whether indoors or out in the open air, etc. Having settled that question, I think I could explain the matter. The

1 Fr. *science*, Descartes' term for systematic knowledge based on indubitable foundations.
2 Descartes eventually observed these coronas in 1635; see below, p. 48.

corona which can be seen around the sun is something quite different; this
84   is proved by the very thing you tell me, namely that the order in which the
colours appear is different. I do not want to dispute the point which M.
Gassendi[1] is so convinced of. I am willing to believe that he has observed a
corona with a diameter of forty-five degrees on numerous occasions; but
my guess is that there are coronas of many different sizes below that one,
and that those which appear only as a white or reddish circle are smaller. If
the observational evidence goes against me here, I admit that I do not yet
know the explanation of the coronas.

Please tell me who the author is who relates that 'Dutch sailors saw three
suns separated from each other by a pattern of six rainbows.' The thing is
beautiful and regular, and it has the same basis as the phenomenon at
Rome.

Thank you for the other comments which you wrote for me. I shall be
obliged if you will continue sending me comments on anything to do with
85   nature which you judge to be particularly worthy of explanation, and
especially on things which are universal and which can be checked by
everyone – it is of these exclusively that I have undertaken to treat. As for
particular observations, which depend on the witness of individual people,
I have never discussed these, and I have decided to say nothing at all about
them.

Thank you also for offering to take care of the little treatise[2] which I
have in hand. I feel bad about putting you to so much trouble; yet, since
you have kindly offered to assist me, I shall send it to you, if by God's grace
I complete it, but not for immediate publication. For although I have
decided not to put my name to the work, I do not want it to be released
until it has received your painstaking scrutiny and that of some other
intelligent people willing to take the trouble (between us we should be able
to find some). I would be content with your judgement alone were it not
that I feared that your affection for me would make you too partial
towards me. I wish this mainly on account of theology, which has been so
deeply in the thrall of Aristotle that it is almost impossible to expound
86   another philosophy without its seeming to be directly contrary to the
Faith. Apropos this topic, please tell me whether there is anything definite
in religion concerning the extension of created things, that is, whether it is
finite or infinite, and whether in all these regions called 'imaginary spaces'
there are genuine created bodies. Although I was not keen to touch on this
topic, I believe nevertheless I shall have to go into it . . .

---

1 The French philosopher Pierre Gassendi (1592–1653), who wrote the Fifth Set of Objections to the *Meditations*.
2 Probably the future *Meteorology*, but possibly *The World*.

What remains is something concerning the speed of motion which you   (88)
say M. Beeckman told you. It will be best to deal with this in reply to your
last question, †where you ask me first why I say¹ that the speed is impressed   89
by heaviness as 1 at the first moment, and as 2 at the second moment, etc. If
you will permit me to say so, that is not how I understand the matter.
Rather, the speed is impressed by heaviness as 1 at the first moment, and by
the same heaviness as 1 at the second moment, etc. Now 1 at the first
moment and 1 at the second moment make 2, and with 1 at the third
moment this makes 3; in this way the speed increases in arithmetical
progression. This is sufficiently proved, I thought, by the fact that heaviness perpetually accompanies the body which possesses it; and heaviness
cannot accompany a body without constantly pushing it down at every
moment. Now if we make the assumption that a mass of lead, say, falls
under the force of its own heaviness, beginning its descent at the first
moment, after which God removes all the heaviness from it so that it is as
light as air or a feather, it will continue to fall nevertheless, at least in a
vacuum, since it has begun to move and there can be no reason why it   90
should stop; but its speed will not increase. (We need to bear in mind that
we are assuming that what is once in motion will, in a vacuum, always
remain in motion. I shall try to demonstrate this in my treatise.) But say
after some time God restores the heaviness to the lead momentarily and
then takes it away again. At the second moment, would the lead not be
pushed by the force of the heaviness just as it was at the first moment? And
hence would the speed of the motion not be twice as great? The same could
be said about all the other moments in question.† It follows from this that if
you let a ball fall 50 feet †in an absolute vacuum†, no matter what stuff the
ball is made of, it will take exactly three times as long to fall the first 25 feet
as it will to fall the last 25 feet. But in air it is an entirely different matter.
To come back to M. Beeckman, although what he told you is false, namely
that once a falling weight reaches a certain point it always continues to fall
at the same speed, all the same it is true that after a certain distance the
increase in speed is so slight as to be imperceptible. I shall explain to you
what he meant to say, for we have discussed this together in the past.

†Like me, he supposes that what has once begun to move continues to   91
move of its own accord unless it is checked by some external force, and so
in a vacuum it is always moving, though in air it is impeded to some extent
owing to the resistance of the air itself. Furthermore he supposes that the
force of heaviness which is present in a body pushes it downwards anew at
each imaginable moment, and hence in a vacuum the speed of the motion
always increases in the ratio which I gave above, and which I tried to

1 See above, p. 8.

establish twelve years ago at his suggestion and still have among my notes from that time. But what follows this is something which he has added of his own accord, namely that the faster a body descends, the more the air resists its motion. I was quite doubtful about this earlier, but now that I have carefully examined the matter I can see that it is true. From this he draws the following conclusion. The force that creates speed always increases uniformly (that is, by one unit at each moment), while the air resistance always impedes it in a non-uniform way (that is, less than a unit at the first moment and a little more at the second moment, and so on). Necessarily therefore, he says, there comes a point where this resistance is equal to the thrust which is due to the heaviness, when it reduces the speed at the same rate as the force of heaviness increases it. At the moment this happens, he says, it is certain that the weight does not fall more quickly than it did at the immediately preceding moment, and at the subsequent moments the speed will neither increase nor diminish, because after that the air resistance remains uniform – any inequality in the speed will be due to the inequality in the speed which is taken away – and the force of heaviness always pushes it in a uniform way.[†]

92   This argument is highly plausible, and those who are ignorant of arithmetic might be convinced by it; but one needs only to be able to count to see that it is unsound. For if the air resistance increases in proportion to the increase in the speed, the resistance cannot increase at a greater rate than the increase in speed, that is, in the same proportion. Let us say that at the beginning of the motion the speed is 1 if there is no air resistance, and only $\frac{1}{2}$ if there is air resistance (that is, that the air resistance is also $\frac{1}{2}$). Then at the second moment, when the heaviness adds another unit to the speed, the speed will be $\frac{3}{2}$ if there is no immediate air resistance. But how much air resistance will there be? One might well say that the air resistance will be proportionally as great as it was the first time, because the weight is already moving; in this case the proposition which M. Beeckman infers

93   will be even less true. But one cannot say that the resistance will be proportionally greater than it was the first time, that is, that it will reduce the speed by a half, from $\frac{3}{2}$ to $\frac{3}{4}$, and at the third moment the heaviness will add yet another unit to the speed, which will be $\frac{7}{4}$, unless the air resistance reduces it by $\frac{1}{2}$, leaving $\frac{7}{8}$. Thus in the succeeding moments the air resistance will be $\frac{15}{16}, \frac{31}{32}, \frac{63}{64}, \frac{127}{128}, \frac{255}{256}$, [†]and so on *ad infinitum*[†]. As you can see from this,

94   the numbers always increase and are always less than a unit. [†]Thus the reduction in speed due to air resistance is never as great as the increase in speed due to heaviness, which is one unit at every moment. The same is true if you say that air resistance reduces the speed by $\frac{2}{3}$ or $\frac{3}{4}$, etc. Yet you cannot say that at the first moment it reduces the speed by one unit, for in that case the weight would not fall. Thus it is demonstrated mathemati-

cally that what Beeckman wrote is false.[†] If you write to him, I shall not mind if you tell him this, so that he will learn not to deck himself out in someone else's feathers.

But to come back to the falling weight, one can see from the calculation that the non-uniformity in the speed is very large at the beginning of the motion but is almost imperceptible later on, and moreover that it is even less perceptible in a weight made of light matter than in one made of heavy matter. Your two excellent experiments can show this empirically. For if you follow the calculation above and represent a moment by a very small space, you can see that a ball which falls 50 feet will move almost three times as fast over the second foot as it did over the first foot, though it will   95 not move perceptibly faster over the third foot than over the second, and that it will take no longer to fall the first 25 feet than to fall the last 25 feet, save what it needs to fall 2 or 3 feet, and this amount will be quite imperceptible. Now that is what will happen largely if the weight is made of light matter, but if it is made of iron or lead, the non-uniformity in the motion will not be so imperceptible; yet if the fall is from a great height you will hardly be able to perceive it any better, since the motion will last for a shorter time than it would if the weight were made of light matter . . .

TO MERSENNE, JANUARY 1630   AT I

I am sorry to hear that you have erysipelas and that M. M[ontais] is ill.   105 Please look after yourself, at least until I know whether it is possible to discover a system of medicine which is founded on infallible demonstrations, which is what I am investigating at present.

As for the halo which is commonly seen around a candle, this has nothing in common with the corona which appears around stars, for there is no gap between it and the candle: it is simply [†]secondary light coming from the rays which pass straight through the iris[†]; it is just like a ray of sunlight which lights up the inside of a room which it has entered through a small hole. But you will see the colours more clearly if you take the trouble to look at a candle, 7 or 8 feet away, across the edge of a quill, or simply even across a hair held upright straight in front of your eye: place the hair right up against the eye and you will see a great variety of lovely colours . . .

Concerning the rebounding of a ball, it is true that this occurs partly   (107) because the air inside the ball (not the air outside it) rebounds like a spring and pushes the ball upwards. But there is a further cause, namely the continuation of the motion of the ball . . .

Most small bodies looked at through eyeglasses appear transparent   (109) because they are in fact transparent; but many small bodies placed together are not transparent, because they are not joined together in a uniform way, and since the parts are not uniform, their arrangement is enough to make opaque what was originally transparent. You can see this from a piece of glass or candy: these are no longer transparent when they are crushed, even though each part of them is transparent . . .

(112)   Thank you for offering to send me M. Gassendi's observations. I did not want to put you to so much trouble, since they are not yet in print. I would 113   just like to know whether he managed to see many sunspots, how many he saw at the same time, whether they all moved at the same speed, and whether their shape always appeared to be round. I should also like to know whether he observed for certain that the refraction due to the air makes the stars appear much higher in the sky when they are near the horizon than when they are not; and supposing he did observe this, whether the refraction in question occurs also in the case of the moon; and also whether it is greater or smaller in the case of stars close to the northern horizon than it is in the case of stars close to the southern horizon. Yet these questions call for such accurate instruments and exact calculations that I dare say no one has yet been able to give exact answers to them. If anyone could do it, I know of no one in whom I could have greater confidence than him.

I think I heard you say once that you had made an accurate investigation of the weights of all the metals and had made a list of these. If this is correct, I would be most obliged if you would send it to me, if it would not put you to too much trouble.

I would also like to know whether you have made an experiment to see whether a stone thrown with a sling, or a ball shot from a musket, or a bolt from a crossbow, travels faster and has greater force in the middle of its flight than it has at the start, and whether its power increases. The common opinion is that this is the case, though my own view differs on this point. I 114   find that things that do not move of their own accord but are impelled must have more force at the start than they have straight after.

AT I   TO MERSENNE, 25 FEBRUARY 1630

(117)   . . . As for your question concerning the rebounding of a ball, I did not say that the cause of this must be ascribed entirely to the air inside the ball, but mainly to the continuation of the motion which is present in all rebounding bodies, that is to say, †from the fact that a thing has begun to move it follows that it continues to move for as long as it can; and if it cannot continue to move in a straight line, rather than coming to rest, it rebounds in the opposite direction.† One must also observe that the air inside a ball acts as a spring which helps it to rebound; the same is true of the matter of all other bodies, both those which rebound and those against

which other bodies rebound, such as the strings of a tennis racket, the wall of a tennis court, the hardness of the ball, etc. As for the air which follows it or goes before it, that is an imaginary idea of the scholastics, which in my view is quite pointless . . .

As to why the air within the barrel of a gun can resist the force of many   (119) men, the reason is not that it is denser than water but that it is composed of parts which cannot pass through the sides of the barrel, and consequently cannot be condensed. For it is certain that when something is condensed it loses some of its parts, and retains the bulkier parts, just as a sponge which is full of water loses water when you press it. If you were to fill a vessel with air (the most highly rarefied air that could be imagined), and the vessel (you supposed) had no pores in it through which any of the air could escape, then, I say, all the forces in the world would not be powerful enough to condense it in the least. But, you should know, in air and in all bodies that can be condensed there are some particles that are so fine that they pass through the pores even of gold and diamonds and all other bodies, however solid they may be . . .

Thank you for your observations on metals.[1] I was not able to draw any   123 conclusions from these, except that it is very difficult to perform accurate experiments in this area. For if your bells were all the same size, the measurements in air should have shown the same difference as those made in water; yet I do not find that any two such measurements correspond in this respect. Moreover, you make out gold to be lighter than lead, the very opposite of what I clearly find to be the case. You make out pure silver to be as heavy in water as in air, and bronze heavier, which is impossible; yet that was perhaps a slip of the pen . . .

TO MERSENNE, 18 MARCH 1630   AT I

. . . You ask whether one can discover the essence of beauty. This is the   (132) same as your earlier question, why one sound is more pleasant than another, except that the word 'beauty' seems to have a special relation to   133 the sense of sight. But in general 'beautiful' and 'pleasant' signify simply a relation between our judgement and an object; and because the judgements of men differ so much from each other, neither beauty nor pleasantness can be said to have any definite measure. I cannot give any better explanation than the one I gave long ago in my treatise on music; I will quote it word for word, since I have the book before me.

Among the objects of the senses, those most pleasing to the mind are neither those

---

1 See above, p. 18. In the inventory of Descartes' papers made after his death is the entry 'The Weights of Metals together with a Brief List'.

which are easiest to perceive nor those which are hardest, but those which are not so easy to perceive that they fail to satisfy fully the natural inclination of the senses towards their objects nor yet so hard to perceive that they tire the senses.[1]

    To explain what I meant by 'easy or difficult to perceive by the senses' I instanced the divisions of a flower bed. If there are only one or two types of shape arranged in the same pattern, they will be taken in more easily than if there are ten or twelve arranged in different ways. But this does not mean that one design can be called absolutely more beautiful than another; to some people's fancy one with three shapes will be the most beautiful, to others it will be one with four or five and so on. The one that pleases most people can be called the most beautiful without qualification; but which this is cannot be determined.

    Secondly, what makes some people want to dance may make others want to cry. This is because it evokes ideas in our memory: for instance those who have in the past enjoyed dancing to a certain tune feel a fresh wish to dance the moment they hear a similar one; on the other hand, if someone had never heard a galliard without some affliction befalling him, he would certainly grow sad when he heard it again. This is so certain that I reckon that if you whipped a dog five or six times to the sound of a violin, it would begin to howl and run away as soon as it heard that music again. . .

134

135
136

    Your letter of 14 March, which I think is the one you are worried about, reached me ten or twelve days later; but because you indicated that others were on the way, and because it was only a week since I had written to you, I put off replying to you until today, when I received your last dated 4 April. I beg you to believe that I feel myself enormously in your debt for all the kind services you do me, which are too numerous for me to be able to thank you for each individually. I assure you that I will repay you in any way you ask if it is in my power; and I will always tell you my address provided, please, that you tell no one else. If anybody has the idea that I plan to write, please try to remove this impression, not to confirm it; I swear that if I had not already told people I planned to do so, so that they would say I have not been able to carry out my plan, I would never undertake the task at all. If people are going to think about me, I am civilized enough to be glad that they should think well of me; but I would

---

1 *Compendium Musicae*: AT x 92.

much prefer them to have no thought of me at all. I fear fame more than I desire it; I think that those who acquire it always lose some degree of liberty and leisure, which are two things I possess so perfectly and value so highly that there is no monarch in the world rich enough to buy them away from me.

This will not prevent me from completing the little treatise I have begun,[1] but I do not want this to be known so that I shall always be free to 137 disavow it. My work on it is going very slowly, because I take much more pleasure in acquiring knowledge than in putting into writing the little that I know. I am now studying chemistry and anatomy simultaneously; every day I learn something that I cannot find in any book. I wish I had already started to research into diseases and their remedies, so that I could find some cure for your erysipelas, which I am sorry has troubled you for such a long time. Moreover, I pass the time so contentedly in the acquisition of knowledge that I never settle down to write any of my treatise except under duress, in order to carry out my resolution, which is, if I am still living, to have it ready for posting to you by the beginning of the year 1633. I am telling you a definite time so as to put myself under a greater obligation, so that you can reproach me if I fail to keep to the date. Moreover, you will be amazed that I am taking such a long time to write a discourse which will be so short that I reckon it will take only an afternoon to read. This is because I take more trouble, and think it more important, to learn what I need for the conduct of my life than to indulge myself by publishing the little I have learnt. Perhaps you find it strange that I have not persevered with some other treatises I began while I was in Paris. I will tell you the reason: while I was working on them I acquired a little more knowledge than I had when I 138 began them, and when I tried to take account of this I was forced to start a new project,[2] rather larger than the first. It is as if a man began building a house and then acquired unexpected riches and so changed his status that the building he had begun was now too small for him. No one could blame such a man if he saw him starting to build another house more suitable to his condition. I am sure that I will not change my mind again; because what I now possess will stand me in good stead no matter what else I may learn; and even if I learn nothing more, I shall still carry out my plan . . .

As for your questions: 1. The corpuscles, which enter a thing during (139) rarefaction and exit during condensation, and which can penetrate the 140 hardest solids, are of the same substance as visible and tangible bodies; but you must not imagine that they are atoms, or that they are at all hard.

---

1 This treatise was the beginning of *The World*, and the *Optics* and *Meteorology*.
2 Probably the future *The World*.

Think of them as an extremely fluid and subtle[1] substance filling the pores of other bodies. You must admit that even in gold and diamonds there are certain pores, however tiny they may be; and if you agree also that there is no such thing as a vacuum, as I think I can prove, you are forced to admit that these pores are full of some matter which can penetrate everywhere with ease. Now heat and rarefaction are simply an admixture of this matter.

To convince you of this would take a longer discussion than is possible within the bounds of a letter. I have said the same about many other questions which you have put to me; please believe that I have never used this as an excuse to conceal from you what I propose to write in my treatise on physics. I assure you that there is nothing of what I know that I am keeping secret from anyone; much less from you whom I honour and esteem and to whom I am obliged in countless ways. But the difficulties of physics which I told you I had taken on are all so linked and interdependent that it would be impossible for me to give the solution to one without giving the solution to all; and I do not know how to do that more quickly or more simply than I shall do in the treatise which I am writing...

141

(143)
144

Your question of theology is beyond my mental capacity, but it does not seem to me outside my province, since it has no concern with anything dependent on revelation, which is what I call theology in the strict sense; it is a metaphysical question which is to be examined by human reason. I think that all those to whom God has given the use of this reason have an obligation to employ it principally in the endeavour to know him and to know themselves. That is the task with which I began my studies; and I can say that I would not have been able to discover the foundations of physics if I had not looked for them along that road. It is the topic which I have studied more than any other and in which, thank God, I have not altogether wasted my time. At least I think that I have found how to prove metaphysical truths in a manner which is more evident than the proofs of geometry – in my own opinion, that is: I do not know if I shall be able to convince others of it. During my first nine months in this country[2] I worked on nothing else. I think that you heard me speak once before of my plan to write something on the topic; but I do not think it opportune to do so before I have seen how my treatise on physics is received. But if the book which you mention was very well written and fell into my hands I might perhaps feel obliged to reply to it immediately, because if the report you heard is accurate, it says things which are very dangerous and, I believe, very false. However, in my treatise on physics I shall discuss a number of

145

1 See footnote 1, p. 161 below.
2 Holland, where Descartes came to live in 1628.

metaphysical topics and especially the following. The mathematical truths which you call eternal have been laid down by God and depend on him entirely no less than the rest of his creatures. Indeed to say that these truths are independent of God is to talk of him as if he were Jupiter or Saturn and to subject him to the Styx and the Fates. Please do not hesitate to assert and proclaim everywhere that it is God who has laid down these laws in nature just as a king lays down laws in his kingdom. There is no single one that we cannot grasp if our mind turns to consider it. They are all †inborn in our minds† just as a king would imprint his laws on the hearts of all his subjects if he had enough power to do so. The greatness of God, on the other hand, is something which we cannot grasp even though we know it. But the very fact that we judge it beyond our grasp makes us esteem it the more greatly; just as a king has more majesty when he is less familiarly known by his subjects, provided of course that they do not get the idea that they have no king – they must know him enough to be in no doubt about that.

It will be said that if God had established these truths he could change them as a king changes his laws. To this the answer is: Yes he can, if his will   146 can change. 'But I understand them to be eternal and unchangeable.' – I make the same judgement about God. 'But his will is free.' – Yes, but his power is beyond our grasp. In general we can assert that God can do everything that is within our grasp but not that he cannot do what is beyond our grasp. It would be rash to think that our imagination reaches as far as his power.

I hope to put this in writing, within the next fortnight, in my treatise on physics; but I do not want you to keep it secret. On the contrary I beg you to tell people as often as the occasion demands, provided you do not mention my name. I should be glad to know the objections which can be made against this view; and I want people to get used to speaking of God in a manner worthier, I think, than the common and almost universal way of imagining him as a finite being.

With regard to infinity, you asked me a question in your letter of 14 March, which is the only thing I find in it which is not in the last letter. You said that if there were an infinite line it would have an infinite number of feet and of fathoms, and consequently that the infinite number of feet would be six times as great as the number of fathoms. †I agree entirely.† 'Then this latter number is not infinite.' †I deny the consequence.† 'But one infinity cannot be greater than another.' Why not? †Where is the absurdity?† Especially if it is only greater †by a finite ratio, as in this case, where   147 multiplication by six is a finite ratio, which does not in any way affect the infinity†. In any case, what basis have we for judging whether one infinity can be greater than another or not? It would no longer be infinity if we could grasp it. Continue to honour me by thinking kindly of me.

　　　　　TO MERSENNE, 6 MAY 1630

148　　　Thank you for M. Gassendi's account of the corona.[1] As for the bad
book, I no longer want you to send it to me; for I have now decided on
other projects, and I think that it would be too late to carry out the plan
which made me say to you in the last post that if it were a well-written
book and fell into my hands I would try to reply immediately. I thought
that even if there were only thirty-five copies of the book, still, if it were
well written it would go to a second impression, and circulate widely
among curious people however much it might be prohibited. I had thought
of a remedy which seemed more effective than any legal prohibition. My
idea was that before the book was reprinted secretly it should be printed
with permission, with the addition, after each paragraph or each chapter,
149　　of arguments refuting its conclusions and exposing their fallaciousness. I
thought that if it were sold thus publicly in its entirety with a reply, nobody
would care to sell it in secret without a reply, and thus nobody would learn
its false doctrine without at the same time being disabused of it. The replies
to such books which appear separately are customarily of little use because
people do not read books which do not suit their humour; and so those
who take the time to examine the replies are never the same as those who
have read the bad books. I expect that you will say that we do not know
whether I would have been able to reply to the author's arguments. To that
I can only say that at least I would have done all I could; and since I have
many arguments that persuade and convince me of the contrary of what
you told me was in the book, I dared to hope that they might also persuade
others. I trusted that truth expounded by an undistinguished mind would
be stronger than falsehood maintained by the cleverest people in the
world.

　　　As for the eternal truths, I say once more that †they are true or possible
only because God knows them as true or possible. They are not known as
true by God in any way which would imply that they are true independently of him†. If men really understood the sense of their words they could
never say without blasphemy that the truth of anything is prior to the
knowledge which God has of it. In God willing and knowing are a single
thing in such a way that †by the very fact of willing something he knows it
and it is only for this reason that such a thing is true†. So we must not say
150　　that †if God did not exist nevertheless these truths would be true†; for the
existence of God is the first and the most eternal of all possible truths and
the one from which alone all others proceed. It is easy to be mistaken about
this because most people do not regard God as a being who is infinite and

1 See above, p. 14.

beyond our grasp, the sole author on whom all things depend; they stick at the syllables of his name and think it sufficient knowledge of him to know that 'God' means what is meant by *Deus* in Latin and what is adored by men. Those who have no higher thoughts than these can easily become atheists; and because they perfectly comprehend mathematical truths and do not perfectly comprehend the truth of God's existence, it is no wonder they do not think the former depend on the latter. But they should rather take the opposite view, that since God is a cause whose power surpasses the bounds of human understanding, and since the necessity of these truths does not exceed our knowledge, these truths are therefore something less than, and subject to, the incomprehensible power of God. What you say about the production of the *Word*[1] does not conflict, I think, with what I say; but I do not want to involve myself in theology, and I am already afraid that you will think my philosophy too free-thinking for daring to express an opinion on such lofty matters.

TO [MERSENNE], 27 MAY 1630   AT I

You ask me †by what kind of causality God established the eternal   151
truths†. I reply: †by the same kind of causality† as he created all things, that   152
is to say, as their †efficient and total cause†. For it is certain that he is the author of the essence of created things no less than of their existence; and this essence is nothing other than the eternal truths. I do not conceive them as emanating from God like rays from the sun; but I know that God is the author of everything and that these truths are something and consequently that he is their author. I say that I know this, not that I conceive it or grasp it; because it is possible to know that God is infinite and all powerful although our soul, being finite, cannot grasp or conceive him. In the same way we can touch a mountain with our hands but we cannot put our arms around it as we could put them around a tree or something else not too large for them. To grasp something is to embrace it in one's thought; to know something, it is sufficient to touch it with one's thought.

You ask also what necessitated God to create these truths; and I reply that he was free to make it not true that all the radii of the circle are equal — just as free as he was not to create the world. And it is certain that these truths are no more necessarily attached to his essence than are other created things. You ask what God did in order to produce them. I reply that †from all eternity he willed and understood them to be, and by that very fact he created them†. Or, if you reserve the word †created† for the existence of things, then he †established them and made them†. In God,   153

---

1 The generation of the Second Person of the Trinity by the First.

willing, understanding and creating are all the same thing without one being prior to the other †even conceptually†.

2. As for the question whether †it is in accord with the goodness of God to damn men for eternity†, that is a theological question: so if you please you will allow me to say nothing about it. It is not that the arguments of free thinkers on this topic have any force, indeed they seem frivolous and ridiculous to me; but I think that when truths depend on faith and cannot be proved by natural argument, it degrades them if one tries to support them by human reasoning and mere probabilities.

3. As for the liberty of God, I completely share the view which you tell me was expounded by Father Gibieuf.[1] I did not know that he had published anything, but I will try to have his treatise sent from Paris as soon as possible so that I can see it. I am very pleased that my opinions coincide with his, because that assures me at least that they are not too extravagant to be defended by very able men.

The fourth, fifth, sixth, eighth and last points of your letter are all theological matters, so if you please I will say nothing about them. As for the seventh point concerning such things as the birth marks caused on children by their mothers' imagination, I agree it is worth examination, but I am not yet convinced.

154   In your tenth point you start from the supposition that God leads everything to perfection and that nothing is annihilated, and then you ask what is the perfection of dumb animals and what becomes of their souls after death. That question is within my competence, and I reply that God leads everything to perfection, in one sense, i.e. †collectively†, but not in another, i.e. in particular. The very fact that particular things perish and that others appear in their place is one of the principal perfections of the universe. As for animals' souls and other forms and qualities, do not worry about what happens to them. I am about to explain all this in my treatise, and I hope that I will make it all so clearly understood that no one will be capable of doubting it.

AT I   TO [BEECKMAN], 17 OCTOBER 1630

(158)   . . . Consider first what are the things which one person can teach another: you will find they are languages, history, observational data, and clear and certain proofs, like those of geometers, which bring conviction to the mind. As for mere opinions and received doctrines, such as those of the philosophers, simply to repeat them is not to teach them. Plato says one

1 Guillaume Gibieuf (1591–1650), Prior of the Oratory in Paris and member of the Sorbonne.

thing, Aristotle another, Epicurus another, Telesio, Campanella, Bruno, Basson, Vanini, and the innovators all say something different. Of all these people, I ask you, who is it who has anything to teach me, or indeed anyone who loves wisdom? Doubtless it is the man who can first convince someone by his arguments, or at least his authority. But if someone merely comes to believe something, without being swayed by any authority or argument which he has learnt from others, this does not mean that he has been taught it by anyone, even though he may have heard many people say it. It may even happen that he really knows it, being impelled to believe it by true reasons, and that no one before him has ever known it, although they may have been of the same opinion, because they deduced it from false principles. All of these points are so clear and so true that if you   159
carefully note them, you will easily see that I have never learnt anything but idle fancies from your *Mathematical Physics*,[1] any more than I have learnt anything from the *Batrachomyomachia*.[2] Have I ever been moved by your authority? Have I ever been convinced by your arguments? Well, you said, I believed and accepted some of your views as soon as I understood them. But, mark you, the fact that I believed them at once does not show that I learnt them from you; I accepted them, rather, because I had already arrived at the same views myself. You should not indulge your sickness by dwelling on the fact that I admit I have sometimes accepted what you said, for it occasionally happens that even when the most incompetent person discusses philosophy, he says many things which by sheer chance coincide with the truth. Many people can know the same thing without any of them having learnt it from the others. It is ridiculous to take the trouble as you do to distinguish, in the possession of know-ledge, what is your own from what is not, as if it was the possession of a piece of land or sum of money. If you know something, it is completely yours, even if you have learnt it from someone else . . .

You reproach me, without any reason or basis, for having sometimes   (165)
put myself on a level with the angels. I still cannot convince myself that you are so out of your mind as to believe this. But I realize that your sickness may be very far gone, and so I will explain what may have given you occasion to make this complaint. Philosophers and theologians are accus-tomed, when they want to show that something's being the case is repug-nant to reason, to say that not even God could make it the case. This way of speaking has always seemed too bold to me; so in order to use a more modest expression, whenever – as happens more often in mathematics than in philosophy – an occasion arises on which others say that God

1 Beeckman's *Mathematico-Physicarum Meditationum*, published posthumously in 1644.
2 A parody of the *Iliad* in hexameter verse.

cannot do something, I would merely say that an angel could not do it. If this is the reason why you say I put myself on a level with the angels, you could as well say that the wisest people in the world put themselves on a level with God. I am very unfortunate to have been suspected of vanity on a point in which I can say I was behaving with extraordinary modesty.

AT I   TO MERSENNE, 25 NOVEMBER 1630

(178)   ... I am sorry for the troubles of M. F[errier] even though he has brought them on himself. Since you thought it proper, I do not object to your having shown my letter about him to M. M[ydorge];[1] but I would have preferred you not to put it actually in his hands. My letters are normally written with too little care to be fit to be seen by anyone except their addressee. Moreover, I am afraid that he may have inferred from it that I
179   want to have my *Optics* printed, because I think I mentioned it in other places beside the last paragraph which you say you cut off. I would like this project to remain unknown, for it cannot be ready for a long time because of the way I am working on it. I want to include a discourse explaining the nature of colours and light. This has held me up for six months and is still not half finished; but it will be longer than I thought and will contain what amounts to a complete physics. I am hoping that it will serve to keep my promise to you, to have my *World* finished in three years, because it will be more or less an abstract of it. After that I do not think I will ever bring myself to have anything else printed, at least in my lifetime. I am too much in love with the fable of my *World* to give it up if God lets me live long enough to finish it; but I cannot answer for the future. I think I will send you this discourse on light as soon as it is complete, and before sending you the rest of the *Optics*, because in it I want to give my own account of colours, and consequently I am obliged to explain how the whiteness of the bread remains in the Blessed Sacrament.[2] I would be glad to have this examined first by my friends before it is seen by the world at large. However, although I am not hurrying to finish my treatise on optics, I am not afraid of anyone †stealing a march on me† because I am sure that
180   whatever others may write will not coincide with my account unless they learn it from the letters I have written to M. F[errier].
       If any people should have the idea that I am intending to write something, please disabuse them of the idea as far as you can, and make it clear to them that I have absolutely no such intention. In fact once the *Optics* is finished I have decided conscientiously to study for the sake of myself and

1 Claude Mydorge (1585–1647), a Court official and amateur mathematician and scientist.
2 See Fourth Replies: AT VII 248–55; CSM II 173–9.

my friends, that is to say, to try to discover something useful in medicine, without wasting time writing for the sake of others who would mock me if what I did was poor, and would be envious of me if what I did was good, and would show me no thanks were I to produce a masterpiece. I have not seen Cabeus' book on the *Magnetic Philosophy*,[1] and at the moment I do not want to be distracted by reading it . . .

I am most obliged to you for sending me an extract from the manuscript (181) you mentioned. The shortest way I know to reply to the arguments which he brings against the Godhead, and to all the arguments of other atheists, is to find an evident proof which will make everyone believe that God exists. I can boast of having found one myself which satisfies me entirely, and 182 which makes me know that God exists with more certainty than I know the truth of any proposition of geometry; but I do not know whether I would be able to make everyone understand it the way I can. I think that it is better not to treat of this matter at all than to treat of it imperfectly. The universal agreement of all races is sufficient to maintain the Godhead against the insults of atheists, and no individual should enter into dispute with them unless he is very certain of refuting them.

I will test in my treatise on optics whether I am capable of explaining my conceptions and convincing others of truths of which I have convinced myself. I doubt it very much; but if I find by experience that it is so, perhaps I may some day complete a little treatise of Metaphysics, which I began when in Friesland, in which I set out principally to prove *the existence of God and of our souls* when they are separate from the body, from which their immortality follows. I am enraged when I see that there are people in the world so bold and so impudent as to fight against God.

TO MERSENNE, 23 DECEMBER 1630   AT I

. . . Let me tell you that at the moment I am busy sorting out Chaos with a (194) view to extracting light from it — one of the most important and most difficult matters I could ever undertake, for it virtually involves the whole of physics. I have countless different things to consider all at once if I am to find a basis on which to give a true account without doing violence to anyone's imagination or shocking received opinion. That is why I want to spend a month or two thinking solely about this topic . . .

TO BALZAC, 15 APRIL 1631   AT I

While you were at Balzac I knew that any conversation other than your 197 own would be burdensome to you; yet if I had thought that you would

1 *Philosophia Magnetica* by Nicolas Cabei (1586–1650), published in 1629.

have had to stay there as long as you have, I would not have been able to stop myself from sending you some small expression of my regard. But since the letter which I had the honour to receive from you gave me to expect that you would soon be at Court, I was somewhat chary about disturbing you in your retreat, and I thought it better to wait until I heard from you that you had departed. That is why, over the course of eighteen months, I have put off writing from one post to the next, when originally I had no intention of putting it off for more than a week. Thus all this time I have saved you from the intrusion of my letters, though you owe me nothing on that score. But since you are now in Paris, I must ask for my share of the time you propose to spend in conversation with prospective visitors. I must say that during the two years I have been away I have not once been tempted to return, until I was told that you were there. That news made me see that I could now be happier somewhere other than where I am now.[1] If the task which keeps me here were not, in my humble judgement, the most important one I could ever devote myself to, the mere hope of having the favour of your conversation and of seeing those powerful thoughts which we admire in your works come naturally into being before my very eyes would be enough to make me leave here.

198

Please do not ask me what this task that I deem so important might be, for it would embarrass me to tell you. I have become so philosophical that I despise most of the things that are ordinarily valued, and I value others which are usually put at no value. For all that, I shall tell you about it more openly some day if you would like me to; for your own views are far removed from those of the majority, and you have often given me proof that you regard me more highly than I deserve. For the time being I shall be content to tell you that I am no longer of a mind to commit nothing to paper, which as you saw, was once my intention. It is not that I would set no great store by reputation, if one could be sure of acquiring an illustrious one such as yours, but as for an indifferent and uncertain reputation, such as I might hope to gain, I value that much less than the peace of mind which I already possess. Here I sleep for ten hours every night, and with never a care to wake me. Once sleep has let my mind wander at length among groves, gardens and enchanted palaces, where I sample all the pleasures that are dreamt of in fables, I gradually intermingle my daydreams with my night dreams; and when it dawns on me that I am awake, it is only to make my contentment more perfect and to enable my senses to share it – for I am not so austere as to deny them anything a philosopher could grant without doing violence to his conscience. In brief, all I lack here is the pleasure of your conversation, and so essential is this for my happiness that there is

1 This letter was written in Amsterdam.

little to prevent me from abandoning all my plans in order to come and tell you in person that I am, with all my heart, your very humble and devoted servant.

TO BALZAC, 5 MAY 1631   AT I

When I received your letter saying that you were planning to come here,[1] 202
I rubbed my eyes to see whether I was awake; yet I still dare not feel any more pleasure at the news than I would if I had merely dreamt it. All the same I do not find it so strange that a mind as great and generous as your own should not be able to adapt itself to the constraints of service to which one is subject at Court; and since you assure me in all seriousness that God has inspired you to retire from the world, I would think it a sin against the Holy Ghost if I tried to deflect you from such a pious resolution.

You must also excuse my enthusiasm if I invite you to choose Amsterdam for your retreat, and to prefer it not only to the monasteries of the Franciscans and the Carthusians, to which many good folk retire, but also, 203
let me say, to the finest abodes in France and Italy, and even to the famous Hermitage where you spent the past year. No matter how perfect a country house may be, it always lacks numerous conveniences which are to be found only in towns, and even the solitude which one hopes to find there turns out never to be quite perfect. There, I agree, you will find a stream that would make the greatest talkers fall into reveries, and a valley so secluded that it could transport them into ecstasies; but, as can easily happen, you will also have some neighbours who will bother you at times, and their visits will be even more bothersome than the ones you receive in Paris. In this large town where I live, by contrast, everyone but myself is engaged in trade, and hence is so attentive to his own profit that I could live here all my life without ever being noticed by a soul.

I take a walk each day amid the bustle of the crowd with as much freedom and repose as you could obtain in your leafy groves, and I pay no more attention to the people I meet than I would to the trees in your woods or the animals that browse there. The bustle of the city no more disturbs my daydreams than would the rippling of a stream. Whenever I reflect upon the doings of passers-by I get the same sort of pleasure as you get when you watch the peasants tilling your fields, for I can see that all their work serves to enhance the beauty of the place I live in, and to supply all 204
my needs. Whenever you have the pleasure of seeing the fruit growing in your orchards and of feasting your eyes on its abundance, bear in mind that it gives me just as much pleasure to watch the ships arriving, laden

1 Amsterdam.

with all the produce of the Indies and all the rarities of Europe. Where else on earth could you find, as easily as you do here, all the conveniences of life and all the curiosities you could hope to see? In what other country could you find such complete freedom, or sleep with less anxiety, or find armies at the ready to protect you, or find fewer poisonings, or acts of treason or slander? Where else do you still find the innocence of a bygone age? I do not know how you can be so fond of Italy, where the air is so often pestilent, the heat of the day always unbearable, the cool of the evening unwholesome, and the darkness of night a cover for thieves and murderers. If you are afraid of the northern winters, pray tell me what shades or fans or fountains could shield you from the burning heat at Rome as effectively as a stove or a roaring fire would protect you from the cold here? In the mean time I must tell you that I have waiting for you a little collection of idle thoughts which you will perhaps find not disagreeable; but whether you come or not, I shall always be your devoted, etc.

AT I   TO VILLEBRESSIEU, SUMMER 1631

213   You saw these two results of my fine rule or natural method in the discussion which was forced on me in the presence of the Papal Nuncio, Cardinal de Bérulle, Father Mersenne and all that great and learned company assembled at the Nuncio's palace to hear M. de Chandoux[1] lecture about his new philosophy. I made the whole company recognize what power the art of right reasoning has over the minds of those who have no learning beyond the ordinary, and how much better founded, and more true and natural, my principles are than any of those which are currently received in the learned world. You were as convinced as everybody else, and you were all good enough to beg me to put them in writing and to publish them . . .

(215)   I read through and examined most of the things in your memoir during my recent trip to Dordrecht, from which I have returned to await you at Amsterdam, where you will find me in good health at our lodgings in the Old Prince. There I shall tell you what I think about all these things. I advise you to put your ideas for the most part in the form of propositions,

216   problems and theorems and to publish them so as to force somebody else to supply them with research and observations. That is what I would like everybody to do, so that many people's experience may help to discover the finest things in nature, and to build a physics which would be clear, certain, based on demonstrative proof, and more useful than that commonly taught. You for your part could greatly help to disabuse poor sick

1 A French physicist and chemist, who later that year was hanged for forgery.

minds concerning the adulteration of metals on which you have worked
so hard and to so little effect, without having found any truth in the idea in
twelve years of assiduous work and numerous experiments. Your experience would be generally useful as a warning to certain people of their
errors.

It seems to me too that you have already discovered some general
principles of nature, such as that there is only one material substance
which receives from an external agent its action or its ability to move from
one place to another, and that from this it acquires the different shapes or
modes which make it into the kind of thing we see in the primary
compounds which are called elements. Moreover you have observed that
the nature of these elements or primary compounds which are called earth,
water, air and fire consists only in the difference between the fragments, or
small and large particles of this matter; and that the matter changes daily
from one element into another (when the larger particles change into finer
ones through heat and movement) or into base substances (when the finer
particles change into larger ones as the action of heat and movement
ceases). You have seen too that the primary mingling of these four
compounds results in a mixture which can be called the fifth element. This
is what you call the principle, or the most noble preparation of the   217
elements; since it is, you say, a productive seed or a material life which
takes specific form in all the noble particular individuals which cannot fail
to be an object of our wonder. I am quite in agreement with your view that
the four elements which constitute matter and the fifth which results from
them are so changed in such a case that none of them continues to be what
it was but that all together constitute the animal or the plant or the
mineral. All this suits my style of philosophizing very well, and it accords
admirably with all the mechanical experiments which I have performed
upon nature in this field.

TO MERSENNE, OCTOBER OR NOVEMBER 1631   AT I

... I am not going back on what I said concerning the speed of weights   (228)
falling in a vacuum.[1] For if we suppose a vacuum, as everyone imagines
that there is, the rest follows demonstratively; but I think that it would be a
mistake to suppose a vacuum. I will try to explain †what heaviness,
lightness, hardness, etc.† are in the two chapters that I promised to send
you at the end of the year; that is why I am not sending you anything about
it at the moment ...

I think I could now determine the rate at which the speed of a falling   (231)

1 See above, p. 8.

body increases, not only †in a vacuum†, but also †in real air†.¹ Yet since my mind is now full of other thoughts, I do not have the time to investigate it, and there would be little profit in it. I beg you to excuse me for writing to you in such a perfunctory way, and to consider that my letters might not be as long as they are, were they composed with greater care . . .

AT I

TO GOLIUS, 2 FEBRUARY 1632

236   I am very much obliged to you for your favourable judgement on my analysis, for I know very well that the greater part of it is due to your good
237   manners. I have a somewhat better opinion of myself all the same, because I see that you have made a full examination of the facts before passing final judgement on it. I am very pleased that you would like to make a similar examination concerning the question of refraction. In order to contribute as much goodwill as I can to the effort which you intend to devote to the observation of refraction, let me tell you how I would wish to go about it had I the same plan.

First I would make an instrument of wood or some other material, just as you see drawn here. A B is a ruler or a perfectly straight piece of wood,

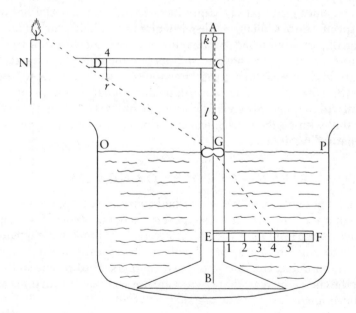

---

1 Descartes never succeeded in doing this.

with a base B on which it can stand firmly at the bottom of the vessel OP. EF and CD are two additional rulers joined at right angles to AB. G is a sight-vane which must be sufficiently large and of roughly the following shape: G has to be sufficiently large not to prevent the surface of the water 238

from being perfectly flat and level at the point in the middle marked *i*, which is exactly where the refraction must occur. The function of points G and H is to fix the point *i*. Ruler EF is divided into a number of divisions 1, 2, 3, 4, etc.; and it does not matter whether these are equal or unequal. Ruler EF must also be bigger than DC and must stick out so that its divisions are on the same plane as sight-vane G and pointer *r*.

Lastly *kl* is a plumb or level, which is to be used to line up the vessel in which the instrument is placed, so that line AB is pointing exactly towards the centre of the earth. Water should then be poured into the vessel until the surface of the water just touches sight-vane G. Holding pointer *r* on ruler DC with one hand and candle N with the other, one should move these back and forth (while keeping pointer *r* on ruler DC), until the shadow of the pointer falls exactly in the middle of sight-vane GH*i* and on 239 one of the divisions of ruler EF, such as 4. Now after marking on line CD the point on which pointer *r* happens at that moment to lie, i.e. point 4, one must then lift the instrument out of the water, and in accordance with the reasoning with which you are familiar, mark the other divisions of line CD, which should correspond to the divisions of EF. For example, having described a circle with centre G and drawn in lines 4G, 4G which intersect the circle at points *a* and *d*, I then draw the perpendicular lines *ab*, *cd*; then, 240 drawing G3, which intersects the circle at point *f*, I draw in the perpendicular *ef*, and then look for the line *hi*, which is to *ef* just as *ab* is to *cd*; and once this is found, I draw it in, parallel to *ab*. Then, extending G*h* to DC, I find point 3 and the others in the same way. Once all the divisions of ruler CD have been found, one must put the instrument back in the water as before, and putting the pointer against the divisions of line DC, one must look to see whether its shadow, which passes through G, falls exactly on the divisions of ruler EF. No doubt if you took the trouble to look for them, you could find other inventions that would be better suited to the present experiment than the one I have described; but since I know that you have many other tasks to occupy you, it occurred to me that if you had

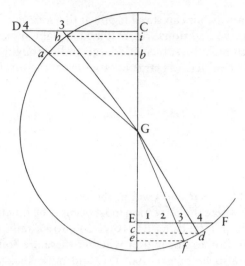

not yet given the matter any thought, I would perhaps lighten your burden a little by telling you about this one, or at least that I would be able to assure you of my affection for you.

The only experiment I ever made on this question was one I made about five years ago. I had a glass cut from a design drawn by M. Mydorge. When the experiment was made, the rays of the sun which passed through the glass all gathered exactly at the point beyond the glass which I had predicted. This convinced me that either the craftsman had made a fortunate blunder or my reasoning was not false.[1]

AT I   TO MERSENNE, 5 APRIL 1632

242   It is a long time since I heard from you, and I shall begin to worry about your health if you do not write to me soon. I expect that you have been waiting for me to send you the treatise[2] which I promised you for this Easter. It is almost finished, and I could keep my promise if I thought that you would want to hold me to the letter; but I would prefer to keep it for a few months, to revise it and rewrite it, and draw some diagrams which are

243   necessary. They are quite a trouble to me, for as you know I am a very poor draughtsman and careless about matters which do not help me to learn anything. If you blame me for having so often failed to keep my promise, I will say in excuse that my only reason for so long putting off writing the little I know has been the hope of learning more and being able to add to

---

1 This paragraph occurs only in Clerselier's text.
2 Probably the *Optics*.

the book. For instance, in the treatise which I now have in hand, after the general description of the stars, the heavens and the earth, I did not originally intend to give an account of particular bodies on the earth but only to treat of their various qualities. In fact, I am now discussing in addition some of their substantial forms, and trying to show the way to discover them all in time by supplementing my reasoning with observations. This is what has occupied me these last days; for I have been making various experiments to discover the essential differences between oils, ardent spirits, ordinary water and acidic liquids, salts, etc. Altogether, if I postpone the payment of my debt it is with the intention of paying you interest on it. I tell you all this only for lack of better matter; when you receive what I plan to send you it will be for you to judge whether it is worth anything. I am very much afraid that it may be so much less than your expectation that you will not be willing to accept it in payment.

Last time you wrote to me about a man who boasted of being able to   244
solve mathematical problems of all kinds. I would be glad to know if you
have set him the problem of Pappus,[1] which I sent to you. I must admit that
I took five or six weeks to find the solution; and if anyone else discovers it, I
will not believe that he is ignorant of algebra.

TO MERSENNE, 10 MAY 1632   AT I

Eight days ago I put you to the trouble of sending on a letter for me to   249
Poitou; but I was in a hurry when writing it, having negligently put off   250
writing, as usual, until the post was almost ready to leave, and so I forgot
to include the address for a reply. This forces me to burden you once more
with a letter to send on.

You tell me that you have Scheiner's[2] description of the phenomenon at
Rome. If it is more detailed than the one which you sent me before,[3] I shall
be most obliged if you will take the trouble to send me a copy.

If you know any author who has made a special collection of the various
accounts of comets, I shall be very obliged if you will inform me of it. For
the last two or three months I have been quite caught up in the heavens. I
have discovered their nature and the nature of the stars we see there and
many other things which a few years ago I would not even have dared to

---

1 Pappus of Alexandria (fl. 320 A.D.), the last great Greek geometer. The problem was to
   find a point on a plane such that the product of the distances between the point and given
   lines is in constant relation to the product of the distances between the points and another
   group of lines.
2 Christopher Scheiner (1575–1650), a German Jesuit and astronomer, who observed
   parhelia near Rome in 1629 and 1630.
3 See above, p. 7.

hope to discover; and now I have become so rash as to seek the cause of the position of each fixed star. For although they seem very irregularly distributed in various places in the heavens, I do not doubt that there is a natural order among them which is regular and determinate. The discovery of this order is the key and foundation of the highest and most perfect science of material things which men can ever attain. For if we possessed it, we could discover *a priori*[1] all the different forms and essences of terrestrial bodies,

251 whereas without it we have to content ourselves with guessing them *a posteriori* and from their effects. I cannot think of anything which could be of greater help towards the discovery of this order than the description of many comets. And, as you know, I have no books, and even if I had, I would begrudge the time spent in reading them; so I would be very glad to find somebody who had collected together the things which could cost me a lot of trouble to glean from several authors each writing about only one or two comets.

You once told me that you knew some people who were so dedicated to the advancement of science that they were willing to make every kind of experiment at their own expense. It would be very useful if some such person were to write the history of celestial phenomena in accordance with the Baconian method and to describe the present appearances of the heavens without any explanations or hypotheses, reporting the position of each fixed star in relation to its neighbours, listing their differences in size and colour and visibility and brilliance and so on. He should tell us how far this accords with what ancient astronomers have written and what differ-

252 ences are to be found; for I have no doubt that the stars are constantly changing their relative position, in spite of being called fixed. He should add the observations which have been made of comets, with a table of the path of each like the ones Tycho[2] made of the three or four that he observed, and he should include the variations in the ecliptic and apogee of planets. Such a work would be more generally useful than might seem possible at first sight, and it would relieve me of a great deal of trouble. But I have no hope that anyone will do it, just as I do not hope to discover the answers to my present questions about the stars. I think that the science I describe is beyond the reach of the human mind; and yet I am so foolish that I cannot help dreaming of it though I know that this will only make me waste my time as it has already done for the last two months. In that time I have made no progress with my treatise; but I will not fail to finish it before the date I told you.

1 '*A priori*' is used here to mean 'reasoning from cause to effect'.
2 Tycho Brahe (1546–1601), the great Danish astronomer whose *Liber de Cometa* appeared in 1603.

I have written all this needlessly so as to fill up my letter and not send you empty paper.

Tell me if M. de Beaune[1] is publishing anything. I would be glad to see MM. Mydorge and Hardy's method of doubling a cube as well as the books you sent me. I think you told me that it would be there, but I have not been able to find it.

TO MERSENNE, JUNE 1632   AT I

Thank you for the letters which you were so good as to send me. I am   254
now at Deventer, and I have decided not to leave here until the *Optics* has been completed. For the last month I have been trying to decide whether I should include in *The World* an account of how animals are generated. I have finally decided not to, because it would take me too long. I have finished all I had planned to include in it concerning inanimate bodies. It only remains for me to add something concerning the nature of man. I shall make a fair copy of it later and send it to you, but I dare not say when that   255
will be, for I have failed to keep my promises so often already that it pains me to think of it.

As for your questions, I do not believe that sound is reflected at a point as light is, since it is not propagated like light in rays which are all straight; rather, it spreads out in all directions in a circle . . .

To measure the refraction of sounds is no easier than to measure their reflection; so far as refraction can be observed at all, it is certain that it must take place †at right angles in water,† which is the very opposite of what happens in the case of light. As for my method of measuring the refractions of light, †I introduce a correspondence between the sines of the angles of incidence and the angles of refraction;†[2] but I should be very glad if this was not yet made public, because the first part of my *Optics* will be devoted entirely to this topic. †What shape a line under water will be seen to have is something that cannot be easily determined; for the location of the image is not fixed either in reflection or in refraction, as students of optics are commonly convinced.† . . .

TO MERSENNE, NOVEMBER OR DECEMBER 1632   AT I

. . . As to what you tell me about the calculation which Galileo has made   (261)
concerning the speed at which falling bodies move, it bears no relation to

---

1 Florimond Debeaune (1601–52), a mathematician and student of astronomy.
2 Cf. *Optics*: AT VI 93–105; CSM I 156–64.

my philosophy.[1] According to my philosophy there will not be the same relation between two spheres of lead, one weighing one pound and the other a hundred pounds, as there is between two spheres of wood, one weighing one pound and the other a hundred pounds, or even between two spheres of lead, one weighing two pounds and the other two hundred pounds. He makes no distinction between these cases, which makes me think that he cannot have hit upon the truth.

I would like to know what he writes concerning the ebb and flow of the tides, for that is one of the things I have had the greatest trouble in fathoming; and while I think I have got to the bottom of it, there are still some circumstances which I have not yet explained . . .

263   My discussion of man in *The World* will be a little fuller than I had intended, for I have undertaken to explain all the main functions in man. I have already written of the vital functions, such as the digestion of food, the heart beat, the distribution of nourishment, etc., and the five senses. I am now dissecting the heads of various animals, so that I can explain what imagination, memory, etc. consist in. I have seen the book *De Motu Cordis*[2] which you previously spoke to me about. I find that it differs slightly from my own view, although I saw it only after having finished writing on this topic.

AT I   TO MERSENNE, END OF NOVEMBER 1633

270   This is the point I had reached when I received your last letter of the eleventh of this month. I was inclined to act like a bad debtor who begs his creditors to give him a little more time when he sees the day of reckoning approaching. In fact I had intended to send you my *World* as a New Year gift, and only two weeks ago I was quite determined to send you at least a part of it, if the whole work could not be copied in time. But I have to say that in the mean time I took the trouble to inquire in Leiden and Amsterdam whether Galileo's *World System* was available, for I thought I had heard that it was published in Italy last year. I was told that it had indeed been published but that all the copies had immediately been burnt at Rome, and that Galileo had been convicted and fined.[3] I was so astonished
271   at this that I almost decided to burn all my papers or at least to let no one

---

1 The reference is to the *Dialogue Concerning the Two Chief World Systems* (1632), by Galileo Galilei (1546–1642), the great Italian astronomer and physicist.
2 *Treatise on the Motion of the Heart* (1628), by William Harvey (1578–1657), the great English physiologist.
3 After publishing his *Dialogue* in 1632, Galileo was sentenced on 22 June 1633 by the Inquisition in Rome to house-arrest in the Palace of the Archbishop of Sienna.

see them. For I could not imagine that he – an Italian and, as I understand, in the good graces of the Pope – could have been made a criminal for any other reason than that he tried, as he no doubt did, to establish that the earth moves. I know that some Cardinals had already censured this view,[1] but I thought I had heard it said that all the same it was being taught publicly even in Rome. I must admit that if the view is false, so too are the entire foundations of my philosophy, for it can be demonstrated from them quite clearly. And it is so closely interwoven in every part of my treatise that I could not remove it without rendering the whole work defective. But for all the world I did not want to publish a discourse in which a single word could be found that the Church would have disapproved of; so I preferred to suppress it rather than to publish it in a mutilated form. I have never had an inclination to produce books, and would never have completed it if I had not been bound by a promise to you and some other of my friends; it was my desire to keep my word to you that constrained me all the more to work at it. But after all I am sure you will not send a bailiff to force me to discharge my debt, and you will perhaps be quite glad to be relieved of the trouble of reading wicked doctrines. There are already so many views in philosophy which are merely plausible and which can be maintained in debate that if my views are no more certain and cannot be approved of without controversy, I have no desire ever to 272 publish them. Yet, after having promised you the whole work for so long, it would be bad faith on my part if I tried to satisfy you with trifling pieces; so as soon as I can, I shall let you see what I have composed after all, but I ask you to be so kind as to allow me a year's grace so that I can revise and polish it. You drew my attention to Horace's saying 'Keep back your work for nine years',[2] and it is only three years since I began the treatise which I intend to send you. I ask you also to tell me what you know about the Galileo affair . . .

TO MERSENNE, FEBRUARY 1634   AT I

I have nothing special to tell you, but since it is now over two months 281 since I last had your news, I thought I ought not to wait any longer before writing to you. If I had not had so much proof of your goodwill towards me – proof too extensive to give me any cause to doubt it – I would almost fear it had cooled somewhat, since I have failed to keep my promise to send you something of my philosophy. Besides, knowing your virtue as I do, I

---

1 Galileo had been censured by the Inquisition and by Cardinal Bellarmino in 1616 for supporting the Copernican theory.
2 *The Art of Poetry*, 388.

hope that you will think even better of me when you see that I have decided wholly to suppress the treatise I have written and to forfeit almost all my work of the last four years in order to give my obedience to the Church, since it has proscribed the view that the earth moves. All the same, since I have not yet seen that the proscription has been ratified by the Pope or the Council (it was made by the Congregation of Cardinals set up for the censorship of books), I should be very glad to know what the view in France is on this matter and whether their authority is sufficient to make the proscription an article of faith. If I may say so, the Jesuits have helped to get Galileo convicted: Father Scheiner's entire book[1] clearly shows that they are no friends of Galileo's. Besides, the observations which the book contains provide so much proof to dispossess the sun of the motion attributed to it that I cannot believe that Father Scheiner himself does not share the Copernican view in his heart of hearts; and I find this so astonishing that I dare not write down my feelings on the matter.

282

As for myself, I seek only repose and peace of mind – goods which cannot be possessed by those who are bitter or ambitious. In the meantime I am not remaining inactive; but for the time being I intend only to instruct myself – in my judgement I am hardly capable of instructing others and especially those who, if the truth were known, would perhaps be afraid of losing the reputation which they have already acquired through views that are false.

AT I

TO MERSENNE, APRIL 1634

285   From your last I learn that my last letter to you has been lost, though I thought I had addressed it very safely. In it I told you at length the reason why I did not send you my treatise. I am sure you will find it so just that, far from blaming me for resolving never to show it to anyone, you would be the first to exhort me to do so, if I were not already fully so resolved.

Doubtless you know that Galileo was recently censured by the Inquisitors of the Faith, and that his views about the movement of the earth were condemned as heretical. I must tell you that all the things I explained in my treatise, which included the doctrine of the movement of the earth, were so interdependent that it is enough to discover that one of them is false to know that all the arguments I was using are unsound. Though I thought they were based on very certain and evident proofs, I would not wish, for anything in the world, to maintain them against the authority of the Church. I know that it might be said that not everything which the Roman Inquisitors decide is automatically an article of faith, but must first be

1 *Rosa Ursina* (1626).

approved by a General Council. But I am not so fond of my own opinions as to want to use such quibbles to be able to maintain them. I desire to live 286 in peace and to continue the life I have begun under the motto 'to live well you must live unseen'.[1] And so I am more happy to be delivered from the fear of my work's making unwanted acquaintances than I am unhappy at having lost the time and trouble which I spent on its composition . . .

As for what it is that causes a stone one has thrown to stop moving, that is quite clear: it is air resistance, something one can easily feel. But the 287 reason why a bent bow springs back is more difficult, and I cannot explain it without referring to the principles of my philosophy, which I think I must keep quiet about from now on.

A rumour has been going round here that a comet appeared a little while ago. Please tell me if you have heard anything about it. Since you told me in a previous letter that you knew some people who could help to perform the experiments that I wanted done, I must tell you that I read about one such experiment recently in *Mathematical Games*:[2] it makes use of a large cannon placed in the middle of some flat ground and pointing straight up at the sky. I would like to see this experiment performed by some people who are interested and have the requisite resources. The author of the book says that the experiment has already been performed many times, and the ball did not once fall back to the ground. Many might think this quite incredible, but I do not judge it to be impossible, and I believe it is something well worth looking into.

As for the results you tell me of Galileo's experiments, I deny them all; but I do not conclude the motion of the earth to be any less probable. I do indeed agree that the movement of a chariot, a boat or a horse remains in some manner in a stone thrown from them, but there are other reasons which prevent it from remaining undiminished. As for a cannon ball shot off a high tower, it must take much longer descending than one which was allowed to fall vertically; for it meets more air on its way, which resists its 288 vertical motion as well as its horizontal motion.

I am astonished that an ecclesiastic should dare to write about the motion of the earth, whatever excuses he may give. For I have seen letters patent about Galileo's condemnation, printed at Liège on 20 September 1633, which contained the words 'though he pretended he put forward his view only hypothetically'; thus they seem to forbid even the use of this hypothesis in astronomy. For this reason I do not dare to tell him any of my thoughts on the topic. Moreover, I do not see that this censure has been endorsed by the Pope or by any Council, but only by a single congregation

1 'Bene vixit, bene qui latuit' (Ovid, *Tristia*, III, iv, 25).
2 By Jean Leurechon, S.J. (pseudonym, van Etten), published in 1624.

of the Cardinals of the Inquisition; so I do not altogether lose hope that the case may turn out like that of the Antipodes, which were similarly condemned long ago. So in time my *World* may yet see the light of day; and in that case I shall need my own arguments to use myself. . . .

AT I   TO MERSENNE, 14 AUGUST 1634

303   I was beginning to be troubled at not getting your news, but I thought that you would have been so preoccupied by the printing of the book[1] which you recently wrote to me about that you would have had no time left for writing. M. Beeckman came here on Saturday evening and lent me the book by Galileo.[2] But he took it away with him to Dordrecht this morning;
304 so I have only had it in my hands for thirty hours. I was able to leaf through the whole book; and I find that he philosophizes well enough on motion, though there is very little he has to say about it that I find entirely true. As far as I could see, he goes wrong more often when following received opinion than when going beyond it, with the exception of his discussion of the ebb and flow of the tide, where I find his reasoning rather forced. In *The World* I had also explained this in terms of the motion of the earth, but in a quite different way from his.[3] I must admit, however, that I have come across some of my own thoughts in his book, including two, among others, which I think I wrote to you about some time ago. The first is that the distance covered by a falling heavy body is proportional to the square of the time which the body takes to fall:[4] for example, if a ball takes three seconds to fall from A to B, it will take only one second for it to continue
305 down from B to C, etc., as I said, albeit with many qualifications, for in fact it is never completely true, as he thinks he has demonstrated that it is.

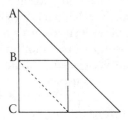

---

1 Mersenne had several books published that year, including *Les Mécaniques de Galilée*.
2 *Dialogue Concerning the Two Chief World Systems* (1632).
3 Cf. *The World*, ch. 12: AT XI 8off.
4 Descartes is mistaken here: in his law the distance travelled is proportional, not to the square of the time, but to another power of the time, namely $\frac{\log 2}{\log \frac{4}{3}}$; see footnote 1, p. 9 above.

The second idea is that the up and down vibrations of a cord take practically the same amount of time, even though some vibrations are very much longer than others.[1]

The arguments which he uses to demonstrate the movement of the earth are very good; but it seems to me that he does not set them out in the way that is required if they are to be convincing, for the digressions which he introduces make you forget the earlier arguments when you are in the process of reading the later ones.

As for what he says about a cannon which is fired parallel to the horizon, I believe you will find some differences that are observable if you perform the experiment precisely.

As for the other things which you write about, I have no time to reply if I am to catch the next post. Besides, I cannot possibly solve any question in physics absolutely without first setting out all my principles, and the treatise which I have decided to suppress would be required for that task.

The text of the document printed at Liège is as follows: 306

The said Galileo, therefore, who had confessed at an earlier interrogation, was summoned to the Sacred Tribunal of the Inquisition, interrogated and detained in custody. He clearly showed himself once again to be still of the same opinion, though he pretended that he put forward his view only hypothetically. The outcome is that after discussing the matter thoroughly, the Most Eminent Cardinals of the Commissionary General of the Inquisition have pronounced and declared that the said Galileo is under strong suspicion of heresy, in so far as he seems to have followed a doctrine which is false and contrary to Holy and Divine Scripture, namely that the sun is the centre of the universe and does not rise from sunrise to sunset, whereas the earth does move and is not the centre of the universe, or he has been of the opinion that this doctrine could be defended as a probability, even though it has been declared to be contrary to Holy Scripture.

I thank you for the letter which you sent me, and ask you to give your attention to the reply I am sending you.

TO [BEECKMAN], 22 AUGUST 1634 AT I

I am glad that you still remember the disagreement which we had 307 recently. Now, since I see that you are still not satisfied with the argument which I used then, I shall give you my frank opinion on your reply. But first let me set out a brief account of the whole matter, so that we are in no doubt about the thesis in question.

I said recently, when we were together, that indeed light does not move instantaneously, as you say, but (what you regard as the same thing)

1 See above, p. 10.

308 instantaneously arrives at the eye from the body which emits it, and I added that so certain was I of this that if it could be shown that it was false, I would be prepared to admit that I knew absolutely nothing in philosophy.

You, by contrast, strongly maintained that light can move only during some time-interval, and you added that you had thought of a way of making an experiment that would show which of us was mistaken. Divested of some superfluous items such as sound, a hammer, and the like, the experiment, as you describe it very well in your letter, is this. Someone holds a torch in his hand after dark and moves it about; if he looks at a mirror which is placed a quarter of a mile in front of him, he will be able to tell whether he feels the movement in his hands before he sees it in the mirror. So confident were you about the outcome of this experiment that you acknowledged that your entire philosophy would have to be regarded as false if the experiment showed that there was no observable time-lag between the instant when the movement was felt by the hand and the instant it was seen in the mirror. If, however, such a time-lag were detected, my philosophy would, I admitted, be completely overturned. Thus the point of contention between us, note, was not so much the question whether light travels instantaneously or during a time-interval, but rather the question of the outcome of this experiment. But in order to be done with the whole dispute and to save you from any pointless labour, I informed you the next day that there was another experiment which had already been carefully performed by numerous attentive observers. This experiment shows clearly that there is no time-lag between the instant the light is emitted from the luminous body and the instant it enters the eye.

In order to describe the experiment, I first asked whether you thought
309 that the moon gets its light from the sun, and whether eclipses occur because the earth comes between the sun and the moon or the moon comes between the sun and the earth. You answered in the affirmative. I then asked how you suppose the light from the stars reaches us, and you replied 'in straight lines'. Thus, on your view, the sun does not appear in its true position when you look at it, but in the position which it was in at the moment when the light which makes it visible was first emitted from it. Finally, I asked you to determine what the smallest observable interval would be between the instant when the torch is moved and the instant at which the movement appears in the mirror a quarter of a mile away. The day before, you stipulated that this time-interval would have to be at the very least as short as a single pulse beat; but then, more generously, you conceded that it could be as short as I liked. So, to show that I did not want to take advantage of your concession, I assumed that the interval was no longer than one-twenty-fourth of a pulse beat; and I said that the interval

which, you entirely agreed, would be quite undetectable in your experiment would turn out to be perfectly detectable in mine. Let us now suppose that the distance between the moon and the earth is fifty times the radius of the earth, and the radius is 600 miles long, which it ought to be at the very least if both astronomy and geometry are to hold. Now if light takes one-twenty-fourth of the interval of a pulse beat to cross a quarter of a mile twice, it will take an interval of 5,000 pulse beats, i.e. at least one hour, to cross the space between the moon and the earth twice, as is obvious when you work it out.

I have argued on the basis of the points which you conceded. Now, so that we can arrive at the same conclusion, let A B C be a straight line, with 310 A, B and C the places where the sun, the earth and the moon respectively are for the time being situated (whether it is the sun that moves or the earth does not matter). Thus:

A B C

Let us now suppose that from the earth B the moon is observed to undergo an eclipse at point C. From what you have conceded, the eclipse must be seen at exactly the moment when the light which was emitted by the sun when it was at A reaches the eye after being reflected from the moon, unless it has been blocked by the earth, that is, going by the points conceded, one hour after the light reached the earth at B. Hence the eclipse at C can only be seen an hour after the sun is seen at A, if the points you conceded are indeed correct, that is, if the movement of the torch is seen in the mirror situated a quarter of a mile away one-twenty-fourth of a pulse beat after it is felt in the hand. But as the careful and painstaking observations of every astronomer testify and countless experiments confirm, if the moon, while it is undergoing an eclipse, is observed at C from the earth B, the sun must be observed at A at the very same moment, and not an hour earlier. When we observe the position of the sun in relation to the earth and the moon, the interval of an hour is much more readily observable than the interval of one-twenty-fourth of a pulse beat is in your experiment. Your experiment, then, is ineffectual, whereas mine, which is the astronomers' experiment, shows much more clearly that light takes no detectable time to be seen. So I said that this argument was demonstrative, whereas you called it fallacious and question-begging . . .

TO GOLIUS, 19 MAY 1635

I was out of town when the letters and observations you kindly sent me (317)
arrived, and I have only been back for about a week; which is why I have

318 not written earlier to thank you. I very much wanted at the same time to give you an account of how informative I found them, but I have changed my lodgings since then, and have not yet had the time to put sea water to the test to see whether I could discover what the cause of its light[1] is.

As for the observations on the coronas and the parhelia, both yours and Schichardus',[2] they completely confirm the view I had; so there is nothing more I wish for on that score. All the same, I shall not return the book yet, for, judging that you had no urgent need of it, I thought it would be better to wait for some other opportunity to return it. But to compensate, I shall tell you about another observation which I made one night about eight or ten days ago when I was on the Zuider Zee on the way from Friesland to Amsterdam. That evening, resting my head on my right hand for quite some time, I covered my right eye with my hand, keeping the other eye open. The room I was in was rather dark, and someone brought in a candle. As soon as I opened both eyes, I perceived two coronas around the candle, with more perfect colours than I thought ever possible, just as you

319 see in the drawing here. A is the outer ring of the larger corona, which was

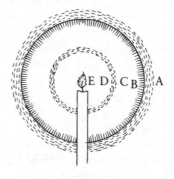

of a deep red-brown colour. B is the inner ring of the same; this was blue. Between the two rings you could just make out the other colours of the rainbow, but they took up very little space. C is the gap between the coronas; this looked as black as, or even blacker than, the air surrounding it. D is the inner corona, this was just a single ring of a deep red colour, just like the outer ring, and you could see that it was of a deeper hue on the outside than on the inside. E is the gap between the red ring and the candle flame; this space was quite white and bright. Now I had plenty of time to

1 I.e. phosphorescence.
2 Wilhelm Schickardt (1592–1635), Professor of Philosophy at Tübingen.

observe these things, for they lasted right up until I fell asleep some two or three hours later.

What this taught me was that the coronas were arranged in exactly the opposite way to those which appear around stars, i.e. red at the outside, and that they did not form in the air, but simply in the water of one of my eyes. For, when I closed my right eye and opened my left, I did not see them at all; and when I closed my left eye and opened my right, I still could not see them. I think I can explain this quite well. I am intrigued by this observation, so much so that I intend to include it in my *Meteorology*.[1]

I thank you very sincerely for inviting me to stay with you, but it would be flagrantly fickle of me, after so short a time, to leave the abode I have just taken up.[2] It is not that I am not acutely aware of my indebtedness to you for the affection which you have shown me in all sorts of ways, or that I do not desire in return to be able to do whatever I think will be agreeable to you.

TO [MERSENNE], JUNE OR JULY 1635   AT I

Thank you for the letter which you kindly sent me. I am very glad to learn that M. de Balzac[3] still remembers me. I was almost of a mind to write to him by this messenger, but I would prefer to wait a little longer. In the mean time if you happen to see him, I shall be obliged if you will assure him of my goodwill towards him . . .

As for the eyepieces, I must say that after Galileo's condemnation I revised and completed the treatise[4] I had begun some time ago. I have detached it completely from *The World*, and I am planning to have it published on its own before long. All the same, since we might not be able to see it in print for more than a year, I shall regard it as a favour if M. N. wants to work on it in the mean time; and I shall be happy to get copied all that I have included on practice and to send it to him whenever it suits him . . .

As for heat, I do not think that it is the same thing as light or rarefaction of air. I think of it as something quite different, which can often arise from light and give rise to rarefaction. I no longer believe that heavy bodies fall because of some *real quality* called *heaviness*, as philosophers imagine, or because of some attraction of the earth. But I could not explain my views on all these topics without publishing my *World* (with the proscribed

320

322

(323)
324

1 See *Meteorology*, Discourse 9: AT VI 345. See also above, pp. 13f.
2 Descartes had moved to Utrecht.
3 Jean-Louis Guez de Balzac (1597–1654), author of the celebrated *Lettres*.
4 The *Optics*.

movement), and I think that the time is not ripe for that. I am very surprised that you are proposing to refute the book *Against the Movement of the Earth*,[1] but I leave this to your own discretion.

AT I   TO HUYGENS, 1 NOVEMBER 1635

591   I am obliged to you beyond words, and am amazed that having so many important tasks you should offer to see to all the details of the printing of the *Optics*. It is an excess of courtesy and sincerity that may be a greater bother to you than you fear. I shall try to follow the detailed instructions which you kindly gave me on these external matters; and by way of repayment I shall be so bold as to ask you to correct the internal matter of the book before I let it go to the printer, at any rate if I can find you this winter in a more accessible abode than your present one, which will enable me to discuss things with you. The three mornings I had the honour to spend in conversation with you left me with such an impression of the
592   excellence of your mind and the soundness of your judgement that, in all honesty, I know of no one in all the world who could be so confidently entrusted to discover my errors as you. Your goodwill and the readiness to learn which you will find in me lead me to hope that you would rather I knew my own errors and removed them than that they should be seen by the public.

I plan to add the *Meteorology* to the *Optics*, and I worked quite diligently at this during the first two or three months of this year, since I found many difficulties which I had not yet gone into and which it was a pleasure to solve. But I must let you in on my state of mind: as soon as I lost hope of learning anything more about this subject, I found it impossible to take any more trouble over it, other than to put things in order and to write a preface[2] which I intend to add to it. For this reason I shall wait another two or three months before speaking to the publisher . . .

AT I   TO MERSENNE, MARCH 1636

338   About five weeks ago I received your last of 18 January, and I had not received the previous letter until four or five days before. I postponed replying to you in the hope of being able to tell you soon that I had sent my

---

1 Perhaps *Responsio pro Telluris Quiete ad Jacob Lansbergii Apologiam pro Telluris Motu* (1634), by Jean-Baptiste Morin (1583–1656). See below, p. 389.
2 The future *Discourse on the Method*.

work[1] to the printer. That was why I came to this town,[2] because the Elzevirs earlier said they would like to be my publishers. But having seen me here they imagine, I think, that I will not escape from them, and so they have been making difficulties, so that I have resolved to go to someone else. Although I could find several other publishers here, I will not settle with any of them until I have news from you, provided I do not have to wait too long. If you think that my manuscripts could be printed in Paris more   339 conveniently than here and if you would be willing to take charge of them as you once kindly offered to do, I could send them to you immediately after receiving word from you. However, there is this difficulty: my manuscript is no better written than this letter; the spelling and punctuation are equally careless and the diagrams are drawn by me, that is to say, very badly. So if you cannot make out from the text how to explain them to the engraver, it would be impossible for him to understand them. Moreover I would like to have the whole thing printed in a handsome fount on handsome paper, and I would like the publisher to give me at least two hundred copies because I want to distribute them to a number of people.

So that you may know what it is that I want to have printed, there will be four treatises, all in French, and the general title will be as follows: 'The Plan of a Universal Science which is capable of raising our Nature to its Highest Degree of Perfection, together with the Optics, the Meteorology and the Geometry, in which the Author, in order to give proof of his universal Science, explains the most abstruse Topics he could choose, and does so in such a way that even persons who have never studied can understand them'. In this *Plan* I explain a part of my method, I try to prove the existence of God and of the soul apart from the body, and I add many other things which I imagine will not displease the reader. In the *Optics*, besides treating of refraction and the manufacture of lenses, I give detailed   340 descriptions of the eye, of light, of vision, and of everything belonging to catoptrics[3] and optics. In the *Meteorology* I dwell principally on the nature of salt, the causes of winds and thunder, the shapes of snowflakes, the colours of the rainbow – here I try also to demonstrate what is the nature of each colour – and the coronas or haloes and the mock suns or parhelia like those which appeared at Rome six or seven years ago. Finally, in the *Geometry* I try to give a general method of solving all the problems that have never yet been solved. All this I think will make a volume no bigger than fifty or sixty sheets. I do not want to put my name to it, as I resolved long ago; please do not say anything about it to anybody unless you judge

1 The *Discourse on the Method, with the Optics, Meteorology, and Geometry*, published by Jean le Maire of Leiden in June 1637.
2 Leiden.
3 Catoptrics is the part of optics that treats of reflection.

it proper to mention it to some publisher to find out whether he is willing to co-operate with me. Do not make any contract for me, please, until you hear my reply; I will make my decision on the basis of what you tell me. I would prefer to employ somebody who has no connection with Elzevir, who will probably have warned his correspondents because he knows that I am writing to you.

I have used up all my paper in telling you this. There remains only enough to tell you that in order to examine the things which Galileo says about motion I would need more time than I can spare at present.

I think that the experiment showing that sounds travel no more quickly with the wind than against the wind is correct, at least so far as the senses are concerned; for the movement of sound is something of a quite different nature from the movement of wind.

Thank you for the account of the ball shot vertically which does not drop back; it is very remarkable.

As for the subtle matter of which I have often spoken, I think it to be the same matter as terrestrial bodies; but as air is more fluid than water, so I imagine this matter much more fluid, liquid and penetrating than air.

A bow bends back because, when the shape of its pores is distorted, the subtle matter which passes through tends to restore them, whichever side it enters from.

AT I

TO MERSENNE, 27 FEBRUARY 1637[1]

I find that you have a very poor opinion of me and consider me very inconstant and irresolute, since you think that because of what you tell me I ought to change my plan, and attach my opening *Discourse* to my *Physics*. You seem to think I should give it to the publisher this very day on seeing your letter. I could not help laughing when I read the passage where you say that I am forcing the public to kill me so that it can see my writings the sooner. To this I can only reply that they are now in such a place and condition that those who would kill me would never be able to lay hands on them; and if I do not die in my own good time and in a good humour with the men who remain living, they will certainly not see them for more than a hundred years after my death.

I am very grateful to you for the objections which you have sent me, and I beg you to continue to tell me all those you hear. Make them as unfavourable to me as you can; that will be the greatest pleasure you can

---

1 There is some disagreement about the date of this letter. Adam and Milhaud date it 27 February 1637, while the editors of Mersenne's correspondence plausibly suggest the end of April.

give me. I am not in the habit of crying when people are treating my wounds, and those who are kind enough to instruct and inform me will always find me very docile.

However, I have not been able to understand your objection to the title; for I have not put *Treatise on the Method* but *Discourse on the Method*, which means *Preface or Notice on the Method*, in order to show that I do not intend to teach the method but only to discuss it. As can be seen from what I say, it is concerned more with practice than with theory. I call the following treatises *Essays in this Method* because I claim that what they contain could never have been discovered without it, so that they show how much it is worth. I have also inserted a certain amount of metaphysics, physics and medicine in the opening *Discourse* in order to show that my method extends to topics of all kinds.

Your second objection is that I have not explained at sufficient length how I know that the soul is a substance distinct from the body and that its 350 nature is solely to think. This, you say, is the only thing that makes obscure the proof of the existence of God. I admit that what you say is very true and that this makes my proof of the existence of God difficult to understand. But I had no better way of dealing with this topic than by explaining in detail the falsehood or uncertainty to be found in all the judgements that depend on the senses and the imagination, so as to show in the sequel which judgements depend only on the pure understanding, and what evidence and certainty they possess. I left this out on purpose and after deliberation, mainly because I wrote in the vernacular. I was afraid that weak minds might avidly embrace the doubts and scruples which I would have had to propound, and afterwards be unable to follow as fully the arguments by which I would have endeavoured to remove them. Thus I would have set them on a false path and been unable to bring them back. Eight years ago, however, I wrote in Latin the beginnings of a treatise of metaphysics in which this argument is conducted at some length; if a Latin version of my present book is made, as is planned, I could have it included. However, I am convinced that those who study my arguments for the existence of God will find them the more cogent the more they try to fault them. I claim that they are clearer in themselves than any of the demonstrations of geometers; in my view they are obscure only to those who cannot †withdraw their minds from their senses†, in accordance with what 351 I wrote on page 38.[1]

I am extremely grateful to you for the trouble which you offer to take concerning the printing of my manuscripts. However, I could not allow anyone but myself to be put to any expense; I would not fail to send you

1 *Discourse*: AT VI 37; CSM I 129.

whatever was necessary. Indeed I do not think that there need be any great expense; some publishers promised me gifts to induce me to offer them my work, even before I had left Paris or begun writing. So I think that there may still be enough foolish publishers to print them at their own expense, and enough gullible readers to buy copies and save them from their folly. Whatever I do I shall not hide myself as if I had committed a crime, but only to avoid being disturbed and to keep the liberty I have always enjoyed. I will not be very alarmed if some people know my name, but for the present I prefer people not to speak of it at all, so that no expectations may be raised and my work may not fall short of expectation.

Like you I am amused by the fantasies of the chemist of whom you wrote. I think that such chimeras are unworthy to occupy the thoughts of a decent man for a single moment.

AT I   TO HUYGENS, 20 MAY 1637

631   If I measured you by the standards of ordinary souls, the sorrow you have experienced since Madame de Zuylichem fell ill would lead me to fear

632   that her death would be quite unendurable; but since I have no doubt that your life is governed entirely in accordance with reason, I am convinced that, now that all hope of remedy has gone, it will be much easier for you to find consolation and to regain your former peace of mind than it was when you still had cause to fear and hope. For it is certain that once hope is gone, desire ceases or at least grows weaker, and the feeling of loss cannot be very vivid when we have little or no desire to recover what we have lost. It is true that ordinary minds do not usually appreciate this argument; they imagine (without themselves knowing what they are imagining) that what formerly existed can exist again and that loving them as he does God is as it were obliged to do whatever they wish. But a soul as stout and noble as yours knows only too well the condition God has given us from birth, to try with pointless longing to resist the necessity of his law. And although we cannot submit ourselves to God's law without some pain, I value love so highly that I think that whatever we go through for the sake of it is pleasant – so much so that even those who are ready to die for the good of

633   those they love seem to me to be happy to their last breath. While you were going without food or sleep in order to nurse your sick wife, even though I feared for your own health, I think it would have been sacrilegious of me to try to divert you from such a devoted and tender task. But now, since it cannot be of any use to her, your grief can no longer be so appropriate, and hence can no longer be accompanied by that sense of joy and inner contentment which follows virtuous actions and makes wise people find happiness in all the vicissitudes of fortune. So if I thought that your reason

was not able to overcome your grief, I would take it upon myself to visit you and do whatever I could to distract you, for I know of no other cure for such distress.

I am taking no account here of the personal loss you have suffered in being deprived of a companion whom you dearly cherished, for it seems to me that the ills which concern ourselves cannot be compared with those that concern our friends, and while it is a virtue to feel pity at the slightest afflictions of others, to grieve over our own is a kind of softness. Besides, you have so many close relations in your family who are devoted to you that you could have no cause to complain on that score; and although you have only Madame de Willelm for a sister, I think she alone is all you need to rescue you from the solitude and household cares which anyone other than you would dread after losing his partner. Please excuse the liberty I have taken here in expressing my thoughts as a philosopher. I have just this 634 minute received through Mr Golius[1] a parcel from your part of the country. I have no idea what Father Mersenne is about, for he has still not sent me any licence to publish, and seems intent on obliging me by doing the very opposite of what I ask.

TO [SILHON], MAY 1637[2]   AT I

I agree, as you observe, that there is a great defect in the work you have 353 seen, and that I have not expounded, in a manner that everyone can easily grasp, the arguments by which I claim to prove that there is nothing at all more evident and certain than the existence of God and of the human soul. But I did not dare to try to do so, since I would have had to explain at length the strongest arguments of the sceptics to show that there is no material thing of whose existence one can be certain. Thus I would have accustomed the reader to detach his thought from things that are perceived by the senses, and then I would have shown that a man who thus doubts everything material cannot for all that have any doubt about his own existence. From this it follows that he, that is to say the soul, is a being or substance which is not at all corporeal, whose nature is solely to think, and that it is the first thing one can know with certainty. If you spend a sufficient time on this meditation, you acquire by degrees a very clear, dare I say intuitive, notion of intellectual nature in general. This is the idea which, if considered without limitation, represents God, and if limited, is the idea of an angel or a human soul. Now it is not possible fully to understand what I later say about the existence of God unless you begin in

1 Jacob Gool (1596–1667), Professor of Mathematics at the University of Leiden.
2 In AT this letter is dated March 1637.

354   this way, as I hinted on page 38.[1] But I was afraid that this introduction would look at first as if it were designed to bring in scepticism, and would disturb weaker minds, especially as I was writing in the vernacular. So I did not dare to put in even the little on page 32 without some words of warning.[2] But as for intelligent people like yourself, Sir, if they take the trouble not only to read but also to meditate in order on the same topics on which, as I reported, I meditated myself, spending a long time on each point, to see whether I have gone wrong, I trust that they will come to the same conclusions as I did. I shall be glad, as soon as I have time, to try to explain this further. I am pleased to have had this opportunity to show you that I am, etc.

AT I   TO MERSENNE, END OF MAY 1637

366   You argue that if the nature of man is solely to think, then he has no will. I do not see that this follows; for willing, understanding, imagining, and sensing and so on are just different ways of thinking, and all belong to the soul.

You reject my statement that in order to do well it is sufficient to judge well; yet it seems to me that the common scholastic doctrine is that 'the will does not tend towards evil except in so far as it is presented to it by the intellect under some aspect of goodness' – that is why they say that 'whoever sins does so in ignorance' – so that if the intellect never represented anything to the will as good without its actually being so, the will could never go wrong in its choice. But the intellect often represents different things to the will at the same time; and that is why they say 'I see and praise the better, but I follow the worse', which applies only to weak minds, as I said on page 26.[3] The well-doing of which I speak cannot be understood in a theological sense – for there grace comes into the question – but simply in the sense of moral and natural philosophy, where no account is taken of grace. So I cannot be accused, on these grounds, of the error of the Pelagians.[4] It is as if I said that good sense was the only thing necessary to make a man of honour; it would be altogether beside the point to object that it was necessary also to have the right sex and not to be a woman.

367   Similarly, when I said that it is probable (I mean according to human reason) that the world was created just as it should be, I am not denying that it may be certain by faith that it is perfect.

1 *Discourse*: AT vi 37; CSM i 129.
2 *Discourse*: AT vi 31; CSM i 126.
3 *Discourse*: AT vi 25; CSM i 123. The quotation is from Ovid, *Metamorphoses*, vii, 20.
4 Followers of Pelagius (*c.* 354–*c.* 418), a theologian whose heterodox doctrine stressed the primacy of human effort, as against divine grace, for human salvation.

As to those who asked you what my religion was, they should have looked at what I wrote on page 29, namely that I would not have thought myself obliged to rest content with the opinions of others for a single moment if I had not intended in due course to examine them using my own judgement.[1] Then they would see that it cannot be inferred from my *Discourse* that infidels should remain in the religion of their parents.

I do not find anything else in your two letters which needs a reply, except that it seems you are afraid that the publication of my opening *Discourse* may commit me never afterwards to publish my *Physics*.[2] You need not be afraid of that, because I do not anywhere promise never to publish it during my lifetime. I merely say that in the past I planned to publish it, but that more recently, for the reasons which I give, I have decided not to do so during my lifetime; and that now I have made up my mind to publish the treatises contained in this volume. It can indeed be inferred from that that if the reasons which prevent me from publishing should be altered, I could make a fresh resolve, without thereby being inconstant; because †when a cause is removed, its effect is removed†. You say also that what I say about my *Physics* may be attributed to vainglory since I do not include it. It may be, by people who do not know me and have read only my opening 368 *Discourse*. But those who look at the whole book, or who know me, will not, I think, accuse me of that vice. Nor will they reproach me, as you do, for despising my fellow men because I do not press upon them a gift that I am not yet sure they want. I spoke of my *Physics* as I did solely in order to urge those who want to see it to put an end to the causes which prevent me from publishing it.

Once more, I ask you to send us either the licence to publish or the refusal of it, as promptly as possible.[3] I would prefer it one day earlier in the simplest form to one day later in the most ample form.

TO ***, END OF MAY 1637 AT I

In revealing my name, Father Mersenne has done the very opposite of 369 what I asked. Yet I cannot hold it against him, since the effect of his action is that I have the honour of being acquainted with someone of your merits. But I have good cause to dissociate myself from his application for the licence to publish which he tells me he wants to try to obtain for me; for he introduces me with fulsome praise, describing me as the discoverer of

1 *Discourse*: AT VI 28; CSM I 124.
2 *The World*.
3 A licence to publish the *Discourse* was granted from the King of France, thanks to Mersenne's efforts, on 4 May 1637.

many fine things, and putting into my mouth the intention to offer to the public other treatises than those already in print. This contradicts what I wrote both at the beginning of page 77 of the *Discourse*[1] (which serves as a preface) and in other places as well. But I am sure he will let you see the letter I am sending him, since I learn from your very kind letter that it was you who obliged me by suggesting to him some of the objections which I deal with.

370

As for the treatise on physics which you have been so kind as to urge me to publish, I would not have been so unwise as to speak of it in the way I did, had I not been keen to publish it should the public desire it and I gain something from it. But I would like you to know that the present publication is designed entirely to prepare the way and to test the waters. To this end I am proposing a general method. I am not actually following the method, but trying rather to give some demonstrations of it in the three consecutive treatises appended to the *Discourse*, where I describe it. The subject-matter of the first treatise[2] is a mixture of philosophy and mathematics, that of the second[3] is entirely pure philosophy, and that of the third[4] entirely pure mathematics. In these treatises I can state that I did not refrain from discussing anything (at least anything knowable by the power of reasoning) because I lacked knowledge of it. So I think this gives me reason to believe that I am employing a method that could be used to explain any other subject just as well, provided I had made the requisite sensory observations and had the time to think about them. Moreover, in order to show that the method can be applied to everything, I have included some brief remarks on metaphysics, physics and medicine in the opening discourse. If I can get the public to view my method in this way, I believe there will no longer be any need to fear that the principles of my physics will be ill received; and if only I could find critics who are as kindly disposed towards me as you, I would have no fear of it from now on.

AT I

TO MERSENNE, EARLY JUNE 1637

(377)   . . . As for the physician who denies that the valves of the heart close tightly, he is going against the anatomists (who all say the very opposite in their writings), rather than going against me, for I have no need of that point to demonstrate that the movement of the heart is exactly as I describe it in my book.[5] For, even if the valves did not close half the openings to

1 Cf. AT VI 77; CSM I 150.
2 The *Optics*. By 'philosophy' here Descartes means natural science.
3 The *Meteorology*.
4 The *Geometry*.
5 *Discourse*: AT VI 47ff; CSM I 134ff.

each blood vessel, the automaton would nevertheless continue to move necessarily, as I have said. Besides, observation makes it clear to the naked eye that the six valves in the great artery and the arterial vein[1] close these vessels tightly. In the heart of a dead animal the valves in the vena cava and venous artery[2] do not appear to close tightly; nevertheless if we consider   378 that the tiny membranes which the valves consist of, and the fibres by which they are attached, are more spread out in live animals than in dead ones (where they have contracted), we shall have no doubt that these close just as tightly as the other ones.

As for his further comment that I considered the brain and eye of an animal rather than that of a human being, I do not see what makes him think this. Perhaps it is because he thinks that since I am not a doctor by profession, I have not had the opportunity to make observations on human organs, which I readily admit, or because the diagram of the brain given in the *Optics*[3] was faithfully drawn after the model of a sheep's brain, the ventricles and internal parts of which are, I know, much larger in relation to the brain as a whole than they are in the human brain. But for this reason I thought the sheep's brain was more suitable for making clear what I had to say, which applies both to animals and to human beings. And that cannot be held against me; for I made no assumption in anatomy which is novel or in any way disputed by those who write on that subject.

Lastly, I am not the least bit surprised that my explanation of refraction, or the nature of colours, was not to everyone's satisfaction, for there is no one who has had sufficient time to investigate these matters thoroughly. But when they have the time, those who are so good as to point out to me   379 any mistakes they notice will be doing me a great favour, especially if they consent to my reply being published along with their comments, so that my reply to one may serve as a reply to all. To conclude, I thank you for all your trouble.

TO HUYGENS, 12 JUNE 1637   AT I

I have at last received from France the licence to publish which we were   637 waiting for, and which caused the publisher to delay the printing of the last page of the book which I am sending you. With all respect I ask you to   638 present it to His Highness,[4] I dare not say in the name of the author, because the author's name is not given and I am not so presumptuous as to think that my name is worthy of his attention, but as having been written

1 The 'great artery' is the aorta, and the 'arterial vein' the pulmonary artery.
2 'Venous artery' denotes the pulmonary veins.
3 AT VI 128.
4 The Prince of Orange, Frederick Henry of Nassau (1584–1647).

by a person of your acquaintance who is warmly devoted to his service. In fact I can say that ever since I decided to leave my native land and distance myself from my acquaintances in order to lead a quieter and more tranquil life than I had before, I would not have taken it into my head to retire to this country and to prefer it to so many other places where no war was going on and where the purity and freshness of the air seemed better suited to intellectual production, if it had not been for the fact that the high opinion I had of His Highness made me utterly confident of his protection and government. And because I have since enjoyed to the full the peace and leisure I had hoped to find here under the aegis of his military power, I am deeply in his debt, and think that the book which contains the fruits of his peace should be offered to him above all others. So if you think it fitting that it is through your hands that I acquit myself of the debt – though the passionate devotion which I know you have for his service does not allow me to hope that you would be willing to pass off bad money for good – the perfect understanding which you have in all things and the ease with which you grasp all that is obscure in my writings makes me confident that your recommendation will add greatly to their value – I shall be for the rest of my life, etc.

TO PLEMPIUS, 3 OCTOBER 1637

410   I received your letter with M. Fromondus'[1] comments, and they were very welcome, though I must admit they arrived sooner than I expected. A few weeks ago I had heard that the book had not yet been sent to you, and many of those to whom I gave it to read here told me that they were not in a position to judge it until they had reread it several times. I am the more grateful to you both: to you for your generous praise, which I fear is beyond my deserts and is doubtless mostly due to your friendship for me; and to M. Fromondus for the care with which he has read my book and the trouble he has taken to send me his opinion of it. The judgement of a man so gifted, and so learned in the topics I treated, enables me, I think, to discern the view which many other readers will take. In many points, however, I see that he has not understood my meaning, so that I cannot yet tell what he and others will say after a closer examination. I cannot altogether agree with your judgement that my explanations can be rejected and ignored, but cannot be refuted or disproved. I used only very evident principles, and like a mathematician I took account of nothing but sizes,

411   shapes and motions, and so I cut myself off from all the subterfuges of philosophers. Consequently, the slightest error which occurs will be easily

---

1 Libert Froidmont (1587–1653), Professor of Philosophy at the University of Louvain.

detectable and refutable by a mathematical proof. On the other hand, if something is so true and solid that it cannot be overthrown by any such proof, then nobody, at least no teacher, can afford to ignore it. It is true that in appearance I expounded my opinions without proving them; but it is not difficult to extract from my explanations syllogisms which so evidently destroy the rival accounts of the same topics that those who want to defend them will find it difficult, without making themselves a laughing stock, to reply to people who have understood what I say. I am aware that my geometry will have very few readers; for I left out things which I thought others knew, and I tried in a few words to include, or touch on, many things – indeed everything which can ever be discovered in that science. So it demands readers who are not only skilled in the whole of geometry and algebra so far discovered, but also industrious, intelligent and attentive. I have heard that in your university[1] there are two such men, Wendel and van der Waegen. I will be very pleased to hear from you what they, or any others, judge of it. I am very anxious to see what you are writing about the motion of the heart. Send me it as soon as possible, please, and let me know how M. Fromondus takes my replies. Greet him warmly in my name. I have nothing to say about the philosophers of Leiden; I left there before the book was published; and so far as I know,   412
they have 'fallen silent, every one',[2] as you predicted of others also.

TO PLEMPIUS FOR FROMONDUS, 3 OCTOBER 1637   AT I

At the beginning of his objections the learned and distinguished M.   413
Fromondus reminds me of the fable of Ixion.[3] This seems very apt. He does well to warn me to keep to the truth and shun cloudy speculations: I protest that as far as in me lies I have always done so and will always do so. But the story fits him too: he thinks that he is attacking my philosophy, but he refutes only empty theories which have nothing to do with me, such as the system of atoms and void attributed to Democritus and Epicurus.

1. Concerning pages 46 and 47[4] he comments that noble actions like sight cannot result from so ignoble and brutish a cause as heat. He supposes that I think that animals see just as we do, i.e. being aware or thinking they see, which is said to have been Epicurus' view and is still almost universal. But in the whole of that part up to page 60[5] I explain quite explicitly that my view is that animals do not see as we do when we

---

1 Louvain.
2 Virgil, *Aeneid*, II 1, 1.
3 In classical mythology Ixion made love to a cloud, mistaking it for Juno.
4 *Discourse*: AT vi 46; CSM I 134.
5 *Discourse*: AT vi 60; CSM I 141.

are aware that we see, but only as we do when our mind is elsewhere. In such a case the images of external objects are depicted on our retinas, and

414 perhaps the impressions they make in the optic nerves cause our limbs to make various movements, although we are quite unaware of them. In such a case we too move just like automatons, and nobody thinks that the force of heat is insufficient to cause their movements.

2. Concerning page 56[1] he asks what is the point of attributing substantial souls to animals, and goes on to say that my views will perhaps open the way for atheists to deny the presence of a rational soul even in the human body. I am the last person to deserve this criticism, since, like the Bible, I believe, and I thought I had clearly explained, that the souls of animals are nothing but their blood, the blood which is turned into spirits[2] by the warmth of the heart and travels through the arteries to the brain and from it to the nerves and muscles. This theory involves such an enormous difference between the souls of animals and our own that it provides a better argument than any yet thought of to refute the atheists and establish that human minds cannot be drawn out of the potentiality of matter. And on the other side, I do not see how those who credit animals with some sort of substantial soul distinct from blood, heat and spirits can answer such Scripture texts as Leviticus 17:14 ('The soul of all flesh is in its blood, and you shall not eat the blood of any flesh, because the soul of flesh is in its blood') and Deuteronomy 12:23 ('Only take care not to eat their blood,

415 for their blood is their soul, and you must not eat their soul with their flesh'). Such texts seem much clearer than others which are quoted against certain other opinions which have been condemned solely because they contradict the Bible or appear to. Moreover, since these people posit so little difference between the operations of a man and of an animal, I do not see how they can convince themselves there is such a great difference between the natures of the rational and sensitive souls. On their view, when the sensitive soul is alone, its nature is corporeal and mortal; when it is joined to the rational soul, it is spiritual and immortal. For how do they think sensation is distinguished from reason? Sense-cognition, they say, is a matter of simple apprehension and therefore cannot be false; but the cognition of reason is a little more complex, and can make its way through tortuous syllogisms. This in no way seems to show its greater perfection; especially when the same people say that the cognition of God and of the angels is utterly simple and intuitive, a sheer apprehension free from any discursive wrapping. With respect, then, it seems that on their view sensation in animals is closer to cognition in God and the angels than

---

1 *Discourse*: AT VI 56; CSM I 139.
2 Animal spirits.

human reasoning is. I could have said many such things to support my theses, not only about the soul, but about almost everything else I have discussed. I did not do so, partly for fear of writing something false while refuting falsehood, partly for fear of seeming to want to ridicule received 416 scholastic opinions.

3. Concerning page 50[1] he says: 'it would take the heat of a furnace to rarefy the drops of blood sufficiently rapidly to make the heart expand'. In saying this he does not seem to have noticed how milk, oil and other liquids, when placed on a fire, almost all expand, gradually and slowly at first, then all of a sudden burst into flame when they reach a certain temperature, so that if they are not removed from the fire at once or at least if the vessel containing them is not opened to let out the vapours which are the main cause of their being rarefied, the major part of them overflows and pours on to the ashes. The temperature in question must vary depending on the various natures of the liquids; hence there are even certain liquids which are rarefied in this way when they are hardly lukewarm. Now if he had noted these points, he would easily have arrived at the view that the blood in the veins of any animal comes very close to the temperature which it must have in the heart if it is to be rarefied there instantaneously.

4. However, nowhere does he show more clearly that he has embraced the clouds of Democritus' philosophy instead of the clear sky of my philosophy than in his comment on page 4 of the *Optics*, where he maintains that my 'analogy of a blind man's stick does not give a correct explanation of the instantaneous transmission of light rays; because', he 417 says, 'a ray which shoots out from the sun should, rather, be compared with an arrow shot from a bow, which flies through the air, not instantaneously, but from one instant to the next, etc.'. Does he not take me here for Leucippus or Epicurus, or indeed Lucretius, who, if my memory serves me right, speaks somewhere in his poem of 'shafts of light'?[2] As for my own view, I nowhere suppose that there is anywhere a vacuum; indeed I expressly say the very opposite, namely that all the space between us and the sun is filled with a sort of highly fluid yet even more continuous body (which I call 'subtle matter'). So I do not see what objection there can be to my analogies, both the analogy of the stick and the analogy with a vat of pressed grapes, which I used to explain the instantaneous transmission of light rays. And if he says that my philosophy is 'crass and dense', on the grounds that some body can easily permeate the pores of glass, he is bound to forgive me if I reply that I consider it an even crasser yet less solid

1 *Discourse*: AT VI 50; CSM I 136.
2 The Latin phrase quoted by Descartes in fact occurs in the *Cathermerinion*, 2, 6, by Prudentius (fourth century), though similar phrases are to be found in Lucretius' *De Rerum Natura* (first century B.C.).

philosophy which holds that there are no pores in glass, on the grounds that such pores are impervious to sound; for we can see that sound is, if not wholly deadened, at least very greatly diminished and dulled by a curtain placed in its path. This shows that it is not in the nature of sound that it can pass easily through any sort of aperture; rather, it can only pass through apertures that are sufficiently wide and open. Indeed, since sound is a movement of the air, or at least depends on a movement of the air, it should surprise no one that sound cannot pass through apertures which do not let through a breath of air, let alone a whole mass of air . . .

(420)   9. He expresses surprise that on page 30[1] I recognize no sensation save that which takes place in the brain. On this point I hope that all doctors and surgeons will help me to persuade him; for they know that those whose limbs have recently been amputated often think they still feel pain in the parts they no longer possess. I once knew a girl who had a serious wound in her hands and had her whole arm amputated because of creeping gangrene. Whenever the surgeon approached her they blindfolded her eyes so that she would be more tractable, and the place where her arm had been was so covered with bandages that for some weeks she did not know that she had lost it. Meanwhile she complained of feeling various pains in her fingers, wrist and forearm; and this was obviously due to the condition of the nerves in her arm which formerly led from her brain to those parts of her body. This would certainly not have happened if the feeling or, as he says, sensation of pain occurred outside the brain.

10. I do not understand his objections to pages 159 and 163.[2] If my philosophy seems too 'crass' for him, because, like mechanics, it considers shapes and sizes and motions, he is condemning what seems to me its most praiseworthy feature, of which I am particularly proud. I mean that in my kind of philosophy I use no reasoning which is not mathematical and evident, and all my conclusions are confirmed by true observational data. Whatever I concluded to be possible from the principles of my philosophy actually happens whenever the appropriate agents are applied to the appropriate matter. I am surprised that he does not realize that the mechanics now current is nothing but a part of the true physics which, not being welcomed by supporters of the common sort of philosophy, took refuge with the mathematicians. This part of philosophy has in fact remained truer and less corrupt than the others, because it has useful and practical consequences, and so any mistakes in it result in financial loss. So if he despises my style of philosophy because it is like mechanics, it is the same to me as if he despised it for being true.

421

1 *Optics*: AT VI 110.
2 *Meteorology*: AT VI 233.

He does not agree that water and other bodies are made up of any parts which are actually distinct. He should observe that in many cases we can perceive such parts with the naked eye: specks of dust in stones, strands in wood, and the warp and woof of flesh, to quote his own example. It is perfectly reasonable to judge of things which are too small for the senses to perceive on the model of those we see. He should remember that he said himself in his objection to page 164[1] that the air and spirits enclosed in water raise its topmost parts as they leave it: and this is unintelligible   422 unless he admits that the air and spirits consist of various parts scattered throughout the water. Perhaps he is worried about his integral union, and the other shadowy entities with which a subtle philosophy stuffs its continuum, and that is why he will not agree that terrestrial bodies are composed of actually divided parts. If so, he should reread page 164, and he will find that I conceive each of these particles as a continuous body, divisible to infinity, about which could be said everything that he has proved in his most subtle treatise *On the Composition of the Continuum*.[2] He will also find that I do not explicitly deny in bodies any of the things which others admit in addition to the elements of my theory; but that my 'crass unsubtle' philosophy is content with this simple apparatus.

11. He is convinced that my assumption that the parts of water are oblong like eels is rash and baseless. He should remember what is said on page 76 of the *Discourse on the Method*.[3] If he would be good enough to read with sufficient attention everything I wrote in the *Meteorology* and the *Optics*, he would find countless reasons from which countless syllogisms could be constructed to prove what I say. They would go like this.

If water is more fluid and harder to freeze than oil, this is a sign that oil is   423 made of parts which stick together easily, like the branches of trees, while water is made of more slippery parts, like those which have the shape of eels. But experience shows that water is more fluid and harder to freeze than oil. Ergo, etc.

Again, if cloths soaked in water are easier to dry than cloths soaked in oil, that is a sign that the parts of water have the shapes of eels, and can thus easily come out through the holes in the cloth, and that the parts of oil have the shapes of branches, and thus get entangled in the same holes; but experience shows, etc.

Again, if water is heavier than oil, this is a sign that the parts of oil are branch-shaped, and so leave many spaces around them, and that the parts of water are like eels, and therefore are satisfied with less space; but, etc.

Again, if water is more easy to turn into vapour, or is, as the chemists

1 *Meteorology*: AT VI 238.
2 Fromondus' *Labyrinthus, sive de Compositione Continui* (1631).
3 AT VI 76; CSM I 150.

say, more volatile than oil, this is a sign that it is made up of parts which can easily be separated from each other like eels; and that oil is made up of branch-like parts which are more closely intertwined. But, etc.

Although each of these points taken by itself gives only probability to the conclusion, taken together they amount to a proof of it. But if I had
424   tried to derive all these conclusions like a dialectician,[1] I would have worn out the printers' hands and the readers' eyes with an enormous volume.

12. What I say on page 162[2] seems paradoxical to him: that a slow motion produces the sensation of cold, and a fast motion the sensation of heat. On the same showing it should seem paradoxical to him that a gentle rubbing on the hand should produce a sensation of titillation and pleasure, and a harder rubbing produce a sensation of pain; for pleasure and pain are no less different from each other than heat and cold. Moreover, if we put a warm hand on a tepid body, it will seem cold to us, though we shall think it to be warm if we touch it with another hand which is colder. . .

AT I   TO HUYGENS, 5 OCTOBER 1637

(434)   . . . As for your request for something on mechanics, I have never been less in the mood to write than I am at present. Not only do I not have such time at my disposal as I had when I was living in Breda, but each day I regret the time which the publications for le Maire[3] have cost me. White hairs are rapidly appearing on my head, which brings it home to me that the only thing I should be devoting myself to is ways of slowing down their growth. That is what I am now doing. I am trying energetically to make up for my lack of observational data. This task takes up so much of my time that I have resolved to concentrate on this alone; I have even laid aside all work on my *World*, so that I shall not be tempted to put the finishing touches to it. For all that, I am sending you the lines you requested, seeing especially that you only asked for three sheets . . .

(435)   *An account*
of the machines by means of which a small force can be used to lift heavy weights[4]

The invention of all these machines is based on a single principle, which is that the same force that can raise a weight of, say, 100 pounds to a height

1 An expert in scholastic logic.
2 *Meteorology*: AT VI 237.
3 The *Discourse*, together with the *Optics*, *Meteorology* and *Geometry*, which were published by the Leiden publisher Jean le Maire in June 1637.
4 A copy of the 'Account' was found among Descartes' papers after his death, and a copy was published by Nicolas Poisson in 1668 under the title *Traité de la mechanique*.

of two feet can raise a 200-pound weight to a height of one foot, or a 400-   436
pound weight to a height of six inches, and so on, supposing such a force is
applied to it.

We cannot fail to accept this principle if we consider that the effect must
always be proportional to the action which is necessary to produce it.
Thus, if in order to lift a certain weight to a height of one foot we are
required to employ a force which can raise a 100-pound weight to a height
of two feet, then the said weight must be 200 pounds. For to lift 100
pounds to a height of one foot twice over is just the same as lifting 200
pounds to a height of one foot or 100 pounds to a height of two feet.

Now machines can be used to move a weight over a shorter distance by
applying a force over a larger distance: such machines are the pulley, the
inclined plane, the wedge, the cog-wheel, the screw, the lever, and some
others. If we do not wish to show how these are related, we can give further
examples; otherwise a few examples will suffice.

The pulley   437

Let ABC be a cord wound round pulley D to which weight E is attached.
First, let us suppose that two men are holding or pulling equally each end
of the cord. If the weight is 200 pounds, then in order to support or lift it, it
is evident that each man will expend only as much force as is needed to
hold up or raise 100 pounds, since each bears only half of the weight. Next,

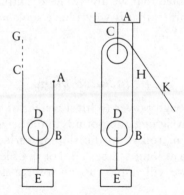

let us suppose that one end of cord A is attached firmly to a nail, while the
other end C is held by one of the men. In this case it is evident that if the
man at C is to support weight E, as before he will need to exert only as
much force as is required to support 100 pounds, because the nail at A
performs the same function as the man holding that end of the cord in the
previous example. Lastly, let us suppose that the man at C is pulling the

cord in order to lift weight E. In this case it is evident that if he employs the force that is required to raise 100 pounds to a height of two feet, he will be able to raise the 200-pound weight E to a height of one foot. For, since in this case the cord ABC is doubled over, he will have to pull it two feet at the end C if he is to raise the weight E to the same height it would reach if two men, one at end A and the other at end C, were pulling it by a foot each.

There is one thing, however, which prevents the calculation from being precise, namely the weight of the pulley, and the difficulty we may have in getting the cord to run and bear the weight. But that is very little in comparison with the weight of the object that is being raised, and it can be estimated only approximately.

It should be noted, moreover, that the force is not due to the pulley, but simply to the cord's being doubled over. For, if another pulley is fitted at A, through which cord ABCH is passed, it will take no less force to pull H towards K, and thus to raise weight E, than it took to pull C towards G in the previous example. But if to these two pulleys a third, D, is added, to which the weight is attached and through which the cord is passed exactly as in the first case, then no more force will be needed to lift the 200-pound weight than would be needed to lift a 50-pound weight without a pulley; because if the cord is pulled four feet, the weight will be raised by only a foot. So if we add more pulleys, we can raise the heaviest of loads with the smallest of forces.

It should also be noted that we always need a little more force to lift a weight than to support it; that is why I have spoken separately of lifting and supporting.

The inclined plane

If we have only enough power to lift a weight of 100 pounds and we want to raise body F weighing 200 pounds to the height of line BA, all we need do is to pull it or roll it up the sloping surface CA, which I am supposing to be twice as long as line AB. For in order to get the body to point A in this way, we will employ as much force as is required to raise

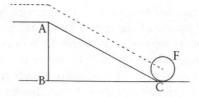

100 pounds to twice that height. And the less steep we make the slope of surface C A, the less force we shall need to raise weight F.

But again, we have to abstract from the calculation the difficulty that would arise in moving body F along surface A C if this surface were to lie along line B C, all the parts of which I am assuming to be equidistant from the surface of the earth. Of course, in this case the resistance would be less, the harder and more even and polished the surface was, and hence, being not very great, it could be estimated only approximately. We need not take into account the fact that, since line B C is part of a circle with the same centre as the earth, surface A C must be ever so slightly curved, having the shape of a spiral described between two circles centred on the earth, since this factor makes no detectable difference.

The wedge   440

If we follow what was said about the inclined plane, the power of wedge ABCD is easily understood. For the force with which we strike the end makes the wedge move in the direction of line BD, and the wood or other

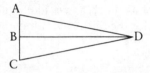

body which it splits opens up, or rather the load which it lifts rises, to the height of line A C. Accordingly the force with which the wedge is pushed or struck must be in the same proportion to the resistance due to the wood or the load as line A C is to line B D.

Again, if we were to be precise, B D should be a segment of a circle, and A D and C D two segments of spirals with the same centre as the earth, and the wedge should consist of a material which was so perfectly hard, polished and light that it would take hardly any force to move it.

The cog-wheel

Consider a cog-wheel A with cogs B and axle or cylinder C round which is wound a cord to which is attached a weight that we want to raise. In this case it is easy to see that the ratio between the weight and the force which turns the wheel must be the same as that between the circumference of the   441
cylinder and the circumference of the circle which this force describes, or what amounts to the same thing, between the diameter of the one and the

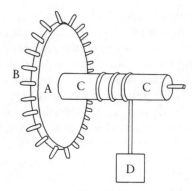

diameter of the other, since the ratio between the circumferences is the same as that between the diameters. So, if cylinder C is only one foot in diameter, and the diameter of cog-wheel A B is six feet, and weight D 600 pounds, then all we need is a force on B capable of raising 100 pounds; and similarly in the other cases.

Instead of the cord we can put a small cog-wheel on cylinder CC, the cogs of which will turn another, larger wheel; in this way we can multiply the strength of the force as much as we like. Due allowance, of course, would have to be made for the difficulty of moving the machine, as in the previous examples.

The screw

Once we know the power of the cog-wheel and the inclined plane, it is a simple matter to work out the power of the screw; for the screw consists simply of a steeply sloping surface which turns on a cylinder. Say the slope of the surface is such that the cylinder has to revolve ten times if it is to move one foot into the nut, and the circumference of the circle described by the turning force is ten feet long. Since ten times ten makes a hundred, with such a screw a single man would be able to press as hard as a hundred men could without it, provided only that we make due allowance for the force it would take to turn it.

Now I spoke of pressing just now, rather than of raising or moving, since that is what a screw is most often used for. But if we want to use the screw to lift a weight, as distinct from inserting it into a nut, we shall attach a cog-wheel to it. And if the wheel has thirty cogs, say, it will turn only a third of a revolution during the time it takes the screw to make a complete revolution. And if the weight is attached to a cord wound round the axle of the wheel, it will be raised one foot for every complete revolution of the wheel.

442

Now since the circumference of the circle described by the force that turns the screw will again be ten feet, and since ten times thirty makes three hundred, with such an instrument (called the endless screw) a single man will be able to lift as heavy a weight as three hundred men could without it. Again, due allowance has to be made for the difficulty there may be in turning the screw, which strictly speaking is not due to the weight of the load but to the form or matter of the instrument; and since a greater force is involved in this case, the difficulty is inherently more conspicuous.

The lever 443

I have left the lever to the last, because of all the machines designed for lifting weights, this one is the most difficult of all to explain. Let us suppose that CH is a lever which turns around point O, to which it is fixed by 444 means of a peg or by some other means.

End C describes semi-circle ABCDE, the other end describing semi-circle FGHIK; the weight which one wants to lift is at H, and the force is applied at end C, line CO being three times as long as OH. Let us then consider that, while the force which moves the lever describes the complete semi-circle ABCDE along which it acts, the weight describes semi-circle FGHIK, though it is not raised through the length of the curved line FGHIK, but only through the length of the straight line FOK. Accordingly, as a measure of the ratio between the force which moves the load and the weight of the load, we ought to take, not the ratio between the diameters of the two circles in question or between their circumferences, as we did in the case of the cog-wheel, but rather the ratio between the circumference of the larger circle and the diameter of the smaller circle. We should also bear in mind that if the force is to move the lever, it need not be so great when the lever is pointing towards A or E as when pointing towards B or D, or so great when pointing towards B or D as when pointing towards C. The reason for this is that the weight rises less in the one case than in the other. This can easily be seen in the following way. Supposing that line COH is parallel to the horizon and that AOF intersects it at right angles, let us take point G equidistant to points F and H, and point B equidistant to points A and C, and draw GS perpendicular to 445 FO. We can now see that line FS, which marks the height to which the weight rises when the force acts along line AB, is much shorter than SO, which indicates the height to which it rises when the force acts along line BC.

In order to determine precisely what the force must be at each point on the curved line ABCDE, we have to know that the force acts exactly as if it were pulling the weight along an inclined plane with a circular slope; and

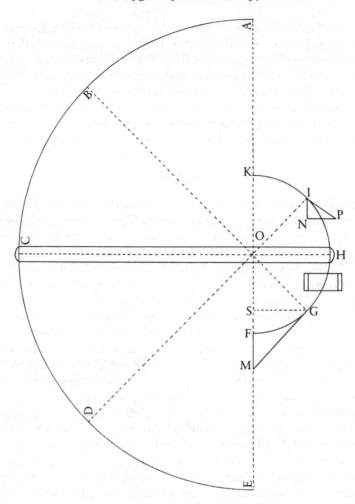

as a measure of the slope at each point on this plane we must take the
straight line which touches the circle at that point. For example, when the
force is applied at point B and the load is at point G, in order to find the
ratio between the force and the weight of the load, we must draw the
tangent GM. The ratio between the weight of the load and the force
required to pull it along this plane, and hence to raise it along the circle
FGH, is just the ratio between GM and SM. Now, because BO is three
times as long as OG, the ratio between the force at B and the weight at G
must be the ratio between a third part of the line SM and the whole line
GM. Similarly, when the force is applied at point D, in order to determine
the weight of the load at point I, we should draw the tangent IP and the

straight line IN at right angles to the horizon (it does not matter where point P is placed, provided it is below point I). We should then draw PN parallel to the horizon, in order to get the ratio between line IP and a third part of line IN, which will give us the ratio between the weight of the load 446 and the force that is to be applied at D to move it. The calculation is similar in the other cases, with the exception of point H; for, since the tangent to H is at right angles to the horizon, the weight must be three times the force at C which is needed to move it; and also with the exception of points F and K, for, since the tangents to these are parallel to the horizon, the smallest determinable force is sufficient to move the weight.

Moreover, to be wholly exact, it should be noted that lines SG and PN must be segments of circles with the same centre as the earth, and GM and IP segments of spirals drawn between two such circles, and that the straight lines SM and IN, each pointing towards the centre of the earth, are not exactly parallel. Furthermore, the point H, the tangent to which I am supposing to be at right angles to the horizon, must be ever so slightly closer to point F than to point K, the tangents to these points being parallel to the horizon. As a consequence of this we can easily solve all the problems of the balance. Assuming that the balance is very exact and that the spot O on which it is centred is merely an indivisible point, as I assumed in the case of the lever, we can show that if the arms lean to the one side or the other, the arm which is lower must always be the heavier. Conse- quently the centre of gravity in each body is not fixed and motionless, as 447 the ancients supposed – a point which, so far as I know, no one has hitherto observed.[1]

These last points, however, have no practical significance; and it would be useful if those who devote themselves to inventing new machines knew no more about this subject than the little I have written here, for they would be in no danger of going wrong on their own account, as they often do when they assume other principles.

Moreover the machines of which I have given an explanation can be applied in all sorts of different ways. There are countless other things to consider in mechanics which I am saying nothing about, as I have filled up my three sheets of paper, and you did not ask for more.

TO MERSENNE, 5 OCTOBER 1637   AT I

You tell me that one of your friends[2] who saw the *Optics* had certain 450 objections to make. The first was that he doubts whether the tendency to

1 Pierre de Fermat (1601–55), one of the great mathematicians of the time, made this point in his *Nova in Mechanicis Theoremata*, which he sent to Mersenne on 24 June 1636.
2 Fermat; see previous note.

move should follow the same laws as the movement itself since the two differ from each other as much as potentiality and actuality. I am convinced that he conceived this doubt because he imagined I was doubtful on the point myself and because I put these words on page 8: 'It is very easy to believe that the tendency to move must follow in this respect the same laws as does the movement itself.'[1] He thought that when I said that something was easy to believe, I meant that it was no more than probable; but in this he has altogether mistaken my meaning. I consider almost as false whatever is only a matter of probability; and when I say that something is easy to believe I do not mean that it is only probable, but that it is so clear and so evident that there is no need for me to stop to prove it. As in fact it cannot reasonably be doubted that the laws which govern movement, which is the actuality, as he says himself, must govern also the tendency to move, which is the potentiality of the same actuality; for although it is not always true that what has once been in potentiality is later in actuality, it is altogether impossible for something to be in actuality without having been in potentiality.

451

As to his further remark, 'there seems to be a particular disanalogy here, in that the motion of a ball is more or less forceful to the degree that it is pushed by different forces, whereas light passes through transparent bodies instantaneously, and there seems to be nothing sequential about it', I do not understand his reasoning here. For he cannot say that the disanalogy resides in the fact that the motion of a ball can be more or less forceful, since the action which I take light to consist in can also be more or less strong. Nor can it reside in the fact that the former is sequential whereas the latter is not; for by means of the analogies[2] with a blind man's stick and wine sinking to the bottom of a vat, I think I have made it sufficiently clear that while the inclination to move is transmitted instantaneously from one place to another, it still follows the same path as the sequential motions would have done, which is all that is at issue here . . .

TO [NOËL], OCTOBER 1637

454

I am extremely glad to learn from the letter you kindly wrote me that I am still so fortunate as to have a place in your memory and affections. Thank you also for promising to have the book I sent you examined by those members of your Society[3] who are the most reliable in such matters, and for being so kind as to send me their criticisms. I only wish that in

455 addition you had been so kind as to include your own criticisms among

---

1 AT VI 89; CSM I 155.
2 See *Optics*: AT VI 84f; CSM I 153f.
3 The Jesuits.

them, for I assure you there is not one of these scholars who commands greater authority in my eyes or to whom I more willingly defer than you. It is true that those of my friends who have already seen the book have told me that a good deal of time and study is required if one is to give a proper assessment of it, since the introductory parts (at least those of the *Optics* and the *Meteorology*) can be wholly persuasive only if one knows all that comes after them, and the latter can be understood only if one remembers what comes before. So I shall be very much obliged to you if you will be so good as to give it your attention or to see that others give it theirs. In truth my aim is simply to provide instruction for myself; and those who bring some error to my attention will always please me more than those who bring me praise. Besides, there is no one, I think, who has a greater interest in examining this book than the members of your Society. I see already that so many people are going to accept the contents of the book that (especially where the *Meteorology* is concerned) I do not know how they will be able to teach these subjects from now on as they are taught year by year in most of your Colleges, unless they either disprove what I have written or else follow it. I know that the main reason why your Colleges take great care to reject all sorts of innovations in philosophical matters is their fear that these innovations may bring about some change in theology as well. That is why I want especially to point out that you have nothing to   456
fear on this score so far as my own innovations are concerned, and that I have reason to thank God that the views which, from my reflection on natural causes, seemed to me most true in physics were always those which are the most compatible with the mysteries of religion, as I hope to show clearly when I have the opportunity. In the mean time I beg you to go on showing me the favour of your affection.

TO HUYGENS, 4 DECEMBER 1637   AT I

The three sheets[1] which I sent you do not in the least deserve the good   648
words in the letter which you kindly wrote me, and I assure you that so far from having aspired to receive your thanks, I am ashamed to have sent you such a meagre offering. In fact because I was afraid of getting myself immersed in a treatise which was much longer than you had asked, I left out the finest parts of my topic, such as, among others, the treatment of *speed*, the problems concerning the *balance*, and several possible ways of *increasing the force of motions* which are different from those I explained. But so that you will not think that I am mentioning these points in order to   649

1 These comprised the short paper on mechanics entitled 'An Account of the Machines etc.' included in Descartes' letter of 5 October 1637 to Huygens; see pp. 66–73 above.

give you cause to invite me to add them to the treatise, I shall reply to the last part of your letter and tell you what I am working on.

I have never taken greater care in looking after myself than I am doing at the moment. Whereas I used to think that death could deprive me of only thirty or forty years at the most, I would not now be surprised if it were to deprive me of the prospect of a hundred years or more. I think I see with certainty that if only we guard ourselves against certain errors which we are in the habit of making in the way we live, we shall be able to reach without further inventions a much longer and happier old age than we otherwise would. But since I need more time and more observational data if I am to investigate everything relevant to this topic, I am now working on a compendium of medicine, basing it partly on my reading and partly on my own reasoning. I hope to be able to use this as a provisional means of obtaining from nature a stay of execution,[1] and of being better able from now on to carry out my plan.

I am not going to reply to the question which your courtesy led you to ask concerning the communication of the three sheets which you have; for not only would it be ungracious of me to want to dispose of something which belongs entirely to you (since I sent it to you earlier without reserving any right to it), but also your clearly expressed inclination not to communicate it to others, and the affection which you show towards me, assure me that you will not do anything on that score which will turn out to
650 my disadvantage. And whatever you do, as long as I live, I shall remain your very devoted and humble servant.

AT I

TO PLEMPIUS, 20 DECEMBER 1637

475   I am glad that my answers to M. Fromondus' objections[2] have at last reached you. But I am very surprised that he should conclude from them that I was annoyed or irritated by his paper. I was not at all; and I do not think that I uttered the slightest word against him without his having said similar or harder things against me first. I concluded that he liked that style of writing, and so I went rather against my own nature, which is disinclined to any contention, because I was afraid that he might enjoy the game less if I received his attack too gently and softly. People who play draughts or chess against each other do not cease thereby to be friends; indeed their very skill in the game is often a cause and bond of friendship between them. I only wanted by my reply to earn his goodwill.

1 Cf. *Discourse*: AT VI 62; CSM I 143; *Description of the Human Body*: AT XI 223; CSM I 314.
2 See above, p. 61.

I do not know why my book is not yet obtainable in your shops: if your 476 booksellers want a copy from mine, I know he will be very glad to send one.

I do not expect to have a sufficiently ripe judgement on my book from anyone who only reads hurriedly through a borrowed copy. The points near the end of each treatise cannot be understood unless everything which goes before is retained in one's memory; and the proofs of the propositions at the beginning depend on everything which follows. The things which I say in the first chapters about the nature of light, and about the shape of the particles of salt and fresh water, are not my principles, as you seem to object, but rather conclusions which are proved by everything that comes after. Sizes, shapes, positions and motions are my *formal* object (in philosophers' jargon), and the physical objects which I explain are my *material* object. The principles or premises from which I derive these conclusions are only the axioms on which geometers base their demonstrations: for instance, 'the whole is greater than the part', 'if equals are taken from equals the remainders are equal'; but they are not abstracted from all sensible matter, as in geometry, but applied to various observational data which are known by the senses and indubitable. For instance, from the oblong and inflexible shape of the particles of salt, I deduced the square shape of its grains, and many other things which are obvious to the senses; I wanted to explain the latter by the former as effects by their cause. I did not want to prove things which are already well enough known, but rather to demonstrate the cause by the effects *a posteriori*, as I remember I 477 wrote at length in my reply to the eleventh objection of M. Fromondus.[1]

I will be glad if the Jesuit to whom you recommended my book writes to me about it; whatever comes from the men of that Society is likely to be well thought out, and the stronger the objections he puts forward, the more pleased I shall be with them. For the same reason I eagerly await your objections about the movement of the heart.

TO MERSENNE, END OF DECEMBER 1637   AT I

I am troubled very little by the assessment of my writings which the 478 author of *Geostatics*[2] gives. I do not like to have to speak well of myself, but because there are few people who are able to understand my *Geometry*, and since you will want me to tell you what my own view of it is, I think it is appropriate that I should tell you that it is such that I could not wish to improve it. In the *Optics* and the *Meteorology* I merely tried to

---

1 See above, p. 65.
2 Jean de Beaugrand.

show that my method is better than the usual one; in my *Geometry*, however, I claim to have demonstrated this. Right at the beginning I solve a problem which according to the testimony of Pappus none of the ancients managed to solve[1]; and it can be said that none of the moderns has been able to solve it either, since none of them has written about it, even though the cleverest of them have tried to solve the other problems which Pappus mentions in the same place as having been tackled by the ancients. These modern writers include the authors of the *Apolonius Redivivus*,[2] *Apolonius Batavus*,[3] and others among whom ought to be counted that Counsellor of yours, author of the *De Maximis et Minimis*;[4] but none of these knew how to solve a problem which had defeated the ancients.

479

Moreover, in Book Two my discussion of the nature and properties of curved lines, and my way of studying these, is in my view as far removed from ordinary geometry as the rhetoric of Cicero is from a child's A B C. And I think very little of your geostatician's promise to provide in a preface some methods for finding the tangents to all curved lines which will be better than mine – here he looks just as ridiculous as the captains in Italian comedies. And so far is it from being the case that the things I have written could easily have been taken from Viète that on the contrary what makes my treatise difficult to understand is that I have tried to include only what I thought he, or anyone else, would not have known. As you can see, if you compare what I wrote on page 372 (which is where I begin to give the rules of my algebra) concerning the number of roots in each equation with what Viète has written on this topic at the end of his book *De Emendatione Aequationum*,[5] you will see that I determine this question for all equations in general. He, by contrast, merely gives some particular examples, which he makes such a fuss about that he decides to bring his book to a close at that point – which shows that he was unable to give a general solution to the problem. Thus I began where he left off, though I did this without being aware of it, for I have leafed through Viète more since I received your last letter than I had ever done before, having come across a copy here that one of my friends happened to have. Between ourselves, I do not find that he knew as much about the matter as I thought, which is not to deny that he was very clever.

480

Furthermore, having determined as I did all that could be achieved in each type of problem and shown the way to do it, I claim that people should not only believe that I have accomplished more than my pre-

1 See footnote 1, p. 37 above.
2 By Marini Ghetaldi (1607).
3 By Wilebrord Snell (1608).
4 A treatise by Pierre de Fermat, who was Counsellor in the Parliament of Toulouse.
5 *The Reformation of Equations* of François Viète (1540–1603).

decessors but should also be convinced that posterity will never discover anything in this subject which I could not have discovered just as well if I had bothered to look for it. Please keep all this to yourself, for I would be very embarrassed if any others were to know that I have written you as much as I have on this topic.

I am not so keen to see M. de Fermat's disproof of what I had written on refraction as to incline me to ask you to send it to me by post, but when you have the opportunity to send it to me by sea with some cargo, I shall not be sorry to see it, along with the *Geostatics*[1] and the book on light by M. de la Chambre,[2] and anything else of that sort. This is not to say I would not be glad to see at once what others write whether for or against my views or of their own invention; but the cost of sending letters is too high.

481

TO MERSENNE, JANUARY 1638[3]

AT I (485)

... You ask whether I think that water is in its natural state when it is liquid or when it is frozen. I reply that I do not regard anything in nature as violent, except in relation to the human intellect, which calls 'violent' anything which is not in accordance with its will, or not in accordance with what it judges ought to be the case. It is no less natural for water to be frozen when it is cold, than to be liquid when it is less cold, because the causes of each are equally natural.

TO PLEMPIUS, 15 FEBRUARY 1638

AT I

I had been eagerly awaiting your objections to my views on the movement of the heart, and have been well rewarded. When I considered your learning, intelligence and character, not to speak of the kindness which you have shown me, I knew that your objections would be erudite, ingenious and unsullied by any prejudice due to ill-will; and I was not wrong in my judgement. I thank you both for sending them to me and for showing me how to shore up my views with the authority of Aristotle.[4] How fortunate that man was: whatever he wrote, whether he gave it much thought or not, is regarded by most people today as having oracular authority. So there is nothing more I could wish for than, without depart-

521
522

---

1 Descartes eventually received the book in June 1638.
2 *Nouvelles pensées sur les causes de la lumière* (1634), by Marin Cureau de la Chambre (1594–1675), physician to the King of France.
3 The exact dating of this letter is uncertain.
4 Plempius maintained that Descartes was following Aristotle's view that the heart-beat is due to a process of fermentation which causes the blood in the heart to expand.

ing from the truth, to be able to follow in his footsteps in all things. But on the point at issue I did not dare pride myself in having achieved that. Granted, like him I say that the heart-beat is due to the expansion of the liquid that heats up within it; but by 'liquid' I simply mean blood, and I do not talk, as he does, of 'the expansion of the liquid which is being continually produced from food, raising the outer membrane of the heart'.[1] If I did make statements of that sort, I could be disproved by many cogent arguments. And it would be reasonable to think that I had never paid any close attention to the structure of the heart of any animal if I said nothing about the ventricles, the blood vessels and the valves, and asserted that it was only the outer membrane of the heart that swelled. Now someone who happens to draw a true conclusion from false premisses (as the logicians put it) seems to me to be reasoning no better than if he had drawn a false conclusion from them. If two people arrive at the same place, the one taking the right road, the other the wrong one, we ought not to think that the former is following in the footsteps of the latter.

    Your first objection is that individual parts of the heart sometimes beat even after the heart has been taken from the body and dissected, though in this case no blood is flowing into or out of the heart. My reply is that I once made a rather exact observation of this point on fish in particular, the hearts of which, after they have been cut out, go on beating for much longer than the heart of any terrestrial animal. But I could always judge or, as often happened, see with my own eyes, that some remaining drops of blood had fallen from parts higher up into the part where the pulse was occurring. This easily convinced me that even a tiny drop of blood falling from one part of the heart into another, slightly warmer part was sufficient to cause this pulsation. We should bear in mind that the smaller the quantity of any liquid, the more easily it can be rarefied. The more frequently our hands perform some movement, the fitter they are to carry it out again on future occasions; similarly, as the heart expands and contracts a countless number of times from the first moment of its formation, the slightest force is enough to impel it to carry out its own repeated movement. Lastly, we see that certain liquids, when mixed with certain others, heat up and expand; similarly, there may be in the recesses of the heart a yeast-like liquid which causes any other liquid entering and mixing with it to expand. Besides, this objection seems to me to be much more damaging to the view which is commonly held by others, that the movement of the heart is due to some faculty of the soul. For how, I ask, can the movement which occurs in the cut-up bits of the heart depend on the

---

1 See Aristotle, *De Respiratione*, ch. 20.

human soul, when it is taken as an article of faith that the rational soul is indivisible, and has no other sensitive or vegetative soul[1] attached to it?

Your second objection is the one that Galen[2] made at the end of his book on the question whether blood is contained in the arteries. I have never made the experiment in question; it would not be easy for me to make it, and I think it would not be worth making. For, given the cause of the pulsation of the arteries that I have put forward, the laws of my mechanics, i.e. my physics, imply that if we insert a quill into an artery and tie the artery above it with a ligature, the artery ought not to beat above the ligature[3] ... If a quill is inserted into the artery ... and a ligature is tied above it, as Galen intends, the blood will be able to pass through the quill ... but it will not strike the sides of the artery ..., at least not with any noticeable force; for when the blood passes from a narrow vessel to a more capacious one, it will lose most of its force, and what force remains will be expended more in the direction of the flow than in the direction of the walls of the artery. Hence the blood will be able to fill the artery in a continuous flow and make it bulge, but it will not make it move with distinct pulsations. The only reason why the veins joined to the arteries by various anastomoses do not also pulsate is that their extremities, through which the blood flows into them, are narrower than the channels into which they flow ...

We are not impressed by the authority of Galen when he asserts in various places that 'it is not that the arteries swell out like bladders because they are full, but rather that they fill up like bellows (or like jaws or lungs or the chest) because they are extended; and when extended, they draw into their extremities and openings whatever in the vicinity is suitable for filling the space they contain'.[4] For this is disproved by an utterly decisive experiment, which I was interested to observe several times before, and which I performed again today in the course of writing this letter. First I opened the chest of a live rabbit and removed the ribs to expose the heart and the trunk of the aorta. I then tied the aorta with a thread a good distance from the heart, and separated it from all its attachments, so that there could be no reason to suspect that any blood or spirits could enter it from anywhere else but the heart. Then, making an incision in the aorta

524

(525)

(526)

---

1 In Aristotelian philosophy the sensitive soul and the vegetative soul are those parts of the soul whose functions are sense-perception and the maintenance of vital functions respectively.
2 Galen of Pergamum (*c.* A.D. 129–199), a Greek physician whose physiology was dominant throughout the Middle Ages and the Renaissance.
3 Plempius took this experiment to show that the beating of the arteries is due to something that flows through the walls of the arteries.
4 See Galen, *An Sanguinis in Arteribus Contineatur*, ch. 9, and *De Usu Pulsum*, ch. 5.

527   with a scalpel, between the heart and the ligature, I saw perfectly clearly
that when the artery dilated, blood gushed out of the incision, but when it
contracted, no blood flowed out. But the very opposite should have
happened if Galen's view had been correct: the artery ought to have drawn
air through the incision at each moment of diastole, and ought not to have
emitted any blood except at the moment of systole.[1] No one, I think, can be
in any doubt about this.

Continuing the vivisection, I cut away half the heart, the half known as
the apex; and from the moment this was separated from the base I noticed
that it did not beat even once. In the light of the previous objection I should
point out that the parts of the heart towards the base pulsate for some time,
since some fresh blood flows into them from the vessels and the attached
auricles, whereas the parts near the apex do not pulsate. After the apex had
been cut off, the base of the heart, with the blood vessels still attached to it,
continued to pulsate for quite some time. Moreover, I could easily see that
the two cavities in the base which are called the ventricles grow larger at
diastole and smaller at systole. This experiment gives the *coup de grâce* to
Harvey's view on the movement of the heart, for he clearly states the very
opposite, namely that the ventricles dilate at systole in order to take in
blood, and contract at diastole in order to force the blood into the
arteries.[2] I have included these remarks as an aside, so that you may see
that the only conceivable view which is not impugned by utterly conclusive
experiments is my own...

(528)   In your third objection you say that if the dilatation of the heart is due to
the rarefaction of the blood, the diastole should last longer than it in fact
does. What persuades you of this is perhaps your imagining that the
rarefaction in question is like that which occurs in an aeolipyle[3] when
water is turned into steam. But various sorts of rarefaction are to be
distinguished. In one sort, a liquid turns into smoke or air, and changes its
form, as happens in an aeolipyle; in another sort the character of the liquid
remains the same, but its volume increases. It is obvious that the first sort
of rarefaction is totally different from the rarefaction of the blood in the
heart, and that for two reasons. First, in the former case the liquid is not all
rarefied at once, but only those parts of it which rise to the surface and are
dissipated in the surrounding air, as I explained at length in my *Meteor-*

---

1 Diastole is the process of expansion of the heart, systole the process of contraction.
2 William Harvey (1578–1657) published his theory of the circulation of the blood in *De
  Motu Cordis* (1628). Harvey correctly held that the pulse is caused by the contraction of
  the heart, and not the expansion, as Descartes thought. See *Discourse*: AT VII 47ff; CSM I
  134ff.
3 A vessel containing water which produces a jet of steam when heated.

ology, chapters 2 and 4. But the heart contains no air, or any surface surrounded by air; in living animals, rather, the cavities of the heart, no matter how large, are completely filled with blood. Second, if the rarefaction of the blood were of the first sort, the arteries would not contain blood, but rather a vapoury air. But no one nowadays doubts that the arteries are filled with blood. By the way, one may well find it astonishing that the ancients were all doubtful on this question, and were so far from the truth that Galen took the trouble to write a book devoted to showing that the arteries do naturally contain blood.

As for the second sort of rarefaction, in which the liquid increases in 529
volume, we have to distinguish between gradual rarefaction and instantaneous rarefaction. In the former case, the parts of the liquid gradually take on some new motion or shape or position which causes the gaps between them to increase in number or size. I explained in my *Meteorology* how not only heat but also intense cold and other causes can give rise to this sort of rarefaction. In the latter case, rarefaction is instantaneous, according to the foundations of my philosophy, when all or at least most of the particles of the liquid, which are randomly dispersed throughout its volume, undergo some simultaneous change, which causes them to take up significantly greater space. Now the facts of the matter indicate that the latter is the way in which blood is rarefied in the heart; for diastole takes place instantaneously. If we attend to all the points made in Part Five of my book *On the Method*, we ought to have no more doubts on this matter than we have on the question whether oil and other liquids are rarefied in this way when we see them suddenly boiling up in a pot over the fire. The entire fabric of the heart, the heat in it, and the very nature of the blood all contribute to this effect; nothing that we perceive by the senses seems to me more certain than this. So far as the question of heat is concerned, even if we do not feel much heat in fishes, their hearts do feel hotter than any other organs in their body.

You say that it is not in the nature of blood to be suddenly rarefied, on the grounds that it is not like oil or pitch, but is a more watery and earthy 530
liquid. As if only things of a thicker consistency could be rarefied instantaneously! Does not water itself normally well up when fish or something else is cooking in it? And blood cannot be said to be more watery than water .. I am not maintaining that the rarefaction of the blood that takes place in the heart is similar in all respects to the rarefaction which is brought about by artificial means. All the same, to be quite frank, I do think it comes about in that way ...

It remains for me to reply to your objections against the circulation of (531)
the blood.

The first objection is that there is a difference between arterial blood and venous blood, a point which I myself indicated on page 52 of my book *On the Method* could be raised as an objection against Harvey, because on his view it is not thought that any change in the blood takes place in the heart. I, by contrast, had no fear of this objection, for as I describe it, there is a sudden expansion and as it were boiling up of the blood in the heart. And what, I ask you, could cause a greater or more sudden change in a body than just such a boiling up and sudden fermentation? But you will say that the blood that flows into the veins from the extremities of the arteries undergoes no change there, and hence the blood in the veins ought to be no different from that in the arteries. To give a careful reply to this objection, I would have you note first that not a drop of blood is contained in the 532   arteries which has not just recently passed through the heart, whereas in the veins there are always some drops of blood which have not come from the arteries, but from the liquid which is constantly flowing into the veins from the intestines; and secondly, all the veins together are, like the liver, to be regarded as a single vessel. Given these points, it is easy to see that the blood must retain the same qualities in the arteries as it acquired in the heart. Suppose the blood becomes pale in the heart, just as it becomes red in the liver; then the arteries will contain only pale blood, and the veins only red blood; for the pale blood which flows continually into the veins from the arteries will mix with the red blood and at once take on a red colour, just as water does when it is mixed with wine...

(533)   There remains the experiment in which most of the veins which go to a limb are tied, while the arteries remain free. When this experiment is performed, you say that the limb does not swell up, but rather, wastes away gradually through lack of nourishment. Surely two situations have to be distinguished here. On the one hand, as soon as the veins have been ligated as described, they will certainly swell a little, and if you open one of them above the ligature, all or practically all of the blood in the body may flow out, as is witnessed by surgeons every day. If I am not mistaken, this provides, I shall not say highly probable evidence, but rather, demonstrative proof of the circulation of the blood. On the other hand, if the veins are left ligated for a long time, I can readily believe that what you say will be true, though I have never performed the experiment myself. For if the blood in ligated veins stagnates, it will soon become quite thick and hardly fit for nourishing the body; and no fresh blood will reach it from the 534   arteries, since the tiny channels between the arteries and the veins will all be blocked by the thick blood. Perhaps the veins themselves will contract a little, owing to a loss of the fluid content of the blood brought about by imperceptible evaporation. But this poses no difficulty for the circulation thesis.

To sum up, even if I regard your objections as the most powerful that could be raised against my views on the movement of the heart and blood, not one of them induces me to change my view. But please let me know whether you think that my brief replies really answer your objections.

TO [VATIER], 22 FEBRUARY 1638   AT I

I am overwhelmed by your kindness in studying my book of essays with such great care, and sending me your opinion of it with so many marks of goodwill. When I sent it to you I should have enclosed a letter assuring you of my very humble service, were it not that I was hoping – vainly as it turned out – to circulate the book anonymously. I must believe that it is your affection for the father rather than any deserts of the child which has made you welcome it so favourably. I am extremely grateful to you. Perhaps I am too flattered by the very favourable things you say in your two letters, but I must say frankly that no one, among all those who have been good enough to express an opinion of my work, has done me such good justice as you. No one else's criticism has been so favourable, so unbiassed and so well informed. By the way, I am surprised that your second letter followed so closely on your first. I received them more or less at the same time, though when I saw your first I was sure that I must not expect another before your vacation.

I will answer you point by point. I must say first that my purpose was not to teach the whole of my method in the discourse in which I propound it, but only to say enough to show that the new views in the *Optics* and the *Meteorology* were not casual thoughts, and were perhaps worth the trouble of examining. I could not demonstrate the use of this method in the three treatises which I gave, because it prescribes an order of research which is quite different from the one I thought proper for exposition. I have, however, given a brief sample of it in my account of the rainbow,[1] and if you take the trouble to reread it, I hope that it will satisfy you more than it did the first time; the matter is, after all, quite difficult in itself. I attached these three treatises to the discourse which precedes them because I am convinced that if people examine them carefully and compare them with what has previously been written on the same topics, they will have grounds for judging that the method I adopt is no ordinary one and is perhaps better than some others.

It is true that I have been too obscure in what I wrote about the existence of God in this treatise on Method, and I admit that although the most important, it is the least worked out section in the whole book. This is partly because I did not decide to include it until I had nearly completed it

558

559

560

---

1 See *Meteorology*: AT VI 325ff.

and the publisher was becoming impatient. But the principal reason for its obscurity is that I did not dare to go into detail about the arguments of the sceptics, or say everything which is necessary †to withdraw the mind from the senses†. The certainty and evidence of my kind of argument for the existence of God cannot really be known without distinctly recalling the arguments which display the uncertainty of all our knowledge of material things; and these thoughts did not seem to me suitable for inclusion in a book which I wished to be intelligible in part even to women while providing matter for thought for the finest minds. I confess also that this obscurity arises partly – as you rightly observed – because I suppose that certain notions, which the habit of thought had made familiar and evident to me, ought to be equally so to everyone. Such, for instance, is the notion

561 that since our ideas cannot receive their forms or their being except from external objects or from ourselves, they cannot represent any reality or perfection which is not either in those objects or in ourselves. On this point I propose to give some further explanation in a second edition.

I realized that what I said I had put in my treatise *On Light* about the creation of the universe would be incredible;[1] because only ten years ago if someone else had written it I would not have been willing to believe myself that the human mind could attain to such knowledge. But my conscience, and the force of truth, gave me the courage to say it; I thought I could not omit it without betraying my own case, and there are already many people who can bear witness to it. Moreover, a part of my *Physics* was completed and prepared for publication some time ago; if it ever sees the light of day, I hope that future generations will be unable to doubt what I say.

I am grateful to you for the care with which you have examined my views on the movement of the heart. If your doctor has any objections to make to it, I will be very pleased to have them, and will not fail to reply. Only a week ago I received seven or eight objections on the same topic from a Professor of Medicine at Louvain, a friend of mine,[2] to whom I sent two sheets in reply. I would like to receive more of the same kind about all the difficulties which people find in what I have tried to explain. I shall not

562 fail to reply carefully to them, and I trust that I can do so without offending any of their propounders. This is the kind of thing which a number of people together can do more easily than one man on his own, and there are no people who can do it better than the members of your Society.[3] I should count it a great honour and favour if they would be willing to take the trouble; it would doubtless be the shortest method of finding out all the errors, or all the truths in my works.

1 See *The World*: AT XI 31ff; CSM I 90ff.
2 Plempius. Cf. letter of 15 February 1638, p. 79 above.
3 The Jesuits.

As for light, if you look at the third page of the *Optics*,[1] you will see that I said there expressly that I was going to speak about it only hypothetically. Indeed, since the treatise which contains the whole body of my physical theory is named *On Light*, and since in it I explain light with greater detail and at greater length than anything else, I did not wish to write again what I had written there, but only to convey some idea of it by comparisons and hints, so far as seemed necessary for the subject-matter of the *Optics*.

I am obliged to you for expressing your pleasure that I did not allow others to anticipate me in publishing my thoughts; but that is something of which I have never been afraid. It matters little to me whether I am the first or the last to write what I write, provided that what I write is true. Moreover, all my thoughts are so closely connected and so interdependent that no one could steal any of them without knowing them all.

Please tell me without delay the difficulties which you find in what I have written on refraction, or any other topic; because if you wait until my more 563 detailed views on light are published, you may have to wait a long time. I cannot prove *a priori* the assumptions I made at the beginning of the *Meteorology* without expounding the whole of my physics; but the observational data which I have deduced necessarily from them, and which cannot be deduced in the same way from other principles, seem to me to prove them sufficiently *a posteriori*.[2] I had indeed foreseen that this manner of writing would shock my readers at first, and I think I could easily have prevented this by refraining from calling the things I discussed initially 'assumptions' and by enunciating them only after I had given some reasons to prove them. However, I will tell you candidly that I chose this manner of expounding my thoughts for two reasons. First, believing that I could deduce them in due order from the first principles of my metaphysics, I wanted to ignore other kinds of proofs; secondly, I wanted to see whether the simple exposition of truth would be sufficient to carry conviction without engaging in any disputes or refutations of contrary opinions. Those of my friends who have read most carefully my treatises on *Optics* and *Meteorology* assure me that in this I have succeeded; for although at first they found them as difficult as everyone else, after reading and re-reading them three or four times they say that they no longer find anything there which they think can be called into question. And indeed it is not always necessary to have *a priori* reasons to convince people of a truth. Thales, or whoever it was who first said that the moon receives its light 564 from the sun, probably gave no proof of it except that the different phases of its light can be easily explained on that assumption. That was enough to

1 AT VI 83; CSM I 152.
2 *Meteorology*: AT VI 233.

ensure that from that time to this his view has been generally accepted without demur. My thoughts are so interconnected that I dare to hope that people will find my principles, once they have become familiar by frequent study and are considered all together, are as well proved by the consequences I derive from them as the borrowed nature of the moon's light is proved by its waxing and waning.

The only other point to which I must reply concerns the publication of my *Physics* and *Metaphysics*. I can tell you briefly that I desire it as much or more than anyone, but only under certain conditions, without which I would be foolish to desire it. I will say also that I do not fear at all, basically, that they contain anything against the faith. On the contrary, I am vain enough to think that the faith has never been so strongly supported by human arguments as it may be if my principles are adopted. Transubstantiation, in particular, which the Calvinists regard as impossible to explain by the ordinary philosophy, is very easily explained by mine. But I see no signs that the conditions which could oblige me to do so will be fulfilled, at least for a long time; and so I resign myself to do for my part whatever I regard as my duty and submit myself for the rest to the providence which rules the world. Knowing it is that providence which gave me the small beginnings of which you have seen the samples, I hope that the same providence will give me the grace to complete it, if it is useful for its glory, and if not, I wish to give up all desire to do so. I assure you that nothing which I have so far gained from my publications has been more delightful to me than the approval which you were good enough to give me in your letter. It is particularly precious and welcome to me because it comes from a person of your worth and cloth, and from the very place[1] where I had the good fortune to receive my entire education in my youth, and from the home of my masters, towards whom I will never fail in gratitude.

565

TO MERSENNE, 1 MARCH 1638

AT II

24   I owe a reply to three of your letters, namely those of 8 January, and 8 and 12 February. The last of these I received only today, and the first only a week ago. I shall reply in due order to the particular points that call for an answer; but on a more general note, I must first thank you very sincerely for scrupulously drawing to my attention many things which it is important I should know. I can assure you that so far from being bothered by the bad things that are said about me, I rather revel in it; indeed, the more extravagant and outrageous it is, the more I consider it to my advantage,

1 The College of La Flèche.

the more it pleases me and the less troubled I am by it. I know that these spiteful people would not go to such lengths to speak ill of me if others did not speak well of me. Besides, truth sometimes needs to be contradicted in order to be better recognized. But those who speak without reason or justification deserve nothing but scorn.

As for M. B[eaugrand], I am amazed that you condescend to speak of 25 him, after the way he treated you.¹ I would be glad if you would give me an account of that affair once more. You told me about it at various times, but in different terms each time; so I do not know whether I would be able to speak or write about it with any certainty, should I have occasion to thank him in the way he deserves. As for the discourses written by him and by those of his ilk, please treat them with contempt, and make it clear to them that I have nothing but contempt for them. Above all, please do not agree to send on to me any writing, either of his or of anyone else's, unless those who offer it to you add a note to the effect that they agree to my publishing it along with my reply. If they make difficulties about this, please tell them that in that case, if they prefer, they can send their manuscript to my publisher, as I said on page 75 of the *Discourse on the Method*.² But after seeing M. de Fermat's last letter, which he says he does not want published, I expressly asked you not to send me any more letters of that sort. Of course if a Jesuit or a priest of the Oratory, or anyone else who was incontestably honest and level-headed, wished to send me something, we would have to be more cautious. I shall make myself freely available to people such as these, but not to those spiteful characters whose aim is anything but the truth.

As for the person who you say accuses me of failing to mention Galileo, 26 he clearly wanted to find fault, yet with no good reason, for Galileo himself does not take credit for the discovery of the telescope, and I had cause to speak only of its inventor.³ There was no need to mention those who wrote on optics before me, for it was not my intention to write a history of the subject, and I confined myself to the general point that there must have been people who made many discoveries in the past; so no one could imagine that I wanted to claim for myself the discoveries of other people. On this score I have done more harm to myself than to those I failed to mention; for if I had mentioned them, one might get the impression that

---

1 Descartes believed, mistakenly, that Beaugrand had retained the MS of Descartes' *Discourse*, passed on the MS of the *Optics* to Fermat without permission, held back the licence to publish, etc.
2 AT VI 75; CSM I 149.
3 At the beginning of the *Optics* Descartes credits Jacob Metius of Alkmaar with the discovery of the telescope: see AT VI 82.

they had done much more than one might find to be the case when one read their writings...

(28)   As for my arguments for the existence of God, I hope that eventually they will be as highly, or even more highly, regarded as any other part of the book.[1] Father Vatier makes it clear that he appreciates this point. It is evident from his last letter[2] that he fully approves of all I wrote; and that is as much as I could wish from anyone, which shows that what you had been told about him is not very plausible.

29   Again I am surprised that you should tell me that my reputation is at stake in my reply to M. de Fermat.[3] I assure you there is not a single word in my reply that I would wish to change, except the slips I pointed out to you, or others which you can recognize by the erasures; for I do not think any changes are required. I am surprised also that you should speak of noting down the points in my book which you regard as having been falsified by experience, for I venture to assure you that there are no such false points in it, because I made all the observations for myself, and especially the one you mention concerning warm water freezing faster than cold water. In the book I wrote, not 'hot and cold', but 'water which has been heated over a fire for a long time freezes more quickly than other water'.[4] In order to perform this experiment properly, the water must be allowed to cool down after it has boiled, until it has attained the same degree of coldness as water from a spring. After taking the temperature with a thermometer, you should take some water from a spring and pour equal quantities of the two sorts of water into identical vessels. But there are some experiments which only a few people are capable of performing, and when they are performed badly, the result is often the very opposite of what it ought to be...

(30)   I am sorry to hear that Galileo's eyesight has failed. Though I do not mention him by name, I am sure he would not think ill of my *Optics*...

AT II   TO HUYGENS, 9 MARCH 1638

659   You have cause to think it odd that your Campanella[5] took such a long time to come back to you; but it is already old and weak and cannot travel very quickly. In fact, although I am only a hundred miles from The Hague, it took over three weeks to get here. When it arrived I was busy replying to

1 See *Discourse*: AT VI 34–40; CSM I 128–31.
2 See above, p. 85.
3 Descartes' reply to Fermat's paper 'De Maximis et Minimis', contained in letter to Mersenne of January 1638 (AT I 486).
4 See *Meteorology*: AT VI 238.
5 A book by Thomas Campanella (1568–1639), an Italian Dominican, either *Philosophiae Instaurandae* (1617) or *Realis Philosophiae Epistolicae* (1623).

some objections which had been sent to me from various places. I must admit that his language, and that of the German who writes the lengthy preface, made it impossible to attempt any conversation with them until I had completed the tasks I had in hand, anxious as I was not to catch anything of their style. As for his doctrines, it is fifteen years since I saw his book *On the Meaning of Things*,[1] along with some other treatises by him, and the present book was perhaps among them. But I found so little substance in his writings then that I could no longer recall anything about them. All I can say at present about them is that to go astray through fondness for the most out-of-the-way paths is less excusable than to follow the well-trodden ones.

As for Fromondus, the disagreement between us was so slight that there was no need for you to know about it. The few faults in the copy[2] you saw cannot have been so many as to mar entirely the less objectionable things you might have found in it. Moreover, our dispute was conducted like a game of chess: we remained good friends once the match was over, and now we send each other nothing but compliments. Dr Plemp, Professor of Medicine at Louvain, also produced some objections against the idea of the movement of the heart;[3] but he did this in a friendly way, his aim being to promote discovery of the truth. I try to reply to each critic in the same style in which he writes to me. A Counsellor of Toulouse[4] also raised some objections against my *Optics* and *Geometry*. Some friends[5] of his in Paris wanted to act as his seconds, but if I am not mistaken, neither he nor they could get out of the duel without admitting that everything they said against me was contrary to reason. I did not venture to send you any of these objections, for I did not think it worth your while to read them, and it would have been exceedingly tiresome to copy them; and who knows, they may be published before long. In fact I wish many of my critics would attack me in this way, and I shall not complain about the time I devote to answering them until I have enough to make up a complete volume, because I am sure this is a very good way of showing whether or not what I wrote can be disproved.

I would have been particularly pleased if some Jesuits had been numbered among my opponents; and letters from L'Isle, La Flèche and Lou-

660

661

---

1 *De Sensu Rerum* (1620).
2 Huygens had seen a defective copy of Descartes' reply to Fromondus (see p. 61 above).
3 See above, p. 79.
4 Pierre de Fermat; see footnote 1, p. 73 above.
5 Fermat had sent Descartes five pages of objections to the *Optics* and a treatise to rival his own *Geometry*, thus beginning a protracted dispute, which drew in, on Fermat's side, Gille Personnier de Roberval (1602–75), Professor of Mathematics at the Collège de France and Member of the French Academy, and Etienne Pascal (1588–1651), a prominent mathematician and father of Blaise Pascal.

vain[1] led me to hope that they would be. I did receive a letter recently from someone at La Flèche,[2] who first of all writes in as glowing terms as one could wish for, but then goes on to say that he has cause to complain not about the points I tried to explain, but about the points I chose not to

662   explain, which leads him to press me for my *Physics* and *Metaphysics*. The members of his Society are, I know, in very close correspondence with each other; hence the testimony of just one of them is enough to make me hope that I shall have all of them on my side. But for all that, I cannot yet see any hope that I shall be able to give my *World* to the world in the near future. Without that, I would not be able to complete the Mechanics which you wrote me about. Before showing that we can adapt nature to operations that are quite out of the ordinary, we must explain the laws of nature and the ordinary workings of nature. I have nothing to say about M. Pollot's[3] request to see the three sheets,[4] except that you may do as you please here. Your desire to leave me some rights in something that belongs to you is a tribute to your courtesy; likewise his desire to see it is proof that he thinks that what I wrote is worthy of attention . . . I understand that young Gillot[5]

663   is in The Hague. If I were able to recommend anyone to you, it would be he, for he is the first and practically the only pupil I have ever had, and he has the best head for mathematics.

AT II   TO PLEMPIUS, 23 MARCH 1638

62   I am greatly indebted to you for the trouble you have taken in replying and for sending on letters from other people. Once again the objections which you make are not all lightly to be dismissed; on the contrary, I think they deserve a careful reply.

       As for your first objection,[6] you make the point very well that in a heart that has been cut out, it is the upper parts in particular that beat; and you conclude from this that in this case the beating is not due to blood dropping down from above. But two points should be noted here; I think

1 From, respectively, Fournet, 3 October 1637, Deriennes, 22 February 1638 and Plempius, 20 December 1637.
2 Vatier, 22 February 1638; see above, p. 85.
3 Alphonse Pollot (1602–68), soldier, courtier at the Court of the Prince of Orange, and friend of Descartes.
4 'An Account of the Machines'; see above, pp. 66–73.
5 Jean Gillot (born c. 1614), a pupil of Descartes.
6 In his letter of March 1638 in reply to Descartes' letter of 15 February 1638 (p. 79 above), Plempius counter-objected that the upper part of the heart beats even though blood does not drop into it from above.

they remove the difficulty completely. The first point is that the so-called   63
upper parts of the heart, i.e. the parts at the base, have two compartments.
On the one hand, there are the parts into which the vena cava and the
venous artery[1] open; these parts do not move, because of the rarefaction of
the fresh blood that flows into them once the auricles and all the attached
vessels have been cut off, unless some blood happens to flow into their
cavities from the coronary artery and the other vessels that are dispersed
throughout the substance of the heart (in that case they would all be open
around the base). On the other hand there are the parts into which the
arterial vein and the great artery[2] open; these ought to beat last of all, even
after the apex of the heart has been cut off, because the blood usually flows
out of these so freely that the remaining blood in the dissected heart flows
into them.

The second point to note here is that the movement of the auricles and
the parts adjacent to the auricles is quite different from the movement of
the main substance of the heart; for in the former it is not so readily
perceived that the blood is rarefied, but only that it immediately flows out
of them, at least in the case of a dissected and lifeless heart. For in a living
and intact heart we can clearly see a different sort of movement of the
auricles, which is due to their being filled with blood. But in the upper parts
of the heart, as far as the ventricles, into which the ends of the tricuspid
valves open, the movement is sometimes like that of the auricles and
sometimes like that of the rest of the heart.

Once these points have been noted, if you have taken the trouble to
observe carefully the final movements of the heart of someone near to
death, no doubt you will have seen perfectly well with your own eyes that
in that situation there is never any movement in the upper parts of the
heart, i.e. the parts from which blood should flow into others, except the
movement which is due to their emptying. And when the ventricles are   64
dissected longitudinally, you will sometimes see the auricles moving three
or four times before the heart has beat even once, and sending some blood
into the ventricles on each occasion, and many other things as well, which
all goes to confirm my view. But you may perhaps ask how blood dropping
down can cause such a large movement in the auricles as that which you
can see quite clearly. I can suggest two reasons for this. First, in a live
animal blood is constantly flowing into the heart from the auricles, not
with a continuous and uniform motion, but with an interrupted motion;
and the fibres of the heart through which it flows are so formed by nature

1 'Venous artery' denotes the pulmonary veins.
2 'Arterial vein' denotes the pulmonary artery, and the 'great artery' the aorta.

that when a tiny quantity of blood flows through them, they must open up just as widely and as rapidly as they do when a large quantity of blood is flowing through. Second, a tiny quantity of blood that seeps from the dissected parts of the heart must form a fairly large drop before flowing into the middle of the ventricles, just as perspiration which gathers gradually clings to the skin for some time before it forms into drops which then fall suddenly to the ground.

As for my additional point, that your objection seems more damaging to a view widely held by others than to mine, you reply that this does not rescue me from the difficulty, which of course is true. Now it is not my style to waste time refuting the views of other people; but in order to win you over to my side, I thought it would be useful to point out that there is no other view which is as well supported as my own ... In order to explain how a human heart cut from a corpse can move when the soul is no longer present, you resort to the idea that heat and vital spirits cause the movement by operating as instruments of the soul. Now is this not resorting to desperate measures? For if these instruments should sometimes suffice on their own to bring about this effect, why not always? And why should you imagine that when the soul is absent, these effects should occur through some power of the soul, when you think that no such power is needed to bring them about when the soul is present?

(65)

As for your second objection[1] concerning a surgeon's method of staunching the flow of blood from a cut artery, I would reply that if the pulse does not stop beyond the cut, this is not due to a blockage in the bed of the artery through which the blood normally flows, but rather to the blockage of the opening in the skin and flesh through which the blood would otherwise flow from the body ...

Galen's view, that the movement of the arteries is due to a certain force flowing within the artery walls, does not seem at all plausible to me. Yet I think it is perfectly reasonable to hold that once the parts of the artery in front of the ligature have been set in motion, the parts beyond it will also be set in motion, at least if the movement of the artery walls is not completely stopped by the ligature; yet this can hardly be the case in the present instance. But if one part of the artery is more tightly constricted than other parts, so that no matter how the constriction is caused, there can be no movement of the artery wall at that part, then I firmly believe that the arterial pulse beyond that part will also cease.

66

In your third objection you cite the coldness of fish as a reason for saying

---

1 Plempius counter-objected to Descartes' second point that Descartes' explanation of the beating of the arteries is contradicted by the fact that when surgeons stop a bleeding artery by compressing the wound with a pack, the artery continues to beat below the wound.

that the blood in the hearts of fish is not rarefied through heat.[1] But if you were with me now, you would have to admit that even in the coldest of animals the movement in question is due to heat. For you would see that the tiny heart of an eel, which I cut out before seven or eight o'clock this morning, revives when a little heat is applied to its surface, and begins to beat again quite rapidly, even though it is obviously dead and already dry on the surface.

Now, to show you that this effect requires not only heat but also a flow of blood into this heart, I am now pouring into the heart blood from the same eel which I had kept for this purpose. I then warm up the heart, and it begins to beat just as rapidly and vigorously as it did in the live animal. (Note that these experiments do not always give the same results. For all sorts of reasons, the results vary; but if they are considered impartially, they will always confirm my view.) When observing the eel's heart this morning, I also found clear evidence for the point I made earlier on about the movement of the upper parts of the heart when blood is flowing from them. Even after the part into which the vena cava opens had been cut off (this is what ought strictly to be called the upper part), I observed that the part beyond it, the so-called upper part, no longer continued to beat along 67 with the rest of the heart, though it did move from time to time, albeit in a different way, when blood dropped into it from the cut.

But if you can manage to perform a similar experiment, you will be able to see that the hearts of colder animals prepared in this way often beat, though there could be no reason to suspect that blood was entering them from somewhere else. In view of this, I shall now tackle the objection which you would be justified in raising at this point, and shall describe how, as I understand it, the pulse is caused in the present instance. In the first place, I observe that the blood in question is very different from that of warmer animals: once it has been drawn from the body, its finest particles are immediately vaporized, and the remainder turns partly into water and partly into deposits. The blood of the said eel has kept not exactly fresh all day, but at least its condition has remained unaltered, so far as I can see, and it continues to give off a good deal of vapour, which rises from it like thick smoke when it is heated ever so slightly.

In the second place, I recall having seen green branches or fruit giving off vapour when they were burnt or boiled. Through the action of the heat, the substance of the wood or fruit gives off vapour through narrow cracks in the bark or skin; everyone has observed this. Sometimes the bark is so

---

1 Plempius counter-objected that even if the hearts of fish are warmer than any other parts of their body, they are not warm enough to rarefy their blood, or to rarefy it as quickly as Descartes' view requires; moreover, our hands are warmer than fishes' hearts, yet they do not rarefy the blood of fish that happens to be on them.

constituted that it swells considerably before a crack opens up, and then rapidly subsides, because the vapour within the swelling suddenly rushes out, and is not replaced by fresh vapour. But as soon as more vapour has built up, that part of the bark swells up again, the crack opens and vapour

68   is given off, just as before. This recurring process provides an excellent model of the heart-beat, not of the live heart, but of the heart I have just now cut out of the eel. These observations make it perfectly clear that our view should be that the fibres which make up the flesh of the heart are so disposed that the vapour of the blood which they contain is sufficient to make them swell up; the swelling causes large pathways to open up, through which the vapour rushes out; thereafter the heart contracts, and so on. I was glad to see this confirmed in another instance that I observed today. I cut off the upper part of the heart of an eel, i.e. the part into which the vena cava opens, and which performs the same function in the eel as the right auricle does in the heart of a land animal (note that in the eel that part is situated below the other, though through force of habit I said 'upper'). The tangled fibres of this part then yielded only a small quantity of thick blood. I put this part aside in a wooden vessel to see whether it would show any pulsation. At first I could detect no pulsation, because, as I noticed a little later, when many pathways were clear and open, all the vapour given off by the blood flew off in a continuous and unimpeded stream. But after a quarter of an hour or so, when the small quantity of blood in which the particles of the heart were bathed began to dry on the surface, and a sort of skin formed, I could see a distinct pulsation in it. The pulsation increased when I applied heat, and it continued until the blood was no longer liquid.

69   I am very surprised that you thought the point I made about fermentation was quite far-fetched, and that I was using it as a last resort, as if I were hard pressed, and that point provided the only way of escape. My view can certainly be set out and demonstrated very easily without that point; but even so, it is necessary to admit that some of the blood that is rarefied in the heart remains in it from one diastole to the next, and the rarefaction is increased by the fresh blood that flows in and mixes with it; and the nature and properties of fermentation are clearly relevant to this fact...

AT II   TO RENERI FOR POLLOT, APRIL OR MAY 1638

34   Your friend need not have been so ceremonious. People of such worth and intelligence need no formal introduction, and I will always count it a favour when they do me the honour of consulting me about my writings. Please tell your friend not to hesitate to do so. This time, however, since he wanted it so, I will ask you to pass on my replies to him.

First, if I had said without qualification that one should hold to opinions that one has once decided to follow, even though they are doubtful, I should indeed have been no less to blame than if I had said that one should be opinionated and stubborn; because holding to an opinion is the same as persisting in a judgement that one has made. But I said something quite different. I said that one must be decisive in one's actions even when one was undecided in one's judgements,[1] and that one should follow the most doubtful opinions with no less constancy than if they were quite certain.[2] 35
By this I meant that once one has settled on opinions which one judges doubtful – that is, once one has decided that there are no others that one judges better or more certain – one should act on them with no less constancy than if one knew that they were the best, which indeed they are when so considered. There is no danger that this constancy in action will lead us further and further into error or vice, since there can be error only in the intellect which, I am supposing, remains free throughout and regards what is doubtful as doubtful. Moreover, I apply this rule mainly to actions in life which admit of no delay, and I use it only provisionally, intending to change my opinions as soon as I can find better, and to lose no opportunity of looking for them. Finally, I was forced to speak of firmness and resolution in action for the sake of ease of conscience and to prevent people from blaming me for saying that in order to avoid rashness we must once in our lifetime put aside all the opinions we have hitherto believed. Otherwise it seemed that people would have objected that such a universal doubt could give rise to great indecision and moral chaos. Altogether it seems to me that I could not have been more careful to set the virtue of decisiveness between its two contrary vices, indecision and obstinacy. 36

2. It does not seem to me a fiction, but a truth which nobody should deny, that there is nothing entirely in our power except our thoughts;[3] at least if you take the word 'thought' as I do, to cover all the operations of the soul, so that not only meditations and acts of the will, but the activities of seeing and hearing and deciding on one movement rather than another, so far as they depend on the soul, are all thoughts. In philosophical language there is nothing strictly attributable to a man apart from what is covered by the word 'thought'; for the activities which belong to the body alone are said to take place in a man rather than to be performed by him. Notice too the word 'entirely' and what follows: 'when we have done our best about external things, everything which we fail to achieve is *absolutely* impossible so far as we are concerned'. This shows that I did not mean that external things were not at all in our power, but that they are in

1 *Discourse*: AT VI 22; CSM I 122.
2 *Discourse*: AT VI 24; CSM I 123.
3 *Discourse*: AT VI 25; CSM I 123.

our power only in so far as they can be affected by our thoughts, and not *absolutely* or *entirely* in our power because there are other powers outside us which can frustrate our designs. To make myself clearer I even put side by side the two expressions 'absolutely' and 'so far as we are concerned',
37   which a critic, if he did not understand the sense of the passage, might complain contradicted each other. Nothing exterior, then, is in our power except in so far as it is at the command of our soul, and nothing is absolutely in our power except our thoughts. But though this is very true, and no one could find it hard to accept when he thinks of it explicitly, yet I did say that it is a belief which one has to grow accustomed to, and that long practice and repeated meditation are necessary to do so. This is because our desires and our passions are constantly telling us the opposite. We have so frequently experienced since childhood that by crying or commanding we could make our nurses obey us and get what we want, that we have gradually convinced ourselves that the world was made only for us, and that everything was our due. Those who are born to greatness and fortune are the more likely to deceive themselves in this way; they too are commonly seen to be the most impatient when they have to bear misfortune. It seems to me that there is no more fitting occupation for a philosopher than to accustom himself to believe what true reason tells him, and to beware of the false opinions which his natural appetites urge upon him.

3. When someone says 'I am breathing, therefore I exist', if he wants to prove he exists from the fact that there cannot be breathing without existence, he proves nothing, because he would have to prove first that it is true that he is breathing, which is impossible unless he has also proved that
38   he exists. But if he wants to prove his existence from the feeling or the belief he has that he is breathing, so that he judges that even if the opinion were untrue he could not have it if he did not exist, then his proof is sound. For in such a case the thought of breathing is present to our mind before the thought of our existing, and we cannot doubt that we have it while we have it.[1] To say 'I am breathing, therefore I exist', in this sense, is simply to say 'I am thinking, therefore I exist.' You will find on examination that all the other propositions from which we can thus prove our existence reduce to the same one; so that one cannot prove from them the existence of the body, i.e. of a nature which occupies space, etc., but only that of the soul, i.e. of a nature which thinks. Of course one may wonder whether the nature which thinks may perhaps be the same as the nature which occupies space, so that there is one nature which is both intellectual and corporeal; but by the method which I suggested, it is known only as intellectual.

1 *Discourse*: AT vi 35; CSM i 128.

4. From the very fact that we conceive clearly and distinctly the two natures of the body and the soul as different, we know that in reality they are different, and consequently that the soul can think without the body, even though, when it is joined to it, it can have its operation disturbed by the bad disposition of the bodily organs.

5. Although the Pyrrhonists[1] reached no certain conclusion from their doubts, it does not follow that no one can. I would try now to show how these doubts can be used to prove God's existence and to clear up the difficulties which remain in what I wrote, were it not that someone has promised to send me soon a summary of all that can be doubted on this topic, which will perhaps enable me to do it better. So I must ask the person who wrote these queries to allow me to put off my reply until I have received the summary.

6. Most of the actions of animals resemble ours, and throughout our lives this has given us many occasions to judge that they act by an interior principle like the one within ourselves, that is to say, by means of a soul which has feelings and passions like ours. All of us are deeply imbued with this opinion by nature. Whatever reasons there may be for denying it, it is hard to say publicly how the case stands without exposing oneself to the ridicule of children and feeble minds. But those who want to discover truth must above all distrust opinions rashly acquired in childhood. In order to know what we ought to believe on this question, it seems to me, we must consider the following. Suppose that a man had been brought up all his life in some place where he had never seen any animals except men; and suppose that he was very devoted to the study of mechanics, and had made, or helped to make, various automatons shaped like a man, a horse, a dog, a bird, and so on, which walked and ate, and breathed, and so far as possible imitated all the other actions of the animals they resembled, including the signs we use to express our passions, like crying when struck and running away when subjected to a loud noise. Suppose that sometimes he found it impossible to tell the difference between the real men and those which had only the shape of men, and had learnt by experience that there are only the two ways of telling them apart which I explained on page 57 of my *Discourse on the Method*[2]: first, that such automatons never answer in word or sign, except by chance, to questions put to them; and secondly, that though their movements are often more regular and certain than those of the wisest men, yet in many things which they would have to do to imitate us, they fail more disastrously than the greatest fools. Now, I say, you must consider what would be the judgement of such a man when he

39

40

1 The Pyrrhonists (named after Pyrrho of Elis, born *c.* 365 B.C.) advocated a strong version of scepticism which required complete suspension of judgement.
2 *Discourse*: AT VI 56; CSM I 139–40.

saw the animals we have; especially if he was filled with the knowledge of God, or at least had noticed how inferior is the best skill shown by men in their artefacts when compared with that shown by nature in the composition of plants. Nature has packed plants with an infinity of tiny invisible ducts through which certain juices gradually ascend to the ends of the branches, where they intermingle and combine and dry out in such a way as to form leaves and flowers and fruits. Let us suppose that our man had noticed this, and so believed firmly that if there were automatons made by God or nature to imitate our actions, they would imitate them more perfectly, and be incomparably more skilfully constructed than any which could be invented by men. Now suppose that this man were to see the animals we have, and noticed in their actions the same two things which make them differ from us, and which he had already been accustomed to notice in his automatons. There is no doubt that he would not come to the conclusion that there was any real feeling or emotion in them, but would think they were automatons, which, being made by nature, were incomparably more accomplished than any of those he had previously made himself. It only remains to consider whether the verdict he would give, with knowledge of the facts and unprejudiced by any false opinion, would be less credible than the one we made when we were children and have kept only through habit. We base our judgement solely on the resemblance between some exterior actions of animals and our own; but this is not at all a sufficient basis to prove that there is any resemblance between the corresponding interior actions.

7. I tried to show that the soul was a substance really distinct from the body. This is sufficient, I believe, in discussion with people who believe God to be creator of all, to force the admission that our souls must necessarily be created by him. And those who acquire certainty of God's existence in the way I have shown cannot fail to recognize him as universal creator.

8. I did not say that light was extended like a stick, but like the actions or movements transmitted by a stick. And although the movement does not take place instantaneously, each of its parts can be felt at one end of the stick at the very moment (that is to say, at exactly the same time) that it is produced at the other end. Moreover, I did not say that light was like grape juice in a vat, but like the action whereby the parts of the juice at the top tend to move towards the bottom: these parts tend to move towards the bottom in a completely straight line, though they cannot move exactly in a completely straight line, as I said on page 8, line 1.[1]

9. Since I made a point of not explaining the foundations of my physics

---

[1] See *Optics*: AT VI 88; CSM I 155.

(page 76, line 19),[1] I did not think I would have to provide a more distinct explanation of subtle matter than the one I gave.

10. Even though water remains liquid simply because its particles are kept moving by the subtle matter surrounding them, this does not prevent its becoming liquid when its particles are set in motion by some other cause. This paragraph should present no difficulty provided we know that fire has the power to move the particles of terrestrial bodies which it approaches, as we see with our own eyes in many instances; and hence it must set the particles of subtle matter in motion all the more easily, because they are smaller and less closely joined together, these being the   43
two qualities which entitle one body to be called more subtle than another.

11. Of course I do not claim to be certain that the particles of water are shaped like certain animals,[2] but only that they are elongated, smooth and flexible. Now, if we can find any other shape that enables us to explain all their properties just as well, I shall be perfectly willing to adopt that instead; but if no others can be found, I do not see what difficulty there could be in imagining them specifically to have that shape, seeing that they must necessarily have some shape or other, and the one I suggested is particularly simple. As to the constitution of air, while I do not deny that some of the particles of air might also have this shape, many things go to show that they cannot all be of that shape. To mention a few: in the case in question, air would not be as light as it in fact is, because particles of that sort of shape can fit closely together with little space around them, and hence must make up a fairly bulky and heavy body such as water; and it would be much more penetrating than it is, for we can see that it is hardly more penetrating than water, and in many cases even less so; nor could it expand or condense by degrees as readily as it does, and so on.

12. I think the point that is being made in this paragraph amounts to this: I had said that the pain we feel when we receive a blow from a sword is not in the sword in the way it is in our sense-organs, but is simply caused by   44
the shape of the edge or point, by the hardness of the matter of which the blade is composed and by the force with which it moves. Against this, it was objected that other bodies which have the same sort of edge could also cause pain; that bodies which have different shapes, especially those that are soft and not hard like a sword, could not be felt; and lastly that the pain is nothing in the sword except its external shape, and is not an internal quality; and that the force which prevents its sheath from breaking when the sword is inside it consists simply in the action through which it

1 See *Discourse*: AT VI 68; CSM I 145.
2 Descartes had said that the particles of which water is composed are elongated, smooth, and as slippery as tiny eels; see *Meteorology*: AT VI 233.

wounds, and in its shape. Given this objection, we can easily see what my reply would be, namely that bodies whose particles have the same size, shape, hardness, etc. as those of salt will have the same effect, so far as taste is concerned. That being the case, we cannot suppose that these bodies are tasteless; for something's being tasteless consists not in its lacking the sensation of taste within itself, but in lacking the power to cause such a sensation. Moreover, liquids whose particles have some other shapes or sizes, etc. do not taste like salt, but they may taste like something else which is not as strong or sharp, if their particles are softer, just as the pain of a bruise is not the same as that of a cut; and we cannot cause as much pain with a feather as we can with a sword, since the former is composed of softer matter. Lastly, I do not see why it is held that taste is more an intrinsic quality in salt than pain is in a sword. And as for the power of salt

45   to keep things from going bad, this is not due to its sharpness or the shape of its particles, but to the hardness and inflexibility of its particles, just as it is the inflexibility of the sword which prevents its sheath from breaking. The shape of the parts is a contributing factor only in so far as it makes them suited to penetrating the pores of other bodies, just as it is the shape of the sword which makes it fit into its sheath . . .

(46)   15. As for the spelling, to be sure, it is for the printer to defend it, for in this matter my wishes were simply that he should follow customary usage. Just as I did not make him take out the *p* from *corps* or the *t* from *esprits* when he put them in, so I did not bother to get him to add them when he left them out; for I did not notice any instances where this could give rise to any ambiguity. Besides it is not my intention to revise French spelling, and I would not advise anyone to try to do this in a book printed in Leiden.[1] But if I am to give my own view, I think it would be much easier for foreigners to learn our language if the spelling followed the pronunciation exactly; it would outweigh the inconvenience to them and us which would be caused by the ambiguity of some expressions. For languages are constituted through speech rather than through writing. If we encountered expressions in the spoken word which frequently gave rise to ambiguity, usage would immediately bring about a change in order to remove the ambiguity . . .

AT II   TO MERSENNE, 27 MAY 1638

138   . . . 2. You ask whether there would be real space, as there is now, if God had created nothing. At first this question seems to be beyond the capacity

---

1 On the errata page of the 1637 edition of the *Discourse*, Descartes gave it as his excuse for certain minor misprints that he was no grammarian and the compositor did not know a word of French.

of the human mind, like infinity, so that it would be unreasonable to discuss it; but in fact I think that it is merely beyond the capacity of our imagination, like the questions of the existence of God and of the human soul. I believe that our intellect can reach the truth of the matter, which is, in my opinion, that not only would there not be any space, but even those truths which are called eternal – as that 'the whole is greater than its part' – would not be truths if God had not so established, as I think I wrote you once before[1] ...

You ask if I regard what I have written about refraction as a demon- (141) stration. I think it is, in so far as one can be given in this field without a previous demonstration of the principles of physics by metaphysics – which is something I hope to do some day but which has not yet been done 142 – and so far as it has ever been possible to demonstrate the solution to any problem of mechanics, or optics, or astronomy, or anything else which is not pure geometry or arithmetic. But to require me to give geometrical demonstrations on a topic that depends on physics is to ask me to do the impossible. And if you will not call anything demonstrations except geometers' proofs, then you must say that Archimedes never demonstrated anything in mechanics, or Vitellio[2] in optics, or Ptolemy in astronomy. But of course nobody says this. In such matters people are satisfied if the authors' assumptions are not obviously contrary to experience and if their discussion is coherent and free from logical error, even though their assumptions may not be strictly true. I could demonstrate, for instance, that even the definition of the centre of gravity given by Archimedes is false, and that there is no such centre; and the other assumptions he makes elsewhere are not strictly true either. The assumptions of Ptolemy and Vitellio are much less certain again; but that is not a sufficient reason for rejecting the demonstrations which they have based on them. Now what I claim to have demonstrated about refraction does not depend on the truth 143 about the nature of light, or on whether its propagation is instantaneous or not, but only on my assumption that it is an action, or a power, which in its propagation from place to place follows the same laws as local motion, and is transmitted by means of an extremely rarefied liquid which is in the pores of transparent bodies. Your difficulty about instantaneous propaga- tion arises from an ambiguity in the word 'instantaneous': you seem to take it as denying every kind of priority, as if the light of the sun could be propagated here without first passing through all the intermediate space. But 'instantaneous' excludes only temporal priority; it is compatible with each of the lower parts of a ray of light being dependent on all the upper

1 See the letters to Mersenne of 15 April, 6 May and 27 May 1630: above, pp. 20, 24 and 25.
2 Vitellio (Witelo) (c. 1225–c. 1275) wrote on optics and on the physics of light refraction.

ones, in the same way as the end of a successive movement depends on all its preceding parts. I say that there are only two ways to refute what I have written. One is to prove by experience or reason that the assumptions I have made are false; the other is to show that what I have deduced from them cannot be deduced from them. M. de Fermat understood this very well; for he tried to refute what I wrote about refraction by attempting to prove that it contained a logical error. But if people simply say that they do not believe what I have written, because I deduce it from certain assump-

144   tions which I have not proved, then they do not know what they are asking or what they ought to ask ...

As for M. Petit, I did not at all agree with what he wrote;[1] I took the view that he was being deliberately frivolous, and raising objections without having anything to object to. For all he did was to throw in some poor platitudes, derived for the most part from the atheists, which he heaped up indiscriminately, confining himself mainly to what I wrote about God and the soul, not one word of which he understood ...

(145)   My opinion of M. Morin[2] is quite different. I think I would be indebted to him for his objections, as I would be to all who make a point of informing me that their aim is to see that the truth is discovered. Moreover, I shall by no means be ungrateful to them for treating me as roughly as they can, and I shall try to answer them all, so that none has cause to be offended.

146   What I wrote about Gillot[3] was not intended to put you to the trouble of seeking a post for him, for I have not yet even asked him whether he has made up his mind to go to France, and I have not seen him for over six months. If he stays in Leiden or The Hague, he can easily earn five or six hundred crowns a year. He managed to earn as much in England. But just when he was getting to know the place, his parents took him away against his will, because they were afraid that if he were far from them he would go astray; no doubt they were afraid that he would become a Catholic if he were in France, for they are very ardent Huguenots. For his part he is very docile, and I would vouch for his loyalty as if he were my own brother. So if M. de Sainte-Croix[4] or someone else offers him a position which in your judgement would be to his advantage, I shall send him all the same,

---

1 Pierre Petit (1598–1677), a military engineer and amateur physicist, had written some objections to Part IV of the *Discourse*, one of which was that we form the idea of a perfect being by some hidden and obscure operation of the imagination.
2 Jean-Baptiste Morin (1583–1656), Professor of Mathematics at the Collège de France and supporter of the hypothesis of the immobility of the earth.
3 Jean Gillot (born c. 1614), a pupil of Descartes; Huygens obtained for him the post of mathematician to the King of Portugal.
4 André Jumeau, Prior of Sainte-Croix, a mathematician who corresponded with Descartes on mathematical problems.

provided of course that Rivet[1] is not told about it. For he has such power over his parents that, on some religious pretext, he would prevent them from giving their consent, though the real reason would be to impede his advancement, for that is his temperament...

Either by this post or the next you will receive the paper I promised you, which will make clear how my *Geometry* is to be understood, for it is almost ready; a well-placed gentleman[2] is writing it up...

TO MERSENNE, 29 JUNE 1638   AT II

... You ask me whether the foreigners' objections are better than those (191) of the French. Of the objections which I received from France, I must say that the only ones I value are those of M. Morin.[3] As for M. Petit,[4] it was clear that he wished merely to be contrary, and had no understanding of the matter which he was criticizing. If it were not for the fact that he 192 confined himself mainly to what I had written about the existence of God, I would not hesitate to make my reply an exercise in derision; but since this is too serious a topic for such an exercise, I shall let him off rather lightly. I know that the only reason why M. Fermat thinks well of him is that he shares his views on this topic; but I assure you I have a low opinion of them both. As for the foreigners, Fromondus of Louvain made several fairly substantial objections, and another man called Plempius, a professor of medicine, sent me some objections concerning the movement of the heart which, I think, covered all the points that could possibly be made against my views on this topic.[5] There was another man, also from Louvain, who did not wish to give his name, but who, between ourselves, is a Jesuit;[6] he sent me some objections concerning the colours of the rainbow. Lastly, someone from The Hague sent me objections on several different topics. That is all I have received up till now. I am very much obliged to M. d'Igby[7] for speaking so favourably on my behalf, as you tell me he does. As for

1 André Rivet (1572–1651), a Protestant minister and Professor of Theology at Leiden.
2 Probably Godefroy de Haestrecht. A fragment of this paper, which Descartes speaks of as an 'introduction' to his *Geometry*, was found among Leibniz' papers in the Royal Library, Hanover, and was published by Henri Adam in *Bulletin des sciences mathématiques* (1896).
3 See letter from Morin of 22 February 1638: AT I 536. Cf. the following letter.
4 See footnote 1, p. 104 above.
5 See Fromondus to Plempius, 13 September 1637 (AT I 402) and Descartes' letter to Plempius for Fromondus of 3 October 1637, p. 61 above.
6 Jean Ciermans (1602–48), a Dutch Jesuit, Professor of Mathematics at Louvain.
7 Sir Kenelm Digby (1603–65), an English scholar and adventurer, author of *A Treatise of the Nature of Bodies* (1644) and *The Operations and Nature of Man's Soul* (1644).

those who speak ill of me, I can assure you I would rather take revenge by making fun of them than by thrashing them; I find it easier to laugh than to get angry.

TO MORIN, 13 JULY 1638

The objections which you have taken the trouble to send me are such that I would have received them gladly from anybody; but your rank among the learned, and the reputation which your writings have earned you, make them more gratifying from you than from anyone else. I think that there is no better way of showing this than by the care I shall take to answer you in every point.

You begin with my assumptions. You say 'the phenomena of the heavenly movements can be deduced with no less certainty from the assumption that the earth is stationary than from the assumption that it moves'. I agree readily. I hope that people will take in the same way what I wrote in the *Optics* about the nature of light, so that the force of the mathematical demonstrations which I tried to set out there will not be dependent on any opinion in physics, as I said sufficiently clearly on page 3.[1] If there is some other way of imagining light which will explain all the properties of it that we know from experience, it will be seen that all that I have demonstrated about refraction, vision, and so on can be derived from it just as well as from the assumptions I made.

You say also that there is a vicious circle in proving effects from a cause, and then proving the cause by the same effects. I agree: but I do not agree that it is circular to explain effects by a cause, and then prove the cause by the effects; because there is a big difference between *proving* and *explaining*. I should add that the word 'demonstrate' can be used to signify either, if it is used according to common usage and not in the technical philosophical sense. I should add also that there is nothing circular in proving a cause by several effects which are independently known, and then proving certain other effects from this cause. I have combined these two senses together on page 76[2]: 'As my last conclusions are demonstrated by the first, which are their causes, so the first are in turn demonstrated by the last, which are their effects.' But that does not leave me open to the accusation of speaking ambiguously, because I explained what I meant immediately afterwards when I said that experience renders most of these effects quite certain and so the causes from which I deduce them serve not so much to prove them as to explain them — indeed it is the causes which

1 *Optics*: AT VI 83; CSM I 152–3.
2 *Discourse*: AT VI 76; CSM I 150.

are proved by the effects. And I put 'serve not so much to prove them' rather than 'do not serve at all', so that people could tell that each of these effects could also be proved from this cause, in case there was any doubt about it, provided the cause had already been proved from other effects. I do not see what other terms I could have used to explain myself better.

You say also that astronomers often make assumptions which cause them to fall into grave errors; as when they wrongly assume a parallax, or the obliquity of the ecliptic, and so on. To this I reply that these items do not belong to the class of assumptions or hypotheses I was speaking of; I marked out this class clearly when I said that one could draw very true and certain consequences from them even though they were false and uncertain. For the parallax, the obliquity of the ecliptic, and so on cannot be assumed as false or uncertain, but only as true; whereas the equator, the zodiac, the epicycles and other such circles are commonly assumed as false, and the movement of the earth as uncertain, and yet for all that true conclusions are deduced from them.

Finally, you say that nothing is easier than to fit a cause to an effect. It is true that there are many effects to which it is easy to fit many separate causes; but it is not always so easy to fit a single cause to many different effects, unless it is the true cause which produces them. There are often cases in which in order to prove what is the true cause of a number of effects, it is sufficient to give a single one from which they can all clearly be deduced. I claim that all the causes of which I spoke belong to this class. You must remember that in the whole history of physics up to now people have only tried to imagine some causes to explain the phenomena of nature, with virtually no success. Compare my assumptions with the assumptions of others. Compare all their *real qualities*, their *substantial forms*, their *elements* and countless other such things with my single assumption that all bodies are composed of parts. This is something which is visible to the naked eye in many cases and can be proved by countless reasons in others. All that I add to this is that the parts of certain kinds of bodies are of one shape rather than another. This in turn is easy to demonstrate to those who agree that bodies are composed of parts. Compare the deductions I have made from my assumption – about vision, salt, winds, clouds, snow, thunder, the rainbow, and so on – with what the others have derived from their assumptions on the same topics. I hope this will be enough to convince anyone unbiassed that the effects which I explain have no other causes than the ones from which I have deduced them. None the less, I intend to give a demonstration of it in another place.

Moreover, I am sorry that in your objections you confined yourself to the topic of light, for I expressly refrained from stating my views on that topic; and since I do not now wish to reverse my decision not to include in

199

200

my replies any explanation of topics I had not planned to discuss, I shall
not be able to answer you as thoroughly as I would have liked. But I ask
you to believe that I was not trying to hide behind a barricade of obscure
201 expressions to avoid being taken by surprise, as you seem to have thought.
If I have a certain skill in mathematical demonstrations, as you do me the
honour of suggesting I have, it is more likely that such demonstrations
taught me to discover the truth rather than to disguise it. The reason why I
did not speak about light as openly as about the other topics was my
decision not to include anything in these *Essays* which I had already tried
to explain in exact detail in another treatise,[1] as I stated on page 42 of the
Discourse on the Method.[2] Of course one is not obliged to believe anything
I wrote there. But when one sees fruits in a country which have not been
introduced from abroad, one takes the view that they have sprung from
indigenous plants rather than grown of their own accord. By analogy, I
think that the particular truths which I discussed in my *Essays* (if at any
rate truths they be) provide much stronger grounds for thinking that I must
have some knowledge of the general causes on which they depend than for
thinking that I was able to discover them without that knowledge. And
since it is only the general causes which are discussed in that other treatise,
I do not think I was suggesting anything very far-fetched when I wrote that
I had done just that.

As for the contempt which you were told I had for the Schools, this can
only have been dreamt up by people who do not know me or my habits or
the way I view things. Of course in my *Essays* I made hardly any use of
202 terms which are familiar only to the learned; yet this is not to say that I
disapprove of such terms, but merely that my aim was to make myself
understandable by means of other terms as well. After all, at the end of the
day it is not for me to select the weapons with which I am to be attacked,
but only to try to defend myself[3] ...

(203)   4. Concerning page 122,[4] you raise two objections. The first is that 'if
light is only an action or inclination to move, it is not in that case a
movement'. But please tell me where I said that it was a 'movement',
without immediately adding 'or an action'? I do not believe there is any
such statement in my writings, and especially not when I discussed the sort
of light which can be seen in transparent bodies, which philosophers call

---

1 The reference is to *The World*. 'Essays' denotes the *Optics*, *Meteorology* and *Geometry*,
  which Descartes called 'Essays in the Method'.
2 See AT VI 41; CSM I 131.
3 At this point Descartes goes on to reply to several objections which Morin had put
  concerning the *Optics*; a selection of Descartes' replies to some of the more interesting
  objections is given below.
4 *Optics*: AT VI 197.

lumen in Latin in order to distinguish this from the light which can be seen in luminous bodies, which they call *lux*. Now, when I say in some places   204 that light is a movement or an action, and in another place that it is only an action, I am not contradicting myself. Moreover, we should bear in mind that the meaning of the word 'action' is quite general: it comprises not only the power or inclination to move but also the movement itself. For example, when we say of someone that he is always in action, this means that he is always moving. That is how I am using the word in the context you cite; so there is no ambiguity there. I point out there that we must keep in mind the explanation of light which I gave earlier. This makes it clear that when I use a word in different contexts, I intend it to be understood in the same sense.

The second objection you make here is that 'if the action belongs to subtle matter, it does not belong to luminous bodies'. But this objection rests upon an ambiguity in the word 'light'. I readily admit that the action of subtle matter, which is *lumen*, is not an action of luminous bodies, which is *lux*; but I do not admit on that account that what I said was ambiguous, for I was very careful to distinguish between these two senses of 'light' throughout...

Concerning page 5,[1] I am amazed that you cite pages 4 and 5 in order to   (205) prove that the movement of luminous bodies cannot be transmitted as far as our eyes, that nothing material given off by these bodies is transmitted. In these two pages I am simply trying to set out the analogy with a blind   206 man, which I put forward primarily to show how movement can be transmitted without something moving. And I do not believe you would think that when the blind man touches his dog with his stick, the dog must pass along the stick to his hand if he is to sense its movements. But to answer you in formal terms: when you say that the movement is never in the moving thing, †I make a distinction†. The movement in question cannot in reality occur without some body, but it can of course be transmitted from one body to another, and thus pass from luminous bodies to our eyes through the medium of some third item, namely (as I say on page 4) the air and other transparent bodies or (as I explain more clearly on page 6) a very subtle matter which fills the pores of these bodies, and extends without a break from the stars to us...

9. Concerning pages 159ff.,[2] you prove quite convincingly that the   (207) round particles of the subtle matter cannot occupy exactly all the pores of terrestrial bodies. I agree, but if you conclude from this that the space which they do occupy is on that account empty, †I deny the conclusion†, if I

1 *Optics*: AT VI 85; CSM I 153.
2 *Meteorology*: AT VI 233.

may put it in scholastic terms. For the pores might very well be occupied by something else, which I need not go into here...

(211)   Concerning your objection that the subtle matter is not hard like a stick[1] I drew a comparison on page 6[2] between the subtle matter and the grape juice in a vat, and showed how the particles at the top of the vat press down and set in motion the particles at the bottom, which go out through the hole at the very moment it is opened. By means of this analogy, I explained how the movement of the subtle matter surrounding a luminous body can instantaneously set in motion very distant matter...

(216)   At the end you ask 'whether the force with which a spark from a fire or a
217   glow-worm at night must, on my view, push the subtle matter towards our eyes if we are to be able to sense the light, can be impeded by the force of the wind when it is blowing very hard in the opposite direction'. Practically the same question can be raised about the vat of grape juice which we discussed above. Let us suppose that the grapes in the juice are attached to threads or enclosed in a net, and are pulled rapidly from the bottom of the vat to the top. Will the motion of the grapes impede the sinking motion of the juice, which is in the opposite direction to that of the grapes? My answer is that if the upward motion of the grapes is slower than the motion by which the particles of the juice tend to sink, this will not prevent the juice from flowing out of the holes at the bottom of the vat. Let us also suppose that the motion of the grapes is much more swift and powerful, and that the holes are blocked up, so that the space vacated by the grapes can be occupied only by the juice (just as nothing but subtle matter can occupy the space vacated by the particles of the air of which wind is composed). In this case we can demonstrate by means of the rules of mechanics that the pressure of the juice on the bottom of the vat will be just as great as it would be if the grapes were not moving at all. By the same token it is certain, to me at any rate, that in no case can the motion of the wind impede the action of light, except in the case where its motion is so violent that it sets fire to the air, in which case the light that is created can obliterate the light of a spark, if indeed it is much more intense...

(218)   But in my view, your main objection – which is perhaps why you decided to keep it till the last – is that 'if the pores of transparent bodies must be straight, it does not look as if they could let the subtle matter pass through them in every direction, because it is impossible that a solid body should contain straight pores in every direction'. I think, however, I can

---

1 In his letter of 22 February 1638 (AT I 549) Morin had objected that the analogy of the blind man's stick was inappropriate: the reason why one end of the stick moves instantaneously when the other end is pushed is that the stick is continuous and solid from one end to the other; but subtle matter is not solid like a stick.
2 *Optics*: AT VI 86; CSM I 154.

clear up this difficulty by means of an analogy, if we do not take the word 'straight' in a stricter sense than I was clearly intending to take it. See page 8, line 2, and even the page you cite (page 122),[1] where I say, not that the pores must be perfectly straight, but that they must be only as straight as is necessary to let the subtle matter flow straight through without meeting any obstacle. Wrap up some apples or balls in a net and compress them 219 until they stick together and seem to form a hard body. Then pour into this body some fine sand of the sort used to make hourglasses, and you will see that no matter how you pour it on, the sand will always pass through without hindrance. Of course the particles of all hard bodies are not as round as apples; but you can imagine them as having all sorts of other shapes, and the particles of subtle matter will still pass through them as freely as the particles of sand flow through the mass of compressed apples.

TO MERSENNE, 13 JULY 1638　　　AT II

An investigation of the question 222
whether a body weighs more or less when close to
the centre of the earth than it does when far from it

In order to fulfil the promise I gave in my last letter to give you my views on the above question, we must distinguish here between two sorts of heaviness, one which may be called 'true or absolute heaviness', and the other which we can call 'apparent or relative heaviness'. When we say that a staff weighs much more when we grasp it at one end than when we grasp it in the middle, it is apparent or relative heaviness that is meant; for this is 223 to say that in the one case it seems heavier, or rather is heavier from one point of view, but it is not intrinsically heavier.

Now before discussing relative heaviness, we must define what we mean by absolute heaviness. Most take it to be a virtue or quality inherent in every body we call heavy, which makes it tend towards the centre of the earth. Some think that this quality depends upon the form of the body, so that the same matter which is heavy when it has the form of water loses the quality of heaviness when it takes on the form of air. Others, by contrast, are convinced that heaviness depends only on the matter, so that there is no body that is not heavy, since there is no body that is not made up of matter, and that absolutely speaking each body is more or less heavy, depending solely upon whether it is composed of proportionately more or less matter. But on this view some bodies will seem more or less heavy in relation to others, depending on whether the matter of which they are composed is

1 *Optics*: AT vi 88, 197; CSM i 155.

more or less compressed and spread out over a smaller or larger space, which fact they attribute to relative heaviness. They imagine that if we could weigh a mass of air and a mass of lead in a vacuum, each having the same quantity of matter, then they would stay equally balanced.

224   The former of these two views is the one most commonly held in the Schools, the latter the one most in favour with those who think they know more than the average person. On both these views, it is obvious that the absolute heaviness of a body is always intrinsically the same, and does not vary depending on its distance from the centre of the earth.

There is even a third view, which is held by those who think that all heaviness is relative. On this view the force or quality which causes bodies we call heavy to descend is not so much within them as within the centre of the earth, or rather in its centre of mass; and it attracts them towards the centre as a magnet attracts iron, or in some other way. Since a magnet and every other natural agent with a given sphere of action is more active at close range than at long range, this view implies that a given body weighs more, the closer it is to the centre of the earth.

As for my own view, my conception of the nature of heaviness is really quite different from that of the three views just described. But to set out my view I would have to go into many other things which I do not intend to discuss here. So all I can say about it is that, so far as I understand it, the nature of heaviness has no bearing on the question at issue; the nature of heaviness is a purely factual question, that is to say, a question that can be decisively answered by human beings only in so far as they are able to perform some experiment. And from experiments in our own atmosphere

225   we cannot even tell what is lower or higher with respect to the centre of the earth and the sky; for if there is any decrease or increase in weight, it is not likely to occur everywhere in the same proportion.

Now here is an experiment we can make. We require a tower at the foot of which there is a very deep shaft, and a weight attached to a long cord. At the top of the tower we make two weighings: first we place the weight and the whole cord in one pan of the balance, and then tie one end of the cord to the pan and let the weight hang down to the bottom of the shaft. In this way we shall be able to tell whether the weight weighs significantly more or less when closer to the centre of the earth than it does when further away. Since, however, the depth of the shaft and the height of the tower will be very small in relation to the radius of the earth, and for other reasons which I shall not mention, this experiment will be of no avail unless the difference in weight between the two weighings is very noticeable.

There is another observation which has already been made and which provides, I think, very convincing evidence that bodies far from the centre of the earth do not weigh as much as those closer to it. The planets which have no light of their own, such as the Moon, Venus, Mercury, etc., are probably bodies composed of the same sort of matter as the earth; and the heavens are liquid, as most present-day astronomers hold. It seems, therefore, that the planets should be heavy and should fall towards the earth, 226 though because of their enormous distance they have lost all tendency to do this. Moreover, we see that large birds such as cranes, swans, etc. fly much more easily when high in the air than when lower down. This cannot be due entirely to the force of the wind, because the same thing occurs when there is no wind; so we have reason to think that their being further from the ground makes them lighter. Paper kites flown by children, and snow in the sky, provide further evidence for this view. There is also the observation which you told me you have made yourself, and which other writers have described, namely that cannon balls which are shot straight up do not fall down again.[1] If this observation is in fact correct, then we must take the view that the force which shoots the ball up high takes it so far from the centre of the earth that it loses all its heaviness as a consequence. That is all I can say here concerning the physics of this question.

I turn now to the mathematical arguments, which apply only to relative heaviness. To this end we must determine the absolute heaviness by making an assumption, since that is the only way we can determine it. For the absolute weight of each body, we shall take, if you like, the force with which the body tends in a straight line towards the centre of the earth, assuming that it is at a certain distance from the earth and in our ordinary atmosphere, and that it is neither pushed nor supported by any other body, 227 and has not yet begun to move. I say 'in our ordinary atmosphere', because if the body is in a thinner or thicker air than our own, it is certain that it will be a little heavier or less heavy as the case may be. I say 'at a certain distance from the earth' meaning that this distance should be taken as standard for reference purposes. And I say 'neither pushed nor supported by any other body, and has not yet begun to move', because all these factors can affect the force with which it tends to descend.

Moreover, we shall suppose that each particle of a given heavy body always has a given force or tendency to descend, whether it is far from the centre of the earth or close to it, and no matter how it is situated. As I have already remarked, this assumption is perhaps not true; yet we ought to make it nevertheless, in order to facilitate the calculation. In a similar way astronomers assume that the average motions of the stars are equal, in order to make it easier to calculate the true motions, which are unequal.

Now given the assumption of the equality of absolute heaviness, we can

---

1 See above, p. 43.

demonstrate that the relative heaviness of all hard bodies, assuming that they are in the open air and not supported by anything, is somewhat less when closer to the centre of the earth than when further from it, although the same is not true of liquid bodies. By contrast, if two perfectly equal bodies are placed at opposite arms of perfectly accurate scales and the
228   arms are not horizontal, the body which is closer to the centre of the earth will weigh more; and the increase in weight will be exactly proportional to its proximity to the centre of the earth. It also follows from this that among the equal particles of a given body outside the scales, the higher particles weigh proportionately less than the lower ones, depending on their distance from the centre of the earth. So the centre of gravity in any body, even in spherical ones, cannot be a motionless point.

The proof of this point depends on just one principle, which is the general foundation of the whole of statics, namely that *it takes neither more nor less force to raise a heavy body to a certain height than it takes to raise a less heavy body to a greater height, or a heavier body to a lesser height; and the difference in height is in both cases proportional to the difference in weight.*[1] For example, a force which can raise a weight of 100 pounds to a height of two feet can raise a weight of 200 pounds to a height of one foot, or a weight of 50 pounds to a height of four feet, and so on, provided of course that the force is applied to it.

You will have no difficulty in accepting this if you consider that an effect must always be proportional to the action which is necessary to bring it
229   about, and hence that *if in order to raise a weight to a height of one foot we need to use a force that can raise a 100-pound weight to a height of two feet, this shows that the weight in question is 200 pounds.* For to raise a 100-pound weight to a height of one foot twice over is the same as raising a 200-pound weight to a height of one foot, and the same again as raising a 100-pound weight to a height of two feet. It obviously follows from this that the relative heaviness of each body, or what amounts to the same thing, the force that is needed to support it at a given position and prevent it from descending, is to be measured by the beginning of the motion which the power supporting it must produce if it is to raise it or accompany it if it descends. So the ratio between the straight line which this force describes and the line which indicates by how much the body moves closer to the centre of the earth is equal to the ratio between the absolute weight and the relative weight. Some examples will help to make this point clearer[2]. . .

1 See 'An Account of the Machines', p. 66 above.
2 Descartes gives three examples: the pulley, the inclined plane and the lever. His discussion of the pulley and the lever are omitted here, since they are virtually identical with that given in 'An Account of the Machines' (see pp. 67, 71–3 above).

The inclined plane   232

Let A C be a plane inclined to the horizon B C, and A B tend vertically towards the centre of the earth. All who write on mechanics are agreed that the heaviness[1] of weight F, in so far as it is resting on plane A C, is in the same ratio to its absolute heaviness as line A B is to line A C, so that if A C is twice as long as A B, and F weighs 200 pounds in the open air, on plane A C it will weigh only 100 pounds relative to the power which draws it or supports it. The reason for this is obvious from the principle put forward above. For the power H will produce the same action in raising the weight

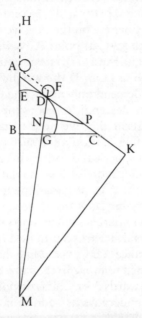

to the height of B A as it would in raising it in the open air to a height equal to line C A.

This is not entirely accurate; it is so only on the assumption that heavy bodies tend downwards along parallel lines – an assumption we usually make when we are considering mechanics simply with a view to its practical application – for in so far as these lines tend towards the centre of the earth, any slight difference due to their inclination will not be detectable. To ensure that the calculation is perfectly exact, line C B should be a   233 segment of a circle, and C A a segment of a spiral, each centred on the centre of the earth. And on the assumption that the surface A C is perfectly

---

1 Relative heaviness (Clerselier's text).

flat, the ratio between the relative heaviness of the weight F and its absolute heaviness will not be the same as the ratio between line AB and line AC, except when it is right at the top A; for when the weight is just a little lower down, at D or C, for example, the ratio will be a little less. We can see this clearly if we imagine that the plane continues to the point where it meets a line drawn from the centre of the earth. Thus, if M is the centre of the earth, MK will be at right angles to AC. Now it is obvious that if weight F is placed at point K, it will have no weight at all in relation to force H. In order to find out how much it weighs at any other point of the plane in relation to the power in question, at point D for example, we should draw a straight line DN towards the centre of the earth; and from point N, which can be anywhere on the line, we should draw NP at right angles to DN, which meets AC at point P. Now, as DN is to DP, so the relative heaviness of weight F at D is to its absolute heaviness. The reason for this is clear: although at point D the weight tends downwards along line DN, it can begin to descend only along line DP.

Note that I say 'begin to descend', and not simply 'descend', because it is only the start of the descent that we need to take into account. If, for example, weight F is resting, not on a flat surface at point D, as ADC is supposed to be, but on a spherical or other curved surface such as EDG, then it will not weigh either more or less in relation to the power H as it does when resting on plane AC, provided the flat surface, which we are imagining touches it at point D, is the same as ADC. For although the motion which the weight undergoes when it rises or descends from point D towards E on the curved surface EDG is quite different from that which it undergoes on the flat surface ADC, yet, while the weight is at point D on EDG, it will be determined to move in the same direction as it would if it were on ADC, that is, towards A or C. It is obvious that the change which the motion in question undergoes as soon as it ceases to touch point D cannot bring about any change in the heaviness that it has when it touches it.

Note also that the ratio between lines DP and DN is the same as that between lines DM and DK, because the right-angled triangles DKM and DNP are similar; and consequently the relative heaviness of the weight F at D is to the absolute heaviness as line DK is to line DM. The general point here is that any body resting on an inclined plane weighs less than it would if it were not so resting, proportionately less as the distance between the point where the body touches the plane and the point where the line from the centre of the earth touches the plane is less than the distance between the body and the centre of the earth...

Now these three examples are, I think, sufficient to convince us of the truth of the principle which I put forward, and to show that all the points usually discussed in statics depend on it. For the wedge and the screw are simply inclined planes, and the wheels that are used to construct various sorts of machines are simply multiple levers; and in fact the balance is nothing but a lever supported at its centre. Thus, all that remains for me to explain here is how the two conclusions I put forward can be derived from this principle. 238

A demonstration
explaining in what sense a body can be said to weigh less when nearer the centre of the earth than when further away

Let A be the centre of the earth and BCD a heavy body, which I am supposing to be so situated in air that if it is not supported by anything, it will descend from H to A along line HFA, its two parts B and D always

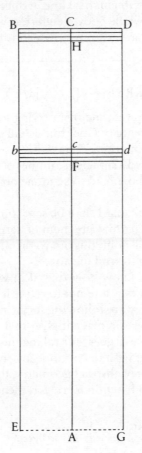

remaining equidistant from point A and line H F. Let us consider that when the body is descending as described, part D can move only along line D G, and part B along line B E; and hence that the lines D G and B E represent two inclined planes on which the two weights D and B are moving. Now, since body B C D is hard, as it moves from B D to E G part D is always supported by all the other parts between D and C; of course it might also

239   be supported by the surface of some very hard matter where line D G is. But it has already been demonstrated that every heavy body which is supported by an inclined plane, and is situated close to the point where the line running perpendicularly from the centre of the earth meets the said plane, weighs less than it does when it is further away from it. It obviously follows from this that when body B C D is at H, part D weighs more than when it is at F. The same conclusion holds for part B and every other part, with the sole exception of the parts located on line H F; and since line H F is supposed simply to be a mathematical line, we need not take account of its parts. Consequently the whole body weighs less when closer to the centre of the earth than when further from it, which is the point that was to be demonstrated . . .

TO MERSENNE, 27 JULY 1638

(267)   . . . 2. This does not prevent me from trying to explain the arguments which I gave for the existence of God, but I shall give these in Latin.

3. Since most of the objections[1] I have been sent, and which I plan to publish once I have received a sufficient number of them, are also in Latin, I would be glad if those who intend to send me objections in future would write them in Latin.

4. I am inclined to think that I shall be sent some from the Jesuits of La Flèche. If so, they will prefer to write them in Latin rather than in French; so I shall be glad if you will point this out to them, but tactfully, since they are perhaps not intending to send me any.

5. I would also like to know how they deal with my *Meteorology* in their philosophy, whether they attempt to refute it or keep silent about it. I

268   dare not yet think that they are following it; the public theses which they are putting forward this season make it clear that they are not.

6. I am obliged to M. Desargues[2] for taking the trouble to make it clear that he is sorry I no longer wish to continue my studies in geometry. But I have decided to give up only abstract geometry, that is to say, the investigation of problems which function merely as mental exercises. My aim is

---

1 I.e. to the *Discourse*, *Optics*, etc.
2 Girard Desargues (1593–1662), geometer and architect.

to have more time to devote to another sort of geometry where the problems have to do with the explanation of natural phenomena. If he cares to think about what I wrote about salt, snow, rainbows, etc., he will see that my entire physics is nothing but geometry.

7. Since he wants to know my views concerning the minute particles of bodies, let me say that I imagine them simply as being like the stones which make up a wall, or the planks which make up a ship; that is, it is much easier to separate one from another than to destroy them, or to put them together again, or to give them some other shape. We can of course do all of these things, provided we have the appropriate tools...

TO [HOGELANDE], AUGUST 1638   AT II

I have read carefully the book you kindly sent me, and I thank you for   346
it.[1] The author is clearly an intelligent and learned man, of great integrity and public spirit. All his criticisms of the accepted sciences and teaching methods are only too true, and his complaints are only too justified.

His plan of collecting into a single book all that is useful in every other book would be a very good one if it were practicable; but I think that it is not. It is often very difficult to judge accurately what others have written, and to draw the good out of it without taking the bad too. Moreover, the particular truths which are scattered in books are so detached and so independent of each other that I think one would need more talent and energy to assemble them into a well-proportioned and ordered collection, as your author plans to do, than to make up such a collection out of one's own discoveries. I do not mean that one should neglect other people's discoveries when one encounters useful ones; but I do not think one should spend the greater part of one's time in collecting them. If a man were capable of finding the foundations of the sciences, he would be wrong to waste his life in finding scraps of knowledge hidden in the corners of   347
libraries; and if he were no good for anything else but that, he would not be capable of choosing and ordering what he found. It is true that the author says that he has already composed or started such a book, and I am prepared to believe that he would succeed in the task better than anybody; but the specimens which he exhibits here do not give one great hope. The aphorisms he prints on pages 31ff. contain only such generalities that he seems to have a long way to go to reach particular truths – and it is the latter alone which are required for practice.

Besides this, I find two things in his programme which I cannot altogether approve. The first is that he seems to want to combine religion and

1 *Conatuum Comeniorum Praeludia* (1637), by Jan Amos Comenius (1592–1656).

revealed truths too closely with the sciences which are acquired by natural reasoning. The other is that he imagines a universal science which could be learned by young scholars before they reach the age of twenty-four. He does not seem to notice that there is a great difference in this respect between acquired and revealed truths. The knowledge of revealed truths depends only on grace, which God denies to no one, even though it is not efficacious for all; so the most stupid and the most simple can acquire it as well as the most sophisticated. But unless you have a mind out of the ordinary, you cannot hope to do anything extraordinary in the human

348   sciences. It is true that we are obliged to take care that our reasonings do not lead us to any conclusions which contradict what God has commanded us to believe; but I think that to try to derive from the Bible knowledge of truths which belong only to human sciences, and which are useless for our salvation, is to apply the Holy Scripture to a purpose for which God did not give it, and so to abuse it. But perhaps the author did not intend to use the Bible in that way, or to mix sacred and profane things. In everything else his intentions seem so good that even though he has some defects, he still deserves great respect. I thank you for the warning which you give me of the slanders of N. They are so weak and ill founded that I think they do more harm to himself in revealing the sickness of his mind than they can do to anyone else.

TO MORIN, 12 SEPTEMBER 1638

AT II

362   The fairness of your motives and the breadth of your courtesy are so
363   conspicuous that I feel obliged to do my best to answer thoroughly all the further points which you were so good as to put to me.

You begin with my reply to your fourth objection.[1] There I was not denying that the word 'action' should be taken to mean 'movement'; but I hold that the word has a more general sense, including the sense of 'inclination to move'. For example, say two blind men are holding a stick and pushing it with equal force against each other, so that the stick does not move at all; each then pulls it with equal force towards himself, and again the stick does not move. In each case one man is exerting a force while the other is doing the same in the opposite direction; and the forces are so exactly equal that the stick stays motionless throughout. It is certain that each blind man, simply from the fact that the stick is motionless, can feel that the other is pushing it or pulling it with equal force. What each

---

1 In his letter of 13 July 1638 Morin counter-objected that few would agree that the word 'action' properly means 'inclination to move', and that no one would agree that the inclination to move is the actual movement. See above, p. 108.

man feels in the stick, namely a lack of movement in various respects, can be called the various actions which are impressed on it by the various exertions of the other man. For when one of them is pulling the stick, this does not cause the other to feel the same action as when he is pushing it, etc. . . .

One body can indeed push another body in a straight line without itself (364) moving in a straight line.[1] An example of this is a stone which is swung round in a sling: the stone pushes the middle part of the sling, and thus pulls the attached cord in straight lines which tend in all directions from the centre of its motion towards the circumference. Now, to spell out more fully what I was trying to say before, let me say that I think of sunlight as being composed solely of a highly fluid sort of matter, which is continually revolving about its centre at a very great speed, thus pressing on all sides the matter which makes up the heavens, which is simply the subtle matter which extends without a break from the stars to our eyes. Through the medium of this matter we come to feel the pressure of the sun that is called 'light'. This, I think, should remove most of the difficulties which you suggested. Of course you could, I know, immediately raise many other difficulties about this point; but I would have just as many answers to them, indeed I have them already prepared; and there would be no end to 365 this process unless I set out my entire physics.

In order to prove that this matter exists, I need only get you to consider that there are pores in all perceivable bodies, or at least in many, as is clear to the naked eye in the case of wood, leather and paper, etc.; and as these pores are too small to let air in, they need not be empty on that account. It follows from this that they must be full of a matter which is more rarefied than the matter which makes up the bodies I have in mind. As for the various motions of this subtle matter, ample evidence of these is provided by the movements of the bodies in the pores from which it comes; for, since this matter is very fluid, it would take a miracle to prevent it from moving in all the various ways in which these bodies might push it . . .

You say that if light is nothing but the action of the sun, then there is no (366) light in the sun's nature; and that light is a more actual and more absolute 367 being than movement is; and that only God acts by his essence, and so on. You are making difficulties in words where there are none in reality. There is no more problem than if I said that a clock shows the time only by the movement of its hands, and that its quality of showing the time is not a more actual or absolute being than its movement, and that this movement belongs to it by its nature and essence, because it would cease to be a clock

---

1 In his letter of 12 August 1638 Morin counter-replied that there can be no movement without the local motion of some moving body. See AT II 294.

if it did not have it. I know that you will say that the form of the clock is only an artificial form, while the form of the sun is natural and substantial; but I reply that this distinction concerns only the cause of these forms, and not at all their nature; or that the substantial form of the sun, in so far as it differs from the qualities to be found in its matter, is an altogether philosophical entity which is unknown to me.

True, the analogies that are usually employed in the Schools explain intellectual matters by means of physical ones, substances by means of accidents, or at any rate one quality by means of a quality of a different kind, and they are not very instructive. But in the analogies which I 368 employ, I compare movements only with other movements, or shapes with other shapes; that is, I compare things that are too small to be perceived by the senses with other things that can be so perceived, the latter differing from the former simply as a large circle differs from a small one.[1] I maintain, therefore, that analogies of this sort are the most appropriate means available to the human mind for laying bare the truth in problems of physics. I would go so far as to say that, when someone makes an assertion concerning nature which cannot be explained by any such analogy, I think I have demonstrative knowledge that the point is false. As for the analogy of a U-shaped tube which I used in my reply, I maintain that it shows very clearly that a very small force is sufficient to move a great quantity of highly fluid matter; for the heaviness of the water in the tube is not what makes it move, since it does not weigh more on one side than on the other. In case there should be any doubt about this, imagine a tube ABC encircling the earth D, so that no part of it is higher than any other except for a piece at each end, which sticks up just enough to hold a tiny quantity of water. Now if we pour just one drop of water into one of the openings, 369 this will be enough to set in motion all the water in the tube, even if the water is otherwise no more inclined to move in one direction than in the other, and the quantity of water is no greater than the quantity of subtle matter that sets a spark in motion[2]...

(372)   Right at the end of your letter I note your statement that when you see

---

1 In his letter of 12 August 1638 Morin counter-objected that analogies are seldom suitable for resolving a dispute, and the analogy of the vat of grape juice is a case in point. For, because of its own intrinsic weight, the juice at the top and bottom of the vat tends to flow instantaneously through the hole at the bottom. By contrast, in the case of the subtle matter which is set in motion by a luminous body, the motion is not due to gravity, but to the motion of the luminous body – a significant difference. Thus, Descartes' analogies do not explain how a luminous body sets in motion in every direction the subtle matter surrounding it.

2 Descartes employs this analogy to solve the difficulty raised by Morin: How can Descartes explain why a tiny spark can be seen by the naked eye 500 feet away, and by a telescope 50 miles away? How can the spark set in motion all the subtle matter within a sphere of a radius of 50 miles centred on the spark?

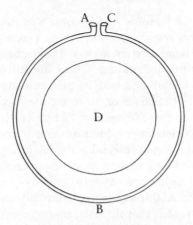

dust in the air dancing about in a sunbeam opposite a chink in a window facing the sun, you now understand what I take the subtle matter to be. But this makes it clear to me that your thoughts and mine are very different on this matter. For the tiniest particles of dust are very much larger than the particles of pure air, and the latter are very much larger again than the particles which I ascribe to subtle matter, which I conceive of as a continuous liquid occupying all the space not taken up by other bodies, and not as something composed of disconnected parts such as the particles that make up dust. That, then, is what I thought should be said in reply to your last letter if I was to demonstrate my desire to give you a proper answer.

373

TO [DEBEAUNE], 12 SEPTEMBER 1638   AT II

I am much obliged to you for your kind remembrance of me, and I value the honour you do me by wishing to have my opinion concerning the education of your son. My desire to be of service to him would prevent me from dissuading you from sending him to this country if I thought that your plan for his education could actually be carried out here; but philosophy is badly taught here. The professors hold lectures only for an hour a day, for about half the year; and they do not dictate any written material, or complete the course within a set time. As a result those who have the slightest wish to gain knowledge are compelled to get private instruction from a tutor, as one has to do when studying law in France if one intends to enter the profession. Now I am not of the opinion that all that is taught in philosophy is gospel truth; yet, since it is the key to the other sciences, I think it is very useful to have taken the complete course in philosophy as it is given in the Jesuit schools before attempting to raise one's mind above

377

378

the level of mere book learning and become a genuinely knowledgeable person. And to give my own teachers their due, I must say that nowhere on earth is philosophy taught better than at La Flèche. Moreover, to leave home for the first time and suddenly find oneself in a country with a different language, religion and way of life is an enormous change. The atmosphere of La Flèche, however, is very close to your own, and since many young people go there from all over France, the exchange of ideas gives rise to a certain blending of different temperaments that has almost the same educational effect as travel. Lastly, the Jesuits treat each other as equals, the high-born being treated much the same as those of humbler origin – an excellent device for removing softness and other weaknesses they might have acquired through being habitually spoiled in the parental

379 home. But I am aware, Sir, that the flattering opinion of myself you have given me by going to the trouble of seeking my advice does not justify my writing to you in freer terms than is appropriate. So I shall venture to add merely that if your son should come to these parts, I shall serve him in any way I can. In Leiden I have lodgings in a house which would provide him with good board; but as far as his studies are concerned, I think he would be much better off at Utrecht; for the university there was founded only four or five years ago, and hence has not yet had time to deteriorate; and there is a professor there by the name of le Roy[1] who is a good friend of mine and, in my view, superior to all those at Leiden.

AT II   TO MERSENNE, 11 OCTOBER 1638

380   I shall begin this letter with my comments on Galileo's book.[2] Generally speaking, I find he philosophizes much more ably than is usual, in that, so far as he can, he abandons the errors of the Schools and tries to use mathematical methods in the investigation of physical questions. On that score, I am completely at one with him, for I hold that there is no other way to discover the truth. But he continually digresses, and he does not take time to explain matters fully. This, in my view, is a mistake: it shows that he has not investigated matters in an orderly way, and has merely sought explanations for some particular effects, without going into the primary causes in nature; hence his building lacks a foundation. Now the closer his style of philosophizing gets to the truth, the easier it is to recognize its faults, just as it is easier to tell when those who sometimes take the right

---

1 Henri le Roy (Henricus Regius, 1598–1679), Professor of Medicine at the University of Utrecht, and an enthusiastic supporter of Descartes, with whom he was later to quarrel.

2 *Discourses and Mathematical Demonstrations Concerning Two New Sciences* (1638). Descartes' references are to page numbers of the original edition; the additional numbers supplied in square brackets refer to the corresponding pages of the English translation by S. Drake, *Galileo Galilei: Two New Sciences* (Madison: University of Wisconsin, 1974).

road go astray than it is to point out aberrations in the case of those who never begin to follow it.

Page 2 [11]. Here he introduces the topics he intends to discuss, namely   381
why it is that large machines, which have exactly the same shape and are made of the same material as smaller ones, are weaker than the latter; and why it is that a child is less seriously injured by a fall than an adult is, or a cat than a horse, etc. In my view there is no difficulty about this, or any reason to construct a new science.[1] For it is obvious that if the force or resistance of a large machine is to be exactly proportional to that of a small one of the same shape, they cannot both be made of the same material; rather, the larger must be made of a material that is harder and less easily destroyed, in proportion as its shape and weight are larger. And there is as much difference between a large machine and a small one made of the same material as between two large machines of the same size, one of which is made from a much lighter and harder material than the other.

Page 8. [17] He is right when he says that the threads of a string stay together because they press against each other; but he does not also say why it is that pressure causes them to stay together. The reason is that there are minute inequalities in the shape of the strands which prevent each strand from moving between the strands pressing against it.

The device for lowering things (page 11 [19])[2] comes down to the same thing, and there is nothing in all this which is not commonplace. But his use of the dialogue genre, where he introduces three characters who do   382
nothing but sing the praises of his discoveries one after the other, helps greatly to make the most of his wares.

Page 12 [20]. In order to explain why the parts of a continuous body hold together, he suggests two causes. One is the abhorrence of a vacuum, the other a sort of glue or bond which holds them together, which he explains later on in terms of a vacuum. I think both explanations are quite false. What he ascribes to a vacuum (page 13) should be ascribed only to the weight of the air. If it were abhorrence of a vacuum that prevented two bodies from separating, there would certainly be no force capable of separating them.

The method he gives to distinguish between the effects of these two causes (page 15 [22]) is worthless. What Simplicio is made to say (page 16) has more truth. The observation (page 17 [24]) that pumps do not draw water above a height of 18 yards should not be explained in terms of a vacuum, but in terms of the matter of the pump, or even that of the water which, rather than rising higher, flows between the pump and the pipe[3]. . . .

1 An allusion to the title of the book which Descartes is discussing.
2 The device is a wooden screw with a cord wound round it.
3 Cf. letter to Mersenne of 16 October 1639: AT II 588.

(383)   Page 31 [38]. All that he says about the infinite will not do; for, even though he admits that the human mind, being finite, is incapable of comprehending the infinite, he discusses it all the same as if he did comprehend it.

Page 40 [47]. He says that when hard bodies liquefy they are divided into an infinite number of points; but this is a fiction which is very easy to disprove, and he gives no proof of it.

Page 42 [48]. He clearly shows that he is not very knowledgeable on optics, to go by what he says about Archimedes' burning mirrors, which I proved to be impossible in my *Optics* (page 119).[1]

384   Page 43. His experiment to determine whether light is transmitted instantaneously is useless; for eclipses of the moon have an exact bearing on the calculation in question, and thus are clearly far superior to any observations we could make on earth[2]...

Page 50 [55]. All that he says about rarefaction and condensation is simply fallacious, for there are no empty parts between the points of a circle; it simply moves more slowly. As for my own view, the only way I can conceive of it is to say that when one body condenses, its pores grow narrower, and some of the subtle matter that fills them escapes, just as water escapes from a sponge when you squeeze it. Conversely, when a body expands, its pores grow wider, and this lets in more subtle matter, as I explained at several places in my *Meteorology*[3]...

(386)   Page 157 [153]. He makes the assumption that the speed at which a weight descends always increases uniformly, something I once believed, as he does;[4] but I now think I have demonstrative proof that this is not the case...

(387)   Page 236 [217]. He adds a further assumption here, which is no more true than those already made, namely that bodies thrown up in the air travel at the same speed horizontally, but as they fall, their speed increases at a rate which is proportional to twice the distance covered. Given this assumption, we can readily conclude that bodies that are thrown up move along a parabolic path; but since his assumptions are false, his conclusion may well be very far from the truth.

Page 269 [245]. Note that without proving it or explaining it, he adopts the converse proposition, to the effect that if a shot fired in a horizontal direction from B to E follows the parabola BD, then a shot fired at an oblique angle along line DE must follow the same parabola. This indeed follows from his assumptions. But it seems that he did not dare to explain

1 See AT VI 194.
2 See above, p. 46.
3 See *Meteorology*, Discourse 2 (AT VI 245) and Discourse 5 (AT VI 272).
4 See above, p. 8.

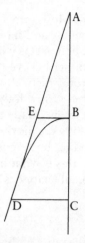

this point, for fear that the falsity of his assumptions would be glaringly obvious. Yet he makes use of the converse proposition only in the last part of the fourth discourse, which apparently he wrote simply in order to explain the force of cannon shots fired at different angles of elevation. We should note, moreover, that in making his assumptions he treats cannon shots as an exception in order to make them more plausible. Yet towards the end it is mainly to cannon shots that he applies his conclusions. In 388 short, he has built his ideas on thin air.

I shall say nothing of the geometrical demonstrations of which the book is full, for I could not summon the patience to read them, and I am prepared to believe they are all correct. When looking at his propositions, it simply struck me that you do not need to be a great geometrician to discover them; and he does not always take the shortest possible route, which leaves something to be desired.

I should be glad, however, if this were seen by you alone, who asked for my views, and to whom I am so greatly indebted that I think myself bound to deny you nothing within my power. Were it not for this, I would not have taken the trouble to rake over someone else's mistakes, for that goes completely against the grain. Besides, if I had been so inclined, I would have been more scrupulous in giving my reasons for my assertions than I have been here, so that those who do not know me as well as you do would have no cause to imagine that I had arrived at my views without good reason.

I shall turn now to the separate points which you raise in your letter, which I have not yet answered since I have not been sleeping well lately. First of all, concerning Galileo, let me say that I have never met him, and have had no communication with him, and consequently I could not have

389 borrowed anything from him. Moreover, I can see nothing in his books that gives me cause to be envious, and hardly anything I would wish to acknowledge as my own. The best part is what he has to say on music; but those who know me would rather believe that he got that from me than that I got it from him; for I wrote practically the same thing nineteen years ago, at which time I had not yet visited Italy. What I wrote then I gave to M. Beeckman,[1] who, as you know, made a great thing of it, and wrote about it in various places as if it were his own...

(399) Galileo says that a descending body goes through all the degrees of speed; but I do not think that this is what normally happens, though it is not impossible that it occasionally happens...

TO MERSENNE, 15 NOVEMBER 1638

(432) ...At last you understand the sense of the word 'force' when I say that it takes as much force to raise a 100-pound weight to a height of one foot as to raise a 50-pound weight to a height of two feet, that is to say, it takes as much action or effort.[2] I am prepared to believe I had not explained this very well on previous occasions, since you had not understood it. So far was I from thinking of force in the sense of the power we call the force of a man when we talk of one man having more force than another, etc., that I would not have suspected that anyone would take it in that sense. And when we say that one action requires less force than another, this is not to say that less power is needed, for there would be no harm in having more power, but is merely to say that less action is required. In that paper, I was not thinking of the power we call the force of a man, but only of the action

433 which we call the force that can raise a weight, whether the action originates in a man, or a spring, or some other weight, and so on. Now the only way to determine *a priori*[3] the quantity of this action (i.e. how heavy a weight, and what sort of weight, we can raise by means of such and such a machine) is to measure the quantity of the action which causes this effect (i.e. the force required to raise such a weight). I have no doubt that M. Desargues will share my view, if he takes the trouble to reread my brief remarks on this topic. Since I am convinced of the excellence of his mind, I think I need have no doubts about my explanation on that score.

As for what Galileo writes concerning the balance and the lever,[4] he sets out very clearly †the facts as they are† but he does not explain †why the facts are as they are†, as I do by my principles. As for those who say that for

1 See footnote 1, p. 1 above.
2 See above, p. 114.
3 'A priori' is used here to mean 'by reasoning from cause to effect'.
4 A reference to Mersenne's translation, *Les Méchaniques de Galilée* (1634), sect. 7, p. 397n.

an explanation of the machines, I ought to consider the speed (as Galileo does) rather than the space, between ourselves, I regard these as people who make purely fanciful statements and who have no understanding of the subject. And while it is obvious that it takes more force to raise a fast-moving body than to raise a slow-moving one, it is utterly fanciful to say that the force has to be exactly twice as great if the speed is to be twice as great, for the contrary is very easily proved...   434

I know of no other way of making sound judgements about the notions (435) which can be taken for principles, except that we must prepare our mind to divest itself of all the views with which it is preoccupied, and to reject as doubtful everything that might be doubtful. It is a common notion that if an intelligent nature is independent, it is God: for if its existence is due to itself, we cannot doubt that it will have given itself as many perfections as it was able to recognize; nor can we think that we know of any perfections which it was unable to recognize. But if we say that some purely material nature is independent, it does not follow from this that it is God.

I looked for the letter in which you quote the passage from St Augustine,[1] but I have not yet been able to find it; nor have I managed to obtain the works of the Saint, so that I could look up what you told me, for which I am grateful...

The second part of your letter contains your comments on Galileo. (439) Here, I admit, what prevents the separation of contiguous terrestrial 440 bodies is the weight of the cylinder of air resting on them up to the atmosphere; this cylinder may well weigh less than 100 pounds. But I do not admit that the force of the continuity of bodies is due to the same cause, for this force consists simply in the connection or union between their parts. I said that if something occurred through abhorrence of a vacuum, no force could prevent it; the reason for this is that it is, I think, just as impossible that a space should be empty as that a mountain should be without a valley.

I imagine the particles of the subtle matter to be as hard and solid as it is possible for bodies of their size to be; but since they cannot affect our senses, and the names of qualities are relative to our senses, such names cannot strictly speaking be applied to them. Similarly, we do not say that powder is hard and has weight, but rather that, compared to pebbles, it is soft and light; yet each of its particles is of the same nature as a tiny pebble.

I do not accept that rotten wood, or a candle, can be motionless when it is giving off light; it simply would not give off light if its tiny particles, or rather the tiny particles of the subtle matter within its pores, did not move extraordinarily swiftly. Since I gave a detailed explanation of the causes of 441

1 See letter to Mersenne of 25 May 1637: AT I 376.

this movement and of the entire nature of terrestrial fire in my *World*, I did not wish to discuss it in my *Essays*, and I could not explain it in only a few words...

(443)   Your third letter has to do with the *Optics*. I am grateful for your kindly correcting the errors in it, and I shall be glad if you will be so good as to mark the corrections in your own copy, so that you can send me it, should a second impression be made. As far as the language or spelling is concerned, I simply wish to follow ordinary usage; but it is so long since I was last in France that there are many things I do not know.

As for the additional questions which you suggest I include, such as the difference in transparency between hard bodies and liquids, and why a transparent body turns opaque when it glows red hot, etc., these are

444   problems in physics which depend entirely on the things discussed in my *World*; and it was not my intention to discuss them in my *Essays*.

I regard the solid particles of air as consisting of all the particles which make it up, in order to distinguish these from the particles of the subtle matter within its pores. In speaking of air we usually mean everything that fills the space which the air occupies, and this includes the subtle matter. If the pores of air or any other body were not full of subtle matter or something like it, there would simply be no pores; for, on my view, a space without matter is a contradiction in terms.

I think there are fewer pores in gold and lead than in iron, etc. A few lines back I said that I think of the particles of subtle matter as being as hard and solid as it is possible for bodies of their size and shape to be. As for the particles of terrestrial bodies, we can imagine some of these as being more or less hard than others, because they may be composed of many other sorts of particles; and as I said on page 188 of my *Meteorology*,[1] the particles of fresh water are softer and more pliable than those of salt water...

(447)   Thank you for the trouble you are taking to support my side. I have no fear that anyone of sound judgement is convinced that I borrowed my *Optics* from Roger Bacon, let alone Fioraventi,[2] who was simply an Italian charlatan.

As for your advice about what I ought to add to my *Optics* concerning old men's eyeglasses, I think I have included enough on the theory of this on page 123;[3] and as for the practical questions, I leave that to the craftsmen.

---

1 *Meteorology*: AT VI 263f.
2 Roger Bacon (*c.* 1214–92), pioneer of experimental science. Leonardo Fioraventi (1518–88), an Italian physician. The allusion is probably to his *Il tesoro della vita umana* (1570).
3 *Optics*: AT VI 197f.

TO MERSENNE, DECEMBER 1638   AT II

... The reason why water flows from a watering-can is not abhorrence (465)
of a vacuum (for as you rightly point out, subtle matter might easily enter
the can in place of the air) but the weight of the air. For if water flows out of
the can, and the space vacated is taken up only by subtle matter, it would
have to raise the entire body of air right up to its highest level...

I said nothing about Galileo and the ranges he gives for cannon shots, (466)
which he presents in the form of tables;[1] for, having rejected all the
arguments on which he bases these, I thought it was not even worth
discussing them...

I do not recognize any inertia or natural sluggishness in bodies any more
than M. Mydorge does; and I think that simply by walking, a man makes   467
the entire mass of the earth move ever so slightly, since he is putting his
weight now on one spot, now on another. All the same, I agree with M.
Debeaune that when the largest bodies (such as the largest ships) are
pushed by a given force (such as a wind), they always move more slowly
than others. This would perhaps be enough to confirm his arguments,
without having recourse to this natural inertia, something that cannot
possibly be proved...

TO MERSENNE, 9 JANUARY 1639   AT II

You tell me in your last letter that you and some other excellent people   480
are very concerned on my behalf when two weeks pass without your
receiving a letter from me; on reading that, I would have to be very weary
of life if I neglected to look after myself. But, by the grace of God, during
the last thirty years I have not had any illness which could properly be
called serious. Over the years I have lost that warmth of the liver which in
earlier years attracted me to the army; and I no longer profess to be
anything but a coward. Moreover, I have acquired some little knowledge
of medicine, and I feel very well, and look after myself with as much care as
a rich man with gout. For these reasons I am inclined to think that I am
now further from death than I ever was in my youth. And should God not
grant me the knowledge to avoid the discomforts of old age, I hope he will
at least grant me a long enough life and the leisure to endure them. Yet all
depends upon his providence, to which, pleasantry aside, I submit myself
with as much courage as Father Joseph would have done. One of the main
points in my own ethical code is to love life without fearing death.   481

2. I am extremely grateful to you for the trouble you have taken in
correcting the printers' errors in my *Essays*, but I rather fear it will be to no

---

1 *Two New Sciences* (1638). Fourth Day, Proposition 13. See above, pp. 124ff.

avail; for the publisher tells me that few copies have been sold; so I do not think it very likely that he will have to bring out a second edition . . .

(482)   4. If you wish to conceive that God removes all the air in a room without putting any other body in its place, you will have to conceive accordingly that the walls of the room touch each other; otherwise your thought will contain a contradiction. Just as we could not imagine him flattening all the mountains in the world while leaving all the valleys, so we cannot think that he removes every kind of body and yet leaves space behind. For the idea that we have of body, or matter in general, is contained in the idea that we have of space, i.e. of something which has length and breadth and depth, just as the idea of a mountain is contained in the idea of a valley.

5. In conceiving of a body moving in a non-resistant medium, what I suppose is that all the parts of the surrounding liquid body are disposed to move at the same speed as the original body in such a way as to leave room for it and take up its room. That is why every kind of liquid resists some
483   movement or other. To imagine some matter which resisted none of the different movements of different bodies, you would have to pretend that God or an angel was moving its parts at various speeds to correspond with the speed of the movements of the body they surround.

Hitherto I have not told you what, on my view, prevents there being a vacuum between the parts of the subtle matter. This was because I could not explain it except by discussing another extremely rarefied matter, which I wished not to mention in my *Essays*, but to keep for my *World*. However, I am too much in your debt to keep secrets from you. So I will tell you that I imagine, or rather I have proof, that besides the matter which makes up terrestrial bodies, there are two other kinds. One is very rarefied and has parts which are round, or almost round, like grains of sand; this fills up the pores of terestrial bodies and is the material of which all the heavens are made. The other is incomparably more rarefied still, and its parts are so small and so fast-moving that they have no fixed shape but at each moment assume with ease the shape required to fill up all the little interstices which are not occupied by other bodies. To understand this, you must first consider that the smaller a body is, the less force is required, other things being equal, to change its shape: for instance, if you have two balls of lead of unequal size, you need less force to flatten the smaller than
484   to flatten the larger; and if they collide with each other, the shape of the smaller one will undergo a greater change. Secondly, you must observe that when several different bodies are set in motion together, the smaller ones receive more of this motion, that is to say, move more quickly, than the larger ones (once again, other things being equal). From this it follows †demonstratively† that since there are moving bodies in the universe, and

since there is no vacuum, there must be a type of matter whose parts are so small and so fast moving that the force of their collision with other bodies is sufficient to change their shape and mould them to fit the places they occupy. But I have said too much on a topic on which I intended to say nothing...

7. Movements in the subtle matter are, I imagine, no different from those we already see in all bodies. But just as the water of a river moves more rapidly at some places than at others, and flows straight here, and in a curve there, even though it is pushed along by the same force and moves with the same flow, we must bear in mind that the same is true of the subtle matter.

485

As for heat, it could be caused by the rapid motion of the particles of this subtle matter, though strictly speaking it consists only in the motion of the terrestrial parts, since the latter have the most force to move the particles of other bodies, and hence to burn them. The more terrestrial particles there are in a body, the hotter it can be, as in the case of iron as distinct from wood. The terrestrial particles of a body may well be in rapid motion, thus making it very hot, even though the subtle matter within its pores is not propelled in the way it would have to be if we were to have any sensation of light. That is why iron can be very hot without being red-hot.

The only difference I recognize between the particles of terrestrial bodies and those of subtle matter is similar to that between certain stones and the powder they give off when you rub one against another. I also think that some terrestrial particles continually take on the form of subtle matter when you crush them up; and some particles of this subtle matter attach themselves to terrestrial bodies, so that there is no matter in the universe which could not take on all the forms one after the other...

9. I can think of two explanations why a candle flame viewed at a distance in the dark can appear very much larger than it is. The first is that, since we cannot see its true distance, we imagine it to be as far away as the stars – since the image of the candle at the back of the eye is very much larger than the image of the star, we judge that the flame itself is larger. The other explanation is that we see not only the light which comes directly from the candle, but also the light which comes from the dense air and other neighbouring bodies which are lit up by it. We can easily distinguish between these two sorts of light at close range, but at a distance we ascribe them both to the candle; in this way the flame seems bigger ... There may well be some other cause of the increase in size, but we would have to see the phenomenon for a proper assessment, and I am sure that I will have touched on the explanation somewhere in my *Optics* ...[1]

(487)

(488)

1 See *Optics*: AT VI 146f.

AT II   TO MERSENNE, 9 FEBRUARY 1639

(500)   ... You tell me that an Italian medical man[1] has written against Harvey's *On the Motion of the Heart*, and that this makes you sorry
that I have decided to write on this topic. To be honest, I must say that I
cannot feel grateful for your solicitude on my behalf. You must think very
501   ill of me if, simply from having heard that someone has written something
which you imagine to be critical of me, you jump to the conclusion that I
have made some mistake, without having seen his argument or even
knowing whether he is competent. (Those who take merely a superficial
view of things hold that what I wrote is the same as Harvey's view, simply
because I believe in the circulation of the blood; but my explanation of the
movement of the heart is radically different from his[2]). I can see from this
and other similar instances that good arguments have very little power to
convince one of the truth. This almost makes me resolve to give up writing
altogether and to pursue my studies exclusively for my own benefit. Still, I
am prepared to admit that if what I have written on this topic or on
refraction – or on any other subject to which I have devoted more than
three lines in my published writings – turns out to be false, then the rest of
my philosophy is entirely worthless. I can assure you I care very little what
people think of my work, especially at present when they have only some
samples of it, which are of no use for further progress. If I had produced the
whole thing, I am sure I would have regretted it...

AT II   TO MERSENNE, 20 FEBRUARY 1639

(525)   ... The number and the orderly arrangement of the nerves, veins, bones
and other parts of an animal do not show that nature is insufficient to form
them, provided you suppose that in everything nature acts exactly in
accordance with the laws of mechanics, and that these laws have been
imposed on it by God. In fact, I have taken into consideration not only
what Vesalius and the others write about anatomy, but also many details
unmentioned by them, which I have observed myself while dissecting
various animals. I have spent much time on dissection during the last
eleven years, and I doubt whether there is any doctor who has made such
detailed observations as I. But I have found nothing whose formation
seems inexplicable by natural causes. I can explain it all in detail, just as in
my *Meteorology* I explained the origin of a grain of salt or a crystal of
snow. In my *World* I supposed the body of an animal already formed, and
merely exhibited its functions; if I were to start it again I should undertake

1 Aemilio Parisano (Parisanus Venetus).
2 See *Discourse*: AT VI 46ff; CSM I 134ff.

to include also the causes of its formation and birth. But for all that I do not yet know enough to be able to heal even a fever. For I claim to know only the animal in general, which is not subject to fevers, and not yet man in particular, who is . . .   526

TO [DEBEAUNE], 30 APRIL 1639   AT II

. . . I would like to be able to meet your request concerning your mechanics; but although my entire physics is nothing but mechanics, I have never made a detailed investigation of questions which depend on measurements of speed . . .   (542)

I hold that in the whole of created matter there is a certain quantity of motion which never increases or diminishes. So, when one body moves another, it loses as much of its own motion as it gives away; thus, when a stone falls to earth from a high place, if it stops and does not bounce, I think that this is because it moves the earth, and so transfers its motion to it; but if the earth it moves contains a thousand times as much matter as itself, when it transfers the whole of its motion to it, it gives it only one-thousandth of its speed. So if two unequal bodies receive the same amount of motion as each other, this equal quantity of motion does not give the same speed to the larger one as to the smaller. In this sense, then, one can say that the more matter a body contains, the more 'natural inertia' it has.[1] One can say too that a body which is large is better able than a small one to transfer its motion to other bodies; and a larger body is harder to move than a smaller one. So there is one sort of inertia which depends on the quantity of the matter, and another which depends on the extent of its surfaces.   (543)   544

My idea of weight is as follows. All the subtle matter which is between here and the moon rotates rapidly round the earth, and pushes towards it all the bodies which cannot move so fast. It pushes them with greater force when they have not yet begun to fall than when they are already falling; for, after all, if they are falling as fast as it is moving, it will not push them at all, and if they are falling faster, it will actually resist them. You can see from this that there are many things to consider before anything can be determined concerning speed; it is this that has always kept me from investigating it; but one can also explain a great deal by means of these principles, and this was not possible before. Moreover, I have been unwilling to discuss these topics elsewhere, since the proof of them

1 'Natural inertia' was an expression of Debeaune's.

depends upon my *World*; and I would not be discussing them so freely with you, were it not that I hoped you would view them in a favourable light, and I wanted with all my heart to show you that I am, etc.

AT II	TO HUYGENS, 6 JUNE 1639

681   Had I not been completely dazzled by your extremely flattering request,
682 I would be very ashamed not to accede to it, such is the power you have over me; but you must excuse my presumption, for it is due to the esteem I have for you:[1] I would prefer not to examine the arguments you put forward, since your authority is enough to convince me that they are very powerful. Let me say simply that so long as the arguments which previously dissuaded me from doing what you urge remain in force, I could not change my mind without demonstrating a lack of resolution that ought to be foreign to the soul of a philosopher. Yet I did not exactly swear that I would not let my *World* see the light of day during my lifetime; nor have I sworn to see that it is released after my death. In this and every other matter, my aim has simply been to be guided by circumstances, and as far as I could, to follow the most reliable and judicious advice. As for death, which you draw to my attention, I am well aware that it may take me by surprise at any moment; yet, by the grace of God, my teeth are still so firm and strong that I do not think I need fear death for another thirty years,
683 unless it catches me unawares. We leave fruit on the tree long enough for it to ripen, though we are well aware that wind and hail and other hazards may spoil it in the mean time. Similarly, I think that my *World* is the sort of fruit that cannot be picked too late, and should be left to ripen on the tree. After all, I am sure that your urging me to publish the book is due more to your desire to please me than to any other reason; for you no doubt think that I would not have gone to the trouble of writing it if I had not intended to publish it, and hence that I would not fail to publish it if there should ever be some advantage in it for me.

AT II	TO MERSENNE, 19 JUNE 1639

(565)   ... Concerning your remarks on weight, the stone C is pushed round by the subtle matter, which also pushes it towards the centre of the earth;[2] but the first movement is imperceptible, because it is common to the whole earth and the surrounding air; so it can only be the second which gives rise to heaviness. The fact that the stone moves more quickly at the end of its

1 Huygens had urged Descartes to publish *The World*.
2 Cf. *The World*, ch. 11: AT XI 72ff.

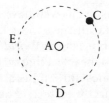

descent than at the beginning, though at that stage it is being propelled less
forcefully by the subtle matter, is due to its retaining the impetus of its   566
preceding motion, together with the impulse contributed by the action of
the subtle matter. Moreover, while I said that the subtle matter revolves
around the earth, I am not on that account required to say whether it
moves from east to west or vice versa, since the motion cannot possibly be
perceived by us. And I have no need to conclude that it must make the earth
rotate along with it, since we did not previously conclude, from the fact
that all the heavens rotate, that the earth must rotate along with them...

TO MERSENNE, 27 AUGUST 1639   AT II

I was very glad to learn of your return; I was beginning to be concerned   570
about your health, since I had not received your news. Two men you know
died here recently, Heylichman and Hortensius,[1] not to mention my good
friend M. Reneri,[2] who died last Lent. You do not need a war to find death.

I finally received the two copies of the book *On Truth*[3] which you were
so good as to send me. At the first opportunity I shall give one copy to M.
Bannius[4] on your behalf, for I think that was your intention. At present I
have no time to read; so all I can say about it is that when I read the earlier
Latin edition, there were many things at the beginning which I thought
were very good; he was clearly above average in his knowledge of metaphysics, a science that hardly anyone understands. But I thought that later
on he mingled religion with philosophy, something that goes quite against
the grain with me; so I did not read it to the end, though I hope to do this as   571
soon as I can find the time to read anything. I shall also look at *Philolaus*,[5]
but for the time being I am studying without any book.

---

1 Jean Heylichman, a Silesian physician resident in Holland; Martinus Hortensius (1605–
  39), Professor of Mathematics at Amsterdam.
2 Henri Regnier (1593–1639), Professor of Philosophy at the University of Utrecht.
3 *De la vérité* (1639), a translation of *De Veritate* (1619), by Edward Herbert, Lord
  Cherbury.
4 Johannes Albertus Ban (1597–1644), Catholic Archbishop of Harlem, musician and
  student of musical theory.
5 *Philolai sive Dissertationis de vero Systemate Mundi* (1639), by Ismaël Boulliau
  (1605–96).

The twinkling of the stars might well have to do with the liveliness of their light, which also makes them appear larger than they are; but I suggest some other explanations in my *World*.

As for your observation to the effect that water that flows from a tube 9 feet in height should flow almost three times as fast as from a tube 1 foot in height, I regard this as perfectly correct; though I add 'almost', to take account of the air and my view of the nature of heaviness, which implies that when the motion of a body which is falling under its own weight

572   reaches a certain degree of speed, it ceases to increase. But I would like some time to go into the question of the motion of water in greater detail;[1] so I shall not say anything more about it here.

The way in which I conceive that a candle flame or light from a lamp presses the subtle matter towards our eyes in a straight line is the same as the way I conceive that a stone which is swung round in a sling presses the mid-part of the sling and pulls the cord in a straight line, namely simply through the force of its own circular motion. For the subtle matter around a candle or a lamp also moves in a circle, and tends to spread out from there and to leave an empty space, that is to say, a space which contains only what might come into it from elsewhere. In the same way, we can

573   conceive how subtle matter presses heavy bodies towards the centre of the earth, simply through its moving in a circle around the earth; and the earth need not be at the centre of the universe in order for this to occur. And if the earth is to make all the less subtle bodies between us and the moon tend towards the earth, it is enough that it is at the centre of the circular motion of all the subtle matter between us and the moon...[2]

AT II   TO MERSENNE, 16 OCTOBER 1639

(593)   ... In order to understand how the subtle matter which revolves around the earth chases heavy bodies towards the centre of the earth, fill a round vessel with tiny lead pellets, and mix in some larger pieces of wood or other material that is lighter than lead.

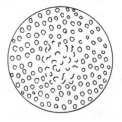

1 See letter to Huygens of 18 February 1643: AT III 617.
2 See *The World*, ch. 11: AT XI 72ff.

Now spin the vessel round very quickly. In this way you will demon-   594
strate that the pellets drive the pieces of wood or other such material
towards the centre of the vessel, just as subtle matter drives terrestrial
bodies towards the centre of the earth . . .

Since my last I have taken the time to read the book which you kindly   (596)
sent me.[1] Since you ask my opinion of it, and since it deals with a subject on
which I have worked all my life, I think I should write something about it in
this letter. I find in it many good things, †but not to everyone's taste,† since
there are few who are capable of understanding metaphysics. In the
general plan of the book the author takes a route very different from the
one I have followed. He examines what truth is; for my part, I have never   597
had any doubts about truth, because it seems a notion so transcendentally
clear that nobody can be ignorant of it. There are many ways of examining
a balance before using it, but there is no way to learn what truth is, if one
does not know it by nature. What reason would we have for accepting
anything which could teach us the nature of truth if we did not know that it
was true, that is to say, if we did not know truth? Of course it is possible to
explain the †meaning of the word† to someone who does not know the
language, and tell him that the word 'truth', in the strict sense, denotes the
conformity of thought with its object, but that when it is attributed to
things outside thought, it means only that they can be the objects of true
thoughts, either ours or God's. But no logical definition can be given which
will help anyone to discover its nature. I think the same of many other
things which are very simple and are known naturally, such as shape, size,
motion, place, time, and so on: if you try to define these things you only
obscure them and cause confusion. For instance, a man who walks across a
room shows much better what motion is than a man who says 'It is the
actuality of a potential being in so far as it is potential', and so on.[2]

The author takes universal consent as the criterion of his truths; whereas
I have no criterion for mine except the natural light. The two criteria agree   598
in part: for since all men have the same natural light, it seems that they
should have the same notions; but there is also a great difference between
them, because hardly anyone makes good use of that light, so that many
people – perhaps all those we know – may share the same mistaken
opinion. Also there are many things which can be known by the natural
light, but which no one has yet reflected on.

He would have it that we have as many faculties as there are different
objects of knowledge. This seems to me like saying that because some wax
can take on an infinite number of shapes, it has an infinite number of

1 Lord Herbert of Cherbury's *On Truth*. See above, p. 137.
2 Aristotle, *Physics*, III, 201ª10. Cf. *The World*: AT XI 39; CSM I 93f.

faculties for taking them on. In that sense it is true, but such a mode of speech seems to me quite useless, and indeed rather dangerous, since it may give ignorant people occasion to imagine a similar diversity of little entities in our soul. So I prefer to think that the wax, simply by its flexibility, takes on all sorts of shapes, and that the soul acquires all its knowledge by the reflection which it makes either on itself (in the case of intellectual matters) or (in the case of corporeal matters) on the various dispositions of the brain to which it is joined, which may result from the action of the senses or from other causes. But it is a useful practice not to accept any belief without considering on what warrant or for what cause one accepts it; and this comes to the same thing as his advice always to consider what faculty one is using, etc.

599   There is no doubt also that in order not to be deceived by the senses one should, as he says, take care that nothing is lacking on the part of the object, or the medium, or the organ, etc.

He recommends that one should above all follow natural instinct especially, from which he derives all his common notions. For my part, I distinguish two kinds of instinct. One is in us *qua* human beings, and is purely intellectual: it is the natural light or †mental vision.† This is the only instinct which I think one should trust. The other belongs to us *qua* animals, and is a certain impulse of nature towards the preservation of our body, towards the enjoyment of bodily pleasures, and so on. This should not always be followed.

His heuristic methods are useful aids in making the enumerations of which I speak on page 20,[1] for once one has duly examined everything they contain, one can be sure of having omitted nothing.

What he says about religion I leave to be examined by the gentlemen of the Sorbonne. I can only say that I found much less difficulty in reading it in French than I did before in going through it in Latin. He has many maxims which seem to me so pious, and so much in conformity with common sense, that I hope they may be approved by orthodox theology. Finally, though I cannot agree in everything with the opinions of this author, I regard him as a person of quite extraordinary talent.

AT II   TO MERSENNE, 13 NOVEMBER 1639

(622)   ... The opinions of your analysts[2] about the existence of God and the honour he should be given are, as you write, very difficult to cure. It is not

---

1 *Discourse*: AT vi 19; CSM i 120.
2 The geometers of Paris, in particular Roberval.

that it is impossible to give reasons strong enough to convince them, but that such people, convinced of their own intelligence, are often less capable of listening to reason than others. The imagination, which is the part of the mind that most helps mathematics, is more of a hindrance than a help in metaphysical speculation. I am now working on a discourse in which I try to clarify what I have hitherto written on this topic. It will be only five or six printed sheets, but I hope it will contain a great part of my metaphysics. To make it as good as possible, I plan to have only twenty or thirty copies printed, and send them to the twenty or thirty most learned theologians I can find, in order to have their criticisms and learn what should be changed, corrected or added before publication...

TO MERSENNE, 25 DECEMBER 1639   AT II

    I owe a reply to three of your letters, namely those of 12 November, and   626
4 and 10 December; the last two I received on the same day.

    1. In the first letter you ask me why a bow or a spring loses its force when stretched wide for a very long time. This is easy to explain in terms of my principles.[1] The pores which I said previously have an oval shape   627 gradually become round, because of the particles of the subtle matter which continually flows from them.

    2. It is this subtle matter which prevents us from throwing a stone, or jumping up, high in the air; for if this matter did not push heavy bodies down again, then when we threw a stone high up, it would rise right up to the sky, and when we jumped up, we would go on rising and would not come down again.

    3. Concerning *inertia*, I think I have already said[2] that in a space free of obstacles, if a body of a certain size, moving at a certain speed, meets a motionless body of the same size, it will communicate half of its motion to it; and hence they will both proceed at half the speed of the first body. But if it meets one which is twice its size, it will communicate two thirds of its motion to it; and hence the two together will not cover a greater distance in three seconds than the first body did in one. In general, the larger a body is, the slower it ought to move when pushed by a given force...

    5. 6. 7. The desire that everyone has to possess every perfection he can   (628) conceive of, and consequently all the perfections which we believe to be in God, is due to the fact that God has given us a will which has no limits. It is

---

1 See letter to Mersenne of 15 May 1634: AT I 295. Cf. *Principles*, Part IV, art. 132: AT VIIIA 274.
2 See above, p. 135.

principally because of this infinite will within us that we can say we are created in his image...

(629)   10. I have noticed that Lord Herbert[1] takes many things as common notions which are nothing of the kind. It is certain that nothing should be taken as such unless it cannot be denied by anybody.

I turn to your letter of 4 December and thank you for the advice you give me about my essay on metaphysics. The arguments of Raymond Lull are sophistries which I do not take seriously. As for the objections of your analysts, I shall try to answer them without setting them out; that is, I shall lay the foundations, from which those who know the objections to them

630   may derive their solution, without teaching them to those who have never heard of them. I think this is how one should treat the matter. In any case, I am not so short of books as you think; I have here a *Summa* of St Thomas[2] and a Bible which I brought from France...

AT III   TO MERSENNE, 29 JANUARY 1640

(9)   ...I have just been looking again at my notes on Galileo. In fact I did not deny that a falling body passes through every degree of slowness; but I said that this cannot be settled without our knowing what heaviness is, which comes to the same thing. Your example of the inclined plane is a good proof of the fact that all speed is infinitely divisible – which I grant. But I do not agree that when a body starts to fall it passes through all these divisions. I hardly think you suppose that a ball struck by a mallet travels, as it begins to move, at a lesser speed than the mallet itself; any body moved by another cannot fail to move, from the very first instant, at a speed proportional to that of the body which imparts the motion. In my

10   view, heaviness is nothing more than the fact that terrestrial bodies are really pushed towards the centre of the earth by subtle matter – and you can easily see what follows from this. But this should not lead us to think that when these bodies start to move, they immediately move as fast as this subtle matter; for the latter pushes them only obliquely, and their move-ment, especially in the case of the lightest bodies, is considerably checked by the air.

I am surprised that you have not heard that flattening a lump of lead with a sledge-hammer when the lead is resting on a cushion or on an anvil that is suspended so that it can move when struck is easier than flattening it when it rests on a rigidly fixed anvil. This is a very widely known

---

1 Lord Herbert of Cherbury, author of *On Truth* (see pp. 137, 139 above).
2 The *Summa Theologiae* of Thomas Aquinas (1224–74), the great medieval philosopher and theologian.

experiment, and there are countless others in mechanics which all depend on the same basic fact. To flatten a lump of lead, it is not enough to strike it with great force; what is required in addition is that the force should continue for a certain period, so as to give the particles of the lump the time to change position. Now when the lead is on a fixed anvil, the hammer rebounds right up almost as soon as the blow is struck, so that it does not have as much time to flatten the lead as it does if the anvil or other supporting body gives way to the blow, thus allowing a longer period of contact between mallet and lead ...

TO MEYSSONNIER, 29 JANUARY 1640   AT III

I would have been the first to write to you, if I had had the advantage of knowing you to be such as you describe yourself in the letter which you so kindly sent me; for the search for truth is so essential and so vast an undertaking as to need the united effort of many thousands; and there are so few people in the world who join it wholeheartedly that those who do should especially cherish each other and seek to help each other by sharing their observations and their thoughts. This I am most willing to do with every kind of affection.

As a beginning, I will answer the question you asked me about the function of the little gland called *conarion*.[1] My view is that this gland is the principal seat of the soul, and the place in which all our thoughts are formed. The reason I believe this is that I cannot find any part of the brain, except this, which is not double. Since we see only one thing with two eyes, and hear only one voice with two ears, and in short never have more than one thought at a time, it must necessarily be the case that the impressions which enter by the two eyes or by the two ears, and so on, unite with each other in some part of the body before being considered by the soul. Now it is impossible to find any such place in the whole head except this gland; moreover it is situated in the most suitable possible place for this purpose, in the middle of all the concavities; and it is supported and surrounded by the little branches of the carotid arteries which bring the spirits into the brain. As for the impressions preserved in the memory, I imagine they are not unlike the folds which remain in this paper after it has once been folded; and so I think that they are received for the most part in the whole substance of the brain. But I do not deny that they can also be present in some fashion in this gland, especially in people whose minds are sluggish. In the case of very good and subtle minds, I think the gland must be free from outside influence and easy to move, just as we observe that the gland

18
19

20

_____

1 The pineal gland.

is smaller in man than it is in animals, unlike the other parts of the brain. I think also that some of the impressions which serve the memory can be in various other parts of the body: for instance the skill of a lute player is not only in his head, but also partly in the muscles of his hands, and so on. As for the likenesses of little dogs, which are said to appear in the urine of those who have been bitten by mad dogs, I must admit that I have always thought it was a fable, and unless you tell me that you have seen very distinct and well-formed specimens I shall still find it difficult to believe in them. However, if it is true that they can be seen, they could be explained in
21 some way similar to the birth marks which children receive from the cravings of their mothers.[1]

AT III   TO HOGELANDE, 8 FEBRUARY 1640

(722)   ... I generally distinguish two aspects of mathematics, the historical and the scientific. By 'history' I understand everything which has been discovered already and is contained in books. By 'science' I mean the skill to solve every problem, and thus to discover by one's own efforts everything capable of being discovered in that science by means of our native human
723 intelligence. Anyone who has such science certainly does not need much external assistance, and so may be called αὐτάρχης ('self-sufficient') in the strict sense of the term. Such a person should not be wholly ignorant of what is contained in books; but a general acquaintance which is automatically acquired by perusing the principal authors is quite sufficient. This will enable him to identify the passages where he can look up previous discoveries, should they be useful to him at any stage. There are indeed many matters which are much better kept in books than memorized, such as astronomical observations, tables, rules, theorems, and in short whatever does not stick spontaneously in the memory at the first encounter. For the fewer items we fill our memory with, the sharper we will keep our native intelligence for increasing our knowledge.

        It would, however, be highly desirable if the historical part of mathematics which is scattered among many volumes and is as yet incomplete
724 and imperfect were collected wholly within a single book. This would not require any resources for seeking out or purchasing books, since there was a great deal of mutual copying of material among the relevant authors, and what remains can be found in any modestly furnished library. Moreover, the chief need would not be so much for diligence in collecting everything together as for judgement in rejecting what is superfluous, and knowledge to fill the gaps where previous attempts at discovery have failed; and these

1 See *Optics* (AT VI 129) and the letter to Mersenne of 30 July 1640 (p. 148 below).

qualities none but your 'self-sufficient' mathematician will be able to supply. If such a book did exist, anyone could easily learn from it the whole of mathematical history, and even a part of mathematical science. But no one will ever emerge as a truly self-sufficient mathematician unless in addition he has been lucky enough to be naturally endowed with an intellectual aptitude for the subject, and has then refined it by a long course of study.

So much for theoretical mathematics. But as for its practical application, should anyone desire to possess everything relevant to this, such as instruments, machines, automatons, and so on, even if he were a king he could never, by spending all the treasure in the world, afford everything he would require. And in fact there is no need for all this; it is enough to know the description of the relevant instruments, so that when the occasion demands it, we can make them ourselves or have them made by craftsmen.

TO MERSENNE, 11 MARCH 1640

... I would think I knew nothing in physics if I could say only how things could be, without demonstrating that they could not be otherwise. This is perfectly possible once one has reduced physics to the laws of mathematics. I think I can do it for the small area to which my knowledge extends. But I did not do it in my *Essays*, because I did not want to present my principles there, and I do not yet see anything to persuade me to present them in future ...

TO MERSENNE, 1 APRIL 1640

. . . Your second letter, of 10 March, contained another from M. Meyssonnier, which I would answer if I thought this was going to find you still at Paris; but if it has to be sent on to you, it is not a good idea to weigh it down so much, and I can put here, in a few words, all that I have to tell him, which you will pass on to him, please, when next you write to him. After thanking him for his kindness, say this to him. I do not altogether deny that the impressions which serve memory may be partly in the gland called *conarium*,[1] especially in dumb animals and in people who have a coarse mind. But it seems to me that others would not have the great facility which they have in imagining an infinity of things which they have never seen, if their souls were not joined to some part of the brain that was very well equipped to receive all kinds of new impressions, and consequently very ill equipped to preserve them. Now there is only this gland to which the soul can be so joined; for there is nothing else in the whole head which

---

1 The pineal gland.

is not double. But I think that it is the other parts of the brain, especially the interior parts, which are for the most part utilized in memory. I think that all the nerves and muscles can also be so utilized, so that a lute player, for instance, has a part of his memory in his hands: for the ease of bending and positioning his fingers in various ways, which he has acquired by practice, helps him to remember the passages which need these positions when they are played. You will find this easy to believe if you bear in mind that what people call 'local memory' is outside us: for instance, when we have read a book, not all the impressions which can remind us of its contents are in our brain. Many of them are on the paper of the copy which we have read. It does not matter that these impressions have no resemblance to the things of which they remind us; often the impressions in the brain have no resemblance either, as I said in the fourth discourse of my *Optics*. But besides this memory, which depends on the body, I believe there is also another one, entirely intellectual, which depends on the soul alone.

49   I would not find it strange that the gland called the *conarium* should be found decayed when the bodies of lethargic persons are dissected, because it decays very rapidly in all other cases too. Three years ago at Leiden, when I wanted to see it in a woman who was being autopsied, I found it impossible to recognize it, even though I looked very thoroughly, and knew well where it should be, being accustomed to find it without any difficulty in freshly killed animals. An old professor who was performing the autopsy, named Valcher, admitted to me that he had never been able to see it in any human body. I think this is because they usually spend some days looking at the intestines and other parts before opening the head.

I need no proof of the mobility of this gland apart from its situation; for since it is supported only by the little arteries which surround it, it is certain that very little will suffice to move it. But for all that I do not think that it can go far one way or the other . . .

(50)   You mention that you have had a letter from England to the effect that I was about to receive an invitation to go there. I have had no word of this myself; but I will tell you in confidence that I would prefer to reside in that country rather than in many others. As far as religion is concerned, moreover, the King himself is said to be Catholic by inclination. So I beg you not to discourage the good intentions of your correspondents . . .

AT III   TO REGIUS, 24 MAY 1640

63 .   I am much obliged to you and M. Emilius for examining and correcting the manuscript[1] which I sent you. I see that you were even kind enough to

---

1 A manuscript of the *Meditations*.

correct the punctuation and spelling. You would have put me under an even greater obligation if you had been willing to make some changes in the words and the thoughts. For however small the changes were, they 64 would have given me hope that what you had left was less at fault; but now I fear that you may have refrained from criticism only because too much needed correction, or the whole needed to be cancelled.

Now for your objections. In your first you say: 'it is because we have in ourselves some wisdom, power and goodness that we form the idea of an infinite, or at least indefinite, wisdom, power, goodness and the other perfections which we attribute to God; just as it is because we have in ourselves some degree of quantity that we form the idea of an infinite quantity'. I entirely agree, and am quite convinced that we have no idea of God except the one formed in this manner. But the whole point of my argument is this. These perfections are so slight that unless we derived our origin from a being in which they are actually infinite, my nature could not enable me to extend them in thought to an infinite degree. Similarly, I could not conceive of an indefinite quantity by looking at a very small quantity or a finite body unless the size of the world was actually or at least possibly indefinite.

In your second objection you say: 'the truth of axioms which are clearly and distinctly understood is self-evident'. This too, I agree, is true, during the time they are clearly and distinctly understood; for our mind is of such a nature that it cannot help assenting to what it clearly understands. But because we often remember conclusions that we have deduced from such premisses without actually attending to the premisses themselves, I say that on such occasions, if we lack knowledge of God, we can imagine that the conclusions are uncertain even though we remember that they were deduced from clear principles: because perhaps our nature is such that we go wrong even in the most evident matters. Consequently, even at the 65 moment when we deduced them from those principles, we did not have *knowledge*[1] of them, but only a *conviction* of them. I distinguish the two as follows: there is conviction when there remains some reason which might lead us to doubt, but knowledge is conviction based on a reason so strong that it can never be shaken by any stronger reason. Nobody can have the latter unless he also has knowledge of God. But a man who has once clearly understood the reasons which convince us that God exists and is not a deceiver, provided he remembers the conclusion 'God is no deceiver' whether or not he continues to attend to the reasons for it, will continue to possess not only the conviction, but real knowledge of this and all other conclusions the reasons for which he remembers he once clearly perceived.

1 Lat. *scientia*, Descartes' term for systematic knowledge based on indubitable foundations.

In your latest objections – which I received yesterday, and which reminded me to reply to your earlier ones – you say that rashness of judgement depends on the innate or acquired temperament of the body. I do not agree. That would take away the freedom and scope of our will, which can remedy such rashness. If it does not remedy it, the error which results is a privation in relation to us, but a mere negation in relation to God . . .

(66)   I do not see why you think that the perception of universals belongs to the imagination rather than to the intellect. I attribute it to the intellect alone, which relates to many things an idea which is in itself singular . . .

AT III   TO MERSENNE, 11 JUNE 1640

(84)   . . . There is no doubt that the folds of the memory get in each other's way, and that there cannot be an infinite number of such folds in the brain; but there are still quite a number of them there. Moreover, the intellectual memory has its own separate impressions, which do not depend in any
85   way on these folds. So I do not believe that the number of folds is necessarily very large.

I do not explain the feeling of pain without reference to the soul. For in my view pain exists only in the understanding. What I do explain is all the external movements which accompany this feeling in us; in animals it is these movements alone which occur, and not pain in the strict sense . . .

AT III   TO MERSENNE, 30 JULY 1640

(120)   . . . With reference to birth marks,[1] since they never occur in the infant when the mother eats fruit which she likes, it is quite probable that they can sometimes be cured when the infant eats the fruit in question. For the same disposition which was in the mother's brain, and caused her desire, is also to be found in the infant's brain; and this corresponds to the area that has the mark, since the mother, by scratching the corresponding area while the desire to eat was upon her, transformed the effects of her imagination
121   to the corresponding part of the baby. For in general the individual parts of the baby's body correspond to those of the mother, as may be proved by reasoning based on mechanics. The point is also established by a number of examples, including a striking one which I once read in Forestus.[2] A woman who had broken her arm while she was pregnant gave birth to a son whose arm was broken in the same place; the doctor treated them

---

1 Fr. *les marques d'envie*, literally 'marks of desire'.
2 Dutch physician, whose sixteen books of *Medical and Surgical Observations and Cures* were published in 1623.

separately, applied the same remedies to the infant's arm as to the mother's, and so cured them both.

As for brute animals, we are so used to believing that they have feelings like us that it is hard to rid ourselves of this opinion. Yet suppose that we were equally used to seeing automatons which perfectly imitated every one of our actions that it is possible for automatons to imitate; suppose, further, that in spite of this we never took them for anything more than automatons; in this case we should be in no doubt that all the animals which lack reason were automatons too. For we would find that they were different from us in all the same respects, as I wrote on page 56 of the *Discourse on the Method*.[1] In my *World* I explained in great detail how the bodies of animals contain all the organs which an automaton needs if it is to imitate those of our actions which are common to us and the beasts . . .[2]

The letter of the learned doctor[3] contains no argument to refute what I have said about the gland called the *conarium*[4] except that it can suffer alteration like the rest of the brain. This is no reason why it should not be the principal seat of the soul; for it is certain that the soul must be joined to some part of the body, and there is no other part which is not as much or more subject to alteration than this gland. Although it is very small and very soft, it is situated in such a well-protected place that it is almost immune from illness, like the vitreous or crystalline humour of the eye. It happens much more often that people become troubled in their minds without any known cause – which could be attributed to some malady of this gland – than it happens that sight is lost through a malady of the crystalline humour. Moreover, all the alterations which take place in the mind, when a man sleeps after drinking, for instance, can be attributed to some alterations taking place in this gland.

He says that the soul can utilize double parts, or use the spirits, which cannot all reside in this gland. I agree, because I do not think that the soul is so imprisoned in the gland that it cannot act elsewhere. But utilizing a thing is not the same as being immediately joined or united to it; and since our soul is not double, but single and indivisible, it seems to me that the part of the body to which it is most immediately joined should also be single and not divided into a pair of similar parts. I cannot find such a part in the whole brain except this gland . . .

I have not yet had my five or six sheets of metaphysics[5] printed, though

123

124

(126)

1 AT VI 56; CSM I 139.
2 Cf. AT XI 119ff.; CSM I 99ff.
3 Christophe Villiers (1595–1661), a doctor in Sens whose comments about the pineal gland had been sent to Descartes by Mersenne.
4 The pineal gland.
5 The *Meditations*.

they have been ready for some time. I delayed because I do not want them to fall into the hands of pseudo-theologians – or, now, into the hands of the Jesuits whom I foresee I shall have to fight – before I have had them seen and approved by various doctors, and if I can, by the Sorbonne as a whole. I intended to visit France this summer, and so planned to bring them myself; and I did not want to have them printed until I was about to depart for fear that the publisher would steal some copies to sell without my knowledge, as often happens. But the summer is already so far gone that I fear I will not be able to make the journey. If not, I will send you ten or twelve copies, or more if you think they will be needed. I will have printed no more than will be necessary for this purpose, and I will ask you to distribute and look after them. Please give them only to those theologians whom you consider to be the most able, and the least prejudiced by, and committed to, scholastic errors – really good people who are moved more by truth and the glory of God than by envy and jealousy . . .

AT III

TO HUYGENS, 31 JULY 1640

(751)   . . . I am astonished that you have been told that I was going to publish something on metaphysics, since I have not yet delivered anything to the publisher, or indeed got anything ready that is not too slight to be worth mentioning. In short, your information must be quite inaccurate – apart from the fact that I remember having told you last winter that I was proposing to clarify what I wrote in Part Four of the *Discourse on the Method*, not to publish it, but merely to have a dozen or so copies printed to send to our leading theologians for their verdict. For I draw a comparison between my work in this area and the demonstrations of Apollonius. Everything in the latter is really very clear and certain, when each point is considered separately; but because the proofs are rather long, and one cannot see the necessity of the conclusion unless one remembers exactly everything that has gone before, you will hardly find a single person in an entire country who is capable of understanding them. Nevertheless, 752   because those few who do understand them vouch for their truth, everyone believes them. Similarly, I think that I have fully demonstrated the existence of God and the non-material nature of the human soul; but this depends on several successive arguments, and forgetting the smallest element will make it impossible to understand the conclusion. So I foresee that my arguments will bear very little fruit, unless I reach readers who are highly intelligent and enjoy a high reputation in the field of metaphysics; if they take the trouble to examine my arguments with care, and state frankly what they think of them, they will encourage the rest to follow their judgement – or at least make them ashamed to contradict them without

reason. Moreover, since this treatise concerns the glory of God, I am, it seems to me, under an obligation to take more care to do it justice than I would be disposed to take if it concerned some other topic.

For the rest, I think I am going to become engaged in a war with the Jesuits. Their mathematician in Paris[1] has publicly attacked my *Optics* in his theses, and I have written to his superior[2] with a view to involving the whole Society in this quarrel. For although I have long been aware of the proverb 'Don't stir up the hornets',[3] nevertheless, since they get stirred up all by themselves and I cannot avoid it, I think it better to face them all in one big battle rather than waiting for one individual attack after another, which would take for ever . . .

TO MERSENNE, 6 AUGUST 1640   AT III

I left myself so short a period to write to you a week ago that I did not 142
have time to answer all the points of your last, and I stopped at the ninth, 143
which concerned the folds of the memory. I do not think that there has to be a very large number of these folds to supply all the things we remember, because a single fold will do for all the things which resemble each other. Moreover, in addition to the corporeal memory, whose impressions can be explained by these folds in the brain, I believe that there is also in our intellect another sort of memory, which is altogether spiritual, and is not found in animals. It is this that we mainly use.

Moreover, it is a mistake to believe that we remember best what we did when we were young; for then we did countless things which we no longer remember at all. Those we do remember are remembered not only because of the impressions we received when we were young, but mainly because 144
we have done the same things again and renewed the impressions by remembering the events over again from time to time.

As for the tides, this is something which depends entirely on my *World*; I can hardly provide a satisfactory explanation of the matter in isolation. But because I can refuse you nothing, I shall try to give a rough account here. Let T be the earth, EFGH the water surrounding it, L the moon, and ABCD the heavens, which I conceive of as a fluid which revolves continually around the earth; the circular motion of this fluid is the only thing 145
keeping the earth where it is. This motion would always keep the earth exactly in the centre of the heavens, were it not for the moon; for, since the

1 Pierre Bourdin (1595–1653), later to write the Seventh Set of Objections to the *Meditations*: see CSM II 64.
2 Julien Hayneuve (1588–1663), to whom Descartes had written on 22 July; see AT III 97ff.
3 Plautus, *Amphitruo*, II, 2, 707.

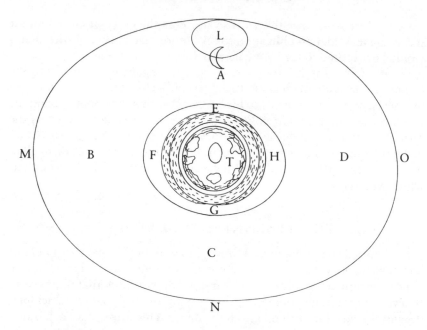

same matter which passes towards B also passes towards C and D, it would require just as much space on one side of the earth as on another, and so would exert an equal pressure on it from every side. But since the moon is situated in the heavens near the outer surface, for example at point L, and since it does not revolve as quickly as the heavens, it causes the matter in this part of the heavens to press the earth down more strongly towards E than towards F or H; this in turn causes the earth to shift slightly from its central position in the heavens, and move towards N, and the result is that the water in areas E and G is slightly more compressed and pushed down than that in areas F or H. Now because the earth turns about its centre in 24 hours, the part of the earth which is now at point E, where we have low tide, will in 6 hours be at point F, where it is high tide, and in 12 hours at point G, where it is low tide again. Moreover, since the moon is itself revolving every 30 days, we must subtract around two-fifths of an hour from each tide, so that the water takes only $11\frac{3}{5}$ hours to rise and fall on each occasion.

146   In addition, I find in my *World* that the heavens LMNO cannot be exactly circular but must be slightly oval, and that the moon is situated on the smallest diameter of the oval when it is full or new, which explains why the tides are bigger than usual at these times. The other peculiarities we observe in the ebb and flow of the tides merely depend on the particular differences in the coastline. I would prefer these views of mine not to be

published, or widely circulated, because they occur in my *World*, and should the book ever see the light of day, it will be good to retain some novelty value . . .

TO MERSENNE, 30 SEPTEMBER 1640   AT III

I did not intend to write to you by this post, but I have thought of 183 something on which I would be glad to have your advice and information. As I told you, I intended to have printed only twenty or thirty copies of my little treatise on metaphysics,[1] so as to send them to the same number of theologians for their opinion of it. But I do not see that I can carry out that plan without the book's being seen by almost everyone who has any curiosity to see it; either they will borrow it from one of those to whom I send it, or they will get it from the publisher, who will certainly print more copies than I want. So it seems that perhaps I will do better to have a public 184 printing of it from the start. I have no fear that it contains anything which could displease the theologians; but I would have liked to have the approbation of a number of people so as to prevent the cavils of ignorant contradiction-mongers. The less such people understand it, and the less they expect it to be understood by the general public, the more eloquent they will be unless they are restrained by the authority of a number of learned people. With this in mind, I thought that I might send you my treatise in manuscript for you to show to Father Gibieuf and that I might write to him myself to ask him to examine it. He will, unless I am much mistaken, be kind enough to approve it. You could also show it to a few others, as you judge fit. Once approved by three or four such people, it could be printed; and if you agree, I would dedicate it to all the masters of the Sorbonne, asking them to be my protectors in God's cause. For I must confess that the quibbles of Father Bourdin have made me determine to fortify myself henceforth with the authority of others, as far as I can, since truth by itself is so little esteemed.[2]

I will not travel during this winter, because in the next four or five 185 months I am due to receive the objections of the Jesuits, and I think I should hold myself in readiness for them. Meanwhile I should like to reread some of their philosophy, which I have not looked at for twenty years. I want to see if I like it better now than I did before. For this purpose, I beg you to send me the names of the authors who have written textbooks

---

1 The *Meditations*.
2 Descartes refers to objections which Pierre Bourdin (1595–1653) had made against his *Optics*, and which Descartes answered in a letter to Mersenne of 29 July 1640 (AT III 105).

of philosophy, and to tell me which are the most commonly used, and whether they have any new ones since twenty years ago. I remember only some of the Conimbricenses,[1] Toletus[2] and Rubius.[3] I would also like to know if there is in current use any abstract of the whole of scholastic philosophy; this would save me the time it would take to read their huge tomes. There was, I think, a Carthusian or Feuillant who made such an abstract, but I do not remember his name.[4]

For the rest, if you think it a good idea for me to dedicate my treatise on metaphysics to the Sorbonne, please let me know what heading I should use for my open letter to them at the start of the book ...

(191)   I entirely agree with the argument which you were sent from Blaye, to the effect that whatever we conceive distinctly to be possible is possible, and that we conceive distinctly that it is possible that the world has been made, and therefore it has been made. It is certain that it is impossible to conceive distinctly that the sun or any other finite thing is independent, because independence, conceived distinctly, involves infinity. It is a serious mistake to believe that one can conceive distinctly that an atom, or even a part of matter, can occupy indifferently a larger or smaller space. First of all, an atom can never be conceived distinctly, since the very meaning of the word involves a contradiction, that of being a body and being indivi-

192   sible. And as for a genuine part of matter, the determinate quantity of the space which it occupies is necessarily involved in any distinct thought which one can have of it. The principal aim of my metaphysics is to show which are the things that can be distinctly conceived ...

AT III   TO MERSENNE, 28 OCTOBER 1640

(212)   ... I come to the second letter sent by one of your friars from Blaye.[5] Because I do not know which are the two points on which you want my opinion, I will go through them all.

1. I agree that a single effect can be explained in several possible ways; but I do not think that the possibility of things in general can be explained except in one way, which is the true one.

---

1 A group of Jesuit commentators on Aristotle named after their connection with the University of Coimbra in Portugal; the commentaries were published from 1592 onwards and frequently reprinted in the early seventeenth century.
2 Francisco Toledo (1532–96), Jesuit Cardinal and theologian.
3 Rubio or Ruvio (1548–1615), prolific commentator on Aristotle who taught in Mexico.
4 Eustache de St Paul, whose *Summa Philosophica Quadripartita* was first published in 1609.
5 Father J. Lacombe.

2. He is right in saying that it is a big mistake to accept the principle that   213
no body moves of itself. For it is certain that a body, once it has begun to
move, has in itself for that reason alone the power to continue to move, just
as, once it is stationary in a certain place, it has for that reason alone the
power to continue to remain there. But as for the principle of movement
which he imagines to be different in each body, this is altogether
imaginary.

3. I cannot accept his indivisible bodies, or the natural inclinations
which he attributes to them. I can conceive such inclinations only in things
which possess understanding, and I do not attribute them even to animals
which lack reason. Everything in them which we call natural appetites or
inclinations is explained on my theory solely in terms of the rules of
mechanics. I cannot accept his elements either; they are at least as difficult
to understand as the things he tries to explain by them.

4. Two indivisible things could only make a single thing divisible into
two parts at most; but before saying that they could make up a body, you
must know what is meant by the term 'body'. In fact it means a thing which
has length and breadth and extension, and so cannot be composed of
indivisible things, since an indivisible thing cannot have any length or
breadth or depth. If it had, we could divide it at least in our imagination,   214
which would suffice to guarantee that it was not indivisible: for if we could
divide it in imagination, an angel could divide it in reality. He thinks
motion and shape by themselves are inadequate as principles of explanation, because he does not see how all the various properties of such
things as wine could be explained in terms of them. You can remove this
difficulty by telling him that they have all been explained already, as
have all the other properties perceptible by the senses. But not a word
about miracles . . .

8. I do not see why he associates atheism with the explanation of nature   (215)
in terms of shapes and motions as if the two doctrines were somehow akin.
He says that the idea of a simple being, which we conceive to contain all
being, could not be conceived if there were not a real exemplar of this
being, because we can conceive – you should add 'distinctly' – only things
which are possible and true. This makes it look as if he has read my works,
which contain this very argument; but he adds many things which I cannot
agree with, as that this being has dimensions, and that dimensions can be
conceived without composition of parts, i.e. without the thing which has
the dimensions being divisible, etc. He is also right in saying that not
everything which we do not conceive distinctly is thereby false. He does
well to apply this to the mystery of the Trinity, which is an article of faith   216
and cannot be known by natural reason alone. I do not find anything to
mention in the other articles, and I have no paper left.

Since you are willing to take my *Metaphysics*[1] under your protection, I hope to send it to you in a week or two at most. I would send it now, but I want to have it copied first. Perhaps I will send it by M. de Zuylichem.[2]

AT III

TO MERSENNE, 11 NOVEMBER 1640

230
231
Thank you for your news of M. Voetius.[3] I find nothing strange in it except his not knowing of our friendship; everyone here who knows me at all knows about that. He is the most pedantic fellow in the world, and he is bursting with rage because there is a professor of medicine[4] in their University of Utrecht who openly teaches my philosophy, and even gives private lectures in physics, which in a few months enable his pupils to make fun of traditional philosophy as a whole. Voetius and the other professors have done all they can to get the magistrates to forbid him to teach; but despite their efforts, the magistrates allow him to continue. This Voetius has also spoilt Mlle de Schurmans:[5] she had excellent gifts for poetry, painting and other gentle arts, but these last five or six years he has taken her over so completely that she cares for nothing but theological controversies, and this has made all decent people shun her. Her brother has always been known as a man of poor intelligence. Your letter to Voetius I have given back to the postman, so that he will pay the postage for it, as if it had not been enclosed in your letter to me. This will give you some small revenge for the six pounds he made you pay for his theses.

232
I do not think that the diversity of the opinions of the scholastics makes their philosophy difficult to refute. It is easy to overturn the foundations on which they all agree, and once that has been done, all their disagreements over detail will seem foolish. I have bought the *Philosophy* of Father Eustache of St Paul, which seems to me the best book of its kind ever made. I would be glad to know if the author is still alive[6] . . .

233
I would willingly answer your question about the flame of a candle and similar things; but I see that I can never really satisfy you on this until you have seen all the principles of my philosophy. So I must tell you that I have resolved to write them before leaving this country, and to publish them perhaps within a year. My plan is to write a series of theses which will

---

1 The *Meditations*.
2 Constantijn Huygens.
3 Gisbert Voet (1589–1676), Professor of Theology at the University of Utrecht, and an implacable opponent of Regius, Professor of Medicine, who boldly supported Descartes' doctrines.
4 Henri le Roy (Regius).
5 Anne-Marie de Schurman (born 1612), who followed closely the controversy over Descartes' philosophy.
6 See footnote 4, p. 154 above. Eustache died on 26 December 1640.

constitute a complete textbook of my philosophy. I will not waste any words, but simply put down all my conclusions with the true premises from which I derive them. I think I could do this without many words. In the same volume I plan to have printed a textbook of traditional philosophy, perhaps Father Eustache's, with notes by me at the end of each proposition. In the notes I will add the different opinions of others, and what one should think of them all, and perhaps at the end I will make a comparison between the two philosophies. But please do not tell anyone yet of this plan, especially before my *Metaphysics* is published; because perhaps if the Regents knew of it they would do their best to make trouble for me – though once the thing is done, I hope they will all be pleased. It might also hold up the approbation of the Sorbonne, which I want, and which I think may be very useful for my purposes, for I must tell you that the little book on metaphysics which I sent you contains all the principles of my physics.

The argument for the Godhead in the book you write about – that if the sun has shone eternally, it cannot have illuminated one hemisphere before the other – proves nothing except that our soul, being finite, cannot   234
comprehend the infinite . . .

Yesterday I sent my *Metaphysics* to M. de Zuylichem[1] to post on to you;   (235)
but he will not do so for a week, since I have allowed him that length of time to look at it. I have not put any title on it, but it seems to me that the most suitable would be †*René Descartes' Meditations on First Philosophy*† because I do not confine my discussion to God and the soul, but deal in general with all the first things to be discovered by philosophizing. You will see its scope from the letters which I have attached to it. I will not say any more now, except that I think it would be a good idea, before printing, to settle with the publisher to give us as many copies as we need, and to let us have them ready bound. There is no pleasure in buying one's own writings, and I am sure the publisher can do what I suggest without loss. Here I will need no more than thirty copies; as for Paris, it is for you to   236
judge how many are needed.

TO [GIBIEUF], 11 NOVEMBER 1640   AT III

The honour you did me, several years ago, of telling me that you did not   237
find my philosophical views incredible, and my acquaintance with your exceptional learning, make me hope very much that you will be so good as to look at the work on metaphysics which I have asked the Reverend Father Mersenne to send you. In my view, the route which I take to make

---

1 Constantijn Huygens.

known the nature of the human soul and to demonstrate the existence of
God is the only one which could enable us to reach our destination. I am
well aware that others could have made a much better job of following this
path than I have, and that I will have left out much that needed to be
explained; but I am sure that I can make good all the defects, provided I am
alerted to them, and that I can make the proofs I employ so evident and so
certain that they can be taken as demonstrations. One problem none the
less remains, which is that I cannot ensure that those of every level of
intelligence will be capable of understanding the proofs, or even that they
will take the trouble to read them attentively, unless they receive a
recommendation from people other than myself. Now I know of no people
on earth who can accomplish more in this regard than the gentlemen of the
238 Sorbonne, or anyone from whom I can expect a more sincere appraisal,
and so I have decided to seek their special protection. And since you are
one of the leading lights of the Society, and have always done me the
honour of giving me signs of your affection, and above all since it is the
cause of God that I have undertaken to defend, I have great hopes of your
help in this matter. I rely on your advice in telling Father Mersenne how he
should conduct this business, and on your kind help in securing favourable
judges for me, and in placing yourself among them. In so doing, Reverend
Father, you will oblige me to be most devotedly for the rest of my life your
very humble and obedient servant, Descartes.

AT III   TO MERSENNE, 11 NOVEMBER 1640

238   I am finally sending you my work on metaphysics, which I have not yet
239 put a title to, so that I can make you its godfather and leave the baptism to
you. I think, as I wrote to you in my previous letter, that it could be called
Meditationes de Prima Philosophia;[1] for in the book I deal not just with
God and the soul, but in general with all the first things that can be
discovered by philosophizing in an orderly way. My name is so well
known that if I refused to put it under the title it would be thought that I
was indulging in deliberate dissimulation, motivated more by vanity than
by modesty.

     As for the letter to the gentlemen of the Sorbonne, if my opening form of
address is inadequate, or I have left out some closing salutation or other
ceremony, please be kind enough to insert it; I am sure that it will be none
the worse for being penned by another hand than my own. I am sending
you the letter to the Sorbonne under separate cover from the treatise itself,
because I think the best plan, if everything goes as it should, would be the

1 *Meditations on First Philosophy.*

following: once all the material has been seen by Father Gibieuf, and one or two others if you see fit, let the treatise be printed minus the letter (for the manuscript copy is too messy to be read by more than a few), and let the printed version then be presented to the Faculty of the Sorbonne, together with the letter in manuscript. The fairest way of proceeding after that would, I think, be for the Faculty to delegate some of their number to examine it; so it will be necessary to provide them with as many copies as they need for this purpose – or, better, with as many copies as there are doctors in the Faculty. Should they find anything to object to, they should send me their comments for my reply, and this could all be printed at the end of the book. After that, I think they could not refuse to give their verdict on the book, which could be printed at the beginning together with my letter to them. But things will perhaps turn out quite differently from what I expect, which is why I put myself entirely in your hands and those of Father Gibieuf, whom I am asking in my letter to help you conduct this business. The recent skirmish against me of which you are aware[1] has made me realize that no matter what the justice of one's cause, one still needs friends to defend it. The importance of this here is that since I am championing the cause of God, no one will be able to reject my arguments unless they can point out that the reasoning is fallacious, which I believe will be impossible, or to belittle them, unless they can provide superior arguments, which I think will be quite difficult.

240

TO COLVIUS, 14 NOVEMBER 1640 {AT III}

I am obliged to you for drawing my attention to the passage of St Augustine relevant to my *I am thinking, therefore I exist*.[2] I went today to the library of this town[3] to read it, and I do indeed find that he does use it to prove the certainty of our existence. He goes on to show that there is a certain likeness of the Trinity in us, in that we exist, we know that we exist, and we love the existence and the knowledge we have. I, on the other hand, use the argument to show that this *I* which is thinking is *an immaterial substance* with no bodily element. These are two very different things. In itself it is such a simple and natural thing to infer that one exists from the fact that one is doubting that it could have occurred to any writer. But I am very glad to find myself in agreement with St Augustine, if only to hush the little minds who have tried to find fault with the principle. My little book

247

248

---

1 An anonymous attack on the *Optics* (of which the author was in fact the Jesuit Pierre Bourdin) which had been sent to Descartes earlier in 1640; see AT III 106ff.
2 This refers to the *Discourse* (AT VI 32; CSM I 127), not to the *Meditations*, in which the famous catchphrase does not occur. See Augustine, *De Civitate Dei* XI, 26.
3 Leiden.

on metaphysics is already on the way to Paris, where I think it will be printed; all that I have left is a draft so full of crossings out that I could scarcely read it myself, which is why I cannot let you have it. But as soon as it is printed, I will see that you receive a copy as soon as anyone, since you are kind enough to want to read it, and I will be very glad to have your opinion of it.

AT III   TO MERSENNE, 3 DECEMBER 1640

(248)   You tell me that St Augustine and St Ambrose say that our heart and our thoughts are not in our power, and that they confuse the mind and distract
249   it and so on. This applies only to the sensitive part of the soul, which receives the impressions of objects, whether external, or internal (such as temptations). So far I entirely agree with them, and I have never said that all our thoughts are in our power, but only that if there is anything absolutely in our power, it is our thoughts, that is to say, those which come from our will and free choice.[1] They in no way contradict me on this point. I wrote it only in order to show that our free will has no absolute jurisdiction over any corporeal thing. This is true and undeniable . . .

(251)   The last letter you sent me brings me news of the death of my father,[2] which gives me great sadness. I very much regret not having been able to go to France this summer, to see him before he died. But since God did not
252   allow this, I am resolved to stay here until my *Philosophy*[3] is completed.

AT III   TO MERSENNE, DECEMBER 1640

(258)   . . . I am not sorry that the ministers are thundering against the movement of the earth; perhaps this will encourage our own preachers to give it their approval. In this connection, if you are writing to Cardinal de B.'s doctor,[4] I should be glad if you would tell him that the only thing that has stopped me publishing my philosophy up to now is the question of defending the movement of the earth. I would not be able to separate this from my philosophy, since the whole of my physics depends on it; but (you may tell him) I shall soon perhaps be forced to publish my philosophy, because of the slander of several people who fail to understand my principles and are trying to persuade the world that I have views which are
259   very far from the truth. Please ask him to sound out the Cardinal on this subject; for since I am his most obedient servant I should be very sorry to

1 See *Discourse*: AT VI 25; CSM I 123.
2 Descartes' father, Joachim Descartes, died on 17 October 1640.
3 The *Meditations*.
4 The reference is to Gabriel Naudé, private physician to Cardinal de Baigné.

displease him, and because of my extreme devotion to the Catholic religion I have a general respect for all its leaders. I do *not* add that I am reluctant to risk their censure; for since I have firm faith in the infallibility of the Church, and in addition have no doubts about my own arguments, I cannot have any fear that one truth may be in conflict with another.

You are right to say that we are as sure of our free will as of any other primary notion; for this is certainly one of them.

When one candle lights another, this is simply one and the same fire spreading from one wick to another. For the particles of the flame are agitated by very subtle matter,[1] and so have the force to agitate and separate the parts of the other wick. The fire thus grows, and is subsequently divided into two fires, when the two wicks are separated.

But I cannot provide a satisfactory explanation of fire without giving the whole of my philosophy, and I will tell you in confidence that I am starting to make a summary of it. I propose to lay out the entire course in proper order, so as to have it printed with a compendium of scholastic philosophy, like that of Eustache;[2] at the end of each question I will append my own notes, which will contain the opinions of the various authors, what one should think of them all, and what usefulness they have. I think I can do this in such a way that it will be very easy to see how one compares with the other; and those who have not yet learnt scholastic philosophy will   260
find it much easier to learn from this book than from their teachers, since they will learn to scorn it at the same time. As for my own philosophy, even the least gifted teachers will be capable of teaching it from this book alone. If Father Eustache de Saint-Paul is still alive, I will not make use of his book without permission; but it is not yet time to request it, or even to broach the subject, because we must wait and see how my meditations on metaphysics are received . . .

I shall look at St Anselm at the first opportunity. Some time ago, you   (261)
drew my attention to a passage from St Augustine concerning my *I am thinking therefore I exist*, and I think you have asked me about it again since then. It is in Book Eleven, chapter 26 of *De Civitate Dei*.

TO MERSENNE, 24 DECEMBER 1640   AT III

I have just received your letters only an hour or two before the postman   263
has to return; so I shall not be able this time to answer you point by point.

1 By 'subtle' Descartes means composed of small, fast-moving particles.
2 See above, pp. 154, 156.

The difficulty you raise about the *conarium*[1] seems to be the most urgent, and the man who wants to defend publicly what I said about it in my *Optics* does me so much honour that I must try to answer his queries.[2] So without waiting for the next post I will say that the pituitary gland bears some relation to the pineal gland in that both are situated between the carotid arteries and on the path which the spirits take in rising from the heart to the brain. But this gives no ground to suspect that the two have the same function; for the pituitary gland is not, like the pineal gland, in the brain, but beneath it and entirely separate, in a concavity of the sphenoid bone specially made to take it, and †even beneath the *dura mater*† if I remember correctly. Moreover, it is entirely immobile, whereas we experience, when we imagine, that the seat of the common sense, that is to say the part of the brain in which the soul performs all its principal operations, must be mobile. It is not surprising that the pituitary gland should be situated where it is, between the heart and the *conarium*, because many

264   little arteries come together there to form the carotid plexus, without reaching the brain. For it is almost a general rule throughout the body that there are glands at the meeting points of large numbers of branches of veins or arteries. It is not surprising either that the carotids send many branches to that point: that is necessary to nourish the bones and other parts, and also to separate the coarser parts of the blood from the more rarefied parts which alone travel through the straightest branches of the carotids to reach the interior of the brain, where the *conarium* is located. There is no need to suppose that this separation takes place in any but a purely mechanical manner. When reeds and foam are floating on a stream which splits into two branches, the reeds and foam will be seen to go into the branch in which the water flows in a less straight line. The present case is similar. There is good reason for the *conarium* to be like a gland, because the main function of every gland is to take in the most rarefied parts of the blood which are given off by the surrounding vessels, and the function of the *conarium* is to take in the animal spirits in the same manner. Since it is the only solid part in the whole brain which is single, it must necessarily be the seat of the common sense, i.e. of thought, and consequently of the soul; for one cannot be separated from the other. The only alternative is to say that the soul is not joined immediately to any solid part of the body, but only to the animal spirits which are in its concavities, and which enter it and leave it continually like the water of a river. That would certainly be thought too

265   absurd. Moreover, the *conarium* is so placed that it is easy to understand how the images which come from the two eyes, or the sounds which enter

1 The pineal gland.
2 See *Optics*: A T VI 129. The man was Dr Villiers of Sens (see p. 149 above).

by the two ears, etc., must come together at the place where it is situated. They could not do this in the concavities, except in the middle one or in the channel just below the *conarium*; and this would not do, because these concavities are not distinct from the other in which the images are necessarily double. If I can offer any further help to the man who put these questions to you, please assure him that I will gladly do my best to satisfy him.

I am very much indebted to you for the care you are taking of my book of metaphysics, and I give you a free hand to correct or change whatever you think fit. But I am astonished that you promise me the objections of various theologians within a week, because I was sure that it would take longer to take note of all the contents. This was also the opinion of the man[1] who made the objections at the end; he is a priest at Alkmaar, who wishes to remain anonymous, so please remove his name if it occurs in any place. You should also please warn the printer to alter the numbers in his objections by which the pages of the *Meditations* are cited, to make them agree with the printed pages.

You say that I have not said a word about the immortality of the soul. 266 You should not be surprised. I could not prove that God could not annihilate the soul, but only that it is by nature entirely distinct from the body, and consequently it is not bound by nature to die with it. This is all that is required as a foundation for religion, and is all that I had any intention of proving.

You should not find it strange, either, that I do not prove in my Second Meditation that the soul is really distinct from the body, but merely show how to conceive it without the body. This is because I do not yet have, at that point, the premisses needed for the conclusion. You find it later on, in the Sixth Meditation.

It should be noted that throughout the work the order I follow is not the order of the subject matter, but the order of the reasoning. This means that I do not attempt to say in a single place everything relevant to a given subject, because it would be impossible for me to provide proper proofs, since my supporting reasons would have to be drawn in some cases from considerably more distant sources than in others. Instead, I reason in an orderly way †from what is easier to what is harder†, making what deductions I can, now on one subject, now on another. This is the right way, in my opinion, to find and explain the truth. The order of the subject-matter is good only for those whose reasoning is disjointed, and who can say as 267 much about one difficulty as about another. So I do not think that it would

---

1 Caterus (Johan de Kater), author of the First Set of Objections to the *Meditations*.

be useful, or even possible, to insert into my *Meditations* the answers to the objections which may be made to them. That would interrupt the flow and even destroy the force of my arguments. The majority of the objections would be drawn from things that are perceivable by the senses, whereas my arguments get their force chiefly from the need to withdraw one's thought from these things. So I have put Caterus' objections at the end, to show where any others which come might be placed.

But I hope that people will take their time in composing them; it does not matter if the treatise remains unpublished for two or three more years, for the manuscript is very ill written and can be seen by only one person at a time. Hence it seems to me that it would be useful to have twenty or thirty copies printed in advance. I would be glad to pay whatever it costs; I would have had it done here, if there were any publisher that I could trust; but I did not want the ministers of this country to see it before our theologians.

As for the style, I would be very glad if it were better than it is; but apart from grammatical faults, if there are any, or Gallicisms such as *in dubium ponere* for *revocare*, I am afraid that nothing could be changed without detriment to the sense. For instance, where the text has 'nempe quicquid hactenus ut maxime verum admisi, vel a sensibus vel per sensus accepi',[1] to add 'falsum esse'[2] as you suggest would entirely change the meaning, which is that I have got from the senses, or by the senses, all that up to now I have thought most true. It would not do so much harm to substitute 'erutis fundamentis' for 'suffosis', since both expressions are good Latin and mean more or less the same.[3] But it seems to me that the latter, which has only the single meaning which I want it to have, is at least as good as the former, which has several.

I will send you perhaps within a week an abstract[4] of the principal points concerning God and the soul, which can be printed in front of the *Meditations*, so that people can see where such matters are to be found. Otherwise I realize that many people will be annoyed at not finding in a single place all the things they are looking for. I shall be very glad to have M. Desargues as well for one of my judges, if he is willing to take the trouble, and I have more trust in him alone than in three theologians. I will not be at all unhappy to have many objections, because I feel sure they will serve to make the truth better known. Thank God, I have no fear of being unable to reply adequately. It is time to finish.

---

1 'Whatever I have till now accepted as most true, I have learnt from the senses or through the senses' (AT VII 18; CSM II 12).
2 'to be false'.
3 Namely 'demolishing or undermining the foundations'.
4 The Synopsis of the *Meditations*: AT VII 12–16; CSM II 9–11.

TO MERSENNE, 31 DECEMBER 1640 AT III

I received no letters from you by this post; but since I did not have time a   271
week ago to answer all your points, I will add now what I then left out.
First, I send you an abstract of my *Metaphysics*, which, if you approve, can
be prefaced to the six Meditations. After the preceding words 'will draw
the same conclusions from them as I do', there should be added 'But
because in the six following Meditations'. In the Abstract the reader will be   272
able to see all that I have proved of the immortality of the soul, and all that
I can add to it when I publish my *Physics*. Without wrecking the order I
could not prove that the soul is distinct from the body before proving the
existence of God.

You say that we do not know that the idea of a most perfect being may
not be the same as that of the corporeal world. This difficulty is easy to
solve in the same way as the soul is proved to be distinct from the body,
that is, because we conceive something altogether different in each case.
But for this purpose we have to form distinct ideas of the things we want to
judge about, and this is what most people fail to do and what I have mainly
tried to teach by my *Meditations*. But I will spend no longer on these
objections, because you promise to send me shortly all those which may be
made. I only ask you to be in no hurry about it: people who do not study
everything carefully, and who merely read the Second Meditation to find
out what I say of the soul, or the Third to find out what I say of God, will
very likely make objections out of difficulties which I have already
explained.

In the place where I put 'in accordance with the laws of my logic', please
put 'in accordance with the laws of the true logic'; it is near the middle of
my Replies to Caterus, where he objects that I have borrowed my argument from St Thomas.[1] The reason why I add 'my' or 'the true' to 'logic' is   273
that I have read theologians who follow the ordinary logic and †inquire
what God is before inquiring whether God exists†.

Where I wrote 'this power to have within us the idea of God could not
belong to our intellect if that, etc.', you are right that it would be better to
write 'the latter' instead of 'that'; it is about the fourth or fifth page of my
Reply to the Objections.[2] It is better also to put 'its cause' instead of 'cause'
in the following line, as you suggest.

What I say later, 'nothing can be in me, that is to say, in my mind, of
which I am not aware',[3] is something which I proved in my *Meditations*,

---

1 AT VII 107; CSM II 78. Here and throughout this letter Descartes quotes phrases from the
   Meditations and *Replies* in the original Latin.
2 AT VII 105; CSM II 77.
3 AT VII 107; CSM II 78.

and it follows from the fact that the soul is distinct from the body and that its essence is to think.

You find obscure the sentence where I say that whatever has the power to create or preserve something separate from itself has *a fortiori* the power to preserve itself.[1] But I do not see how to make it clearer without adding many words, which would be inelegant since I only mention the matter briefly by the way.

At the place where I speak of infinity, it is a good idea to insert, as you say, 'the infinite *qua* infinite can in no way be comprehended by us'.[2]

274   The world 'perhaps lacks limits as regards extension, but not as regards power, intelligence, etc. And so it does not altogether lack limits.'[3]

A little further on, we could, as you suggest, put '– a point on which there can be no doubt', after the expression 'something real', and add parentheses.[4] But as it stands it does not seem obscure to me; you could find a thousand places in Cicero which are more so.

It seems very clear to me that †possible existence is contained in everything which we clearly understand, because from the fact that we clearly understand something it follows that it can be created by God†.

As for the mystery of the Trinity, I share St Thomas' opinion that it is a sheer article of faith and cannot be known by the natural light. But I do not deny that there are things in God which we do not understand, just as even in a triangle there are many properties which no mathematician will ever know – which does not prevent everyone knowing what a triangle is.

It is certain that there is nothing in an effect †which is not contained formally or eminently in its E F F I C I E N T and T O T A L cause†.[5] I added these two words on purpose. The sun and the rain are not the total cause of the animals they generate.

I was finishing this when I received your last letter, which reminds me to

275   ask you to tell me if you know why you did not receive my *Metaphysics* by the post by which I sent it, or even with the letters which I wrote you a week later, and whether the packet was opened; for I gave it to the same postman.

Thank you for correcting 'majorem' to 'maius'. I am not surprised that there are such mistakes in my writing: I have often come across them myself; they happen when I am writing with my mind on something else. But I am surprised that three or four of my friends who read it did not notice the solecism.

1 AT VII 111; CSM II 80.
2 AT VII 112; CSM II 81.
3 These phrases do not appear in the published *Replies*.
4 AT VII 114; CSM II 82.
5 See AT VII 40; CSM II 28.

I have no objection to seeing what M. Morin has written about God, because you say that he uses a mathematical method. Between ourselves, however, I do not hope for much from it, because I never heard before that he went in for that sort of writing. Nor have I great hopes of the other books printed at la Rochelle. M. de Zuylichem[1] has returned, and if you send it to him with the paper written by the Englishman,[2] I can get them from him. But do ask him to send them on promptly, because he has so 276
much other business that he might forget.

I will not fail to answer immediately anything you send me about my *Metaphysics*. But otherwise I should be very glad to have as few distractions as possible, for the coming year at least, since I have resolved to spend it in writing my philosophy in an order which will make it easy to teach.[3] The first part, which I am working on at present, contains almost the same things as the *Meditations* which you have, except that it is in an entirely different style, and what is written at length in one is abbreviated in the other, and vice versa . . .

TO [POLLOT], MID JANUARY 1641   AT III

I have just learnt the sad news of your loss, and though I do not 278
undertake to say anything in this letter which could have any great power to soften your pain, I still cannot refrain from trying, so as to let you know at least that I share what you feel. I am not one of those who think that tears and sadness are appropriate only for women, and that to appear a stout-hearted man one must force oneself to put on a calm expression at all times. Not long ago I suffered the loss of two people who were very close to me,[4] and I found that those who wanted to shield me from sadness only 279
increased it, whereas I was consoled by the kindness of those whom I saw to be touched by my grief. So I am sure that you will listen to me better if I do not try to check your tears than if I tried to steer you away from a feeling which I consider quite justified. Nevertheless, there should be some moderation in your feelings, and while it would be barbaric not to be distressed at all when one has due cause, it would also be dishonourable to abandon oneself completely to grief; we do ourselves no credit if we do not strive with all our might to free ourselves from such a troublesome passion. The profession of soldiering, to which you were brought up, makes men used to seeing their best friends suffer untimely deaths, and there is nothing in

1 Constantijn Huygens.
2 Thomas Hobbes (1588–1679).
3 That is, in writing the *Principles of Philosophy*.
4 Descartes' daughter, Francine, died on 7 September 1640 and his father, Joachim, died on 17 October 1640. Descartes' elder sister Jeanne also died about this time; cf. AT IV 373n.

the world that is so distressing that we do not become inured to it in time. The loss of a brother, it seems to me, is not unlike the loss of a hand. You have already suffered the latter without, as far as I could see, being overwhelmed; so why should the former affect you so much more? If it is for your own sake, the loss of your brother is certainly the easier loss to make good, since acquiring a faithful friend can be as worth while as the friendship of a good brother. And if it is for your brother's sake – and your noble spirit would surely not allow you to be troubled on any other account – you know that neither reason nor religion gives us cause to fear that any harm can come after this life to those who have lived honourably, but that on the contrary they both hold out to such people the promise of
280   joys and rewards. In short, Sir, all our afflictions, whatever they may be, depend only to a very small extent on the reasons to which we attribute them; their sole cause is the emotion and internal disturbance which nature arouses within us. For when this emotion is quelled, even though all the reasons which we had earlier remain the same, we no longer feel upset. Now I certainly do not want to advise you to use all your powers of determination and steadfastness to check the internal agitation you feel straight away – for this would perhaps be a cure more troublesome than the original sickness. But equally I do not advise you to wait until time alone heals you, still less to sustain and prolong your suffering by your own thoughts. I ask you merely to try to alleviate the pain little by little, by looking at what has happened to you from whatever perspective can make it appear more bearable, while at the same time taking your mind off it as much as you can by other activities. I am well aware that I am telling you nothing new here. But we should not despise good remedies just because they are in common use; and since I have myself made successful use of this one, I felt myself bound to include it in this letter.

AT III

TO MERSENNE, 21 JANUARY 1641

(282)   . . . I shall be very pleased to receive yet more objections from learned critics, both philosophers and geometers, as indeed you tell me I may expect. But it will be a good thing if the later critics see what the earlier ones have said, including the material already sent to me, so that they do not repeat the same things. I think this is the best possible way of ensuring that if my readers find any difficulty at any point, they will find it clarified in my replies; for I hope I will be able to give a completely satisfactory
283   answer to all the difficulties, with God's help. Indeed, I am more worried that the objections put to me will be too feeble than that they will be too powerful. But, to follow the passage from St Augustine which you sent me, I cannot open the eyes of my readers or force them to attend to the things

which must be examined to ensure a clear knowledge of the truth; all I can do is, as it were, to point my finger and show where the truth lies.

Yesterday, M. de Zuylichem[1] sent me M. Morin's book, together with the three pages written by the Englishman. I have not yet read the former, but you will see what I say in reply to the latter.[2] I have put my comments on a separate sheet, so that you can let him see it, if you think it suitable, and also to avoid being obliged to answer the rest of the letter, which I do not yet have to hand. Between ourselves, I am sure it will not be worth the bother, and since the man claims to have some regard for me, I should be sorry to upset him. I am not worried that his philosophy resembles mine – although, like me, he wants to restrict his attention to shapes and movements. These are indeed the true principles, but if one makes mistakes in following them, the errors can be spotted very clearly by those with a modicum of understanding; so if we want to achieve success, we must not go as fast as he does. I pray God to keep you in health. We have had several people who have been ill here too, and in the past few days I have been wholly occupied in paying visits and writing letters of condolence.

I come back to your letter of 23 December, which I have not yet answered. The passage from Augustine relevant to the point at issue – namely that God is ineffable – depends merely on a small distinction which is very easy to understand. †We cannot encompass in words everything that is in God, or indeed grasp it in our minds, and hence God is ineffable and beyond our comprehension. But there are many things reallly in God, or which relate to God, which we are capable of reaching in our minds and expressing in words – more, indeed, than in the case of any other thing. And so in this sense God can be known and spoken of to a very great extent† ...

Be sure that there is nothing in my *Metaphysics* which I do not believe to be †either very evident by the natural light or else demonstrated very precisely†; and I am confident that I can make it understood by those who are able and willing to meditate on it. But I cannot bestow intelligence on people, or make them see what lies on the floor of a closet if they refuse to go in to have a look ...

To say that thoughts are merely movements of the body is as perspicuous as saying that fire is ice, or that white is black; for no two ideas we have are more different than those of black and white, or those of movement and thought. Our only way of knowing whether two things are different or identical is to consider whether we have different ideas of them, or one and the same idea ...

1 Constantijn Huygens.
2 Thomas Hobbes (1588–1679); see the following two letters.

AT III   TO MERSENNE FOR HOBBES, 21 JANUARY 1641

287   I have read part of the letter sent to your Reverence from England, which
was passed on to me here by M. de Zuylichem.[1] I am very surprised that
although from the way he writes the author shows himself to be an
intelligent and learned man, he seems to miss the truth in every single claim
which he puts forward as his own.

I pass over the first part, concerning the corporeal nature of the soul and
God, the 'internal spirit' and the other matters which do not concern me.
288   For though he may say that my 'subtle matter' is the same as his 'spirit', I
cannot grant this. Firstly, he makes his 'spirit' the cause of hardness,
whereas my subtle matter is, on the contrary, the cause of softness. Second,
I do not see how this supposedly very mobile spirit could be confined, as he
claims, within hard bodies, without ever emerging; nor do I see how it
could enter soft bodies when they become hard. But I come to the
comments on my *Optics*.[2]

First of all, he says that I would have put things more clearly if I had
spoken of determinate motion instead of the determination of motion. I do
not agree with him. For though it can be said that the speed of a ball going

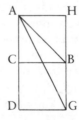

from A to B is made up of two other speeds, along the lines A C and A H, I
thought this way of putting it should be avoided, in case it should be
understood to imply that the quantity of the speeds in such composite
motion, and the proportion of one to the other, remains fixed; yet this is
certainly not the case. If, for example, we take a ball travelling horizontally
from A with one unit of speed, and vertically with one unit, it will reach B,
with two units of speed, at the same time as another ball, moving horizontally from A with one unit of speed and vertically with two units, arrives at
G with three units of speed. And it would follow from this that the ratio of
A B to A G is 2 to 3, whereas in fact it is 2 to root 10.[3] . . .

1 Constantijn Huygens.
2 See AT VI 93ff; CSM I 156.
3 Using Pythagoras' Theorem, Descartes is calculating as follows:
    $AB^2 = AC^2 + CB^2 = 1^2 + 1^2 = 2$
    $AG^2 = AD^2 + DG^2 = 2^2 + 1^2 = 5$
    Thus, $AB:AG = \sqrt{2}:\sqrt{5} = \sqrt{4}:\sqrt{10} = 2:\sqrt{10}$.

I am surprised that he adds that my demonstration is invalid, when he   (290)
produces no argument to attack it except the statement that certain points
are inconsistent with our experience, when in fact they square with
experience and are true in the highest degree. He seems not to have noticed
the difference there is between the deflection of a ball or other body falling   291
into water, and the refraction of light. In fact there is a very important
twofold difference. Firstly, one deflection is towards the perpendicular
while the other is away from it;[1] and since light rays pass more easily
through water than air by a factor equal to approximately a third of their
impetus, it does not follow that a ball must lose a third of its speed when
passing through the same water; in fact there is no connection between the
two. Secondly, the angle of refraction of feeble light in a given fluid is the
same as that of strong light; but it is quite different with a ball, which,
when thrown into water with a great force, cannot be deprived of as great a
proportion of its speed by the water as would be the case if it were moving
more slowly. So it is no surprise that he has observed a lead ball thrown off
a cliff with very great force, entering the water at an angle of five degrees;
for in such a case it probably loses less than a thousandth part of its
speed . . .

TO MERSENNE, 28 JANUARY 1641   AT III

This note is only to tell you that I am not able to send you my reply to the   293
objections[2] by today's post. This is partly because I have had other
business which has not left me a day free, and partly because the objectors
seem to have understood absolutely nothing of what I wrote, and merely to
have read it through post-haste. They merely oblige me to repeat what I
have already said, and this is more troublesome than if they had put
forward difficulties which gave more exercise to my mind. This is between
ourselves, because I should be very sorry to offend them, and you will see
by the trouble I take in replying that I consider myself indebted to them and
also to the author of the latest objections which I received only last
Tuesday.[3] (That was why I did not mention them in my last, because our
postman leaves on a Monday.)

I have read M. Morin's book.[4] Its main fault is that he always discusses

---

1 See fig. 6, !T vi 103; CSM i 163.
2 The Second Set of Objections to the *Meditations*, which were attributed in the first edition
  to 'theologians and philosophers', but were in fact largely the work of Mersenne.
3 The Third Set of Objections to the *Meditations*, by Thomas Hobbes.
4 Jean-Baptiste Morin, *Quod Deus sit Mundusque ab ipso Creatus fuerit in Tempore* ('The
  existence of God and his creation of the world in time') (1635).

the infinite as if he had completely mastered it and could comprehend its properties. This is an almost universal fault which I have tried carefully to avoid. I have never written about the infinite except to submit myself to it, and not to determine what it is or is not. Then, before giving any explana-

294   tion of controversial points, in his sixteenth theorem, where he sets about proving that God exists, he rests his argument on his alleged refutation of the earth's movement, and on the revolution of the whole sky around it, which he has in no way proved. He supposes also that there cannot be an infinite number, which he could never prove. Right up to the end, every-thing that he says is very far from the geometrical self-evidence and certainty which he seemed to promise at the beginning. This also is between ourselves, please, since I have no desire to hurt his feelings . . .

(295)   I claim that we have ideas not only of all that is in our intellect, but also of all that is in the will. For we cannot will anything without knowing that we will it, nor could we know this except by means of an idea; but I do not claim that the idea is different from the act itself.

There will be no difficulty, so far as I can see, in adapting theology to my style of philosophizing. I do not see that anything in it needs changing

296   except in the case of transubstantiation, which is very clear and easy to explain on my principles. I shall have to explain it in my *Physics*, along with the first chapter of Genesis; I propose to send my explanation to the Sorbonne to be examined before it is printed. If you think that there are other things which call for the writing of a whole new course of theology, and are willing to undertake this yourself, I shall count it a favour and do my best to help you . . .

(297)   I will be very glad if people put to me many objections, the strongest they can find, for I hope that the truth will stand out all the better from them. But if anyone wants to make fresh objections, please show them my replies and the objections which you have already sent to me, so that they will not put forward points which I have already answered.

I proved quite explicitly that God was the creator of all things, and I proved all his other attributes at the same time, because I proved his existence from the idea which we have of him; and also from the fact that since we have this idea in ourselves, we must have been created by him. But I see that people take more notice of the headings in books than of anything else. This makes me think that the title of the Second Meditation, 'The nature of the human mind', could have added to it 'how it is better known than the body', so that people will not think that I was intending to prove its immortality in that place. So in the Third: 'The existence of God'. And the Fifth: 'The essence of material things, and the existence of God considered a second time'. In the Sixth: 'The existence of material things, and the real distinction between mind and body'. These are the things that

I want people mainly to notice. But I think I included many other things besides; and I may tell you, between ourselves, that these six Meditations contain all the foundations of my physics. But please do not tell people, for that might make it harder for supporters of Aristotle to approve them. I hope that readers will gradually get used to my principles, and recognize their truth, before they notice that they destroy the principles of Aristotle. 298

TO MERSENNE, 4 MARCH 1641 AT III

. . . Now that I have read at leisure the last communication from the Englishman,[1] I find that the opinion I had of him when I wrote to you two weeks ago is completely confirmed. I think the best thing would be for me to have nothing more to do with him, and, accordingly, to avoid answering him. For if his temperament is what I think it is, it will be hard for us to exchange views without becoming enemies. It is far better for us both to leave things where they are. I beg you, moreover, not to tell him any more than you have to of what you know of my unpublished views; for unless I am very much mistaken, this is someone who is looking to acquire a reputation at my expense, and by sharp practice . . . 320

I sent you my book in order to have the gentlemen of the Sorbonne give their verdict on it and not to burden myself with arguing with every petty-minded critic who wants to enter the fray and ply me with objections. Nevertheless, if some swaggering warrior wants to enter the lists, so be it; I will not refuse to answer him if his comments are judged worthy of being printed. As for those who have produced the earlier comments,[2] I am obliged to them; if they want to comment further on my replies, I will be very happy to produce my own additional comments. I am not sending you my replies to M. Arnauld yet,[3] partly because I have had a lot of other things to do, and partly because I do not want to rush them; but I think I shall be ready to send them to you in a week. As soon as you receive them, I think it will be time to send all the material to the gentlemen of the Sorbonne to obtain their verdict, and then have it printed – at least if the verdict is favourable, as I hope it will be. For I think that too many objections will merely serve to fatten the book and spoil it, unless they are first rate. (328)

329

For the rest, please do not change anything in my copy without letting me know. It is extremely easy to make a misinterpretation – indeed, it could easily happen even to me: if I were looking at the phrases in

1 Thomas Hobbes.
2 Second Set of Objections to the *Meditations*.
3 Antoine Arnauld (1612–94), theologian and logician, and author of the Fourth Set of Objections to the *Meditations*.

isolation, as one does to insert full stops and commas, I might well mistake the sense of a word from time to time. Thus you told me two weeks ago that you had put 'intelligere' ['understand'] for 'adipisci' ['acquire'].[1] Since then my eye happened to light on this passage quite by chance – I think it is in the Third Meditation – and I find that 'adipisci' must be retained. For I have said earlier[2] that 'if I derived my existence from myself, I would be able not merely to understand but really to get for myself or *acquire* all the perfections of God' . . .

(329)   I must also ask you to correct these words, which come in my reply to the penultimate objection made by the theologian. 'We are unable to think of its existence as possible without at the same time thinking there can be some power by means of which it exists, and that power cannot be understood as residing in anything other than that same supremely powerful being; hence we conclude that it can exist by its own power.'[3] In place of that, put simply: 'When we attend to the immense power of this being,
330   we shall be unable to think of its existence as possible without also recognizing that it can exist by its own power.' But please correct it in all the copies in such a way that none will be able to read or decipher the words 'thinking there can be some power by means of which it exists, and that power cannot be understood as residing in anything other than that same supremely powerful being; hence we conclude'. For many people are more curious to read and examine words that have been erased than any other words, so as to see where the author thinks he has gone wrong, and to discover there some ground for objections, attacking him in the place which he himself judged to be the weakest.

Between ourselves, I think that this is why M. Arnauld paid so much attention to my statement that 'God derives his existence from himself in a positive sense.' I remember that my first draft of this passage was too crude; but in the later version I amended and refined it to such an extent that, had he merely read the corrections, without stopping to read the deleted words, he would perhaps have found nothing at all to say. For I do believe that everything is in fact quite in order. You yourself, when you read the passage the first time, wrote to me saying that you found it crudely expressed, but at the other end of the letter you remarked that after reading it a second time you found nothing to object to. I attribute this to your having paid attention, on your first reading, to the deleted words, which
331   are only lightly crossed through, whereas on the second reading you took

1 See A T vii 47; CSM ii 32, line 18.
2 In fact Descartes goes on to say this, or something close, *later* in the Third Meditation: A T vii 48; CSM ii 33.
3 First Replies: A T vii 119; CSM ii 85.

note only of the corrected version. But I shall explain this and other matters at more length in my reply to M. Arnauld, who has put me greatly in his debt by producing his objections. I think they are the best of all the sets of objections, not because they are more telling, but because he, more than anyone else, has entered into the sense of what I wrote. I had quite well foreseen that few people would grasp my meaning, given the small number who are willing or able to pause and meditate . . .

TO MERSENNE, 18 MARCH 1641   AT III

I am sending you at last my reply to the objections of M. Arnauld;[1] and I   334
ask you to change the following things in my *Metaphysics*, thus letting it be known that I have deferred to his judgement, so that others, seeing how ready I am to take advice, may tell me more frankly what reasons they have for disagreeing with me, and may be less stubborn in opposing me if they have none.

The first correction is in the Synopsis of the Fourth Meditation. After the words 'make intelligible what is to come later', please add 'But here it should be noted in passing that I do not deal at all with sin, i.e. the error which is committed in pursuing good and evil, but only with the error that   335
occurs in distinguishing truth from falsehood. And there is no discussion of matters pertaining to faith or the conduct of life, but simply of specula-tive truths which are known solely by means of the natural light.' Put the words between brackets so that it can be seen that they have been added.[2]

2. In the Sixth Meditation, page 96, after the words 'since I did not yet know the author of my being', please add, again in brackets, the words 'or at least I was pretending not to know'.[3]

3. Then, in my Reply to the First Objections, where I discuss whether God can be said to be caused by himself, at the words 'Hence if I thought that nothing could somehow have the same relation to itself . . .'[4] please put in the margin 'Note that these words mean only that there may be a thing whose essence is such that it needs no efficient cause in order to exist.'

4. A little further on, at the words 'Although God has always existed since it is he who in fact preserves himself', put in the margin 'It should also be noted that "preservation" here must not be understood to be the kind of

---

1 The Fourth Set of Objections to the *Meditations*.
2 See AT VII 15; CSM II 11. In the original letter, this and all subsequent quotations are from the Latin text of the *Meditations*.
3 AT VII 77; CSM II 53.
4 AT VII 108; CSM II 78.

336 preservation that comes about by the positive influence of an efficient cause; all that is implied is that the existence of God is such that he must always exist.'[1]

5. Three lines later there occur the words 'For there are some who think it is impossible for anything to be its own efficient cause, and hence . . .'. Please correct the text as follows: 'There are some who attend only to the literal and strict meaning of the phrase "efficient cause" and thus think it is impossible for anything to be the cause of itself. They do not see that there is any place for another kind of cause analogous to an efficient cause, and hence . . .'.[2] For I did not mean to say that 'Something could be its own efficient cause if "efficient" is taken in the strict sense'; I meant only that when we ask 'whether anything can exist "from itself"' the question must not be taken to concern 'efficient causality strictly so called, or it would be vacuous', as I said. It is because of the common scholastic axiom 'Nothing can be its own cause' that 'from itself' has not been taken in the appropriate sense. None the less, I did not want to blame the scholastics for this openly.

6. Please do not forget the correction which I mentioned in my last 337 letter, at the end of the same Replies: 'We are unable to think . . .'. For until my book is published, I think I have the right to change it as I think fit.

I also think that I have the right to make the following request. In M. Arnauld's Objections, towards the end of the one where he is inquiring 'whether God is the cause of himself', and he quotes my words 'Hence if I thought that nothing could have the same relation to itself', the quotation should read 'somehow have the same relation'. For the word 'somehow', which he has forgotten, changes the sense. I think it is better to ask you to insert it in his text than for me to accuse him in my Reply of quoting me inaccurately; especially as he seems to have left it out inadvertently, since he concludes 'Since it is quite evident that nothing can in any way stand in at all the same relation', where his 'in any way' corresponds to my 'somehow'.[3]

In the same way I might ask you, at the beginning of the same objection, where he quotes me as saying 'so that God in a sense stands in the same relation to himself', to put 'so that we are quite entitled to think that God in a sense stands', as my text has it.[4] A little further on, where he quotes me as saying 'such a restriction on the meaning of the term "efficient" does not

1 AT VII 109; CSM II 78.
2 AT VII 109; CSM II 79.
3 AT VII 213; CSM II 150.
4 AT VII 208; CSM II 146. The requested change was not made.

seem appropriate',[1] he quotes only the less important of the reasons I gave, and omits the main one, which is 'that the question would be vacuous'. But 338 I have quietly put this right in my reply; so it is less important to change it, and the change should not be made without his permission . . .

I leave you to take care of the titles of my *Metaphysics*; you will be, if you (340) please, its godfather. For the objections, it is a good idea to call them 'First Objections', 'Second Objections', and so on, and then to put 'Replies to the Objections' rather than 'Solutions' so as to leave the reader to judge whether my replies contain solutions or not. Let those who give false answers call them 'Solutions'; for it is usually those who are not nobly born who boast loudest of their nobility.

I am not yet sending you the last sheet of my Reply to M. Arnauld, where I give an explanation of transubstantiation according to my principles, because I want first to read the Councils on this topic, and I have not yet been able to obtain them.[2]

TO MERSENNE, 31 MARCH 1641   AT III

I have not much to tell you by this post, because I have not had a letter 349 from you; but I did not want to put off sending you the remainder of my reply to M. Arnauld's objections.[3] You will see that in it I reconcile the doctrine of the Councils about the Blessed Sacrament with my own philosophy – so much so that I maintain that it is impossible to give a satisfactory explanation of the doctrine by means of the traditional philosophy. Indeed, I think that the latter would have been rejected as clashing with the Faith if mine had been known first. I swear to you in all seriousness that I believe it is as I say. So I have decided not to keep silent on this matter, and to fight with their own weapons the people who confound Aristotle with the Bible and abuse the authority of the Church in order to vent their passions – I mean the people who had Galileo condemned. They 350 would have my views condemned likewise if they had the power; but if there is ever any question of that, I am confident I can show that none of the tenets of their philosophy accords with the Faith so well as my doctrines.

As soon as M. Arnauld has seen my Replies, I think it will be time to give the complete work to the doctors of the Sorbonne, so that it can be printed when they have expressed their opinion. I leave entirely to you such matters as the size of the volume, the type face, the titles I have left out, and

---

1 AT VII 209; CSM II 147.
2 The decrees of the Council of Trent (1545–63), a recognized authority on matters of Roman Catholic doctrine.
3 The Fourth Set of Objections to the *Meditations*.

any notes for the reader which need adding to what I have written. You have already taken so much trouble over the book that the greater part of it belongs to you . . .

 I send you a note for the publisher, which you will find is not dated from Leiden, because I no longer live there, but at a house half a league away.[1] I have retired here to work more easily both at philosophy and at experi-

351 mentation. You do not need to change the address on your letters – or rather you do not need to put any address except my name, because the Leiden postman knows where he should deliver them.

AT III   TO MERSENNE FOR HOBBES, 21 APRIL 1641

354 The communication from the Englishman which you sent me says that his 'spirit' and my 'subtle matter' are the same thing, that he arrived at an explanation of light and sounds using his method as early as 1630, and that he believes his results must have reached me. This is childish and ridiculous. If his philosophy is of a kind which makes him frightened that it will be stolen, let him publish it. As far as I am concerned, I will not hurry forward the publication of my own work one second on his account.

 His most recent arguments which you sent me in your letter are as bad as all the others I have seen from him. Firstly, granted that *man* and *Socrates* are not two different substances, nevertheless the term 'Socrates' means

355 something other than the term 'man', since it signifies individual or particular differentiating characteristics. Similarly, determinate motion is not different from motion, but nevertheless the determination is something other than the motion.

 Secondly, it is not true that the efficient cause of motion is also the efficient cause of the determination of motion. For example, If I throw a ball against a wall, the wall determines the ball to come back towards me, but it is not the cause of the motion.

 Thirdly, he employs a delicate subtlety in asking if the determination is in the motion 'as in a subject' – as if the question here were to establish whether motion is a substance or an accident. For there is no awkwardness or absurdity in saying that an accident is the subject of another accident, just as we say that quantity is the subject of other accidents. When I said that motion is to its determination as a flat body is to its top or surface, I certainly did not mean to compare the motion and the body as if they were

356 two substances; I was comparing them merely as one would compare two concrete things, to show that they were different from things which could be treated merely as abstractions.

1 At Endegeest.

Finally, it is very inept of him to infer that if one determination is altered, so must the others be, on the grounds that, as he puts it, 'all the determinations are merely one single accident under different names'. In that case it follows that on his view *man* and *Socrates* are merely a single thing under different names, and accordingly that no individual differentiating characteristic of Socrates could perish – for example his knowledge of philosophy – without his simultaneously ceasing to be a man.

What he goes on to say, namely that 'a motion has only one determination', is just like my saying that an extended thing has only a single shape. Yet this does not prevent the shape being divided into several components, just as can be done with the determination of motion . . .

TO MERSENNE, 21 APRIL 1641 {AT III}

. . . I am surprised at the objections of your doctors, namely that we have (359) no certainty, according to my philosophy, that the priest is holding the host at the altar, or that he has water to baptize, etc. Even among scholastic philosophers, whoever said that there was any more than moral certainty about such things? Theologians say that it is a matter of faith to believe that the body of Jesus Christ is in the Eucharist, but they do not say that it is a matter of faith to believe that it is in this particular host. For that you have to suppose, †as a matter of ordinary human credence, that the priest had the intention to consecrate, and that he pronounced the words, and is duly ordained, and other such things which are by no means matters of faith†.

Those who say that God continually deceives the damned,[1] and that he might similarly be continually deceiving us, contradict the foundation of 360 faith and all our belief, which is that †God cannot lie†. This is stated over and over again in so many places in St Augustine, St Thomas and others that I am surprised that any theologian denies it. They will have to abandon all certainty if they do not admit as an axiom that †God cannot deceive us†.

I wrote that indifference in our case is rather a defect than a perfection of freedom; but it does not follow that the same is the case with God. Nevertheless, I do not know that it is †an article of faith†[2] to believe that he is indifferent, and I feel confident that Father Gibieuf will defend my position well on this matter; for I wrote nothing which is not in accord with what he has said in his book *De Libertate*.[3]

1 See Sixth Objections: AT VII 415; CSM II 279.
2 Sixth Objections: AT VII 417; CSM II 281.
3 *De Libertate Dei et Creaturae* (1630).

I nowhere denied God's immediate concurrence in all things; indeed I explicitly affirmed it in my reply to the theologian.[1]

I did not think I should have made my Replies to the Englishman[2] any longer, since his objections seemed so implausible to me that to answer them at greater length would have been giving them too much importance.

361   The doctor who says that we can doubt whether or not we are thinking as well as we can doubt anything[3] is so much in conflict with the natural light that I am sure that no one who thinks about what he says will share his opinion.

You told me earlier that in my reply to the Englishman I use the word 'idea' two or three times very close to each other. It did not seem superfluous to me, because it refers to different ideas. Repetitions may be offensive in some places, but they are elegant in others.

The sense in which I include imaginations in the definition of *cogitatio* or thought differs from the sense in which I exclude them. [†]The forms or corporeal impressions which must be in the brain for us to imagine anything are not thoughts; but when the mind imagines or turns towards those impressions, its operation is a thought[†].

The earlier letter in which you wrote me objections about the *conarium*[4] must have been lost, unless you forgot to write them. I do not have any objections except your more recent ones, namely that no nerve goes to the *conarium* and that it is too mobile to be the seat of the common sense. In fact, these two things tell entirely in my favour. Each nerve is assigned to a particular sense or movement, some going to the eyes, others to the ears, arms, and so on. Consequently if the *conarium* were specially connected with one in particular, it could be inferred that it was not the seat of the common sense which must be connected to all of them in the same way.

362   The only way in which they can all be connected with it is by means of the spirits, and that is how they are connected with the *conarium*. It is certain too that the seat of the common sense must be very mobile, to receive all the impressions which come from the senses; but it must also be of such a kind as to be movable only by the spirits which transmit these impressions. Only the *conarium* fits this description.

Anima in good Latin signifies *air*, or *breath*; it is in a transferred sense, I think, that it means *mind*. That is why I said that it is 'often taken for a corporeal thing'.[5]

The axiom 'whatever can do the greater can do the lesser' applies only

1 See First Replies: AT VII 109; CSM II 79.
2 Thomas Hobbes, the author of the Third Set of Objections.
3 See Sixth Replies: AT VII 413; CSM II 278.
4 The pineal gland.
5 Cf. Med. II: AT VII 27; CSM II 18.

†in the same order of operations, or in things which require a single power†.[1] For †among men†, who doubts that a person who could not make a lantern may be able to make a good speech? . . .

TO REGIUS, MAY 1641   AT III

Our entire dispute concerning the threefold nature of the soul is more   369
verbal than real.

In the first place, a Roman Catholic is not allowed to say that the soul in man is threefold; and I am afraid that people will impute to me the views expressed in your thesis. So I would prefer you to avoid this way of talking.

Second, although the powers of growth and sensation may be primitive   370
acts in the case of animals, this is not so in the case of man, since the mind is prior to such acts, at least in respect of its status.

Third, although items falling under some general category may be regarded by logicians as divisions of the same genus, every general category of this sort is not a true genus. A classification is not sound unless the members of a true genus are divided into genuine species; and although the divisions may be opposed and different without this impugning the classification, there must not be too great a distance between them. For example, if someone were to separate the whole of the human body into two divisions, one of which contained just the nose, while the other contained all the other parts of the body, the classification would be faulty, just like yours, because of the excessive inequality of the divisions.

Fourth, I do not admit that the powers of growth and sensation in animals deserve the name 'soul', as does the mind in human beings. This common view is based on ignorance of the fact that animals lack a mind. So the term 'soul' is ambiguous as used of animals and of human beings . . .

TO REGIUS, MAY 1641   AT III

I certainly cannot complain that you and M. de Raey[2] have been so kind   371
as to place my name at the head of your theses; but on the other hand I do not know how I can thank you for it. I see only that it means further work for me. For people will believe henceforth that my opinions are the same as yours, and so I shall be unable to extricate myself from having to defend your propositions as best I can. So I shall have to examine with extreme care what you sent me to read, for fear of letting something pass which I would not wish to defend.

---

1 See Med. III: AT VII 48; CSM II 33.
2 Johannes de Raei (1622–1701), a pupil of Regius who had defended Cartesian theses in a public disputation at Utrecht.

The first thing which I cannot approve is your saying that 'men have a threefold soul'. In my religion this is a heretical thing to say; and quite apart from religion, it goes against logic to conceive the *soul* as a genus whose species are the *mind*, the *vegetative power* and the *locomotive power of animals*. When you speak of the *sensory soul* you can only mean the *locomotive power*, unless you are confusing it with the *rational soul*; but this *locomotive power* is not even of a different species from the *vegetative power*, and it belongs to a totally different genus from the *mind*. But since there is no real disagreement between us, I will tell you how I would explain the matter.

There is only one *soul* in human beings, the *rational soul*; for no actions can be reckoned human unless they depend on reason. The *vegetative power* and the *power of moving the body*, which are called the *vegetative* and *sensory souls* in plants and animals, exist also in human beings; but in the case of human beings they should not be called *souls*, because they are not the first principle of their actions, and they belong to a totally different genus from the *rational soul*.

372   The *vegetative power* in human beings is nothing but a certain arrangement of the parts of the body which, etc.

A little further on: The *sensory power*, etc.

Then: So these two are simply, in the human body, etc.

Then: And since the *mind, or rational soul*, is distinct from the body, etc., it is with good reason that it *alone* is called the *soul*.

Finally, where you say 'Willing and understanding differ only as different ways of acting in regard to different objects', I would prefer 'They differ only as the activity and passivity of one and the same substance.' For strictly speaking, understanding is the passivity of the mind and willing is its activity; but because we cannot will anything without understanding what we will, and we scarcely ever understand something without at the same time willing something, we do not easily distinguish in this matter passivity from activity.

Voetius' criticism on this point in no way tells against you. Theologians indeed say that no created substance is the immediate principle of its operation; but by this they mean that no creature can operate without the concurrence of God, and not that it needs some created faculty, distinct from itself, to operate by. It would be absurd to say that such a created faculty could be the immediate principle of an operation, while the substance itself could not.

In what you sent me I cannot find his other criticisms, and so I can make no judgement about them.

When you discuss colours, I cannot see why you exclude blackness, since the other colours too are only modes. I would simply say: 'Blackness

too is commonly counted as a colour, yet it is nothing but a certain   373
arrangement' . . .

To say of the passions that their seat is in the brain is very paradoxical
and even, I think, contrary to your own view. For although the spirits
which move the muscles come from the brain, the seat of the passions must
be taken to be the part of the body which is most affected by them, which is
undoubtedly the heart. So I would say: 'The principal seat of the passions,
in so far as they are corporeal, is in the heart, since that is principally
affected by them; but in so far as they affect also the mind, their seat is
solely in the brain, since the brain alone can directly act upon the mind.'

It is also paradoxical to say that 'reception is an action', when in fact it is
merely a passion, quite contrary to action. But what you write could
perhaps be retained with the following modification: 'Reception is an
automatic animal action, or rather passion, whereby we receive the movements of things; for here we are linking passions with actions, in order to
include under one category everything that occurs in man.'. . .

I do not agree with you when you define actions as 'operations per-   (374)
formed by man by the power of soul and body'. For I am one of those who
deny that man understands by means of the body. Nor am I impressed with   375
the argument you use to try to prove the contrary; for even though the
mind is hindered by the body, when it is a matter of understanding
immaterial things it cannot be helped by the body, but only hindered by
it . . .

TO MERSENNE, 16 JUNE 1641   AT III

I am not yet replying to the two little sheets of objections which you sent   382
me, because you tell me that I can combine them with some others which I
have not yet received, although you sent me them a week ago.[1] But the
person who asks what I meant by the word 'idea' seems to promise more
objections, and the way he begins makes me hope that the ones coming
from him will be the best and strongest that can be made. So in case he is
waiting for my reply to this before sending any others, you can tell him the   383
gist of it, which is as follows. I use the word 'idea' to mean everything
which can be in our thought, and I distinguish three kinds. †Some are
adventitious†, such as the idea we commonly have of the sun; †others are
constructed or made up†, in which class we can put the idea which the
astronomers construct of the sun by their reasoning; and †others are
innate, such as the idea of God, mind, body, triangle, and in general all
those which represent true, immutable and eternal essences. Now if from a

---

1 The Sixth Set of Objections to the *Meditations*.

constructed idea I were to infer what I explicitly put into it when I was constructing it, I would obviously be begging the question; but it is not the same if I draw out from an innate idea something which was implicitly contained in it but which I did not at first notice in it. Thus I can draw out from the idea of a triangle that its three angles equal two right angles, and from the idea of God that he exists, etc. So far from being a begging of the question, this method of demonstration is even according to Aristotle the most perfect of all, for in it the true definition of a thing occurs as the middle term†.

AT III   TO MERSENNE, 23 JUNE 1641

384   I am sending you the remainder of M. Gassendi's objections, together with my reply. In connection with which, please, if it is possible, have the said objections¹ printed before the author sees the reply I have produced. For between ourselves, I find that they contain so little good argument that I doubt if he will want to allow them to be printed, once he has seen my reply. For my part, I very much want them printed. Apart from the fact that I should be sorry to have wasted the time spent composing my reply, I have no doubt that those who believed that I would not be able to answer him would think that it was I who refused to have them published because I was unable to deal with the objections. I shall also be very happy for his name to go at the head of the objections, just as he has put it. Admittedly, should he be unwilling to allow this, he is entitled to prevent it, since the other objectors have not given their names; but he cannot prevent the objections being published. Could you please also give the publisher the same copy I have seen, for printing, so that there are no discrepancies . . .

(388)   You will see that I have done everything I could to deal with M. Gassendi in an honourable and considerate way. But he has given me so

389   many grounds to despise him, and to point out his lack of common sense and inability to argue in any rational manner, that I should have been lackadaisical in defending my own just cause if I had said any less than I did – and I assure you that I could have said a lot more.

AT III   TO MERSENNE, JULY 1641

(392)   . . . Is it possible that [your correspondent]² could not, as he says, understand what I mean by the idea of God, the idea of the soul, and the ideas of imperceptible things? I mean only what he must necessarily have

---

1 The Fifth Set of Objections to the *Meditations*.
2 The identity of the correspondent is not known; see the letter to Mersenne of 16 June 1641 (p. 183 above).

understood himself when he wrote to you that he did not understand my meaning. For he does not say that he had no conception corresponding to the expressions 'God', 'soul', 'imperceptible things'; he just says that he did not know what was to be understood by the idea of these things. But if he had any conception corresponding to these expressions, as he doubtless had, he knew at the same time what was to be understood by the ideas – namely nothing other than the conception which he himself had. For by 'idea' I do not just mean the images depicted in the imagination;[1] indeed, in so far as these images are in the corporeal imagination, I do not use that term for them at all. Instead, by the term 'idea' I mean in general everything   393 which is in our mind when we conceive something, no matter how we conceive it.

But I realize that he is not one of those who think they cannot conceive a thing when they cannot imagine it, as if this were the only way we have of thinking and conceiving. He clearly realized that this was not my opinion, and he showed that it was not his either, since he said himself that God cannot be conceived by the imagination. But if it is not by the imagination that God is conceived, then either one conceives nothing when one speaks of God (which would be a sign of terrible blindness) or one conceives him in another manner; but whatever way we conceive him, we have the idea of him. For we cannot express anything by our words, when we understand what we are saying, without its being certain thereby that we have in us the idea of the thing which is signified by our words.

It will be easy, then, for him to understand what I mean by the idea of God if he takes the word 'idea' in the way in which I said explicitly that I took it, and is not confused by those who restrict it to the images of material things formed in the imagination. I mean by the idea of God nothing but what all men habitually understand when they speak of him. This he must necessarily have understood himself; otherwise, how could he have said that God is infinite and incomprehensible and that he cannot be represented by our imagination? How could he affirm that these   394 attributes belong to him, and countless others which express his greatness to us, unless he had the idea of him? It must be agreed, then, that we have the idea of God, and that we cannot fail to know what this idea is, or what must be understood by it; because without this we could not know anything at all about God. It would be no good saying that we believe that †God exists†, and that some attribute or perfection belongs to him; this would be to say nothing, because it would convey no meaning to our mind. Nothing could be more impious or impertinent.

---

1 Fr. *fantaisie*, the term which Descartes frequently uses to denote the part of the brain in which the physiological processes associated with imagining take place.

In the case of the soul the matter is even clearer. As I have shown, the soul is nothing but a thing which thinks, and so it is impossible for us ever to think of anything without at the same time having the idea of our soul as a thing capable of thinking of whatever we think of. It is true that a thing of such a nature cannot be imagined, that is, cannot be represented by a corporeal image. But that is not surprising, because our imagination is capable of representing only objects of sense-perception; and since our soul has no colour or smell or taste, or anything which belongs to the body, it is not possible to imagine it or form an image of it. But that does not make it any less conceivable; on the contrary, since it is by means of it that we conceive all other things, it is itself more conceivable on its own than all other things put together.

395   Next, I must tell you that your friend has altogether missed my meaning when, in order to mark the distinction between the ideas in the imagination and those in the mind, he says that the former are expressed by terms, and the latter by propositions. It is not whether they are expressed by terms or by propositions which makes them belong to the mind or the imagination; they can both be expressed in either way. It is the manner of conceiving them which makes the difference: whatever we conceive without an image is an idea of the pure mind, and whatever we conceive with an image is an idea of the imagination. As our imagination is tightly and narrowly limited, while our mind has hardly any limits, there are very few things, even corporeal things, which we can imagine, even though we are capable of conceiving them. One might perhaps think that the entire science which considers only sizes, shapes and movements, would be most under the sway of our imagination. But those who have studied it at all deeply know that it rests not at all on the phantasms of our imagination, but only on the clear and distinct notions of our mind.

He infers from my writings that the idea of God must be expressed by the proposition 'God exists', and concludes that the main argument I use

396   to prove his existence is a simple begging of the question. How can he make such an inference? He must be very sharp-eyed to see something there which I never meant to say and which never entered my mind before I saw his letter. I based the proof of the existence of God on the idea which I find in myself of a supremely perfect being, which is the ordinary notion we have of him. It is true that the simple consideration of such a being leads us so easily to the knowledge of his existence that it is almost the same thing to conceive of God and to conceive that he exists; but none the less the idea we have of God, or of a supremely perfect being, is quite different from the proposition 'God exists', so that the one can serve as a means or premiss to prove the other.

In the same way it is certain that after having come to know the nature of our soul by the steps I used, and after having thus recognized that it is a spiritual substance – because I see that all the attributes which belong to spiritual substances belong to it – one does not have to be a great philosopher to conclude as I did that it is not corporeal. But one certainly needs to have a very open mind, and rather an extraordinary one too, to see that the conclusion does not follow from the premisses and to find some flaw in this argument. It is this that I ask him to show me, and that I hope to learn from him if he is willing to take the trouble to teach me. I for my part will not refuse him my little clarifications, if he needs them and is willing to proceed in good faith.

397

TO MERSENNE, 22 JULY 1641   AT III

I am sending you the Sixth Objections with my replies; and because the   415
objections are made up of various papers which you sent me at different times, I have copied them out in my own writing in the way it seemed they could most conveniently be combined . . .

With regard to printers' errors, I am well aware that they are not of great importance, and I assure you that I am no less in your debt for the care you have taken to correct them than I would be if every single one had been   416
eliminated. For I know the great trouble this has put you to, and also that it is morally[1] impossible to prevent some errors remaining none the less, particularly when dealing with someone else's writings.

I very much approve your having pruned what I put at the end of my reply to M. Arnauld, especially if this can help us to get a formal approval for the book.[2] But even if we do not get it, I am sure I will not be very upset . . .

I do not understand your question whether our ideas are expressed by a   (417)
simple term. Words are human inventions, so one can always use one or several to express the same thing. But I explained in my Reply to the First   418
Objections how a triangle inscribed in a square can be taken as a single idea or as several.[3] Altogether, I think that all those which involve no affirmation or negation are †innate† in us; for the sense-organs do not bring us anything which is like the idea which arises in us on the occasion of their stimulus, and so this idea must have been in us before.[4]

1 I.e. for all practical purposes. For Descartes' use of 'morally' in this sense, cf. *Principles*, Part IV, art. 205: AT VIIIA 327; CSM I 289.
2 See above, pp. 158f. for Descartes' hopes in this regard.
3 AT VII 118; CSM II 84.
4 See *Comments on a Certain Broadsheet*: AT VIIIB 359; CSM I 304.

AT III   TO [DE LAUNAY], 22 JULY 1641

(420)   . . . At the end of the last set of objections which I sent to Father
Mersenne, I spoke only of the most general reason why I think most people
have trouble recognizing the distinction that exists between the soul and
the body. This is as follows. The earliest judgements which we made in our
childhood, and later on the influence of traditional philosophy, have
accustomed us to attribute to the body many things which belong only to
the soul, and to attribute to the soul many thing which belong only to the
body. So people commonly mingle the two ideas of body and soul when
they construct the ideas of real qualities and substantial forms, which I
think should be altogether rejected. If you examine physics carefully, you
can reduce all those things in it which fall under the province of intellectual
knowledge to very few kinds, of which we have very clear and distinct
421   notions. Once you have considered them I do not think you can fail to
recognize whether, when we conceive one thing apart from another, this
happens only by an abstraction of our mind or because the things are truly
distinct. When things are separated only by a mental abstraction, you
cannot help noticing their conjunction and union when you consider them
together. But in the case of body and soul you cannot see any such
connection, provided you conceive them as they should be conceived, the
one as that which fills space, the other as that which thinks. Indeed after
the idea we have of God, which is very different from all those we have of
created things, I do not know any other pair of ideas in the whole of nature
which are as different from each other as these two. But here I am merely
putting forward my own opinion, and I do not have so high a regard for it
that I would not be ready to change it, if I could learn better from those
whose light is brighter than my own.

AT III   TO HYPERASPISTES, AUGUST 1641

422   Now that the objections I have so far received have been sent to the
printer, I had decided to keep any further objections which might come for
a second volume. But since your objections claim to exhaust all the points
that remain, I gladly hasten to reply to them so that they can be printed
with the others.[1]
         1. It would indeed be desirable to have as much certainty for the

---

1 The objections in question were against Descartes' Replies to the Fifth Set of Objections.
  The identity of the author, Hyperaspistes (the Greek word for 'champion'), evidently a
  supporter of Gassendi, is not known. In fact the objections and reply arrived too late to be
  included.

conduct of our lives as is needed for the acquisition of knowledge;[1] but it is easily shown that in such matters so much is not to be sought or hoped for. This can be shown *a priori* from the fact that a human, being a composite entity, is naturally corruptible, while the mind is incorruptible and immortal. It can be shown even more easily *a posteriori* from the consequences that would follow. Suppose that a man decided to abstain from all food to the point of starvation, because he was not certain that it was not poisoned, and thought that he was not bound to eat because it was not transparently clear that he had the means of keeping alive, and it was better to wait for death by abstaining than to kill himself by eating. Such a man would be rightly regarded as insane and responsible for his own   423 death. Suppose further that he could not obtain any food that was not poisoned, and that his nature was such that fasting was beneficial to him; none the less, if the food had appeared harmless and healthy, and fasting appeared likely to have its usual harmful effects, he would be bound to eat the food and thus follow the apparently beneficial course of action rather than the actually beneficial one. This is so self-evident to all that I am surprised that anyone could think otherwise.

2. I nowhere said 'because the mind acts less perfectly in infancy than in adulthood it follows that it is no less perfect'; so I cannot be criticized on that account.[2] But because it does not follow either that it is more imperfect, I had the right to criticize someone who had assumed that to be the case. I had reason to assert that the human soul, wherever it be, even in the mother's womb, is always thinking. What more certain or evident reason could be wished for than the one I gave? I proved that the nature or essence of the soul consists in the fact that it is thinking, just as the essence of the body consists in the fact that it is extended. Now nothing can ever be deprived of its own essence; so it seems to me that someone who denies that his soul was thinking during those periods when he does not remember having noticed it was thinking deserves no more attention than if he were to deny that his body was extended during those periods when he did not notice that it had extension. This does not mean, however, that I believe that the mind of an infant meditates on metaphysics in its mother's womb; not at all. We know by experience that our minds are so closely joined to   424

---

1 Hyperaspistes had objected to Descartes' admission that less certainty was needed for conduct than for speculation (AT VII 351; CSM II 243). It is more important, he said, to avoid sin than to avoid error in metaphysics: 'why then do you suppose or demand a lesser truth in morals than in science?' (AT III 398).

2 In the Fifth Replies Descartes had said '[From the fact] that the mind does not work so perfectly when it is in the body of an infant as it does when in an adult's body ... it does not follow that it is made more or less perfect by the body' (AT VI 354; CSM II 245). Hyperaspistes had objected 'it does not follow that it is *not*'.

our bodies as to be almost always acted upon by them; and although when thriving in an adult and healthy body the mind enjoys some liberty to think of other things than those presented by the senses, we know there is not the same liberty in those who are sick or asleep or very young; and the younger they are, the less liberty they have. So if one may conjecture on such an unexplored topic, it seems most reasonable to think that a mind newly united to an infant's body is wholly occupied in perceiving in a confused way or feeling the ideas of pain, pleasure, heat, cold and other similar ideas which arise from its union and, as it were, intermingling with the body. None the less, it has in itself the ideas of God, of itself and of all such truths as are called self-evident, in the same way as adult human beings have these ideas when they are not attending to them; for it does not acquire these ideas later on, as it grows older. I have no doubt that if it were released from the prison of the body, it would find them within itself.

This view does not involve us in any difficulties.[1] The mind, though really distinct from the body, is none the less joined to it, and is affected by traces impressed on it, and is able to impress new traces on its own account. This is no harder for us to understand than it is for those who believe in real accidents to understand, as they commonly do, that such accidents act on a corporeal substance while being quite different in kind from it. It makes no difference that these accidents are called corporeal. If 'corporeal' is taken to mean anything which can in any way affect a body, then the mind too must be called corporeal in this sense; but if 'corporeal' is taken to mean whatever is made up of the substance called body, then the mind cannot be said to be corporeal, but neither can those accidents which are supposed to be really distinct from body. It is only in this latter sense that the mind is commonly said not to be corporeal. Thus, when the mind joined to a body thinks of a corporeal thing, certain particles in the brain are set in motion. Sometimes this results from the action of external objects on the sense-organs, sometimes from the ascent of animal spirits from the heart to the brain, and sometimes from the mind's own action, when it is impelled simply of its own free will to a certain thought. The motion of these brain particles leaves behind the traces on which memory depends. But where purely intellectual things are concerned, memory in the strict sense is not involved; they are thought of just as readily irrespective of whether it is the first or second time that they come to mind – unless, as often happens, they are associated with certain names, in which case, since the latter are corporeal, we do indeed remember them. But there are

425

1 In his objection, Hyperaspistes had stressed the difficulty in conceiving the relation between incorporeal thoughts in the mind and corporeal traces in the brain.

many other points to be noted on this topic which cannot now be explained in detail.

3. I did distinguish between what belongs to me, or to my nature, and what belongs only to my awareness of myself; but it cannot be deduced from this that my metaphysics reaches no conclusions apart from those pertaining to the latter. Nor do the other objectionable conclusions follow. It is easy for the reader to tell when I was discussing merely such awareness, and when I was discussing the truth about the world.[1]

I never used the word 'believe' when the topic was knowledge;[2] the word does not even occur in the passage here cited.[3] In the reply to the Second Objections I said 'when we are supernaturally illumined by God, we are confident that what is put forward for us to believe has been revealed by God himself'; but there I was speaking not of human know-   426
ledge, but of faith.[4] And I did not assert that by the light of grace we clearly know the very mysteries of faith – though I would not deny that this too may happen – but only that we are confident that they are to be believed. No one who really has the Catholic Faith can doubt or be surprised that it is most evident that what God has revealed is to be believed and that the light of grace is to be preferred to the light of nature. The further questions on this topic do not concern me,[5] since I gave no occasion in my writings for them to be asked. Earlier, in the Reply to the Second Objections I stated that I would not reply to such questions, and so I will say no more about them here.[6]

4. The fourth objection rests on something I nowhere say, namely 'that the highest point of my certainty is when we think we see something so clearly that the more we think about it, the truer it seems'. So there is no need for me to answer what follows; though an answer could easily be given by anyone who distinguishes the light of faith from the natural light and prefers the former to the latter.[7]

---

1 See Fifth Replies (AT VII 357; CSM II 247) and Med II (AT VII 27; CSM II 18).
2 Lat. *scientia*, Descartes' term for systematic knowledge based on indubitable foundations.
3 Hyperaspistes had accused Descartes of teaching, in the Second Replies, that one should not believe anything unless one clearly saw that what was proposed for belief was true. This, he said, would erase the distinctions between knowledge and belief, and between belief and faith.
4 AT VII 148; CSM II 105.
5 Hyperaspistes asked Descartes' opinion about non-Catholic martyrs. 'Do you think that you or anyone perceive the truth of the mystery of the Trinity more clearly than the contrary appears to a Jew or an Aryan?'
6 Cf. AT VII 428f; CSM II 289.
7 Hyperaspistes had objected that Descartes had given no method by which a man may know whether he clearly perceives something or not. Turks think they see clearly that the doctrine of the Trinity is false, and claim that nothing in geometry or metaphysics is clearer.

5. The fifth objection too rests on something I nowhere say.[1] I utterly deny that we do not know what a thing is, or what thought is, or that I need to teach people this. It is so self-evident that there is nothing which could serve to make it any clearer. Finally I deny that we think only of corporeal things.

427   6. It is quite true that we do not understand the infinite by the negation of limitation; and one cannot infer that, because limitation involves the negation of infinity, the negation of limitation involves knowledge of the infinite. What makes the infinite different from the finite is something real and positive; but the limitation which makes the finite different from the infinite is non-being or the negation of being. That which is not cannot bring us to the knowledge of that which is; on the contrary, the negation of a thing has to be perceived on the basis of knowledge of the thing itself. When I said that it is enough for us to understand a thing which is bounded by no limits in order to understand the infinite, I was following a very common usage. Similarly, I kept the term 'infinite', when 'the greatest being' would be more correct if we wanted all names to conform to the nature of the things in question.[2] But usage demanded that I use the negation of a negation. It was as if, to refer to the largest thing, I had said it was not small, or had no smallness in it. But by this I did not mean that the positive nature of the infinite was known through a negation, and so I did not contradict myself at all.

I did not deny that there is a power in the mind of amplifying the idea of things;[3] but I frequently insisted that the ideas thus amplified, or the power of so amplifying them, could not be in the mind unless the mind itself came from God, in whom there really exist all the perfections which can be

428   reached by such amplification. I proved this from the principle that there can be nothing in an effect which was not previously present in the cause. And no one who deserves to be called a subtle philosopher in this field thinks that atoms exist of themselves. For it is clear by the natural light that there can be only one supreme being independent of everything else.

When it is said that a spinning top does not act upon itself, but is acted upon by the absent whip, I wonder how one body can be acted upon by

---

1 The fifth objection was against the *cogito, ergo sum*. 'Is it possible for you to understand a proposition without understanding its subject and predicate? But you do not know what is meant by "thing", what is meant by "exist", what is meant by "thought". Otherwise you would say so clearly what they are that I too would clearly perceive the truth of that proposition. Moreover, you do not know whether it is you yourself who think or whether the world-soul in you does the thinking, as the Platonists believe' (AT III 403).

2 AT VII 369; CSM II 254.

3 Descartes had said (AT VII 370; CSM II 255) that the mind's power of amplifying perfections must have come from God. Hyperaspistes asked 'Could it not come from the mind itself as an eternal and independent substance?'

another which is absent, and how activity and passivity are to be distinguished.¹ For I admit I am not subtle enough to grasp how something can be acted upon by something else that is not present – which may, indeed, be supposed not to exist any more, like the whip if it should cease to exist after whipping the top. Nor do I see why we could not as well say that there are now no activities in the world at all, but that all the things which happen are passivities of the activities there were when the world began. But I have always thought that it is one and the same thing which is called an activity in relation to a *terminus a quo*² and a passivity in relation to a *terminus ad quem* or *in quo*.³ If so, it is contradictory that there should be a passivity without an activity for even a single moment. Finally, I agree that the ideas of corporeal things – indeed of everything in the whole visible world, though not, as you say in your objection, of the visible world itself – could be produced by the human mind; but it does not follow that we cannot know whether there is in the nature of things anything corporeal. It is not my views, but conclusions wrongly deduced from them, that lead to difficulties. I proved the existence of material things not from the fact that we have ideas of them but from the fact that these ideas come to us in such a way as to make us aware that they are not produced by ourselves but come from elsewhere.

429

7. I say first that in Bologna spar⁴ the light of the sun is not preserved, but the sun's rays kindle a new light which can afterwards be seen in shadow. Secondly, it would not follow that anything can be kept in being without the influence of God, for truths may often be illustrated by a false example, and it is much more certain that nothing can exist without the concurrence of God than that there can be no sunlight without the sun. There is no doubt that if God withdrew his concurrence, everything which he has created would immediately go to nothing; because all things were nothing until God created them and lent them his concurrence. This does not mean that they should not be called substances, because when we call a created substance self-subsistent we do not rule out the divine concurrence⁵ which it needs in order to subsist. We mean only that it is the kind of thing that can exist without any other created thing; and this is something

---

1 Hyperaspistes had objected to Descartes' giving a spinning top as an example of an agent acting on itself (AT VII 367; CSM II 253).
2 'The source of the action'.
3 'The destination of the action or its locus of reception'.
4 Descartes had said that creatures could not be kept in being without a continuous action of God, just as light would fail if the sun stopped shining (AT VII 369; CSM II 254). Hyperaspistes countered that phosphorescent substances, like Bologna spar, could shine in a closed room.
5 The continuous divine action needed to maintain things in existence: cf. AT VII 14; CSM II 10.

that cannot be said about the modes of things, like shape and number. It is not the case that God would be showing the immensity of his power if he made things which could exist without him later on; on the contrary, he would thus be showing that his power was finite, since things once created would no longer depend on him. I agree that it is impossible that God should destroy anything except by withdrawing his concurrence, because otherwise he would be tending towards non-being by a positive activity. But in admitting that, I am not falling into any trap of my own devising. For there is a great difference between what happens by God's positive 430 activity and what results from the cessation of his positive activity: the former cannot be anything but excellent, and the latter includes evils and sins and the destruction of some being, if any existent being is ever destroyed.

There is no force in what you say about the nature of a triangle.[1] As I have insisted in several places, when God or the infinite is in question, we must consider not what we can comprehend – for we know that they are quite beyond our comprehension – but only what conclusions we can reach by an argument that is certain. To find what kind of causal dependence these truths have on God, see my replies to the Sixth Objections, article 8.[2]

8. I do not remember ever having written, or even thought, what is here attributed to me.[3]

9. I do not remember that I ever expressed surprise 'that not everybody is aware of the idea of God in himself'; for I have often observed that what men judge does not accord with what they understand.[4] I do not doubt that everyone has within himself an implicit idea of God, that is to say, an aptitude to perceive it explicitly; but I am not surprised that not everyone is aware that he has it or notices that he has it. Some people will perhaps not notice it even after reading my *Meditations* a thousand times. In the same way, people judge that so-called empty space is nothing; all the same they conceive it as a positive thing. Similarly, when people think that accidents are real, they are representing them to themselves as substances, even though they do not judge them to be substances; and in many other 431 matters people's judgements disagree with their perception. But if we never make any judgement except about things we clearly and distinctly

1 Hyperaspistes had argued against Descartes' doctrine of the free creation of eternal truths. 'Let God do whatever he can; let us suppose *per impossibile*, that he never thought of a triangle; yet suppose you are in the world as you now are: would you not agree that it was true that the three angles of a triangle equal two right angles?'
2 AT VII 425; CSM II 287.
3 That an infinite series of subordinate causes is impossible.
4 See Fifth Replies: AT VII 374; CSM II 257.

perceive – a rule which I always keep as well as I can – then we shall be incapable of making different judgements at different times about the same thing. It is true that things which are clear and beyond doubt appear more certain to us the more often and the more attentively we think of them; but I do not remember that I ever put this forward as the criterion of clear and indubitable certainty. I do not know where the word 'always' occurs in the way mentioned here; but I know that when we say we *always* do something, we do not usually mean that we do it eternally, but only that we do it whenever the occasion presents itself.[1]

10. It is self-evident that we cannot know God's purposes unless God reveals them. From the human point of view adopted in ethics, it is true that everything was made for the glory of God, in the sense that we must praise God for all his works; and it is true that the sun was made to give us light, in the sense that we see that the sun does give us light. But it would be childish and absurd for a metaphysician to assert that God, like some vainglorious human being, had no other purpose in making the universe than to win men's praise; or that the sun, which is many times larger than the earth, was created for no other purpose than to give light to man, who occupies a very small part of the earth.   432

11. Here there is a confusion between the functions of the intellect and the will. The function of the will is not to understand, but only to will; and though, as I agreed before, we never will anything of which we have no understanding at all, yet experience shows clearly that about any given thing our will may extend further than our knowledge. Again, falsehood is never apprehended as truth, and those who deny that we have an idea of God do not really apprehend this even though perhaps they affirm it, believe it and argue for it. As I remarked before, in answer to objection 9 above, people's judgements often do not accord with their perception or apprehension.

12. I do not need to take great pains to answer here, since nothing is objected to me save the authority of Aristotle and his followers; and I do not hide the fact that I trust him less than I trust reason.[2]

It does not matter whether a man born blind has the ideas of colours or not, and it is pointless to cite the testimony of a blind philosopher.[3] For let

---

1 Hyperaspistes had asked why Descartes was certain he had the idea of God, since others denied having such an idea, and Descartes himself could not be sure, short of eternal experience, that he would *always* think as he now thought.
2 Hyperaspistes had quoted the Aristotelian dictum that nothing is in the intellect which was not first in the senses.
3 Arguing for empiricism, Hyperaspistes had said 'Has anyone born blind ever perceived anything of light and colour? Of course not, as our three hundred blind men at Paris will testify, including a philosopher who, when I asked him, said he could not conceive of colour or light.'

us suppose that he has ideas exactly like our ideas of colours: he still cannot know that they are like ours, or that they are called ideas of colours, because he does not know what ours are like. I do not see how I am in any worse position than you here, because even though the mind is indivisible, it is none the less capable of acquiring various properties. It is not surprising that it does not construct in sleep demonstrations like those of

433 Archimedes;[1] for even in sleep it is still united to the body and is no freer than during waking life. Keeping awake for a long time does not make the brain more fit to retain the traces impressed on it. In sleep and waking life alike, traces are better retained the more strongly they are impressed. And so sometimes we remember even dreams, but we remember better what we have thought in waking life. The reasons for this will be clear in my *Physics*.

13. When I said that God is his own existence,[2] I was using the regular theological idiom, which means that it belongs to God's essence to exist. The same cannot be said of a triangle, whose whole essence can be correctly understood even if it be supposed that in reality there is no such thing.

I said that the sceptics would not have doubted the truths of geometry if they had duly recognized God, because since those geometrical truths are very clear, they would have had no occasion to doubt them if they had known that whatever is clearly understood is true. Now this last is contained in a sufficient acquaintance with God, and that is the premiss which they do not have ready at hand.

The question whether a line consists of points or segments is irrelevant and need not be answered here.[3] I must remark, however, that in the place cited, page 543,[4] I was not talking about any and every geometrical topic, but only about those demonstrations which the sceptics doubted even though they clearly understood them. You cannot have a sceptic saying 'Let the evil demon deceive me as much as he can,'[5] because anyone who

434 says this is by that token not a sceptic, since he does not doubt everything. Certainly I have never denied that the sceptics themselves, as long as they clearly perceive some truth, spontaneously assent to it. It is only in name,

---

1 Hyperaspistes had said it should do this if the senses were a hindrance rather than a help.
2 AT VII 383; CSM II 263.
3 Hyperaspistes had tried to show that either supposition led to absurdity, and thus to generate sceptical doubts about geometry.
4 AT VII 384; CSM II 263.
5 Hyperaspistes had said that a sceptic could say 'Let the evil demon deceive me as much as he can, he will never deceive me about this geometrical proposition' – echoing Descartes' assertion 'let whoever can do so deceive me, he will never bring it about . . . that two and three added together are more or less than five' (AT VII 36; CSM II 25).

and perhaps in intention and resolve, that they adhere to their heresy of doubting everything. But I was dealing only with things which we remember having clearly perceived earlier, not with those which we clearly perceive at the present moment, as can be seen on pages 84 and 344.[1]

14. The mind is co-extensive with an extended body even though it has itself no real extension in the sense of occupying a place and excluding other things from it. How this can be, I explained above by the illustration of heaviness conceived as a real quality. I also showed above that when Ecclesiastes says that man has no advantage over a beast of burden, he is speaking only of the body; for immediately afterwards he goes on to deal separately with the soul, saying 'Who knows if the spirit of the sons of Adam . . .'.[2]

You ask how to tell which way of conceiving things is more imperfect and more revealing of the weakness of our mind: being unable to conceive one thing without another (e.g. the mind without the body) or conceiving each thing as complete, apart from the other. You must consider which of these proceeds from a positive faculty and which is caused by our lacking the same faculty. Then it is easy to understand that it is through a real faculty of the mind that it perceives two things, one apart from the other, as complete things; and that it is through a lack of the same faculty that the mind apprehends these two things merely in a confused manner, as a single thing. In the same way, eyesight is more perfect when it distinguishes accurately between the different parts of an object than when it perceives them all together as a single thing. Of course someone whose eyes are unsteady may take one thing for two, as people often do when drunk; and philosophers may do the like, not when they distinguish essence from existence – because normally they do not suppose any greater distinction between them than there really is – but when in the same body they make a distinction between the matter, the form and the various accidents as if they were so many different things. In such cases the obscurity and confused nature of the perception makes it easy for them to realize that it arises not only from a positive faculty but also from a defect of some faculty; if they paid more careful attention they would notice that they do not have completely distinct ideas of the things they thus suppose to be distinct.

435

If all the places insufficiently explained in my previous replies have been noted in these objections, I am much indebted to their author for giving me grounds to hope that no more objections will be forthcoming.

---

1 AT VII 69, 245; CSM II 48, 171.
2 Ecclesiastes 3:19–21. Cf. Sixth Replies: AT VII 431; CSM II 291.

AT III TO MERSENNE, SEPTEMBER 1641

436   I am very much in your debt for all the trouble you put yourself to for my sake, and for the concern you show yourself to have for my interests. But since I have far less of the latter than you, I should think myself guilty of an injustice if I did not beg you to ignore completely whatever you may hear against me, and not even bother to listen to it, or write to me about it. For my part, I have long known that there are fools abroad in the world, and I have so little regard for their judgement that I should be extremely sorry to lose a single moment of my leisure or my peace and quiet on their account.

As for my *Metaphysics*,[1] I have completely stopped thinking about it since the day I sent you my answer to Hyperaspistes[2] – so much so that I have not picked up the work since then. So I cannot answer a single one of the queries you sent me in your letter last week, except to say that I beg you not to give them any more thought than I do. In publishing the book I did what I thought I had to for the glory of God and to satisfy the demands of my conscience. If my project has failed, and there are too few people in the

437   world capable of understanding my arguments, it is not my fault: the arguments are no less true for that. But it would be my fault if I got angry, or used up more time answering the irrelevant objections of those who have been in touch with you . . .

(438)   I beg you once more not to send me any more objections against my *Metaphysics*, or indeed regarding my *Geometry* or similar matters, or at least not to continue to expect me to compose any more replies.

AT III TO MERSENNE, 17 NOVEMBER 1641

448   I have not received any letters from you by the two most recent deliveries, and I have little to say in reply to the letters I had received earlier. But I must tell you that my *Meditations* are being printed in this country. One of my friends had told me that several houses wanted to publish them, and that I could not stop it, since the licence to publish owned by Soli is valid only for France, and they are so free here that even a licence for the States[3] would not hold them back. So I preferred there to be one publisher who would undertake it with my approval and my corrections, and who by advertising the project would stop the plans of others; this seemed better than letting an edition come out without my knowledge, which would be bound to be full of mistakes. So I have given my permission to one of the Elzevirs who lives in Amsterdam to print it, on condition that he does not

1 The *Meditations*.
2 See pp. 188ff. above.
3 I.e. the United Provinces of the Netherlands.

send any copies to France so as not to do any wrong to Soli. I have no cause, however, to be very satisfied with Soli: it is now three months since the book was published, and he has still not sent me any copies.[1] . . .

My only question to you is whether you think it appropriate that I should restore the cuts you made from the end of my reply to M. Arnauld regarding the Eucharist[2] and whether I should include the objections of 'Hyperaspistes' with my reply. Also, should I put under the title 'Second Edition, with corrections and additions to the first edition published in Paris'? The new edition will not be ready for two months, and if the 100 copies which you told me Soli would be dispatching are already on their way, they can easily be sold during that time; if they are not on their way, he can keep them if he wishes . . . 449

450

TO REGIUS, DECEMBER 1641 AT III

I have received your theses, and I thank you; I find nothing in them which I do not agree with. What you say about actions and passions presents no difficulty, I think, provided the terms are understood correctly. For in corporeal things, all actions and passions consist simply in local motion; we call it an 'action' when the motion is considered in the body that imparts the motion, and a 'passion' when it is considered in the body that is moved. It follows from this that when the terms are extended to immaterial things, there is something in such things which has to be considered as analogous to motion. So we should use the term 'action' for what plays the role of a moving force, like volition in the mind, while we apply the term 'passion' to what plays the role of something moved, like intellection and vision in the same mind. Those who think perception should be called an action are apparently taking the term 'action' to mean any real power, and the term 'passion' to mean the mere negation of a power; for since they think perception is an action, they would no doubt say that the reception of motion in a hard body, or the power whereby it receives the motions of other bodies, is an action. Yet it is incorrect to say this, since the 'passion' correlative to this action would exist in the body imparting the motion, while the 'action' would be in the body that is moved. Those who say that every action can be taken from that which acts are correct if by 'action' they mean merely motion, but incorrect if they mean to include every kind of power under the term 'action'. For length, breadth and depth, and the power of receiving all kinds of shapes and motions, cannot be taken from matter or quantity, any more than thought can be taken from a mind . . . 454

455

---

1 The *Meditations* was published by Michel Soli at Paris on 28 August 1641.
2 The cuts made by Mersenne to the Fourth Replies were in fact restored in the second edition. See AT VII 253–6; CSM I 176–8 and 177n.

460   In your theses[1] you say that a human being is an *ens per accidens*.[2] You could scarcely have said anything more objectionable and provocative. The best way I can see to remedy this is for you to say that in your ninth thesis you considered the whole human being in relation to the parts of which he is composed, and in your tenth thesis you considered the parts in relation to the whole. Say too that in your ninth you said that a human being comes into being *per accidens* out of body and soul in order to indicate that it can be said in a sense to be accidental for the body to be joined to the soul, and for the soul to be joined to the body, since the body can exist without the soul and the soul can exist without the body. For the term 'accident' means anything which can be present or absent without its possessor ceasing to exist – though perhaps some accidents, considered in themselves, may be substances, as clothing is an accident with respect to a human being. Tell them that in spite of this you did not say that a human being is an *ens per accidens*, and you showed sufficiently, in your tenth thesis, that you understood it to be an *ens per se*. For there you said that the body and the soul, in relation to the whole human being, are incomplete substances; and it follows from their being incomplete that what they constitute is an *ens per se*. That something which is an *ens per se* may yet come into being *per accidens* is shown by the fact that mice are generated, or come into being, *per accidens* from dirt, and yet they are *entia per se*. It may be objected that it is not accidental for the human body to be joined to

461   the soul, but its very nature; because if the body has all the dispositions required to receive a soul, which it must have to be strictly a human body, then short of a miracle it must be united to a soul. Moreover, it may be objected that it is not the soul's being joined to the body, but only its being separated from it after death, which is accidental to it. You should not altogether deny this, for fear of giving further offence to the theologians; but you should reply that these things can still be called accidental, because when we consider the body alone we perceive nothing in it demanding union with the soul, and nothing in the soul obliging it to be united to the body; which is why I said above that it is accidental in a sense, not that it is absolutely accidental.

A simple alteration is a process which does not change the form of a subject, such as the heating of wood; whereas generation is a process which changes the form, such as setting fire to the wood. Although both

---

1 Regius had recently defended a number of theses which gave offence to orthodox thinkers at the University of Utrecht, and in particular Voetius.

2 Literally 'an entity by accident', i.e. a thing whose unity is purely contingent, in contrast to an *ens per se* ('an entity by itself'), a being which has an essential unity.

kinds of process come about in the same way, there is a great difference in the way of conceiving them and also in reality. For forms, at least the more perfect ones, are collections of a number of qualities with a power of mutual preservation. In wood there is only moderate heat, to which it returns of its own accord after being heated; but in fire there is strong heat, which it always preserves as long as it is fire.

You should not be angry with the colleague who advised you to add a corollary to explain your thesis: it seems to me that it was a friendly piece of advice.

You left out a word in the tenth of your handwritten theses. You say 'all the others', and you do not say what these are: you mean 'all the other qualities'.

I have nothing to say about the rest. There is hardly anything in them   462 which you have not put forward elsewhere; that is something I am glad to see. It would be a great task to want always to find something new.

If you come here, I will always be very pleased to see you.

TO GIBIEUF, 19 JANUARY 1642   AT III

... My hope has never been to gain the approval of the learned as a body.   (473) I have long since known and predicted that my views would not be to the taste of the multitude, and that where a majority held sway, they would be readily condemned. Nor have I desired the approval of individuals, since I should be sorry if they did anything on my account which might be disagreeable in the eyes of their colleagues; moreover, books no more heretical than mine have generally gained approval so easily that I believe that any reason which might lead to a judgement against me would not be   474 to my disadvantage. But this did not stop me offering my *Meditations* to your Faculty for thorough scrutiny; for if such a celebrated body could not find any good reason to criticize the work, this would give me further assurance of the truths it contained.

You inquire about the principle by which I claim to know that the idea I have of something is not †an idea made inadequate by an abstraction of my intellect†.¹ I derive this principle purely from my own thought or aware- ness. I am certain that I can have no knowledge of what is outside me except by means of the ideas I have within me; and so I take great care not to relate my judgements immediately to things, and not to attribute to things anything positive which I do not first perceive in the ideas of them. But I think also that whatever is to be found in these ideas is necessarily also in the things themselves. So, to tell whether my idea has been made

1 Cf. First Replies: AT VII 120; CSM II 86.

incomplete or †inadequate† by an abstraction of my mind, I merely look to see whether I have derived it, not from some thing outside myself which is more complete, but †by an intellectual abstraction† from some other, 475   richer or more complete idea which I have in myself. This intellectual abstraction consists in my turning my thought away from one part of the contents of this richer idea the better to apply it to the other part with greater attention. Thus, when I consider a shape without thinking of the substance or the extension whose shape it is, I make a mental abstraction. I can easily recognize this abstraction afterwards when I look to see whether I have derived this idea of the shape on its own from some other, richer idea which I also have within myself, to which it is joined in such a way that although one can think of the one without paying any attention to the other, it is impossible to deny one of the other when one thinks of both together. For I see clearly that the idea of the shape in question is joined in this way to the idea of the corresponding extension and substance, since it is impossible to conceive a shape while denying that it has an extension, or to conceive an extension while denying that it is the extension of a substance. But the idea of a substance with extension and shape is a complete idea, because I can conceive it entirely on its own, and deny of it everything else of which I have an idea. Now it seems to me very clear that the idea which I have of a thinking substance is complete in this sense, and that I have in my mind no other idea which is prior to it and joined to it in 476   such a way that I cannot think of the two together while denying the one of the other; for if there were any such within me, I must necessarily know it. You will say perhaps that the difficulty remains, because although I conceive the soul and the body as two substances which I can conceive separately, and which I can even deny of each other, I am still not certain that they are such as I conceive them to be. Here we have to recall the rule already stated, that we cannot have any knowledge of things except by the ideas we conceive of them; and consequently, that we must not judge of them except in accordance with these ideas, and we must even think that whatever conflicts with these ideas is absolutely impossible and involves a contradiction. Thus we have no reason to affirm that there is no mountain without a valley, except that we see that the ideas of these things cannot be complete when we consider them apart; though of course by abstraction 477   we can obtain the idea of a mountain, or of an upward slope, without considering that the same slope can be travelled downhill. In the same way we can say that the existence of atoms, or parts of matter which have extension and yet are indivisible, involves a contradiction, because it is impossible to have the idea of an extended thing without also having the idea of half of it, or a third of it, and so conceiving it as being divisible by two or three. From the simple fact that I consider the two halves of a part of matter, however small it may be, as two complete substances, †whose ideas are not made inadequate by an abstraction of my intellect†, I conclude with certainty that they are really divisible. Someone may tell me that though I can conceive them apart, I have no reason to deny their inseparability because I do not know that God has not united or joined them together so tightly that they are entirely inseparable. I would reply that however he may have joined them, I am sure that he can also disjoin them; so that absolutely speaking I have reason to call them divisible, since he has given me the faculty of conceiving them as such. I say the same about the soul and the body and in general all the things of which we have distinct and complete ideas; that is, I say that their being inseparable involves a contradiction. But I do not on that account deny that there can be in the soul or the body many properties of which I have no ideas; I deny only that there are any which are inconsistent with the ideas of them that I do have, including the idea that I have of their distinctness; for otherwise God would be a deceiver and we would have no rule to make us certain of the truth.

478

I believe that the soul is always thinking for the same reason that I believe that light is always shining, even though there are not always eyes looking at it, and that heat is always warm though no one is being warmed by it, and that body, or extended substance, always has extension, and in general that whatever constitutes the nature of a thing always belongs to it as long as it exists. So it would be easier for me to believe that the soul ceased to exist at the times when it is supposed to cease to think than to conceive that it existed without thought. And I do not see any difficulty here, except that people think it superfluous to believe that it thinks at times when no memory of the thought remains with us afterwards. But consider that every night we have a thousand thoughts, and even while awake we have a thousand thoughts in the course of an hour of which no trace remains in our memory, and which seem no more useful than thoughts we may have had before we were born. Then you will find it easier to be convinced of my view than to judge that a substance whose nature is to think can exist while not thinking at all.

479

I do not see any difficulty in understanding on the one hand that the faculties of imagination and sensation belong to the soul, because they are species of thoughts, and on the other hand that they belong to the soul only in so far as it is joined to the body, because they are kinds of thoughts without which one can conceive the soul in all its purity.

We observe in animals movements similar to those which result from our imaginations and sensations; but that does not mean that we observe imaginations and sensations in them. On the contrary, these same movements can take place without imagination, and we have arguments to prove that they do so take place in animals, as I hope to show clearly by describing in detail the structure of their limbs and the causes of their movements.

480 But I fear I have already been tiresome to you by writing at such length, and I will count myself very happy if you continue to honour me with your kindness and grant me the favour of your protection.

AT III TO MERSENNE, 19 JANUARY 1642

480 I am sending you my letter to Reverend Father Gibieuf; I have sealed it purely as a matter of propriety, since there is nothing in it that may not be seen by everyone . . .

481 As for the Jesuits . . . you may assure them that I have no plans to write against them, that is, to use insults and slanders to try to discredit them, as Father Bourdin did previously against me. But please do not tell them that I will not be taking one of their textbooks on philosophy so as to point out its errors;[1] on the contrary, I would like them to know that I *will* do so, if I judge it advantageous that the truth should be known. They should not take this amiss if they prefer the truth to the vanity of always wanting to be thought wiser than they are. But I am waiting for their objections to decide what I shall do . . .

(483) I have recently found a successful way to weigh air. I took a small very light glass phial, fashioned by the glass blower into the space shown in the diagram, about the size of a small tennis ball, and having only one tiny

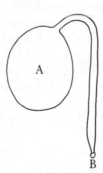

484 opening, a hair's breadth in diameter, at the end of the spout B. I weighed it on a very accurate balance, and the weight when cold was $78\frac{1}{2}$ grains. I then heated it over a coal fire, and replacing it on the balance in the same orientation as shown in the diagram, namely with the spout pointing

---

1 See above, p. 161 and the letter to Mersenne of 22 December 1641 (AT III 470).

downwards, I found that it weighed just under 78 grains. I then immersed spout B in water and let it cool, and as the air condensed as it cooled, a quantity of water entered the spout which was equal to the quantity of air previously expelled by the heating process. Finally, I weighed the phial, including the water it now contained, and found that it weighed $72\frac{1}{2}$ grains more than it did before. I conclude from this that the weight of the air expelled by the heat stands in relation to the water which took its place in the ratio $\frac{1}{2}$ to $72\frac{1}{2}$, or 1 to 145. My calculation could be wrong, since it is very difficult to be exact, but I am sure that the weight of air can be detected by this means, and I have described my procedure at length so that you can repeat it if you are interested in doing the experiment . . .

TO REGIUS, JANUARY 1642 AT III

I have had here all afternoon a distinguished visitor, M. Alphonse,[1] who 491
discussed the Utrecht affair[2] at length in a most friendly and prudent manner. I agree with him entirely that you should refrain from public disputations for some time, and should be extremely careful not to annoy people by harsh words. I should like it best if you never put forward any new opinions, but retained all the old ones in name, and merely brought forward new arguments. This is a course of action to which nobody could take exception, and yet those who understood your arguments would 492
spontaneously draw from them the conclusions you had in mind. For instance, why did you need to reject openly substantial forms and real qualities? Do you not remember that on page 164 of my *Meteorology*,[3] I said quite expressly that I did not at all reject or deny them, but simply found them unnecessary in setting out my explanations? If you had taken this course, everybody in your audience would have rejected them as soon as they saw they were useless, and in the mean time you would not have become so unpopular with your colleagues.

But what is done cannot be undone. Now you must try to defend as moderately as possible the truths you put forward, and to correct without any obstinacy anything you may have said which is untrue or inexact. Remind yourself that there is nothing more praiseworthy in a philosopher than a candid acknowledgement of his errors.

1 Pollot.
2 Voetius, now Rector of the University of Utrecht, had attempted, unsuccessfully, to have Regius removed from his Chair. Meanwhile Voetius' partisans held a public disputation in which they attacked three of Regius' theses: that a human being is an *ens per accidens*; that the earth moves round the sun; and that substantial forms are to be rejected.
3 AT VI 239; CSM II 173, note 2.

For instance, when you said that a human being is an *ens per accidens*[1] I know that you meant only what everyone else admits, that a human being is made up of two things which are really distinct. But the expression *ens per accidens* is not used in that sense by the scholastics. Therefore, if you cannot use the explanation which I suggested in a previous letter – and I see that in your latest paper you have departed from it to some degree, and not altogether avoided the hazards – then it is much better to admit openly that you misunderstood this scholastic expression than to try unsuccessfully to cover the matter up. You should say that fundamentally you agree with the

493 others and that your disagreement with them was merely verbal. And whenever the occasion arises, in public and in private, you should give out that you believe that a human being is a true *ens per se, and not an ens per accidens*, and that the mind is united in a real and substantial manner to the body. You must say that they are united not by position or disposition, as you assert in your last paper – for this too is open to objection and, in my opinion, quite untrue – but by a true mode of union, as everyone agrees, though nobody explains what this amounts to, and so you need not do so either. You could do so, however, as I did in my *Metaphysics*, by saying that we perceive that sensations such as pain are not pure thoughts of a mind distinct from a body, but confused perceptions of a mind really united to a body. For if an angel were in a human body, he would not have sensations as we do, but would simply perceive the motions which are caused by external objects, and in this way would differ from a real man . . .

494 I think it would be worth while for you to answer Voetius' appendix by means of an open letter; for if you ignored it, your enemies would perhaps rejoice at your supposed defeat. But you should reply so gently and modestly as to offend no one – yet at the same time so firmly that Voetius realizes he is beaten by your arguments, and, to avoid further defeats, stops being so keen to contradict you and lets himself be calmed down by you. I will now sketch out the reply in the form I would think it ought to take, were I in your position. I will write partly in French and partly in Latin, depending on which phrases come to mind more promptly; for if I wrote in Latin alone you might omit to alter my phrasing and the informal style would be detected as not coming from your own pen . . .

(499) 'I readily admit[2] that since I employ only arguments which are very evident and intelligible to those who merely have common sense, I do not need many foreign terms to make them understood. It thus takes very little time to learn the truths I teach and find that one's mind is satisfied on all the principal difficulties of philosophy; this is much quicker than learning all

1 See p. 200 above.
2 This paragraph is written in French.

the terms others employ to explain their views on the same problems. For despite all their terminology, they never manage to produce this kind of satisfaction in minds which make use of their own natural powers of reasoning; they merely fill them with doubts and mists . . .

'I fully agree with the view of the learned Rector that those "harmless 500 entities" called substantial forms and real qualities should not be rashly expelled from their ancient territory. Indeed, up to now we have certainly not rejected them absolutely; we merely claim that we do not need them in order to explain the causes of natural things. We think, moreover, that our arguments are to be commended especially on the ground that they do not in any way depend on uncertain and obscure assumptions of this sort. Now in such matters, saying that one does not wish to make use of these entities is almost the same as saying one will not accept them; indeed, they are accepted by others only because they are thought necessary to explain the causes of natural effects. So we will be ready enough to confess that we do wholly reject them . . .

'Voetius asks whether the denial of substantial forms can be reconciled (501) with Holy Scripture. No one can doubt this who knows that these philo- 502 sophical entities, which are unknown outside the Schools, never crossed the minds of the prophets and apostles and others who composed the sacred Scriptures at the dictation of the Holy Ghost. To prevent any ambiguity of expression, it must be observed that when we deny substantial forms, we mean by the expression a certain substance joined to matter, making up with it a merely corporeal whole, and which, no less than matter and even more than matter – since it is called an actuality and matter only a potentiality – is a true substance, or self-subsistent thing. Such a substance, or substantial form, present in purely corporeal things but distinct from matter, is nowhere, we think, mentioned in Holy Scripture . . . Nor can it be said that the words "genus" or "species" denote substantial differences, since there are genera and species of accidents and modes, as shape is a genus in relation to circles and squares, which no one supposes to have substantial forms, etc.

'He fears that if we deny substantial forms in purely material things, we 503 may also doubt whether there is a substantial form in man, and may thus be in a less happy and secure position than the adherents of forms when it comes to silencing the errors of those who imagine there is a universal world-soul, or something similar.

'In reply to this it may be said on the contrary that it is the view which affirms substantial forms which allows the easiest slide to the opinion of those who maintain that the human soul is corporeal and mortal. Yet if the soul is recognized as merely a substantial form, while other such forms consist in the configuration and motion of parts, this very privileged status it has compared with other forms shows that its nature is quite different from theirs. And this difference in nature opens the easiest route to demonstrating its non-materiality and immortality, as may be seen in the recently published *Meditations on First Philosophy*. Thus one cannot think of any opinion on this subject that is more congenial to theology.

'It would certainly be absurd for those who believe in substantial forms to say that these forms are themselves the immediate principle of their actions; but it cannot be absurd to say this if one does not regard such forms as distinct from active qualities. Now we do not deny active qualities, but we say only that they should not be regarded as having any degree of reality greater than that of modes; for to regard them so is to conceive of them as substances. Nor do we deny dispositions, but we divide them into two kinds. Some are purely material and depend only on the configuration or other arrangement of the parts. Others are immaterial or spiritual, like the states of faith, grace and so on which theologians talk of; these do not depend on anything bodily, but are spiritual modes inhering in the mind, just as movement and shape are corporeal modes inhering in the body . . .

504

(505)   'All the arguments to prove substantial forms could be applied to the form of a clock, which nobody says is a substantial form.

'The arguments, or physical proofs, which we think would force a truth-loving mind to abandon substantial forms, are mainly the following *a priori* metaphysical or theological ones. It is inconceivable that a substance should come into existence without being created *de novo* by God; but we see that every day many so-called substantial forms come into existence; and yet the people who think they are substances do not believe that they are created by God; so their view is mistaken. This is confirmed by the example of the soul, which is the true substantial form of man. For the soul is thought to be immediately created by God for no other reason than that it is a substance. Hence, since the other "forms" are not thought to be created in this way, but merely to emerge from the potentiality of matter, they should not be regarded as substances. It is clear from this that it is not those who deny substantial forms but those who affirm them who "can be forced by solid arguments to become either beasts or atheists". . .

(506)   'The second proof is drawn from the purpose or use of substantial forms. They were introduced by philosophers solely to account for the proper actions of natural things, of which they were supposed to be the principles and bases, as was said in an earlier thesis. But no natural action at all can be explained by these substantial forms, since their defenders admit that they are occult and that they do not understand them themselves. If they say that some action proceeds from a substantial form, it is as if they said that it proceeds from something they do not understand; which

explains nothing. So these forms are not to be introduced to explain the causes of natural actions. Essential forms explained in our fashion, on the other hand, give manifest and mathematical reasons for natural actions, as can be seen with regard to the form of common salt in my *Meteorology*.[1] And here what you say about the movement of the heart can be added . . .

'We affirm that human beings are made up of body and soul, not by the (508) mere presence or proximity of one to the other, but by a true substantial union. (For this there is indeed a natural requirement, on the bodily side, of an appropriate positioning and arrangement of the various parts; but nevertheless the union is different from mere position and shape and the other purely corporeal modes, since it relates not just to the body but also to the soul, which is incorporeal.) The idiom which we used is perhaps unusual, but we think it is sufficiently apt to express what we meant. When we said that a human being is an *ens per accidens*, we meant this only in relation to its parts, the soul and the body; we meant that for each of these parts it is in a manner accidental for it to be joined to the other, because each can subsist apart, and what can be present or absent without the subject ceasing to exist is called an accident. But if a human being is considered in himself as a whole, we say of course that he is a single *ens per se*, and not *per accidens*; because the union which joins a human body and soul to each other is not accidental to a human being, but essential, since a human being without it is not a human being. But many more people make the mistake of thinking that the soul is not really distinct from the body than make the mistake of admitting their distinction and denying their substantial union, and in order to refute those who believe souls to be mortal it is more important to teach the distinctness of parts in a human being than to teach their union. And so I thought I would please the theologians more by saying that a human being is an *ens per accidens*, in order to make the distinction, than if I said that he is an *ens per se*, in 509 reference to the union of the parts.' . . .

TO HUYGENS, 31 JANUARY 1642   AT III

. . . Four or five days ago I received the paper of the Jesuits.[2] It is now a (523) prisoner in my hands, and I want to treat it as courteously as I can; but I find it so guilty that I see no way of saving it. Every day I call my council of war about it, and I hope that in a short time you will be able to see the account of the trial.

Perhaps these scholastic wars will result in my *World* being brought into

1 AT VI 249.
2 The Seventh Set of Objections, of Father Bourdin.

the world. It would be out already, I think, were it not that I want to teach it to speak Latin first. I shall call it *Summa Philosophiae* to make it more welcome to the scholastics, who are now persecuting it and trying to smother it before its birth. The ministers[1] are as hostile as the Jesuits.

AT III   TO REGIUS, END OF FEBRUARY 1642

528   As far as I hear from my friends, everyone who has read your reply[2] to Voetius praises it highly – and very many have read it. Everyone is laughing at Voetius and says he has lost hope for his cause, seeing that he has had to call on the assistance of your magistrates for its defence. As for substantial forms, everyone is denouncing them; and they are saying quite openly that if all the rest of our philosophy were explained in the manner

529   of your reply, everyone would embrace it. You should not be upset that you have been forbidden to lecture on problems in physics; indeed, I would prefer it if you had been forbidden even to give private instruction. All this will redound to your honour and the shame of your adversaries. Certainly, if I were one of your magistrates and wished to destroy Voetius, I would deal with you on his account just as they are doing – and who knows what they have in mind? I am sure that M. V[an der] H[oolck] is on your side; you should carefully follow his advice and instructions . . .

AT III   TO MERSENNE, MARCH 1642

(542)   . . . On the matter of my bearing public witness to the fact that I am a
543   Roman Catholic, I think I have already done so very explicitly several times, for example in the dedication of my *Meditations* to the gentlemen of the Sorbonne, in my explanation of how the forms remain in the substance of the bread in the Eucharist,[3] and elsewhere. I hope that in future my residence in this country will not give anyone occasion to think badly of my religion, seeing that the country is a refuge for Catholics – as witnessed both by the Queen who arrived here a short time ago[4] and the Queen who, it is said, must return here shortly[5]. . . . I send you the first three sheets of Father Bourdin's objections;[6] I cannot send you the whole yet because of the negligence of the publisher. Please keep the manuscript copy which you

---

1 The Protestant ministers in Holland.
2 Regius' reply to Voetius was published on 16 February 1642. The magistrates of Utrecht, at Voetius' instance, ordered the work to be suppressed and forbade Regius to teach anything but medicine.
3 Cf. AT VII 249ff; CSM II 173ff.
4 Henrietta Maria, wife of Charles I of England and Scotland.
5 Marie de Medici, Queen Mother of France, who had visited the Netherlands in 1641.
6 The Seventh Set of Objections to the *Meditations*.

have, so that he cannot say that I have changed anything in his copy, which I was careful to have printed as accurately as possible without changing a single letter. You will perhaps be surprised that I accuse him of such duplicity; but you will see worse to come. I have treated him as courteously as possible, but I have never seen a paper so full of faults. I hope, however, to keep his cause separate from that of his colleagues, so that they cannot bear me any ill-will unless they want openly to declare themselves enemies of the truth and partisans of calumny.

I have looked in St Augustine for the passages you mentioned about the   544 fourteenth Psalm; but I have not been able to find them, or anything on that Psalm. I have also looked for the errors of Pelagius, to discover why people say that I share his opinions, with which I have never hitherto been acquainted. I am surprised that those who want to slander me should seek such false and far-fetched pretexts. Pelagius said that it was possible without grace to do good works and merit eternal life, and this was condemned by the Church; I say that it is possible to know by natural reason that God exists, but I do not say that this natural knowledge by itself, without grace, merits the supernatural glory which we hope for in heaven. On the contrary, it is evident that since this glory is supernatural, more than natural powers are needed to merit it. I have said nothing about the knowledge of God except what all the theologians say too. One should note that what is known by natural reason – that he is all good, all powerful, all truthful, etc. – may serve to prepare infidels to receive the Faith, but cannot suffice to enable them to reach heaven. For that it is necessary to believe in Jesus Christ and other revealed matters, and that depends upon grace.

I see that people find it very easy to misunderstand what I write. Truth is indivisible, so the slightest thing which is added or taken away falsifies it. Thus, you quote as an axiom of mine: 'Whatever we clearly conceive is or exists.' That is not at all what I think, but only that whatever we perceive   545 clearly is true, and so it exists if we perceive that it cannot not exist; or that it can exist if we perceive that its existence is possible. For although the objective being of an idea must have a real cause, it is not always necessary that this cause should contain it *formally*, but only *eminently*.[1]

Thank you for what you tell me of the Council of Constance's condemnation of Wycliffe,[2] but I do not see that this tells at all against me. He would have been condemned no less if all the members of the Council had

---

1 In scholastic terminology, to contain something *formally* is to contain it literally, in accordance with its own definition, to contain it *eminently* is to contain it in some higher form.

2 John Wycliffe (*c.* 1330–84), a forerunner of the Protestant Reformation, condemned by the Council of Constance in 1418 for denying transubstantiation.

followed my opinion. When they denied that the substance of the bread and the wine remains to be the subject of the accidents, they did not specify that the accidents were real, and that is what I said I had never read in the Councils. But I am very obliged to you for the great care you take of everything which concerns me . . .

AT V   TO ***, MARCH 1642[1]

I

544   You always overwhelm me with your kindness and courtesy so that I can never equal you in my replies; but it is very pleasant to be outdone in this way. I shall follow your advice and directions as carefully as possible, particularly in matters regarding sacred theology and orthodox religion; for I am confident that there is nothing in them which does not square with my philosophy much more easily than with the philosophy that is commonly accepted. As for the controversies which are foisted on theology by false philosophy, I will not get involved with them; but unless I am mistaken, they will subside of their own accord if my opinions become accepted. There remains one problem, concerning the motion of the earth; and here I have got a Cardinal to advise me. He professes himself a friend of mine of many years standing, and is one of the Congregation that condemned Galileo.[2] I will hear from him what is or is not permitted, and if I have Rome and the Sorbonne on my side, or at least not against me, I hope that I shall be equal to bearing the malice of others . . .

II

(545)   . . . To show you that I am writing quite candidly and without any pretence, I will indicate the two or three places [in your comments on my *Meditations*] where I noted a slight departure, not from my views, but from my way of putting them.

546   The first is contained in the words 'God does not have the faculty of taking away from himself his own existence.' Now by a 'faculty' we normally mean some perfection; yet it would be an imperfection in God to be able to take away existence from himself. So to forestall any quibbling, I would prefer to put it as follows: 'It is a contradiction that God should take

---

1 The dates and addressees of these Latin fragments are uncertain. In A T it is suggested that the first is to Dinet and the second to Mesland. In A M the conjecture is that both are to Sainte-Croix.
2 François Barberin.

away from himself his own existence; or be able to lose it in some other way.'

The second place is where you say 'God is the cause of himself.' Several people have in the past misinterpreted this phrase, and hence it would appear to require some such explanation: 'For something to be the cause of itself is for it to exist through itself, and to have no other cause than its own essence, which may be called a formal cause.'[1] The third passage I thought worth commenting on is towards the end, where you say 'The matter of the universe exists as a machine.' I would have preferred to write 'The universe is composed of matter, like a machine' or 'All the causes of motion in material things are the same as in artificial machines' or something similar.

TO HUYGENS, 26 APRIL 1642

AT III
(785)

. . . I have asked [M. Van Surk] to present you . . . with a copy of the Amsterdam edition of my *Meditations*. Although the book is not worth your reading more than once, and I know that you have seen it already, I would not be happy with myself if I failed to send you a copy. Besides, this edition is more correct than the Paris one, and even a little larger, particularly at the end of my reply to the Fourth Objections, where I have so far abandoned my restraint as to say that the common view of our theologians regarding the Eucharist is not so orthodox as mine.[2] This was a passage that Father Mersenne had cut out so as not to offend our learned doctors.

TO REGIUS, JUNE 1642

AT III
565

I am delighted that my account of the Voetius affair[3] has pleased your friends. I have seen no one, even among the theologians, who does not seem to approve of the cudgelling he got. My account can scarcely be called too hard on him, since everything I recorded is simple fact, and I wrote at much greater length against one of the Jesuit fathers.

I have briefly read what you sent me, and I found nothing that is not excellent and highly pertinent, except for the following few points.

First, in many places the style is not sufficiently polished.

Apart from that, on page 46, where you say 'matter is not a natural body' I would add 'in the view of those who define "natural body" in this way'. For since we believe it is a true and complete substance, I do not see why we would say that matter is not a natural body.

---

1 See Fourth Replies: AT VII 235ff; CSM II 165ff.
2 AT VII 253–6; CSM II 176–8.
3 In the letter to Dinet: AT VII 563–603; CSM II 384–97.

566   On page 66 you seem to make a greater difference between living and lifeless things than there is between a clock or other automaton on the one hand, and a key or sword or other non-self-moving appliance on the other. I do not agree. Since 'self-moving' is a category with respect to all machines that move of their own accord, which excludes others that are not self-moving, so 'life' may be taken as a category which includes the forms of all living things . . .

To provide a solution to your objection about the idea of God, we must observe that the point at issue is not the essence of the idea, in respect of which it is only a mode existing in the human mind and therefore no more perfect than a human being, but its objective perfection, which the principles of metaphysics teach must be contained formally or eminently in its

567   cause.[1] Suppose someone said that anyone can paint pictures as well as Apelles, because they consist only of patterns of paint and anyone can make all kinds of patterns with paint. To such a suggestion we should have to reply that when we are talking about Apelles' pictures we are not considering just a pattern of colours, but a pattern skilfully made to produce a representation resembling reality, such as can be produced only by those very practised in this art.

My reply to your second point is this. You agree that thought is an attribute of a substance which contains no extension, and conversely that extension is an attribute of a substance that contains no thought. So you must also agree that a thinking substance is distinct from an extended substance. For the only criterion we have enabling us to know that one substance differs from another is that we understand one apart from the other. And God can surely bring about whatever we can clearly understand; the only things that are said to be impossible for God to do are those which involve a conceptual contradiction, that is, which are not intelligible. But we can clearly understand a thinking substance that is not extended, and an extended substance that does not think, as you agree. So even if God conjoins and unites them as much as he can, he cannot thereby divest himself of his omnipotence and lay down his power of separating them; and hence they remain distinct . . .

AT III   TO POLLOT, 6 OCTOBER 1642

577   I have already heard so many remarkable reports of the outstanding intelligence of the Princess of Bohemia[2] that I am not surprised to learn that she reads books on metaphysics; I rather think myself fortunate that

1 See Med. III: AT VII 42; CSM II 29.
2 Princess Elizabeth of Bohemia (1618–80), who was in exile in The Hague.

she has deigned to read my own book and has expressed her approval of its contents. I set far more store by her judgement than by that of those learned doctors whose rule is to accept the truth of Aristotle's views rather than the evidence of reason. I shall not fail to come to The Hague as soon as I hear that you have arrived, so that by your good offices I may have the honour of paying my respects to the Princess and putting myself at her disposal. Since I hope that this will be soon, I will put off till then the opportunity of engaging in further discussion with you, and expressing my thanks for all the ways in which I am bound to you.

578

TO HUYGENS, 10 OCTOBER 1642   AT III

I spent yesterday reading the dialogues entitled *On the World*[1] which you were kind enough to send me. But I have not noticed any passages where I can detect a wish on the author's part to contradict me. In the passage where he says that one could not construct more perfect telescopes than those already in use, he speaks so favourably of me that I would be ill tempered if I took it in bad part. It is true that in several places he has views very different from my own, but he gives no evidence that he has me in mind, any more than he does in other places where his views agree with what I have written. I am happy to allow every writer the same freedom that I desire for myself, namely the freedom to be able to write frankly whatever one believes to be the most true, without worrying whether it agrees or clashes with anyone else's views. I find several very good things in his third dialogue; but in the second, where he tries to imitate Galileo, I think all the material is too subtle to be true, since nature employs only means that are very simple. I would like there to be many books of this kind, for I think they could prepare people's minds to accept other opinions than those of the Schoolmen, without, I believe, harming my own.

796

797

For the rest, I am doubly obliged to you, Sir, because neither your distress[2] nor the many occupations which I am sure it brought have prevented you from thinking of me and taking the trouble to send me this book. I know that you have a great affection for your family and that the loss of any member of it cannot but be very painful to you. I know also that you have great strength of mind and are well acquainted with all the remedies which can lessen your sorrow. But I cannot refrain from telling you one which I have always found most powerful, not only to enable me to bear the death of those I have loved, but also to prevent me from fearing

798

1 *De Mundo*, by Thomas White (1593–1676), English philosopher and controversialist.
2 Huygens' brother had died recently.

my own, though I love life as much as anyone. It consists in the consideration of the nature of our souls. I think I know very clearly that they last longer than our bodies, and are destined by nature for pleasures and felicities much greater than those we enjoy in this world. Those who die pass to a sweeter and more tranquil life than ours; I cannot imagine otherwise. We shall go to find them some day, and we shall still remember the past; for we have, in my view, an intellectual memory which is certainly independent of the body. And although religion teaches us much on this topic, I must confess a weakness in myself which is, I think, common to the majority of men. However much we wish to believe, and however much we think we do firmly believe all that religion teaches, we are not usually so moved by it as when we are convinced by very evident natural reasons.

599

AT III

TO MERSENNE, 26 APRIL 1643

648   My view on your questions depends on two principles of physics, which I must establish before I can explain it.[1]

The first is that I do not suppose there are in nature any *real qualities*, which are attached to substances, like so many little souls to their bodies, and which are separable from them by divine power. Motion, and all the other modifications of substance which are called *qualities*, have no greater reality, in my view, than is commonly attributed by philosophers to

649   shape, which they call only a *mode* and not a *real quality*. My principal reason for rejecting these real qualities is that I do not see that the human mind has any notion, or particular idea, to conceive them by; so that when we talk about them and assert their existence, we are asserting something we do not conceive and do not ourselves understand. The second reason is that the philosophers posited these real qualities only because they did not think they could otherwise explain all the phenomena of nature; but I find on the contrary that these phenomena are much better explained without them.

The other principle is that whatever is or exists remains always in the state in which it is, unless some external cause changes it; so that I do not think there can be any *quality* or *mode* which perishes of itself. If a body has a certain shape, it does not lose it unless it is taken from it by collision with some other body; similarly if it has some motion, it should continue to keep it, unless prevented by some external cause. I prove this by metaphysics; for God, who is the author of all things, is entirely perfect

---

1 Mersenne had asked whether two missiles of equal matter, size and shape must travel the same distance if projected at the same speed in the same direction through the same medium.

and unchangeable; and so it seems to me absurd that any simple thing which exists, and so has God for its author, should have in itself the principle of its destruction. Heat, sound, and other such qualities present no difficulty; for they are only motions in the air, where they encounter   650 various obstacles which make them stop.

Since motion is not a *real quality* but only a *mode*, it can be conceived only as the change by which a body leaves the vicinity of some others; and there are only two kinds of change to consider, the one, change in its speed, and the other, change in its direction. For although this change may be brought about by various causes, nevertheless if these causes impel it in the same direction with the same speed, it is impossible that they should impart to it any difference of nature.

So I think that if two missiles equal in matter, size and shape set off with the same speed in the same medium and the same direction (the same direction because otherwise they would not be setting off in the same medium), neither could go further than the other . . .

TO PRINCESS ELIZABETH, 21 MAY 1643   AT III

The honour Your Highness does me in sending her commandments in   663 writing is greater than I ever dared hope; and it is more consoling to my unworthiness than the other favour which I had hoped for passionately, which was to receive them by word of mouth, had I been permitted to pay   664 homage to you and offer you my very humble services when I was last at The Hague. For then I would have had too many wonders to admire at the same time; and seeing superhuman sentiments flowing from a body such as painters give to angels, I would have been overwhelmed with delights like those I think a man coming fresh from earth to heaven must feel. Thus I would hardly have been able to reply to Your Highness, as she doubtless noticed when once before I had the honour of speaking with her. In your kindness you have tried to redress this fault of mine by committing the traces of your thoughts to paper, so that I can read them many times, and grow accustomed to consider them. Thus I am less overwhelmed, but no less full of wonder, observing that it is not only at first sight that they seem perceptive, but that the more they are examined, the more judicious and solid they appear.

I may truly say that the question[1] which Your Highness poses seems to me the one which can most properly be put to me in view of my published writings. There are two facts about the human soul on which depend all

---

1 In a letter of 6 May 1643 (AT III 660), Princess Elizabeth had asked how the soul, being only a thinking substance, can determine the bodily spirits to perform voluntary actions.

the knowledge we can have of its nature. The first is that it thinks, the second is that, being united to the body, it can act and be acted upon along 665 with it. About the second I have said hardly anything; I have tried only to make the first well understood. For my principal aim was to prove the distinction between the soul and the body, and to this end only the first was useful, and the second might have been harmful. But because Your Highness's vision is so clear that nothing can be concealed from her, I will try now to explain how I conceive the union of the soul and the body and how the soul has the power to move the body.

First I consider that there are in us certain primitive notions which are as it were the patterns on the basis of which we form all our other conceptions. There are very few such notions. First, there are the most general – those of being, number, duration, etc. – which apply to everything we can conceive. Then, as regards body in particular, we have only the notion of extension, which entails the notions of shape and motion; and as regards the soul on its own, we have only the notion of thought, which includes the perceptions of the intellect and the inclinations of the will. Lastly, as regards the soul and the body together, we have only the notion of their union, on which depends our notion of the soul's power to move the body, and the body's power to act on the soul and cause its sensations and passions.

I observe next that all human knowledge[1] consists solely in clearly distinguishing these notions and attaching each of them only to the things 666 to which it pertains. For if we try to solve a problem by means of a notion that does not pertain to it, we cannot help going wrong. Similarly we go wrong if we try to explain one of these notions by another, for since they are primitive notions, each of them can be understood only through itself. The use of our senses has made the notions of extension, of shapes and of motions much more familiar to us than the others; and the main cause of our errors is that we commonly want to use these notions to explain matters to which they do not pertain. For instance, we try to use our imagination to conceive the nature of the soul, or we try to conceive the way in which the soul moves the body by conceiving the way in which one body is moved by another.

In the *Meditations* that Your Highness condescended to read, I tried to give a conception of the notions which belong to the soul alone by distinguishing them from those which belong to the body alone. Accordingly, the next thing I must explain is how to conceive those which belong to the union of the soul with the body, as distinct from those which belong to the body alone or to the soul alone. At this point what I wrote at the end

---

1 Fr. *science*, Descartes' term for systematic knowledge based on indubitable foundations.

of my Reply to the Sixth Objections may be useful.[1] It is in our own soul that we must look for these simple notions. It possesses them all by nature, but it does not always sufficiently distinguish them from each other, or   667 assign them to the objects to which they ought to be assigned.

So I think that we have hitherto confused the notion of the soul's power to act on the body with the power one body has to act on another. We have attributed both powers not to the soul, for we did not yet know it, but to the various qualities of bodies such as heaviness, heat, etc. We imagined these qualities to be real, that is to say to have an existence distinct from that of bodies, and so to be substances, although we called them qualities. In order to conceive them we sometimes used notions we have for the purpose of knowing bodies, and sometimes used notions we have for the purpose of knowing the soul, depending on whether we were attributing to them something material or something immaterial. For instance, when we suppose that heaviness is a real quality, of which all we know is that it has the power to move the body that possesses it towards the centre of the earth, we have no difficulty in conceiving how it moves this body or how it is joined to it. We never think that this motion is produced by a real contact between two surfaces, since we find, from our own inner experience, that we possess a notion that is ready-made for forming the conception in question. Yet I believe that we misuse this notion when we apply it to   668 heaviness, which – as I hope to show in my *Physics* – is not anything really distinct from body.[2] For I believe that it was given us for the purpose of conceiving the manner in which the soul moves the body.

If I used more words to explain myself, I would show that I was not fully aware of the incomparable quality of Your Highness's mind; but I would be too presumptuous if I dared to think that my reply should entirely satisfy her. I will try to avoid both errors by adding nothing for the present except that if I am capable of writing or saying anything which may give her pleasure, I will always count it a great privilege to take up my pen or to visit The Hague for that purpose; and that nothing in the world is so dear to me as the power of obeying her commands. I cannot here find any reason for observing the Hippocratic oath[3] she enjoined on me, since she has written nothing which does not deserve to be seen and admired by all. I will only say that as I infinitely prize your letter, I will treat it as misers treat their treasures. The more they prize them, the more they hide them, grudging the sight of them to the rest of the world and placing their supreme happiness in looking at them. So I will be glad to enjoy in solitude

1 AT VII 444f; CSM II 299f.
2 See *Principles*, Part IV, art. 20–7: AT VIIIA 212–16; CSM I 268–70.
3 Elizabeth had called Descartes her doctor, and had claimed that he was bound by the Hippocratic oath not to reveal the weakness of her mind.

the benefit of looking at your letter; and my greatest ambition is to be able to call myself, and to be truly, Madame, Your Highness's most humble and obedient servant, DESCARTES.[1]

AT III   TO HUYGENS, 24 MAY 1643

(816)   I think I have already told you that I explain all the properties of magnetism by means of a very subtle and imperceptible kind of matter which emerges continuously from the earth, not just from the pole, but from every part of the Northern hemisphere, and then passes to the south, where it proceeds to enter every part of the Southern hemisphere. There is a corresponding kind of matter which emerges from the earth in the Southern hemisphere and re-enters the earth in the north. Now the particles of these two kinds of matter are shaped in such a way that they cannot easily pass through the gaps of air or water or several other kinds of body; moreover, the pores of earth and of magnetite which allow passage to the particles coming from one hemisphere cannot be entered by those from the other hemisphere. I think I demonstrate all this in my *Physics*,[2] where I explain the origin of those kinds of subtle matter, and the shapes of
817   their particles, which are long and spiralling like a screw – the northern ones twisting in the opposite direction to the southern ones . . .

AT VIIIB   LETTER TO VOETIUS, MAY 1643[3]

(25)   . . . Even if the philosophy at which you rail were unsound, which you have failed to show at any point, and never will manage to show, what vice
26   could it possibly be imagined to contain great enough to require its author to be slandered with such atrocious insults? The philosophy which I and all its other devotees are engaged in pursuing is none other than the know-

---

1 Elizabeth replied, on 20 June, that she was too stupid to understand how the discarded idea of a falsely attributed quality could help us to understand how an immaterial substance could move a body, especially as Descartes was about to refute the notion of heaviness in his forthcoming *Physics*. 'I have to admit', she wrote, 'that it would be easier for me to attribute matter and extension to the soul than to attribute to an immaterial thing the capacity to move and be moved by a body' (AT III 685).
2 *Principles* Part IV, art. 133: AT VIIIA 275.
3 Descartes had this extremely long open letter published by Elzevirs of Amsterdam in May of 1643. The original Latin text is entitled *Epistola Renati Descartes ad Celeberrimum Virum D. Gisbertium Voetium* ('Letter from René Descartes to that distinguished gentleman M. Gisbertus Voetius'); a Flemish translation was issued simultaneously. The letter was written as a reply to two works in which Voetius had savagely attacked Descartes: the *Confraternitas Mariana* (1642) and the *Admiranda Methodus* (1643). Voetius had earlier secured a formal condemnation of the Cartesian philosophy at the University of Utrecht, of which he was Rector; cf. CSM II 393ff and 393n.

ledge of those truths which can be perceived by the natural light and can provide practical benefits to mankind; so there is no study that can be more honourable, or more worthy of mankind, or more beneficial in this life. The ordinary philosophy which is taught in the schools and universities is by contrast merely a collection of opinions that are for the most part doubtful, as is shown by the continual debates in which they are thrown back and forth. They are quite useless, moreover, as long experience has shown to us; for no one has ever succeeded in deriving any practical benefit from 'prime matter', 'substantial forms', 'occult qualities', and the like. So it is quite irrational for those who have learnt such opinions, which they themselves confess to be uncertain, to condemn others who are trying to discover more certain ones. The desire for innovation is indeed to be condemned in matters of religion; for since everyone says he believes that his own religion was instituted by God, who cannot err, he believes as a result that any possible innovation must be bad. But in matters of philosophy, which, as everyone readily admits, men do not yet have sufficient knowledge of, and whose scope can be expanded by many splendid discoveries, there is nothing more praiseworthy than to be an innovator . . .

You say that the first thing a prospective disciple of mine must do is to (36) 'forget all he has learnt from others'. Yet in all the passages you cite[1] there is no word of 'forgetting' but only of removing preconceived opinions – 37 nor does talk of 'forgetting' come in any other passage from my writings; so the reader will easily judge how much faith to place in your citations. It is one thing to set aside preconceived opinions, that is, to cease to give one's assent to opinions that we rashly accepted on a previous occasion; this depends merely on our will, and is wholly necessary in order to lay the first foundations of philosophy. But it is something else entirely to forget such opinions, which is virtually never in our power . . .

I have read many of your writings, yet I have never found any reasoning (42) in them, or any thought that is not base or commonplace – nothing which suggests a man of intelligence or education.

I say 'education', not 'learning'. For if under the term 'learning' you mean to include everything learnt from books, irrespective of quality, I will gladly agree that you are the most learned of men . . . By 'educated' I mean the man who has improved his intelligence and character by careful study and cultivation. Such education is, I am convinced, to be acquired not by the indiscriminate reading of any book whatever, but by a frequent and repeated reading of only the best, by discussion with those who are already educated, when we have the opportunity, and, finally, by continually 43

---

1 Voetius had cited passages from the *Discourse* (AT VI 16; CSM I 118f) and the Replies to the Seventh Objections (AT VII 475; CSM II 320).

contemplating the virtues and pursuing the truth. Those who seek learning from standard texts and indexes and concordances can pack their memories with many things in a short time, but they do not emerge as wiser or better people as a result. On the contrary, there is no chain of reasoning in such books, but everything is decided either by appeal to authority or by short summary syllogisms, and those who seek learning from these sources become accustomed to placing equal trust in the authority of any writer . . ., so little by little they lose the use of their natural reason and put in its place an artificial and sophistical reason. For notice that the true use of reason, which is the basis of all education, all intelligence and all human wisdom, does not consist in isolated syllogisms, but only in the scrupulous and careful inclusion of everything required for knowledge of the truths we are seeking. This can almost never be expressed in syllogisms, unless many of them are linked together; so it is certain that those who use only isolated syllogisms will almost always leave out some part of what needs to be looked at as a whole, and thus grow careless and lose the use of a mind that is in good order . . .

(60)   [He claims that in my philosophy] 'God is thought of as a deceiver.' This is foolish. Although in my First Meditation I did speak of a supremely powerful deceiver, the conception there was in no way of the true God, since, as he himself says, it is impossible that the true God should be a deceiver. But if he is asked how he knows this is impossible, he must answer that he knows it from the fact that it implies a conceptual contradiction – that is, it cannot be conceived. So the very point he made use of to attack me is sufficient for my defence . . .

(165)   You deny that anyone can rightly conclude, from the fact that he is
166   thinking, that he exists; for you want the sceptic to conclude merely that he *seems to himself to exist* – as if anyone using his reason, however sceptical he might be, could seem to himself to exist without at the same time understanding that he really exists, whenever this seems to him to be the case. Thus you deny what is the most evident proposition there could possibly be in any science . . .

You claim that the arguments I use to prove the existence of God have force only for those who already know he exists, since they depend simply on notions that are innate within us. But notice that all those things whose knowledge is said to be naturally implanted in us are not for that reason expressly known by us; they are merely such that we come to know them by the power of our own native intelligence, without any sensory experi-
167   ence. All geometrical truths are of this sort – not just the most obvious ones, but all the others, however abstruse they may appear. Hence, according to Plato, Socrates asks a slave boy about the elements of geometry and thereby makes the boy able to dig out certain truths from his

own mind which he had not previously recognized were there, thus attempting to establish the doctrine of reminiscence.[1] Our knowledge of God is of this sort . . .

You say that my method of philosophizing opens the way to scepticism (169) . . . since I am willing to accept as true only what is so clear that it leaves no 170 room for doubt; yet, you say, not even truths known by faith qualify, since we very often have occasion to doubt them. If you are referring here to the actual time at which an act of faith, or natural cognition, is elicited, you are destroying all faith and human knowledge, and are indeed a sceptic; for you are saying that it is impossible ever to have any cognition that is free from doubt. But if we are talking of different times – for someone who at one time has true faith or evident cognition of some natural thing may at another time not have it – this merely shows the weakness of human nature, since we do not always remain fixed on the same thoughts. It does not follow that there should be any doubt in the knowledge itself, and so you establish nothing against me; for I was speaking not of any certainty that would endure throughout an entire human life, but merely of the kind of certainty that is achieved at the moment when some piece of knowledge is acquired . . .

You say that 'René may rightly be compared with that cunning cham- 175 pion of atheism, Cesare Vanini,[2] since he uses the self-same techniques to erect the throne of atheism in the minds of the inexperienced.' Who will not marvel at the absurdity of your impudence? Even if it is true (and I insist it is) that I wrote against atheists and put forward my arguments as first rate, and even if it is true (which I strongly deny) that I reject the common traditional arguments, and that my own have been found to be invalid, it still would not follow that I should be even suspected – let alone guilty – of atheism. Anyone who claims to refute atheism and produces inadequate arguments should be accused of incompetence, not face a summary charge of atheism . . .

Those who follow your way of talking could say of St Thomas (who was (176) further than anyone from the slightest suspicion of atheism) that since his arguments against the atheists have, on close examination, been found to be invalid, he should be likewise compared with Vanini. Indeed, if it were not invidious, I would venture to say that the comparison would be more apt than in my own case, since my own arguments have never been refuted as his have . . .

I do not doubt that the time will come when my arguments, despite all (177) your snarling, will have the power to call back from atheism even those

1 I.e. that the ideas are 'remembered' from a previous existence; cf. *Meno* 81ff.
2 Condemned for atheism and burnt at Toulouse in 1619.

178   slow-witted enough not to understand them. For they will know that they are accepted as the most certain demonstrations by all those who understand them aright, that is, by all the most intelligent and learned people, and that although they are looked at askance by you and many others, no one has been able to refute them . . .

(193)   You will get no benefit from calling me 'a foreigner and a papist'. I do not need to tell you that the treaties between my King and the rulers of these Provinces are such that, even were this my first day in your country, I ought to enjoy equal rights with those who were born here. But I have spent so many years here, and am so well known by all the more honourable citizens, that even if I had come from a hostile country, I should have long ceased to be regarded as a foreigner. Nor do I need to appeal to the freedom of religion that is granted us in this republic. I shall merely declare that such criminal lies, such scurrilous insults and such atrocious slanders are contained in your book, that they could not be employed between enemies, or by a Christian against an infidel, without convicting the perpetrator of wickedness and criminality. I may add that I have always experienced such courtesy from the people of this country, have been received in such a friendly manner by all those I have met, and have found

194   everyone else to be so kind and considerate, and so far removed from the coarse and impertinent freedom with which you indiscriminately attack those whom you do not know and who have done you no harm, that I have no doubt the people will feel far more aversion towards you, their compatriot, than they would towards any foreigner . . .

AT III   TO VORSTIUS, 19 JUNE 1643

(686)   . . . You know that in my physics I consider nothing apart from the sizes, shapes, positions and movements of the particles of which bodies are made up. For although every body is infinitely divisible, there is no doubt that there are some parts into which it is more easily divided than others. Medical men are very well aware of this, as they often say that some bodies are composed of thin parts, and others of thick parts, and so on.

    You also know that from the fact that a vacuum is impossible, and yet many small pores are to be seen in all terrestrial bodies, I conclude that those gaps are filled with a certain subtle matter. And I hold that the only

687   difference between this subtle matter and terrestrial bodies is that it is made up of much smaller particles which do not stick together and are always in very rapid motion. And as a result of this, when they pass through the gaps in terrestrial bodies and impinge on the particles of which the bodies are made up, they often make them vibrate, or even dislodge them and sweep some of them away.

The particles which are swept away by the subtle matter in this fashion make up *air*, *spirits* and *flame*. But there is a great difference between air and flame, in that the terrestrial particles which make up flame are travelling much faster than those which constitute air. The spirits are intermediate between the two: their degree of agitation is taken to be greater than that of the particles in calm air, and less than those of flame. And since there are an infinite number of intermediate steps between a slow motion and a fast one, we may apply the term 'spirits' to every body consisting of terrestrial particles that are infused with subtle matter and are more agitated than those which make up air, but less agitated than those which make up flame.

That there are many such spirits in the human body is easily demonstrated. First, in the stomach there is a solution of nutrients subjected to heat; heat, however, is simply a greater than usual jostling of material particles, as I explained in the *Meteorology*.[1] And the spirits are created from those particles of terrestrial bodies which are the easiest of all to dissolve. Hence it is necessary that a large quantity of spirits from the food contained in the stomach should pass into the veins with the chyle; these are called 'natural spirits'.

These spirits are increased in the liver and in the veins by heat – that is, by the agitation which occurs there. As a result of the heat, while the chyle is turned into blood, many of its particles separate off, and more spirits are formed there. When this blood then comes into the heart, it immediately becomes rarefied and dilates as a result of the heat which is greater in the heart than in the veins. This is the source of the beating of the heart and the arteries; and the rarefaction causes yet more particles of blood to separate off, thus converting them into the spirits which the medical men call 'vital spirits'. 688

The particles of blood leaving the heart by the great artery are agitated in the highest degree and travel straight through the carotid arteries toward the middle of the brain, where they fill its cavities and, once separated from the rest of the blood, form the animal spirits. I think the cause of their being separated from the rest of the blood is simply that the gaps through which they enter the brain are so narrow that the rest of the blood cannot find a way in.

1 Cf. *Meteorology*, Discourse 1: 'As for heat and cold, my supposition here is that we have no need to introduce any other conception beyond the fact that the particles of the bodies we touch are separated more or less strongly than usual, either by the particles of this subtle matter or by some other cause. As a result the little strands of those of our nerves which function as the organs of touch are agitated to a greater or lesser extent; when the agitation is stronger than usual this causes in us the feeling of heat, and when it is weaker than usual this causes the feeling of cold' (AT VI 236).

These animal spirits flow from the cavities of the brain through the nerves to all the muscles of the body, where they serve to move the limbs. Finally they leave the body by transpiration which cannot be detected – not merely those which pass along the nerves, but others as well which merely travelled in the arteries and veins. Whatever leaves the animal's body by this undetectable process of transpiration necessarily has the form of spirits. So I am very surprised that anyone denies the existence of spirits in animals, unless he is questioning the name, and objects to the term 'spirits' being applied to particles of terrestrial matter that are separated from each other and driven about at great speed.

689

These are my present thoughts on the origin and movement of the spirits; their varieties and relative strengths and functions can easily be inferred from what I have said. For there is virtually no difference between 'natural' and 'vital' spirits; these two are not separated from the blood. Only the animal spirits are pure; but they vary in strength depending on the differences in the particles which make them up. Thus spirits derived from wine and reaching the brain in excessive quantities cause drunkenness; those derived from opium cause sleep, and so on for the rest. Also this will be made clearer if you read chapters 1, 2 and 3 of my *Meteorology*; for what I wrote there of vapours, exhalations and winds can easily be applied to spirits . . .

AT III   TO PRINCESS ELIZABETH, 28 JUNE 1643

690

I am very obliged to Your Highness because although she saw how badly I explained myself in my last letter about the question she was good

691

enough to put me, she still has enough patience to listen to me on the same subject and to give me the opportunity to mention the things I left out. The principal omissions seem to me as follows. First of all I distinguished three kinds of primitive ideas or notions, each of which is known in its own proper manner and not by comparison with any of the others: the notions we have of the soul, of body and of the union between the soul and the body. After that I should have explained the difference between these three kinds of notion and between the operations of the soul by which we acquire them. I should have explained also how to make each of them familiar and easy to us. Finally, after saying why I used the analogy of heaviness, I should have explained how, although one may wish to conceive of the soul as material (which is, strictly speaking, to conceive of its union with the body), one may still recognize afterwards that it is separable from the body. I think this covers the topics which Your Highness proposed for me in her letter.

First of all then, I observe one great difference between these three kinds of notions. The soul is conceived only by the pure intellect; body (i.e. extension, shapes and motions) can likewise be known by the intellect alone, but much better by the intellect aided by the imagination; and finally what belongs to the union of the soul and the body is known only obscurely by the intellect alone or even by the intellect aided by the 692 imagination, but it is known very clearly by the senses. That is why people who never philosophize and use only their senses have no doubt that the soul moves the body and that the body acts on the soul. They regard both of them as a single thing, that is to say, they conceive their union; because to conceive the union between two things is to conceive them as one single thing. Metaphysical thoughts, which exercise the pure intellect, help to familiarize us with the notion of the soul; and the study of mathematics, which exercises mainly the imagination in the consideration of shapes and motions, accustoms us to form very distinct notions of body. But it is the ordinary course of life and conversation, and abstention from meditation and from the study of the things which exercise the imagination, that teaches us how to conceive the union of the soul and the body.

I am almost afraid that Your Highness may think that I am not now speaking seriously; but that would go against the respect which I owe her and which I will never cease to show her. I can say with truth that the chief rule I have always observed in my studies, which I think has been the most useful to me in acquiring what knowledge I have, has been never to spend more than a few hours a day in the thoughts which occupy the imagination and a few hours a year on those which occupy the intellect alone. I have 693 given all the rest of my time to the relaxation of the senses and the repose of the mind. And I include among the exercises of the imagination all serious conversations and anything which needs to be done with attention. This is why I have retired to the country. In the busiest city in the world I could still have as many hours to myself as I now employ in study, but I could not spend them so usefully if my mind was tired by the attention required by the bustle of life. I take the liberty of writing this to Your Highness, so that she may see how genuinely I admire her ability to devote time to the meditations needed to appreciate the distinction between the mind and the body, despite all the business and cares which attend people who combine great minds with high birth.

I think it was those meditations rather than thoughts requiring less attention that have made Your Highness find obscurity in the notion we have of the union of the mind and the body. It does not seem to me that the human mind is capable of forming a very distinct conception of both the distinction between the soul and the body and their union; for to do this it is necessary to conceive them as a single thing and at the same time to conceive them as two things; and this is absurd. This is why I made use earlier[1] of the analogy with heaviness and other qualities which we commonly imagine to be united to certain bodies in the way that thought is united to ours. I supposed that Your Highness still had in mind the arguments proving the distinction between the soul and the body, and I did not want to ask her to put them aside in order to represent to herself the notion of the union which everyone invariably experiences in himself without philosophizing. Everyone feels that he is a single person with both body and thought so related by nature that the thought can move the body and feel the things which happen to it. I did not worry about the fact that the analogy with heaviness was lame because such qualities are not real, as people imagine them to be. This was because I thought that Your Highness was already completely convinced that the soul is a substance distinct from the body.

Your Highness observes that it is easier to attribute matter and extension to the soul than to attribute to it the capacity to move and be moved by the body without having such matter and extension. I beg her to feel free to attribute this matter and extension to the soul because that is simply to conceive it as united to the body. And once she has formed a proper conception of this and experienced it in herself, it will be easy for her to consider that the matter she has attributed to the thought is not thought itself, and that the extension of this matter is of a different nature from the extension of the thought, because the former has a determinate location, such that it thereby excludes all other bodily extension, which is not the case with the latter. And so Your Highness will easily be able to return to the knowledge of the distinction between the soul and the body in spite of having conceived their union.

I believe that it is very necessary to have properly understood, once in a lifetime, the principles of metaphysics, since they are what gives us the knowledge of God and of our soul. But I think also that it would be very harmful to occupy one's intellect frequently in meditating upon them, since this would impede it from devoting itself to the functions of the imagination and the senses. I think the best thing is to content oneself with keeping in one's memory and one's belief the conclusions which one has once drawn from them, and then employ the rest of one's study time to thoughts in which the intellect co-operates with the imagination and the senses.

The great devotion which I feel to Your Highness's service gives me hope that my frankness will not be disagreeable to her. I would have written at greater length, and tried to clarify on this occasion all difficulties on this topic, but I am forced to stop by a piece of tiresome news. I learn from

---

1 See above, p. 219.

Utrecht that I am summoned before the Magistrates to justify what I have written about one of their ministers.[1] This despite the fact that he has slandered me very unworthily, and that everything that I wrote about him for my just defence was only too well known to everyone. I must proceed to find a way of freeing myself from their quibblings as soon as I can.

TO BUITENDIJCK, 1643[2]   AT IV

In the letter which you were good enough to write to me, I find three questions which clearly indicate the strength and sincerity of your desire for learning. Nothing could give me greater pleasure than to answer them.

Your first question is whether it is ever permissible to doubt about God – that is, whether, in the order of nature, one can doubt of the existence of God. I think that a distinction is called for here between the aspect of doubt which concerns the intellect and that which concerns the will. As to the intellect, since it is not a faculty of choice, we must not ask whether something is permissible to it or not; we can only ask whether something is possible for it. Now it is certain that there are many people whose intellect can doubt of God. This includes all those who cannot give an evident proof of his existence, even though they may have the true faith; for faith belongs to the will, and leaving that aside, a person with faith can examine by the use of natural reason whether there is any God, and thus doubt about God. As for the will, once again we must make a distinction, between doubt as an end, and doubt as a means. For if someone sets out to doubt about God with the aim of persisting in the doubt, then he sins gravely, since he wishes to remain in doubt on a matter of such importance. But if someone sets out to doubt as a means of acquiring a clearer knowledge of the truth, then he is doing something altogether pious and honourable, because nobody can will the end without willing also the means, and in Scripture itself men are often invited to seek this knowledge of God by natural reason. Nor is there any sin if a person, for the same purpose, temporarily puts out of his mind all the knowledge which he can have of God: we are not bound to think unceasingly that God exists – for then we would never be allowed to sleep or to do anything else since as often as we do something else, we put aside for that time all the knowledge which we can have of the Godhead.

Your second question is whether it is permissible to suppose anything false in matters pertaining to God. Here we must distinguish between the true God, clearly known, and false gods. Once the true God is clearly known, not only is it not permissible, but it is not possible for the human

62

63

64

---

1 The *Letter to Voetius*. See pp. 220ff. above.
2 The date of this letter is conjectural.

mind to attribute anything false to him, as I have explained in my *Meditations* on pages 152, 159, 269 and elsewhere.[1] But the case is not the same with false divinities, i.e. evil spirits, or idols, or other such gods invented by the error of the human mind – all these are called gods in Holy Scripture – or with the true God, if he is known only in a confused way. To attribute to these something false as a hypothesis can be either good or bad, depending on whether the purpose of framing such a hypothesis is good or bad. For what is thus imagined and attributed hypothetically is not thereby affirmed by the will as true, but is merely proposed for examination to the intellect; and so it does not include any of the strict essence of good or evil – or if it does so, this is derived from the purpose for which the hypothesis was framed. Thus, take the case of someone who imagines a deceiving god – even the true God, but not yet clearly enough known to himself or to the others for whom he frames his hypothesis. Let us suppose that he does not misuse this fiction for the evil purpose of persuading others to believe something false of the Godhead, but uses it only to enlighten the intellect, and bring greater knowledge of God's nature to himself and others. Such a person is in no way sinning in order that good may come. There is no malice at all in his action; he does something which is good in itself, and no one can rebuke him for it except slanderously.

65   Your third question is about the motion which you think I regard as the soul of brute animals. I do not remember ever having written that motion is the soul of animals; indeed I have not publicly revealed my views on the topic. But because, by the word 'soul', we usually mean a substance, and because I think that motion is a mode of bodies, I would not wish to say that motion is the soul of animals. (By the way, I do not admit various kinds of motion, but only local motion,[2] which is common to all bodies, animate and inanimate alike.) I would prefer to say with Holy Scripture (Deuteronomy 12:23) that blood is their soul, for blood is a fluid body in very rapid motion, and its more rarefied parts are called spirits. It is these which move the whole mechanism of the body as they flow continuously from the arteries through the brain into the nerves and muscles.

TO FATHER ****, 1643[3]

(67)   ... All I can say about the book *De Cive* is that I believe its author to be the person who wrote the Third Objections against my *Meditations*, and that I find him much more astute in moral philosophy than in metaphysics

---

1 AT VII 138, 144, 233; CSM II 99, 103, 163.
2 See *Principles*, Part I, art. 69: AT VIIIA 33; CSM I 217.
3 The date and addressee of this letter are in doubt. Clerselier notes that it is addressed to a 'Reverend Jesuit Father'.

or physics.[1] Not that I could approve in any way his principles or his maxims. They are extremely bad and quite dangerous in that he supposes all persons to be wicked, or gives them cause to be so. His whole aim is to write in favour of the monarchy; but one could do this more effectively and soundly by adopting maxims which are more virtuous and solid. And he writes with such vehemence against the Church and the Roman Catholic religion that I do not see how he can prevent his book from being censured, unless he is given special support from some very powerful quarter.

TO [MESLAND], 2 MAY 1644   AT IV

I know that it is very difficult to enter into another person's thoughts, and experience has taught me how difficult many people find mine. So I am all the more grateful to you for the trouble which you have taken to examine them; and I cannot but think highly of you when I see that you have taken such full possession of them that they are now more yours than mine. The difficulties which you were kind enough to put to me come rather from the subject-matter and the defects of my expression than from any lack of understanding on your part. You have in fact provided the solution to the principal ones. But none the less I will tell you my views on all of them.

I agree that in the case of physical and moral causes which are particular and limited, it is often found that those which produce a certain effect are incapable of producing many others which appear to us less remarkable. Thus one human being can produce another human being, but no human being can produce an ant; and a king, who makes a whole people obey him, cannot always get obedience from a horse. But in the case of a universal and indeterminate cause, it seems to be a common notion of the most evident kind that †whatever can do the greater can also do the lesser†; it is as evident as the maxim that †the whole is greater than the part†. Rightly understood, this notion applies also to all particular causes, moral as well as physical. For it would be a greater thing for a human being to be able to produce human beings and ants than to be able only to produce human beings; and a king who could command horses as well would be more powerful than one who could command only his people. Just so, when they want to attribute great power to the music of Orpheus, they say that it could move even the beasts.

It does not make much difference whether my second proof, the one based on our own existence, is regarded as different from the first proof, or

111

112

---

1 Thomas Hobbes, the author of *De Cive* (1642), did indeed write the Third Set of Objections to the *Meditations*.

merely as an explanation of it.[1] Just as it is an effect of God to have created me, so it is an effect of him to have put the idea of himself in me; and there is no effect coming from him from which one cannot prove his existence. Nevertheless, it seems to me that all these proofs based on his effects are reducible to a single one; and also that they are incomplete, if the effects are not evident to us (that is why I considered my own existence rather than that of heaven and earth, of which I am not equally certain) and if we do not add to them the idea which we have of God. For since my soul is finite, I cannot know that the order of causes is not infinite, except in so far as I have in myself that idea of the first cause; and even if there be admitted a first cause which keeps me in existence, I cannot say that it is God unless I truly have the idea of God. I hinted at this in my Reply to the First Objections;[2] but I did so very briefly, so as not to show contempt for the arguments of others, who commonly accept the principle that †a series cannot go on for ever†. I do not accept that principle; on the contrary, I think that †in the division of the parts of matter there really is an endless series†, as you will see in my treatise on philosophy,[3] which is almost printed.

I do not know that I laid it down that God always does what he knows to be the most perfect, and it does not seem to me that a finite mind can judge of that. But I tried to solve the difficulty in question, about the cause of error, on the assumption that God had made the world most perfect, since if one makes the opposite assumption, the difficulty disappears altogether.

I am grateful to you for pointing out the places in St Augustine which can be used to give authority to my views. Some other friends of mine had already done so, and I am pleased that my thoughts agree with those of such a great and holy man. For I am not the kind of person who wants his views to appear novel; on the contrary, I make my views conform with those of others so far as truth permits me.

I regard the difference between the soul and its ideas as the same as that between a piece of wax and the various shapes it can take. Just as it is not an activity but a passivity in the wax to take various shapes, so, it seems to me, it is a passivity in the soul to receive one or other idea, and only its volitions are activities. It receives its ideas partly from objects which come into contact with the senses, partly from impressions in the brain, and partly from prior dispositions in the soul and from movements of the will. Similarly, the wax owes its shapes partly to the pressure of other bodies, partly to the shapes or other qualities which it already possesses, such as

1 Med. III: AT VII 47–52; CSM II 32–6.
2 AT VII 106; CSM II 77.
3 *Principles*, Part II, art. 20: AT VIIIA 51; CSM I 231.

heaviness or softness, and partly also to its own movement, in so far as it has in itself the power to continue moving when it has once been set in motion.

The difficulty we have in learning the sciences, and in clearly setting before ourselves the ideas which are naturally known to us, arises from the false preconceptions of our childhood, and other causes of error, as I have tried to explain at length in the treatise I am having printed.[1]

As for memory, I think that the memory of material things depends on the traces which remain in the brain after an image has been imprinted on it; and that the memory of intellectual things depends on some other traces which remain in the mind itself. But the latter are of a wholly different kind from the former, and I cannot explain them by any illustration drawn from corporeal things without a great deal of qualification. The traces in the brain, on the other hand, dispose it to move the soul in the same way as it moved it before, and thus to make it remember something. It is rather as the folds in a piece of paper or cloth make it easier to fold again in that way than it would be if it had never been so folded before.

The moral error which occurs when we believe something false with good reason – for instance because someone of authority has told us – involves no privation provided it is affirmed only as a rule for practical action, in a case where there is no moral possibility of knowing better. Accordingly it is not strictly an error; it would be one if it were asserted as a truth of physics, because the testimony of an authority is not sufficient in such a case.

As to free will, I have not seen what Father Petau[2] has written about it; but from what you say in explaining your opinion on the topic, it does not appear that my views are very different. For first, I beg you to observe that I did not say that a person was indifferent only if he lacked knowledge, but rather, that he is more indifferent the fewer reasons he knows which impel him to choose one side rather than another; and this, I think, cannot be denied by anybody. And I agree with you when you say that we can suspend our judgement; but I tried to explain in what manner this can be done. For it seems to me certain that †a great light in the intellect is followed by a great inclination in the will†;[3] so that if we see very clearly that a thing is good for us, it is very difficult – and, on my view, impossible, as long as one continues in the same thought – to stop the course of our desire. But the nature of the soul is such that it hardly attends for more than a moment to a single thing; hence, as soon as our attention turns from the

115

116

1 *Principles*, Part I, art. 71–4: AT VIIIA 31–8; CSM I 218–21.
2 Denis Petau (1583–1652), a Jesuit whose three-volume work on free will had appeared in 1643.
3 Med. IV: AT VII 59; CSM II 41.

reasons which show us that the thing is good for us, and we merely keep in our memory the thought that it appeared desirable to us, we can call up before our mind some other reason to make us doubt it, and so suspend our judgement, and perhaps even form a contrary judgement. And so, since you regard freedom not simply as indifference but rather as a real and positive power to determine oneself, the difference between us is a merely verbal one – for I agree that the will has such a power. However, I do not see that it makes any difference to that power whether it is accompanied by indifference, which you agree is an imperfection, or whether it is not so accompanied, when there is nothing in the intellect except light, as in the case of the blessed, who are confirmed in grace. And so I call free in the general sense whatever is voluntary, whereas you wish to restrict the term to the power to determine oneself only if accompanied by indifference. But so far as words are concerned, I wish above all to follow usage and precedent.

117   As for animals that lack reason it is obvious that they are not free, since they do not have this positive power to determine themselves; what they have is a pure negation, namely the power of not being forced or constrained.

The only thing which prevented me from speaking of the freedom which we have to follow good or evil was the fact that I wanted to avoid as far as possible all theological controversies and stay within the limits of natural philosophy. But I agree with you that wherever there is an occasion for sinning, there is indifference; and I do not think that in order to do wrong it is necessary to see clearly that what we are doing is evil. It is sufficient to see it confusedly, or merely to remember that we once judged it to be so, without in any way seeing it – that is, without paying attention to the reasons which prove it to be so. For if we saw it clearly, it would be impossible for us to sin, as long as we saw it in that fashion; that is why they say that †whoever sins does so in ignorance†.[1] And we may earn merit even though, seeing very clearly what we must do, we do it infallibly, and without any indifference, as Jesus Christ did during his earthly life. Since we cannot always attend perfectly to what we ought to do, it is a good action to pay attention and thus to ensure that our will follows so promptly the light of our understanding that there is no longer any indifference at all. In any case, I did not write that grace entirely prevents

118   indifference, but simply that it makes us incline to one side rather than to another, and so diminishes indifference without diminishing freedom; from which it follows, in my view, that this freedom does not consist in indifference.

1 Aristotle, *Nicomachean Ethics*, III, 1110ᵇ28.

I turn to the difficulty of conceiving how God would have been acting freely and indifferently if he had made it false that the three angles of a triangle were equal to two right angles, or in general that contradictories could not be true together. It is easy to dispel this difficulty by considering that the power of God cannot have any limits, and that our mind is finite and so created as to be able to conceive as possible the things which God has wished to be in fact possible, but not be able to conceive as possible things which God could have made possible, but which he has nevertheless wished to make impossible. The first consideration shows us that God cannot have been determined to make it true that contradictories cannot be true together, and therefore that he could have done the opposite. The second consideration assures us that even if this be true, we should not try to comprehend it, since our nature is incapable of doing so. And even if God has willed that some truths should be necessary, this does not mean that he willed them necessarily; for it is one thing to will that they be necessary, and quite another to will this necessarily, or to be necessitated to will it. I agree that there are contradictions which are so evident that we cannot put them before our minds without judging them entirely impossible, like the one which you suggest: 'that God might have brought it about that his creatures were independent of him'. But if we would know the immensity of his power we should not put these thoughts before our minds, nor should we conceive any precedence or priority between his intellect and his will; for the idea which we have of God teaches us that there is in him only a single activity, entirely simple and entirely pure. This is well expressed by the words of St Augustine: 'They are so because thou see'est them to be so';[1] because in God *seeing* and *willing* are one and the same thing. 119

I distinguish lines from surfaces, and points from lines, as one mode from another mode, but I distinguish a body from the surfaces, lines and points belonging to it as a substance from its modes. And there is no doubt that at least one mode which belongs to bread remains in the Blessed Sacrament, since its outward shape, which is a mode, remains. As for the extension of Jesus Christ in that Sacrament, I gave no explanation of it, because I was not obliged to, and I keep away, as far as possible, from questions of theology, especially as the Council of Trent has said that he is present 'with that form of existence which we can scarcely express in words'. I quoted that phrase, towards the end of my Reply to the Fourth Objections, precisely to excuse myself from giving an explanation.[2] But I venture to say that if people were a little more used to my way of 120

1 *Confessions*, xiii. 30.
2 AT VII 252; CSM II 175.

philosophizing, they could be shown a way of explaining this mystery which would stop the mouths of the enemies of our religion so that they could say nothing against it.

There is a great difference between *abstraction* and *exclusion*. If I said simply that the idea which I have of my soul does not represent it to me as being dependent on the body and identified with it, this would be merely an abstraction, from which I could form only a negative argument which would be unsound. But I say that this idea represents it to me as a substance which can exist even though everything belonging to the body be excluded from it; from which I form a positive argument, and conclude that it can exist without the body. And this exclusion of extension can be clearly seen in the nature of the soul, as you have very well observed, from the fact that one cannot think of a half of a thinking thing.

I do not want to give you the trouble of sending me what you have been kind enough to write about my *Meditations* because I hope to go to France soon, and there, I hope, I shall have the honour of seeing you.

TO [GRANDAMY], 2 MAY 1644

AT IV

121
122

I was extremely pleased to learn of the kind memories you have of me, and to receive the excellent letters from Father Mesland. I shall try to reply to him with the utmost honesty, and without concealing any of my thoughts. But I cannot give as much attention to my reply as I would have wished. For I am at present in a place[1] where I have many distractions and little leisure – having recently left my usual abode in order to arrange passage to France, where I plan to go shortly. I shall not fail to call on you there if at all possible; for I shall be delighted to return to La Flèche, where I spent eight or nine years during my youth. It is there that the first seeds of everything I have ever learnt were implanted in me, and I am wholly obliged to your Society[2] for this.

If the testimony of M. de Beaune is enough to recommend respect for my *Geometry*, even though few others understand it, I am confident that Father Mesland's testimony will no less effectively lend authority to my *Meditations*, particularly since he has taken the trouble to adapt them to the style which is commonly used for teaching, and I am deeply obliged to him for doing this. I hope that experience will show there is nothing in my views which should cause teachers to be apprehensive about them and to reject them; on the contrary, I hope they will be found very useful and acceptable.

1 Leiden.
2 The Society of Jesus (Jesuits).

The printing of my *Principles of Philosophy* should have been completed two months ago, if the publisher had kept his word. But the drawings have delayed him, for he could not get them engraved as soon as he thought he could. I hope, however, to send a copy to you quite soon, unless the wind carries me away from here before they are finished.

123

TO PRINCESS ELIZABETH, 8 JULY 1644

AT V

My journey could not be accompanied by any misfortune, since I have been so happy during it to have been in Your Highness's mind.[1] The very flattering letter which tells me this is the most precious gift I could receive in this country. It would have made me altogether happy if it had not told me also that the sickness which troubled Your Highness before I left The Hague had left some traces of indisposition in the stomach. The remedies which Your Highness has chosen, diet and exercise, are in my opinion the best of all – leaving aside those pertaining to the soul, for there is no doubt that the soul has great power over the body, as is shown by the great bodily changes produced by anger, fear and the other passions. The soul guides the spirits into the places where they can be useful or harmful; however, it does not do this directly through its volition, but only by willing or thinking about something else. For our body is so constructed that certain movements in it follow naturally upon certain thoughts: as we see that blushes accompany shame, tears compassion, and laughter joy. I know no thought more proper for preserving health than a strong conviction and firm belief that the architecture of our bodies is so thoroughly sound that when we are well we cannot easily fall ill except through extraordinary excess or infectious air or some other external cause, while when we are ill we can easily recover by the unaided force of nature, especially when we are still young. This conviction is beyond doubt more true and more reasonable than that of some people who are convinced by an astrologer or doctor that they must die at a certain time, and for this reason alone fall ill, and frequently even die. I have seen that happen to several people. But I could not help being extremely sad, if I thought that Your Highness's indisposition still continued. I prefer to hope that it is already quite over. At the same time, the desire to be certain makes me want very much to return to Holland.

I propose to leave here in four or five days for Poitou and Brittany, where I must do the business that brought me here. As soon as I have put my affairs in order, I shall be very anxious to return to the region where I have

64

65

66

1 Descartes was in Paris, about to visit Poitou on family business.

been so happy as to have the honour of speaking from time to time with Your Highness. Although there are many people here whom I honour and esteem, I have not yet seen anything to keep me here.

140   Now that I have finally published the principles of my philosophy[1] (a philosophy to which some people have taken offence), you are one of those to whom I most desire to offer it – both because I am obliged to you for all the fruits I may reap from my studies, thanks to the care you devoted to my early education, and also because I know how much you can do to prevent my good intentions from being badly interpreted by those of your Society who do not know me. I do not fear that my writings will be criticized or scorned by those who examine them; for I am always very ready to acknowledge my mistakes and to correct them, when anyone is kind enough to tell me about them. But I wish to avoid, as much as possible, the false preconceptions of those who need only to know that I have written something about philosophy (in which I have not completely followed the ordinary style) in order to form a bad opinion about it. And because I already see from experience that the things I have written have had the good fortune to be accepted and approved by a good number of people, I do not have much reason to fear that my views will be refuted. Indeed I see
141   that those whose common sense is good enough, and who are not yet steeped in contrary opinions, are strongly drawn to embrace my views. So it seems that with the passage of time these views cannot but be accepted by most people – and, I venture to say, by those with the most sense. I know that people have thought my views were new; yet they will see here that I do not use any principles which were not accepted by Aristotle and by all those who have ever concerned themselves with philosophy. People have also imagined that my aim was to refute the received views of the Schools, and to try to render them absurd; but they will see that I do not discuss them any more than I would if I had never learnt them. Again, people have hoped that when my philosophy saw the light of day, they would find numerous faults in it, which would make it easy to refute; for myself, on the contrary, I hope that all the best minds will think it so reasonable that those who undertake to condemn it will be repaid simply by shame. And I hope too that the wisest people will be proud to be among the first to judge it favourably, and that posterity will follow their judge-

---

1 Descartes' *Principles of Philosophy* had been published earlier in 1644.

ment if it should be true. If you make any contribution to this through your authority and your leadership, as I know you can, that will add to the substantial debt which I already owe you.

TO ***, 1644[1]

AT V

You advise me to refer to the beginning of chapter 7 of Book One of Aristotle's *Meteorology* in order to defend myself. I was delighted to find this advice in the letter which you did me the honour of writing, for I referred to just this passage at the end of my *Principles*[2] – it is, indeed, the sole reference I made to Aristotle. Thus I regard it as no small mark of your affection that you advise me to do exactly what I thought I ought to do.

As for any censure by Rome regarding the movement of the earth, I see no likelihood of that, for I very explicitly deny this movement. I think indeed that at first it will be judged that I deny it merely verbally, so as to avoid censure, because I uphold the system of Copernicus. But when you examine my arguments, I am confident you will find that they are serious and sound, and that they show clearly that followers of Tycho's system are more obliged to say that the earth moves than those who follow the Copernican system – when it is explained in the way I explain it. Now, if we cannot follow either of these systems then we must return to that of Ptolemy, and I do not believe that the Church will ever oblige us to do this, since it is manifestly contrary to experience. Moreover, all the passages of Scripture which go against the movement of the earth do not concern the system of the world, but only the manner of speaking about it. Consequently, since I prove that if you follow the system I put forward then, properly speaking, you must say that the earth does not move, my account agrees entirely with these passages. For all that, however, I am much obliged to you for having warned me about what may be said against me . . .

You have understood very well what I wrote concerning the extension of surfaces – namely that the resistance of the air to a given quantity of matter is proportional to the extension of its surfaces. For I do not consider there to be any inertia absolutely speaking, or according to the nature of things: inertia always is relative to the surrounding bodies. Thus, when I say that the larger a body is, the better it can transfer its motion to other bodies and the less it can be moved by them, my reason is that it pushes them all in the same direction; whereas the small bodies surrounding it can

549
550

551

---

1 The date and addressee of this letter are in doubt.
2 *Principles*, Part IV, art. 204: AT VIIIA 327; CSM I 289.

never work all together to push it at the same instant in the same direction. For, since one of them pushes one of its parts in one way and another 552 pushes another part in another way, they do not make it move as much.

AT IV   TO CHARLET, 9 FEBRUARY 1645

156   I am greatly obliged to Father Bourdin for enabling me to have the good fortune to receive your letters. I am overjoyed to learn from them that you share my interests, and that you do not find my endeavours displeasing. I was also extremely pleased to see that the said Father was disposed to bestow upon me his good graces, which I shall try to deserve in all sorts of ways. Feeling very deeply obliged to the members of your Society – and especially to you for having acted like a father to me throughout my youth[1]
157 – I would be extremely sorry to be on bad terms with any members of the Society of which you are the head in France. My own inclination and regard for my duty lead me to desire their friendship keenly. Moreover, in publishing a new philosophy I have followed a path which makes it possible for me to derive so much benefit from their goodwill or, on the other hand, so much disadvantage from their lack of interest, that anyone who knows that I am not completely lacking in sense would, I think, be sure that I will do everything in my power to make myself worthy of their favour. This philosophy is so firmly based on demonstrations that I cannot doubt the time will come when it is generally received and approved; yet since they make up the largest part of those competent to judge it, I could not expect to live long enough to see this time if their lack of interest prevented them from wanting to read it. If, on the other hand, their goodwill leads them to examine it, I venture to hope that they will find many things in it which they will think true and which may readily be substituted for the ordinary views, and serve effectively to explain the truths of the faith without, moreover, contradicting the writings of Aristotle. Should they accept these things, then in a few years this philosophy will gain as much credence as it would in a century without their goodwill. This is a matter, I confess, in which I have some interest. For I am a man like any 158 other, and not one of those insensitive people who do not allow themselves to be affected by success. And this is also a matter in which you can do me a great favour. But I venture to believe too that the public has an interest in it – and especially your Society, which should not tolerate a situation in which others accept important truths which it does not accept. I beg you to excuse the freedom with which I express my feelings. It is not that I do not

---

1 Charlet was a professor at La Flèche while Descartes was a student there.

acknowledge the respect which I owe you, but that I regard you as if you were my father, and so believe that you will not be offended if I discuss things with you in the same way as I would with him if he were still alive.

TO MESLAND, 9 FEBRUARY 1645   AT IV

Your letter of 22 October reached me only a week ago, which is why I   162
have not been able earlier to assure you of my great obligation to you. It is not because you took the trouble to read and examine my *Meditations* that I am obliged to you, for since we were not acquainted beforehand I would like to think that it was the matter alone which attracted you; and it is not because you have made such a good abstract of it that I am obliged to you, for I am not so vain as to think that you did it for my sake, and I have a   163
sufficiently good opinion of my arguments to believe that you thought them worth making intelligible to many, to which end the new form you have given them will be very useful. I am obliged to you rather because in explaining them, you have been very careful to make them appear in their full strength, and to interpret to my advantage many things which might have been distorted or concealed by others. It is this in particular which makes me recognize your candour and your desire to do me honour. I have not found a single word, in the manuscript that you were good enough to send me, with which I do not entirely agree; and though it contains many thoughts which are not in my *Meditations*, or at least are not proved there in the same manner, none the less there is not one which I would not be willing to accept as my own. When, in the *Discourse on the Method*, I said that I did not recognize the thoughts which people attributed to me,[1] I was not thinking of people who have examined my writings as carefully as you; I was thinking only of people who had tried to gather my opinions from what I said in familiar conversation.

In discussing the Blessed Sacrament I speak of the surface which is intermediate between two bodies, that is to say between the bread (or the body of Jesus Christ after the consecration) and the air surrounding it.[2] By 'surface' I do not mean any substance or real nature which could be destroyed by the omnipotence of God, but only a mode or manner of being, which cannot be changed without a change in that in which or through which it exists; just as it involves a contradiction for the square shape of a piece of wax to be taken away from it without any of the parts of   164
the wax changing their place. This surface intermediate between the air and the bread does not differ in reality from the surface of the bread, or from the surface of the air touching the bread; these three surfaces are in

1 *Discourse*: AT VI 69; CSM I 146.
2 Fourth Replies: AT VII 251; CSM II 174.

fact a single thing and differ only in relation to our thought. That is to say, when we call it the surface of the bread, we mean that although the air which surrounds the bread is changed, the surface remains always †numerically the same†, provided the bread does not change, but changes with it if it does. And when we call it the surface of the air surrounding the bread, we mean that it changes with the air and not with the bread. And finally, when we call it the surface intermediate between the air and the bread, we mean that it does not change with either, but only with the shape of the dimensions which separate one from the other; if, however, it is taken in that sense, it is by that shape alone that it exists, and also by that alone that it can change. For if the body of Jesus Christ is put in the place of the bread, and other air comes in place of that which surrounded the bread, the surface which is between that air and the body of Jesus Christ is still †numerically the same† as that which was previously between the other air and the bread, because its numerical identity does not depend on the identity of the bodies between which it exists, but only on the identity or similarity of the dimensions. Similarly, we can say that the Loire is the same river as it was ten years ago, although it is no longer the same water, and perhaps there is no longer a single part of the earth which then surrounded that water.

As for the manner in which one can conceive the body of Jesus Christ to be in the Blessed Sacrament, I do not think it is for me to explain, since the Council of Trent teaches that he is there 'with that form of existence which we can scarcely express in words'. I quoted these words on purpose at the end of my Reply to the Fourth Objections[1] to excuse myself from speaking further on the topic, and also because not being a theologian by profession, I was afraid that anything I might write would be less well taken from me than from another. All the same, since the Council does not lay it down that 'we cannot express it in words', but only that 'we can scarcely express it in words', I will venture to tell you here in confidence a manner of explanation which seems to me quite elegant and very useful for avoiding the slander of heretics who object that our belief on this topic is entirely incomprehensible and involves a contradiction. I do so on condition that if you communicate it to anyone else you will please not attribute its authorship to me; and on condition that you do not communicate it to anyone at all unless you judge it to be altogether in accord with what has been laid down by the Church.

First of all, I consider what exactly is the body of a man, and I find that this word 'body' is very ambiguous. When we speak of a body in general, we mean a determinate part of matter, a part of the quantity of which the

---

1 Fourth Replies: AT VII 252; CSM II 175.

universe is composed. In this sense, if the smallest amount of that quantity were removed, we would judge without more ado that the body was smaller and no longer complete; and if any particle of the matter were changed, we would at once think that the body was no longer quite the same, no longer †numerically the same†. But when we speak of the body of a man, we do not mean a determinate part of matter, or one that has a determinate size; we mean simply the whole of the matter which is united with the soul of that man. And so, even though that matter changes, and its quantity increases or decreases, we still believe that it is the same body, †numerically the same† body, so long as it remains joined and substantially united with the same soul; and we think that this body is whole and entire so long as it has in itself all the dispositions required to preserve that union. Nobody denies that we have the same bodies as we had in our infancy, although their quantity has much increased and, according to the common opinion of doctors, which is doubtless true, there is no longer in them any 167 part of the matter which then belonged to them, and even though they no longer have the same shape; so that they are †numerically the same† only because they are informed by the same soul. Personally, I go further. I have examined the circulation of the blood, and I believe that nutrition takes place by a continual expulsion of parts of our body, which are driven from their place by the arrival of others. Consequently I do not think that there is any particle of our bodies which remains †numerically† the same for a single moment, although our body, *qua* human body, remains always †numerically† the same so long as it is united with the same soul. In that sense, it can even be called indivisible; because if an arm or a leg of a man is amputated, we think that it is only in the first sense of 'body' that his body is divided – we do not think that a man who has lost an arm or a leg is less a man than any other. Altogether then, provided that a body is united with the same rational soul, we always take it as the body of the same man, whatever matter it may be and whatever quantity or shape it may have; and we count it as the whole and entire body, provided that it needs no additional matter in order to remain joined to this soul.

Moreover, consider that when we eat bread and drink wine, the small parts of the bread and wine dissolve in our stomach, and pass at once into our veins; so that they transubstantiate themselves naturally and become parts of our bodies simply by mixing with the blood. However, if we had 168 sharp enough eyesight to distinguish them from the other particles of blood, we would see that they are still †numerically† the same as those which previously made up the bread and the wine. In this way, if we did not consider their union with the soul, we could still call them bread and wine as before.

Now this transubstantiation takes place without any miracle. But I see no difficulty in thinking that the miracle of transubstantiation which takes place in the Blessed Sacrament consists in nothing but the fact that the particles of bread and wine – which in order for the soul of Jesus Christ to inform them naturally would have had to mingle with his blood and dispose themselves in certain specific ways – are informed by his soul simply by the power of the words of consecration. The soul of Jesus Christ could not have remained naturally joined with each of these particles of bread and wine unless they were assembled with many others to make up all the organs of a human body necessary for life; but in the Sacrament it remains supernaturally joined with each of them even when they are separated. In this way it is easy to understand how the body of Jesus Christ is present only once in the whole host, when it is undivided, and yet is whole and entire in each of its parts, when it is divided; because all the matter, however large or small, which as a whole is informed by the same human soul, is taken for a whole and entire human body.

169　　No doubt this explanation will be shocking at first to those who are accustomed to believe that for the body of Jesus Christ to be in the Eucharist all its parts must be there with their same quantity and shape, and with †numerically† the same matter as they were composed of when he ascended into heaven. But they will easily free themselves from these difficulties if they bear in mind that nothing of the kind has been decided by the Church. It is not necessary for the integrity of the human body that it should possess all its external parts with their quantity and matter; such things are in no way useful or fitting in this Sacrament, in which the soul of Jesus Christ informs the matter of the host, in order to be received by men and to be united more closely with them. This does not in any way diminish the veneration due to the Sacrament. Moreover, people should bear in mind that it is impossible, and seems manifestly to involve a contradiction, that these bodily parts should be present, for what we call the arm or hand of a man is what has the external shape, size and use of one; so that whatever one might imagine in the host as the hand or the arm of Jesus Christ, it goes against all the dictionaries and entirely changes the use of the words to call it an arm or a hand, since it has neither extension, nor external shape, nor use.

170　　I would be most grateful if you would tell me your opinion of this explanation, and I would be glad also to know Father Vatier's opinion, but time does not allow me to write to him.

AT IV　　　　　　　　TO [MESLAND], 9 FEBRUARY 1645

173　　As for freedom of the will, I entirely agree with what the Reverend Father here wrote. Let me explain my opinion more fully. I would like you to notice that 'indifference' in this context seems to me strictly to mean that state of the will when it is not impelled one way rather than another by any perception of truth or goodness. This is the sense in which I took it when I said that the lowest degree of freedom is that by which we determine ourselves to things to which we are indifferent.[1] But perhaps others mean by 'indifference' a positive faculty of determining oneself to one or other of two contraries, that is to say, to pursue or avoid, to affirm or deny. I do not deny that the will has this positive faculty. Indeed, I think it has it not only with respect to those actions to which it is not pushed by any evident reasons on one side rather than on the other, but also with respect to all other actions; so that when a very evident reason moves us in one direction, although morally speaking we can hardly move in the contrary direction, absolutely speaking we can. For it is always open to us to hold back from pursuing a clearly known good, or from admitting a clearly perceived truth, provided we consider it a good thing to demonstrate the freedom of our will by so doing.

It must be noted also that freedom can be considered in the acts of the will either before they are elicited, or after they are elicited.

Considered with respect to the time before they are elicited, it entails indifference in the second sense but not in the first. Although, when we contrast our own judgement with the commandments of others, we say that we are freer to do those things which have not been prescribed to us by 174 others and in which we are allowed to follow our own judgement than to do what we are prohibited from doing, yet we cannot similarly make a contrast within the field of our own judgements or our own cognitions and say that we are freer to do those things which seem to us to be neither good nor evil, or in which we recognize many reasons *pro* but as many reasons *contra*, than to do those things in which we perceive much more good than evil. For a greater freedom consists either in a greater facility in determining oneself or in a greater use of the positive power which we have of following the worse although we see the better. If we follow the course which appears to have the most reasons in its favour, we determine ourselves more easily; but if we follow the opposite, we make more use of that positive power; and thus we can always act more freely in those cases in which we see much more good than evil than in those cases which are called ἀδιάφορα or indifferent. In this sense too the things which others command us to do, and which we would not otherwise do spontaneously, we do less freely than the things which we are not ordered to do; because the judgement that these things are difficult to do is opposed to the judgement that it is good to do what is commanded; and the more equally

1 See Med. IV: AT VII 58; CSM II 40.

these two judgements move us the more indifference, taken in the first sense, they confer on us.

But freedom considered in the acts of the will at the moment when they are elicited does not entail any indifference taken in either the first or the second sense; for what is done cannot remain undone as long as it is being

175 done. It consists simply in ease of operation; and at that point freedom, spontaneity and voluntariness are the same thing. It was in this sense that I wrote that I moved towards something all the more freely when there were more reasons driving me towards it;[1] for it is certain that in that case our will moves itself with greater facility and force.

AT IV   TO CLERSELIER, 17 FEBRUARY 1645

183   Here is the reason why I said that a motionless body could never be
184 moved by another smaller body, no matter how fast this smaller body might be moving.[2] It is a law of nature that if one body moves another, then the former must have more power to move the latter than the latter has to resist being moved by the former. But this surplus can depend only on the size of the body. For the motionless body has as many degrees of resistance as the moving body has degrees of speed. The reason for this is that if it is set in motion by a body moving twice as fast as some other body, it must receive twice as much motion from it; but its resistance to this motion will also be twice as great.

For example, body B cannot push body C unless it makes it move as rapidly as it will itself move after having pushed it. That is, if B is to C as 5

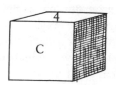 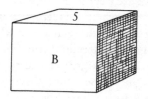

to 4, and there are 9 degrees of motion in B, then B will have to transfer 4 of these degrees to C in order to make C move as fast as it is moving. It can do this easily because it has the power to transfer up to $4\frac{1}{2}$ units (i.e. half of those it possesses) instead of rebounding in the opposite direction. But if B is to C as 4 is to 5, then B cannot move C unless it transfers 5 of its 9 degrees of motion, which is more than half of what it possesses, and consequently

185 body C has more resistance than B has power to act; this is why B must

---

1 Med. IV: AT VII 57; CSM II 40.
2 See *Principles*, Part II, art. 49: AT VIIIA 68.

rebound in the opposite direction, rather than move C. And, without that, no body would ever be made to rebound when it meets another body.

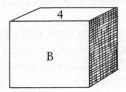 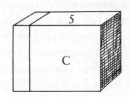

For the rest, I am very happy that the first and chief difficulty you have found in my *Principles* concerns the rules governing the change in motion of colliding bodies.[1] For I take this to mean that you have found no difficulties in what precedes these rules, and also that you will not find many in the rest of the book. Nor will you have further difficulty with these rules when you take account of the fact that they depend uniquely on the principle that *when two bodies collide, and they contain incompatible modes, then there must occur some change in these modes in order to make them compatible; but this change is always the least that may occur.* In other words, *if these modes can become compatible when a certain quantity of them is changed, then no larger quantity will change.* Two distinct modes must be considered in motion: one is motion on its own, or speed, and the other is the determination of this motion in a given direction; and either of these two modes is as difficult to change as the other.

Thus, in order to understand the fourth, fifth and sixth rules, where the   186
motion of body B is incompatible with body C's being at rest, one must note that there are two ways in which these can become compatible: namely *if B changes the whole determination of its motion,* or else *if it changes the state of rest of body C by transferring so much of its motion that it cannot catch up with this body no matter how fast it goes.* In these three rules I have said only that when C is larger than B, it happens in the first way; when it is smaller, it happens in the second way; and finally, when they are the same size, the change occurs half in the first way and half in the second. For when C is the larger, B cannot push it in front of itself unless it transfers to C more than half of its speed, together with more than half of its determination to travel from right to left, in so far as this determination is linked with its speed. Instead it rebounds without moving body C, and changes only its whole determination, which is a smaller change than the one that would come about from more than half of this determination together with more than half of the speed. Conversely, if C

---

1 There are seven such rules; see *Principles*, Part II, art. 46–52: AT VIIIA 68–70.

is smaller than B, it must be pushed by it, for then B gives C less than half of its speed, and less than half of the determination connected with its speed, which is less than half of the whole of this determination, which is what B would have to change if it rebounded.

187   This is not contradicted by experience; for in these rules, by 'motionless body' I mean a body which is not acting so as to separate its surface from those of the other bodies surrounding it, and which consequently forms part of another hard body bigger than it. Elsewhere I said that when the surfaces of two bodies become separated, then all that is positive in the nature of motion is present in the one commonly said not to be moving as much as in the one said to be moving.[1] And later I explained why a body suspended in the air can be moved by the smallest force.[2]

Here I must acknowledge, however, that these rules are not trouble-free. I would try to explain them further if I were now able to do so; but since my mind is now occupied with other thoughts, I shall, if I may, put off to a future occasion sending you a lengthier account of my views.[3]

I am greatly obliged to you for the victories which you are winning on my behalf. Your answer to the argument that †the pagans had the idea of many gods†, etc. is very sound. For, although the idea of God is *imprinted on the human mind in such a way* that everyone has within himself the

188   power to know him, this does not prevent many people passing through their whole lives without ever having a distinct representation of this idea. Indeed, those who think they have an idea of many gods have no idea of God at all. For, as you have so well noted, to conceive of many supremely perfect gods implies a contradiction. When the ancients referred to many gods they did not mean many all-powerful gods, but only many very powerful gods, above whom they imagined a single Jupiter as sovereign; and consequently, to this Jupiter alone they applied the idea of the true God, this idea being presented to them in a confused manner.

AT IV   TO MESLAND, MAY 1645

(216)   ... I am obliged that you have been so kind as to give me your opinion of my *Principles*. But I wish that you had been more specific about your difficulties, and I confess that I cannot think of any regarding rarefaction. For nothing is easier to conceive, I think, than the way in which a sponge swells up in water and shrinks as it dries out.

As for the manner in which Jesus Christ exists in the Holy Sacrament,

---

1 *Principles*, Part II, art. 30: AT VIIIA 57; CSM I 235.
2 *Principles*, Part II, art. 56: AT VIIIA 72; CSM I 246.
3 In the French version of the *Principles* the articles on the rules of motion are indeed expanded and modified.

certainly there is no need at all to accept the explanation I sent you[1] in order to make it agree with my principles. For I put it forward not for this reason, but because I deemed it quite useful for getting round the objections of the heretics, who say that the Church's articles of faith contain impossibilities and contradictions. You may do what you please with my letter, but since it is not worth keeping, please simply destroy it, without bothering to return it to me.

I wish you had enough leisure to make a more detailed examination of   217 my *Principles*. I dare to think you would find in it at least something logically coherent, so that one must either reject everything contained in the last two parts and simply take it as a pure hypothesis or even a fable, or else accept the whole of it. And even if one takes it as merely a hypothesis, as I presented it, I think none the less that one should not reject it until one has found some other, better explanation of all the phenomena of nature.

So far, however, I have no reason to complain about my readers. For since this last treatise was published, I have not heard of anyone who has tried to find fault with it, and it seems that I have at least succeeded in making many people wonder whether what I wrote might not be true. Nevertheless I do not know what is said in my absence, and I am living in a corner of the world where I would manage to live quite peacefully and happily even if the verdict of the entire learned world were against me. I have no feelings about those who hate me, but only for those who wish me well, whom I desire to serve whenever I can.

TO PRINCESS ELIZABETH, MAY OR JUNE 1645   AT IV

I have read the letter which Your Highness did me the honour to write,   218 and I could not help being very distressed to see that a virtue so rare and so perfect is not accompanied by the health and prosperity which it deserves. I can readily understand how many things must continually distress Your Highness, and I know that they are more difficult to overcome when they are of such a kind that true reason does not command us to oppose them directly or try to remove them. They are domestic enemies with whom we are forced to keep company, and we have to be perpetually on guard lest they injure us. I know only one remedy for this: so far as possible to distract our imagination and senses from them, and when obliged by prudence to consider them, to do so with our intellect alone.

In this matter it is easy, I think, to observe the difference between the   219 intellect on the one hand and the imagination and the senses on the other. To appreciate this difference, consider on the one hand a person who had

---

1 See above, p. 241.

every reason to be happy but who saw continually enacted before him tragedies full of disastrous events, and who spent all his time in the consideration of sad and pitiful objects. Let us suppose that he knew they were imaginary fables, so that though they drew tears from his eyes and moved his imagination, they did not touch his intellect at all. I think that this by itself would be enough gradually to constrict his heart and make him sigh in such a way that the circulation of his blood would be delayed and slowed down. The grosser parts of his blood, sticking together, could easily block the spleen, by getting caught and stopping in its pores; while the more rarefied parts, being continually agitated, could affect his lungs and cause a cough which in time could be very dangerous. On the other hand, there might be a person who had countless genuine reasons for distress but who took such pains to direct his imagination that he never thought of them except when compelled by some practical necessity, and who spent the rest of his time in the consideration of objects which could furnish contentment and joy. This would greatly help him by enabling him to make more sober judgements about the things which mattered, because he would look on them without passion. Moreover I do not doubt that this by itself would be capable of restoring him to health, even if his spleen and lungs were already in a poor condition because of the bad condition of the blood caused by sadness. This would be especially likely if he also used medical remedies to thin out the part of the blood causing the obstructions. I think that the waters of Spa are very good for this purpose, above all if Your Highness while taking them observes the customary recommendation of doctors, and frees her mind from all sad thoughts, and even from all serious meditations on scientific subjects. She should be like people who convince themselves they are thinking of nothing because they are observing the greenness of a wood, the colours of a flower, the flight of a bird, or something else requiring no attention. This is not a waste of time but a good use of it; for one can, in the process, content oneself with the hope that in this way one will recover perfect health, which is the foundation of all the other goods of this life.

220   I know that everything I write here is better known to Your Highness than to me, and that it is not the theory but the practice which is difficult; but the great favour which Your Highness does me in showing that she finds it not unpleasant to learn my sentiments makes me take the liberty of writing them down just as they are. I take the further liberty of adding that I found by experience in my own case that the remedy I have just suggested cured an illness almost exactly similar, and perhaps even more dangerous. I was born of a mother who died, a few days after my birth,[1] from a disease

1 Descartes' mother died on 13 May 1597, thirteen months after his birth.

of the lungs, caused by distress. From her I inherited a dry cough and a pale   221
colour which stayed with me until I was more than twenty, so that all the
doctors who saw me up to that time gave it as their verdict that I would die
young. But I have always had an inclination to look at things from the most
favourable angle and to make my principal happiness depend upon myself
alone, and I believe that this inclination caused the indisposition, which
was almost part of my nature, gradually to disappear completely.

I am very much obliged to Your Highness for sending me her opinion of
the book of M. le Chevalier Digby,[1] which I will not be able to read until it
has been translated into Latin. M. Jonsson, who was here yesterday,
informed me that some people wish to do this; he told me also that I may
send my letters to Your Highness by the regular post, which I would not
have dared to do without his suggestion. I was putting off writing this
because I was waiting for one of my friends to go to The Hague to give it to
Your Highness. I greatly regret the absence of M. de Pollot, because I could
learn from him how your indisposition progresses. However, the letters
which are sent for me to the Alkmaar postman are always delivered to me;   222
and just as there is nothing in the world which I so ardently desire as to be
able to serve Your Highness, so there is nothing which can make me
happier than to have the honour to receive her commands.

TO ***, JUNE 1645[2]   AT IV

It is a mark of your friendship, for which I am greatly obliged, that you   223
have taken the trouble to inquire into the opinions held about my writings
in the place where you live. But although the authors of books are always
glad to know what readers say about them, I can assure you nevertheless
that this has very little interest for me. In fact I think I am so familiar with
the intelligence of most of those who pass for learned that I would think
badly of my thoughts if I saw that they approved of them.

I do not mean to say that the person whose opinion you send me is one of
these people. But since he says that my explanation of rainbows is common
and that my principles of physics are drawn from Democritus, I do not
believe that he has read much of my works. His objections against
rarefaction confirm this view; for if he had attended to what I have written   224
about the rarefaction which occurs in the hollow balls called aeolipyles,[3] or

---

1 Sir Kenelm Digby (1603–65); see footnote 7, p. 105 above.
2 Printed without name or date by Clerselier. In AT one conjecture is that it is to Huygens.
3 Vessels containing water which produce jets of steam when heated; cf. *Meteorology*: AT VI
  265.

in machines where the air is forcibly compressed,[1] or in gun powder,[2] he would not tell me about the rarefaction which occurs in his artificial fountain. And if he had noticed the way in which I explained our idea of body in general, or of matter, as being no different from our idea of space,[3] he would not try to make us conceive the interpenetration of dimensions through the example of motion. For we have a very distinct idea of the various speeds of motion; but it is self-contradictory, and impossible to conceive, that two spaces should interpenetrate one another.

I will not reply to the critic who says that demonstrations are missing in my *Geometry*. For it is true that I have omitted many; but you know them all, and you know also that those who complain that I have omitted them, for the reason that they cannot produce them for themselves, thereby show that they are not very talented geometers.

What I find most strange is the conclusion of the judgement you sent me, namely that what will prevent my principles from being accepted in the Schools is that they are not sufficiently confirmed by experience, and that I have not refuted the arguments of others. For I have reported in detail almost as many observations as there are lines in my writings, and after giving general explanations in my *Principles* of all the phenomena of nature, I explained in the same manner all the observations that can be made regarding inanimate bodies. By contrast, the principles of the ordinary philosophy have never provided a good explanation of any of these observations. So I am amazed that, despite all this, the followers of this philosophy still complain about a lack of observational evidence in my work.

I find it very strange too that they want me to refute the arguments of the scholastics. For I believe that if I undertook this task, I would do them a bad turn. A long time ago the malicious actions of some of them gave me cause to do this, and perhaps in the end they will force me to do it again. But those who have most at stake here are the Jesuit fathers, and because of my respect for Father Charlet (a relation of mine, formerly assistant to the General, and leader of the Society since his death), Father Dinet, and several other senior members of their Body whom I believe to be genuinely my friends, I have till now held back. It was for this reason also that I composed my *Principles* in such a way that it can be said to be not at all in conflict with the ordinary philosophy, but actually to have enriched it with many things that were missing from it. Since these philosophers accept countless other opinions which are contrary to each other, why could they

225

1 *Principles*, Part IV, art. 47: AT VIIIA 231.
2 *Principles*, Part IV, art. 113: AT VIIIA 274.
3 *Principles*, Part II, art. 10: AT VIIIA 45; CSM I 227.

not also accept mine? Nevertheless I would not wish to ask this of them. For if my views are false I would be sorry that they had been led astray; and if they are true then it is more in their interest to examine them than it is in my interest to recommend them. . . .

TO PRINCESS ELIZABETH, JUNE 1645   AT IV

I humbly beg Your Highness to pardon me if the letters which I am   236
honoured to receive from her make me incapable of feeling sympathy for her indisposition. For I always observe in them such clarity of thought and soundness of reasoning that it is impossible for me to believe that a mind capable of such thought and reasoning should be lodged in a body which is weak and ill. However that may be, Your Highness displays such know-ledge about illness and remedies for overcoming it that I am sure she must also possess the skill required for using these remedies.

I know indeed that it is almost impossible not to give in to the distur-bances which new misfortunes initially arouse in us. I know too that ordinarily the best minds are those in which the passions are most violent and act most strongly on their bodies. But the next day, when sleep has calmed the turbulence that affects the blood in such cases, I think one can   237
begin to restore one's mind to a state of tranquillity. This is done by striving to consider all the benefits that can be derived from the thing which had been regarded as a great misfortune on the previous day, while turning one's attention away from the evils which this thing had been imagined to contain. For no events are so disastrous, or so absolutely bad in the judgement of ordinary people, that they cannot be considered in some favourable light by a person of intelligence. And Your Highness may draw this general consolation from the disfavours of fortune: that they have perhaps contributed greatly towards making her cultivate her mind to the extent that she has. This is an asset which she should value more highly than an empire. Great prosperity is often so dazzling and intoxicat-ing that it possesses those who enjoy it, rather than being possessed by them; and although that does not happen to persons with minds of the quality of yours, prosperity always provides fewer opportunities for mental exercise than misfortune. And I believe that, just as good sense is the only thing in the world that one may call good in the absolute sense, so there is no bad thing from which a person having good sense cannot derive some benefit.

I have previously tried to persuade Your Highness to adopt a more carefree outlook, for I believe that occupations which are too serious may weaken the body by tiring the mind. But for all that, I would not wish to dissuade her from occupying herself with matters that help to turn her

238 mind away from objects that make her sad. And I have no doubt that the distractions of study, which would be quite arduous for other people, might sometimes provide her with relaxation. I should count myself extremely fortunate if I could help to facilitate her studies; and I would much rather go to The Hague to learn about the powers of the waters at Spa than gain knowledge here about the plants in my garden – the more so because I do not care what happens at Groningen or Utrecht, whether to my advantage or not. So I shall be obliged to follow this letter in four or five days.

AT IV   TO REGIUS, JULY 1645

248   When I sent you my last letter, I had read only a few pages of your book.[1] I thought I found in them reason to judge your style of writing to be appropriate only for presenting theses, where it is customary to set forth one's opinions in the most paradoxical fashion, so as to get more people to oppose them. As for myself, there is nothing I would more strenuously avoid than letting my opinions seem paradoxical, and I would never want them to be the subject of disputations. For I consider them to be so certain and evident that whoever rightly understands them will have no occasion

249 to dispute them. I admit that they can be correctly presented through definitions and divisions, proceeding from the general to the particular, but I deny that proofs ought in that case to be omitted. I know of course that such proofs are not necessary for those, like you, who are more mature and well versed in my doctrines. But I ask you to consider how few such persons there are, since of the many thousands who practise philosophy, scarcely one can be found who understands my doctrines. Certainly those who understand the proofs are not ignorant of the conclusions, and so they do not need your book. But when others read the conclusions without the proofs, along with wholly paradoxical definitions in which you mention ethereal globules and other such things without explaining them anywhere, they will make fun of them and hold them in contempt. Thus what you have written will very often be harmful, and never beneficial.

This is the judgement I formed upon reading the first pages of the book you have written. But when I came to the chapter on man, and saw there what you hold concerning the human mind and God, not only did I find my previous judgement confirmed, but I was completely astounded and saddened, both because you seem to believe such things and because you

1 Possibly a manuscript copy of Regius' book *Foundations of Physics* (1646).

cannot refrain from writing and teaching them even though they expose you to danger and censure without bringing you any praise. I beg you to forgive me if I open my heart to you as freely as if you were my brother. If these writings should fall into the hands of malicious people (as may easily happen since they may get them from some of your pupils), they would be able to prove from them – and in my opinion convincingly – that you hold views similar to those of Voetius, etc. Lest this should rebound upon me, I find it necessary to declare once and for all that I differ from you on metaphysical questions as much as I possibly could, and I shall even put   250 this declaration into print if your book should see the light of day. I am indeed grateful that you have shown it to me before publishing it; but I am not grateful that you have been teaching its contents privately, without my knowledge. And now I wholly share the opinion of those who want you to confine yourself to medicine. Why is it necessary for you to mix metaphysical and theological matters in your writings, given that you cannot touch upon such things without falling into some error or other? At first, in considering the mind as a distinct substance from the body, you write that a man is an *ens per accidens*;[1] but then, when you observe that the mind and the body are closely united in the same man, you take the former to be only a *mode of the body*. The latter error is far worse than the former. Again, please excuse me: I assure you that I would not have written to you so freely were I not genuinely fond of you.

I would have returned your book with this letter, but I was afraid that if it should fall into hostile hands, the severity of my censure might harm you. I shall keep it, therefore, until I learn that you have received this letter.

TO PRINCESS ELIZABETH, 21 JULY 1645   AT IV

Since I last had the honour of seeing Your Highness, the weather has   251 been so unsettled, and some days have been so unseasonably cold, that I have often suspected and feared that the waters of Spa would be less healthy and beneficial than in more settled weather. As you have honoured me by indicating that my letters might provide you with some diversion, even though the doctors advise against occupying your mind with anything that fatigues it, I would not be making the best of the favour you did me in permitting me to write to you if I failed to take advantage of it at the first opportunity.

I imagine that most of the letters you receive from other people arouse

1 See footnote 2, p. 200 above for an explanation of this expression.

252 emotions in you, and that even before reading one of these letters you dread finding unpleasant news in it, since ill-fortune has long accustomed you to receiving such news. But as for the letters coming from this quarter, you may be sure that if they do not give you any cause for joy, at least they will not make you sad. And you may be sure too that you can open them at any time without fear that they will impede the digestion of the waters you are taking. For in this isolated place I hear nothing of what goes on in the rest of the world, and I have no more frequent thoughts than those which, dwelling upon the virtues of Your Highness, make me wish to see her enjoy all the happiness and contentment that she deserves. To entertain you, therefore, I shall simply write about the means which philosophy provides for acquiring that supreme felicity which common souls vainly expect from fortune, but which can be acquired only from ourselves.

One of the most useful of these means, I think, is to examine what the ancients have written on this question, and try to advance beyond them by adding something to their precepts. For in this way we can make the precepts perfectly our own and become disposed to put them into practice. That is why, in order to make up for the deficiency of my mind, which cannot produce anything on its own that I judge worthy of being read by Your Highness, and to ensure that my letters are not entirely empty and useless, I propose henceforth to fill them with considerations drawn from 253 the reading of a certain book – namely the one that Seneca wrote *On the Happy Life*[1] – unless you prefer to choose another, or this proposal does not please you. But if I see that you approve it (as I hope you will), and especially if you are so gracious as to share with me your observations on this book, then besides providing me with instruction, these observations will give me the opportunity to make my own more exact; and the more I see our conversation is to your liking, the more carefully I shall develop my observations. For there is nothing in the world that I desire more keenly than to show in every way I can, Madame, that I am Your Highness's very humble and obedient servant.

AT IV   TO PRINCESS ELIZABETH, 4 AUGUST 1645

263   When I chose Seneca's *On the Happy Life* to suggest to Your Highness as an agreeable topic of discussion, I took account only of the reputation of the author and the importance of his topic, without thinking of his manner

---

1 Seneca (*c.* 4 B.C.–A.D. 65), Roman philosopher, statesman and orator, wrote *De Vita Beata* (*On the Happy Life*) in A.D. 58–59.

of treating it. I have since given some thought to this and find it not sufficiently rigorous to deserve to be followed. But to assist Your Highness to make a judgement on the topic, I will try to explain how I think it should have been treated by such a philosopher, unenlightened by faith, with only natural reason to guide him.

At the beginning he says very well that 'all men want to live happily ["vivere beate"], but do not see clearly what makes a life happy'. But first we must know what 'vivere beate' means; I would translate it into French as 'vivre heureusement', if there were not a difference between *l'heur* and *la béatitude*. The former depends only on outward things: we are thought more fortunate (*heureux*) than wise if some good happens to us without our own effort; but happiness (*la béatitude*) consists, it seems to me, in a perfect contentment of mind and inner satisfaction, which is not commonly possessed by those who are most favoured by fortune, and which is acquired by the wise without fortune's favour. So *vivere beate*, to live happily, is just to have a perfectly content and satisfied mind.

Next we must consider what makes a life happy, that is, what are the things which can give us this supreme contentment. Such things, I observe, can be divided into two classes: those which depend on us, like virtue and wisdom, and those which do not, like honours, riches and health. For it is certain that a person of good birth who is not ill, and who lacks nothing, can enjoy a more perfect contentment than another who is poor, unhealthy and deformed, provided the two are equally wise and virtuous. Nevertheless a small vessel may be just as full as a large one, although it contains less liquid; and similarly if we regard each person's contentment as the full satisfaction of all his desires duly regulated by reason, I do not doubt that the poorest people, least blest by nature and fortune, can be entirely content and satisfied just as much as everyone else, although they do not enjoy as many good things. It is only this sort of contentment which is here in question; to seek the other sort would be a waste of time, since it is not in our own power.

It seems to me that each person can make himself content by himself without any external assistance, provided he respects three conditions, which are related to the three rules of morality which I put forward in the *Discourse on the Method*.[1]

The first is that he should always try to employ his mind as well as he can to discover what he should or should not do in all the circumstances of life.

The second is that he should have a firm and constant resolution to carry out whatever reason recommends without being diverted by his passions

264

265

---

1 AT VI 23–8; CSM I 122–5.

or appetites. Virtue, I believe, consists precisely in sticking firmly to this resolution; though I do not know that anyone has ever so described it. Instead, they have divided it into different species to which they have given various names, because of the various objects to which it applies.

The third is that he should bear in mind that while he thus guides himself as far as he can, by reason, all the good things which he does not possess are one and all entirely outside his power. In this way he will become accustomed not to desire them. For nothing can impede our contentment except desire and regret or repentance; but if we always do whatever our reason tells us, even if events show us afterwards that we have gone wrong, we will never have any grounds for repentance, because it was not our own fault. We do not desire to have, for example, more arms or more tongues than we have, and yet we do desire to have more health or more riches. The reason for this is simply that we imagine that the latter, unlike the former, can be acquired by our exertions, or are due to our nature. We can rid ourselves of that opinion by bearing in mind that since we have always followed the advice of our reason, we have left undone nothing that was in our power; and that sickness and misfortune are no less natural to man than prosperity and health.

Of course not every kind of desire is incompatible with happiness – only those which are accompanied by impatience and sadness. It is also not necessary that our reason should be free from error; it is sufficient if our conscience testifies that we have never lacked resolution and virtue to carry out whatever we have judged the best course. So virtue by itself is sufficient to make us content in this life. But virtue unenlightened by intellect can be false: that is to say, the will and resolution to do well can carry us to evil courses, if we think them good; and in such a case the contentment which virtue brings is not solid. Moreover, such virtue is commonly set in opposition to pleasure, appetite and passion, and is accordingly very difficult to practise. The right use of reason, on the other hand, by giving a true knowledge of the good, prevents virtue from being false; by accommodating it to licit pleasures, it makes virtue easy to practise; and by making us recognize the condition of our nature, it sets bounds to our desires. So we must conclude that the greatest felicity of man depends on the right use of reason; and consequently the study which leads to its acquisition is the most useful occupation one can take up. Certainly it is the most agreeable and delightful.

After this, it seems to me, Seneca should have taught us all the principal truths whose knowledge is necessary to facilitate the practice of virtue and to regulate our desires and passions, and thus to enjoy natural happiness. That would have made his book the finest and most useful that a pagan philosopher could have written. But this is only my opinion, which I

submit to the judgement of Your Highness; and if she is good enough to
tell me where I go wrong, I will be most grateful, and I will show, by
correcting my error, that I am, etc.

268

TO PRINCESS ELIZABETH, 18 AUGUST 1645   AT IV.

I do not know whether my last letter has been delivered to Your
Highness. I am sure I could not write anything about the subject I had
chosen for our conversation which you do not know better than I. All the
same I shall continue our correspondence, in the belief that you will not
find my letters any more tiresome than the books in your library; for since
they contain no news which you will be interested in learning promptly,
nothing will impel you to read them at times when you are busy. Thus I
shall regard the time spent in writing them as being well used if you devote
to them only the time you feel like wasting.

I mentioned earlier what I thought Seneca ought to have discussed in his
book. Now I shall examine what he does discuss. I observe only three
general topics in it: the first is his attempt to explain the supreme good,
which he defines in various ways; the second, his argument against the
views of Epicurus;[1] and the third, his reply to those who object that
philosophers do not live in accordance with the rules they lay down. In
order to see in greater detail how he treats these topics, I shall spend a little
time on each chapter.

In the first, he chides those who follow custom and example rather than
reason. 'When it comes to how to live', he says, 'people rely on mere
beliefs, never on sound judgement.' Nevertheless he approves of our
taking the advice of those whom we believe to be the wisest persons;
though he would have us also make use of our own judgement in examining their opinions. Here I am strongly of his opinion. For although many
people are incapable of finding the right path on their own, yet there are
few who cannot recognize it well enough when somebody else clearly
points it out to them. Moreover, provided we take care to seek the advice
of the most able people, instead of allowing ourselves to be guided blindly
by example, and we use all our mental powers to discover how we ought to
proceed, then however things may turn out, our consciences will be at
peace and we shall have the assurance that our opinions on morality are
the best we could possibly have. Although Seneca strives to write with
eloquence here, he does not always express his thoughts with sufficient
accuracy. For example, when he says 'we shall become wise provided we

271

272

273

---

1 Epicurus (341–270 B.C.), Greek philosopher who created a school of moral philosophy
based on pleasure.

separate ourselves from the crowd', he seems to teach that in order to become wise it is enough to behave in an unorthodox manner, which certainly is not his intention.

In the second chapter, he virtually repeats in different words what he said in the first; he adds only that what is commonly judged to be good is not so.

In the third chapter, after having again employed many superfluous words, he finally gives his views on the supreme good: namely that 'it accords with the nature of things', that 'wisdom consists in conforming with the law and the example of nature', and that 'a happy life is one that accords with one's nature'. These statements all seem very obscure to me. For undoubtedly by 'nature' he does not mean our natural inclinations, seeing that they ordinarily lead us to pursue pleasure, which he argues against; but the rest of his discussion makes me think that by 'nature' he means the order established by God in all the things there are in the world. Considering this order to be infallible and independent of our will, he says that 'wisdom consists in agreeing with the nature of things and in conforming to the law and example of nature' – that is to say, wisdom is acquiescence in the order of things, and doing those things for which we believe ourselves to be born; or rather, to use a Christian way of speaking, wisdom is submission to the will of God, and following it in all our actions. And he
274 says that 'a happy life is one that accords with one's nature' – that is to say, happiness consists in following the order of nature, and in accepting in good part all that happens to us. This explains almost nothing, and does not make sufficiently clear the connection with what he adds immediately afterwards – that this happiness cannot come about 'unless the mind is healthy', etc. – unless he means also that 'to live according to nature' is to live in accordance with true reason.

In the fourth and fifth chapters, he gives some other definitions of the supreme good. They all bear some relation to the sense of the first definition, but none of them explains it well enough. The different versions make it seem that Seneca has not clearly understood what he wanted to say, for the better one conceives a thing, the more one is inclined to express it in only one way. The best definition he has found is, I think, the one given in the fifth chapter, where he says that 'a happy person is one who, thanks to reason, has neither desires nor fears', and that 'a happy life is one that is grounded in right and certain judgement'. But so long as he does not tell us the reasons why we ought to have no fears or desires, all this gives us very little assistance.

In these same chapters he begins to argue against those who locate happiness in pleasure and he continues to do so in the following chapters. So before examining them I shall give my views on this question.

My first observation is that there is a difference between happiness, the   275
supreme good, and the final end or goal towards which our actions ought
to tend. For happiness is not the supreme good, but presupposes it, being
the contentment or satisfaction of the mind which results from possessing
it. The end of our actions, however, can be understood to be one or the
other; for the supreme good is undoubtedly the thing we ought to set
ourselves as the goal of all our actions, and the resulting contentment of
the mind is also rightly called our end, since it is the attraction which
makes us seek the supreme good.

A further point is that the word 'pleasure' was understood in a different
sense by Epicurus from those who argued against him. For all his opponents restricted the meaning of the word to the pleasures of the senses;
whereas he, by contrast, extended it to every contentment of the mind, as
can easily be judged from what Seneca and others have written about him.

Now the pagan philosophers had three main views about the supreme
good and the end of our actions: that of Epicurus, who said it was
pleasure; that of Zeno,[1] who insisted that it was virtue; and that of
Aristotle, who made it consist of all the perfections, as much of the body as
of the mind. These three views can, I think, be accepted as true and as   276
consistent with each other, provided they are interpreted favourably.

For Aristotle considered the supreme good of the whole of human
nature in general – that is to say, the good which may be possessed by the
most accomplished of all men. And so he had reason to make it consist of
all the perfections of which human nature is capable. But this does not
serve our purpose.

Zeno, by contrast, considered the supreme good which each person in
particular can possess. That is why he also had very good reason to say that
it consists solely in virtue, because this is the only good, among all those we
can possess, which depends entirely on our free will. By equating all the
vices, however, he made this virtue so severe and so inimical to pleasure
that I think only depressed people, or those whose minds are entirely
detached from their bodies, could be counted among his adherents.

Lastly, when Epicurus considered what happiness consists in and to
what purpose or end our actions tend, he was not wrong to say that it is
pleasure in general – that is to say, contentment of the mind. For although
the mere knowledge of our duty might oblige us to do good actions, yet this
would not cause us to enjoy any happiness if we got no pleasure from it.
But because we often give the name 'delight' to false pleasures, which are   277
accompanied or followed by worry, anxiety and repentance, many have

---

1 Zeno of Citium (*c.* 335–263 B.C.), Greek thinker who founded the Stoic school of moral
philosophy.

believed that this view of Epicurus inculcates vice. Indeed, it does not inculcate virtue. Suppose there is a prize for hitting a bull's-eye: you can make people want to hit the bull's-eye by showing them the prize, but they cannot win the prize if they do not see the bull's-eye; conversely, those who see the bull's-eye are not thereby induced to fire at it if they do not know there is a prize to be won. So too virtue, which is the bull's-eye, does not come to be strongly desired when it is seen all on its own; and contentment, like the prize, cannot be gained unless it is pursued.

That is why I believe I can conclude that happiness consists solely in contentment of mind – that is to say, in contentment in general. For although some contentment depends on the body, and some does not, there is none anywhere but in the mind. But in order to achieve a contentment which is solid, we need to pursue virtue – that is to say, to maintain a firm and constant will to bring about everything we judge to be the best, and to use all the power of our intellect in judging well. On another occasion I shall consider what Seneca has written about this; for my letter is already too long.

AT IV   TO PRINCESS ELIZABETH, 1 SEPTEMBER 1645

281   When last I wrote I was uncertain whether Your Highness was at The Hague or at Rhenen: so I addressed my letter via Leiden; and the one you did me the honour of writing was delivered to me only after the departure of the messenger who had brought it to Alkmaar. So I have been unable to tell you earlier how proud I am that my judgement of the book you read is no different from yours, and that my manner of reasoning seems quite natural to you. I am sure that if you had had as much leisure to think about these topics as I have had, I could not write anything which you would not have observed better than I; but because Your Highness's age, birth and occupation have not permitted this, perhaps what I write can save you time, and even my faults will give you opportunities for observing the truth.

For instance, I spoke of a happiness which depends entirely on our free will, which all men can acquire without external assistance. You observe
282   very truly that there are diseases which take away the power of reasoning and with it the power of enjoying the satisfaction proper to a rational mind. This shows me that what I said in general about every person should be taken to apply only to those who have the free use of their reason and in addition know the way that must be followed to reach such happiness. For each person wants to make himself happy; but many people do not know how to, and often a bodily indisposition prevents their will from being

free. This happens too when we are asleep; because nobody, however philosophical, can prevent himself having bad dreams when his bodily condition so disposes him. Experience, however, shows that if one has often had a certain thought while one's mind was at liberty, it returns later on, however indisposed one's body may be. Thus I can tell you that my own dreams never portray anything distressing, and there is no doubt that it is a great advantage to have long accustomed oneself to drive away sad thoughts. But we cannot altogether answer for ourselves except while we are in our own power. It is less distressing to lose one's life than to lose the use of one's reason, for even without the teachings of faith, natural philosophy by itself makes us hope that our soul will be in a happier state after death than now, and makes us fear nothing more distressing than being attached to a body which altogether takes away its freedom.

There are other indispositions which do not trouble one's senses but   283
merely alter the humours, and make one unsually inclined to sadness, or anger, or some other passion. These certainly cause distress, but they can be overcome; and the harder they are to conquer, the more satisfaction the soul can take in doing so. The same is true of all external handicaps, such as the splendour of high birth, the flatteries of Court, the adversities of fortune, and also great prosperity, which commonly does more than misfortune to hamper the would-be philosopher. When everything goes according to our wishes, we forget to think of ourselves; and when fortune changes, we are the more surprised the more we trusted it. Altogether, we can say, nothing can completely take away our power of making ourselves happy provided it does not trouble our reason. It is not always the things that seem the most distressing which do the most harm.

But in order to discover exactly what contribution each thing can make to our contentment, we must consider what are its causes. This information is also most valuable in making it easy to practise virtue; for all the actions of our soul that enable us to acquire some perfection are virtuous, and all our contentment consists simply in our inner awareness of possess-   284
ing some perfection. Thus we cannot ever practise any virtue – that is to say, do what our reason tells us we should do – without receiving satisfaction and pleasure from so doing. But pleasures are of two kinds: those that belong to the mind alone, and those that belong to the whole human being, that is to say, to the mind in so far as it is united with the body. These last present themselves in a confused manner to the imagination and often appear much greater than they are, especially before we possess them; and this is the source of all the evils and all the errors of life. For according to the rule of reason, each pleasure should be measured by the size of the perfection which produces it; it is thus that we measure those whose causes are clearly known to us. But often passion makes us believe certain things

to be much better and more desirable than they are; then, when we have taken much trouble to acquire them, and in the process lost the chance of possessing other more genuine goods, possession of them brings home to us their defects; and thence arise dissatisfaction, regret and remorse. And so the true function of reason is to examine the just value of all the goods whose acquisition seems to depend in some way on our conduct, so that we never fail to devote all our efforts to trying to secure those which are in fact

285   the most desirable. If, in such cases, fortune opposes our plans and makes them fail, we shall at least have the satisfaction that our loss was not our fault; and we shall still enjoy all the natural happiness whose acquisition was within our power.

Anger, for instance, can sometimes excite in us such violent desires for vengeance that it makes us imagine more pleasure in chastising our enemy than in preserving our honour or our life, and makes us risk both imprudently in the attempt. Whereas, if reason examines what is the good or perfection on which the pleasure derived from vengeance is based, it will find – unless the vengeance serves to prevent future offences – nothing except that it makes us imagine we have some superiority and advantage over the person on whom we are taking vengeance. And this is often only a vain imagination, which is worthless in comparison with honour or life, or even with the satisfaction to be had from seeing one's own mastery of one's anger when one abstains from revenge.

The same is true of the other passions. They all represent the goods to which they tend with greater splendour than they deserve, and they make us imagine pleasures to be much greater, before we possess them, than our subsequent experiences show them to be. This is why pleasure is com-

286   monly disparaged, because the word is used to mean only the pleasures which frequently deceive us by their appearance, and make us neglect other much solider pleasures, such as the pleasures of the mind commonly are, which are not so impressive in anticipation. I say 'commonly' because not all pleasures of the mind are praiseworthy: they can be founded on some false opinion. An instance is the pleasure we take in slander, which is based only on the belief that the worse others are esteemed, the better esteemed we shall be ourselves. Also, they can deceive us by their appearance, when they are accompanied by some strong passion, as can be seen in the pleasure arising from ambition.

But the main difference between the pleasures of the body and those of the mind is the following. The body is subject to perpetual change, and indeed its preservation and well-being depend on change; so all the pleasures proper to it last a very short time, since they arise from the acquisition of something useful to the body at the moment of reception, and cease as soon as it stops being useful. The pleasures of the soul, on the

other hand, can be as immortal as the soul itself provided they are so solidly founded that neither the knowledge of truth nor any false conviction can destroy them.

The true function of reason, then, in the conduct of life is to examine and consider without passion the value of all the perfections, both of the body and of the soul, which can be acquired by our conduct, so that since we are 287 commonly obliged to deprive ourselves of some goods in order to acquire others, we shall always choose the better. Because the pleasures of the body are minor, it can be said in general that it is possible to make oneself happy without them. However, I do not think that they should be altogether despised, or even that one should free oneself altogether from the passions. It is enough to subject one's passions to reason; and once they are thus tamed they are sometimes the more useful the more they tend to excess. I will never have a more excessive passion than that which impels me to the respect and veneration which I owe you and makes me, etc.

TO PRINCESS ELIZABETH, 15 SEPTEMBER 1645   AT IV

Your Highness has so accurately observed all the reasons which pre- 290 vented Seneca from expounding clearly his opinion on the supreme good, and you have read his book with such great care that I fear I would bore 291 you if I continued examining his chapters one by one; and seeing the care you had taken, I put off replying to your question how to strengthen one's understanding so as to discern what is the best in all the actions of life. And so, without pausing to follow Seneca any further, I will try simply to explain my own opinion on the topic.

In order to be always disposed to judge well, only two things seem to me necessary. One is knowledge of the truth; the other is practice in remembering and assenting to this knowledge whenever the occasion demands. But because nobody except God knows everything perfectly, we have to content ourselves with knowing the truths most useful to us.

The first and chief of these is that there is a God on whom all things depend, whose perfections are infinite, whose power is immense and whose decrees are infallible. This teaches us to accept calmly all the things which happen to us as expressly sent by God. Moreover, since the true object of love is perfection, when we lift up our minds to consider him as he 292 is, we find ourselves naturally so inclined to love him that we even rejoice in our afflictions at the thought that they are an expression of his will.

The second thing we must know is the nature of our soul. We must know that it subsists apart from the body, and is much nobler than the body, and that it is capable of enjoying countless satisfactions not to be found in this life. This prevents us from fearing death, and so detaches our affections from the things of this world that we look upon whatever is in the power of fortune with nothing but scorn.

For this it may be useful to judge worthily of the works of God and to have a vast idea of the extent of the universe, such as I tried to convey in the third book of my *Principles*. For if we imagine that beyond the heavens there is nothing but imaginary spaces, and that all the heavens are made only for the service of the earth, and the earth only for man, we will be inclined to think that this earth is our principal abode and this life our best. Instead of discovering the perfections that are truly within us, we will attribute to other creatures imperfections which they do not possess, so as to raise ourselves above them, and we will be so absurdly presumptuous as to wish to belong to God's council and assist him in the government of the world; and this will bring us countless vain anxieties and troubles.

293   After acknowledging the goodness of God, the immortality of our souls and the immensity of the universe, there is yet another truth that is, in my opinion, most useful to know. That is, that though each of us is a person distinct from others, whose interests are accordingly in some way different from those of the rest of the world, we ought still to think that none of us could subsist alone and that each one of us is really one of the many parts of the universe, and more particularly a part of the earth, the state, the society and the family to which we belong by our domicile, our oath of allegiance and our birth. And the interests of the whole, of which each of us is a part, must always be preferred to those of our own particular person – with measure, of course, and discretion, because it would be wrong to expose ourselves to a great evil in order to procure only a slight benefit to our kinsfolk or our country. (Indeed if someone were worth more, by himself, than all his fellow citizens, he would have no reason to destroy himself to save his city.) But if someone saw everything in relation to himself, he would not hesitate to injure others greatly when he thought he could draw some slight advantage; and he would have no true friendship, no fidelity, no virtue at all. On the other hand, if someone considers himself a part of the community, he delights in doing good to everyone, and does not hesitate even to risk his life in the service of others when the occasion demands. If he could, he would even be willing to lose his soul to save others. So this consideration is the source and origin of all the most

294   heroic actions done by men. A person seems to me more pitiful than admirable if he risks death from vanity, in the hope of praise, or through stupidity, because he does not apprehend the danger. But when a person risks death because he believes it to be his duty, or when he suffers some other evil to bring good to others, then he acts in virtue of the consideration that he owes more to the community of which he is a part than to

himself as an individual, though this thought may be only confusedly in his mind without his reflecting upon it. Once someone knows and loves God as he should, he has a natural impulse to think in this way; for then, abandoning himself altogether to God's will, he strips himself of his own interests, and has no other passion than to do what he thinks pleasing to God. Thus he acquires a mental satisfaction and contentment incomparably more valuable than all the passing joys which depend upon the senses.

In addition to these truths which concern all our actions in general, many others must be known which concern more particularly each individual action. The chief of these, in my view, are those I mentioned in my last letter: namely that all our passions represent to us the goods to whose pursuit they impel us as being much greater than they really are; and that 295 the pleasures of the body are never as lasting as those of the soul, or as great in possession as they appear in anticipation. We must pay careful attention to this, so that when we feel ourselves moved by some passion we suspend our judgement until it is calmed, and do not let ourselves easily be deceived by the false appearance of the goods of this world.

I have only this to add, that one must also examine minutely all the customs of one's place of abode to see how far they should be followed. Though we cannot have certain demonstrations of everything, still we must take sides, and in matters of custom embrace the opinions that seem the most probable, so that we may never be irresolute when we need to act. For nothing causes regret and remorse except irresolution.

I said above that besides knowledge of the truth, practice also is required if one is to be always disposed to judge well. We cannot continually pay attention to the same thing; and so, however clear and evident the reasons may have been that convinced us of some truth in the past, we can later be turned away from believing it by some false appearances unless we have so 296 imprinted it on our mind by long and frequent meditation that it has become a settled disposition with us. In this sense the scholastics are right when they say that virtues are habits;[1] for in fact our failings are rarely due to lack of theoretical knowledge of what we should do, but to lack of practical knowledge – that is, lack of a firm habit of belief. And since in examining these truths I am also increasing in myself the corresponding habit, I am particularly obliged to Your Highness for allowing me to correspond with her about them. There is no activity in which I think my leisure better spent than one in which I can show that I am, etc.

---

1 Fr. *habitudes*: a reference to the Aristotelian view that virtues are dispositions acquired through habit.

AT IV   TO PRINCESS ELIZABETH, 6 OCTOBER 1645

304   I have sometimes asked myself the following question. Is it better to be
305   cheerful and content, imagining the goods one possesses to be greater and
        more valuable than they are, and not knowing or caring to consider those
        one lacks; or is it better to have more consideration and knowledge, so as
        to know the just value of both, and thus grow sad? If I thought joy the
        supreme good, I should not doubt that one ought to try to make oneself
        joyful at any price, and I should approve the brutishness of those who
        drown their sorrows in wine, or dull them with tobacco. But I make a
        distinction between the supreme good – which consists in the exercise of
        virtue, or, what comes to the same, the possession of all those goods whose
        acquisition depends upon our free will – and the satisfaction of mind
        which results from that acquisition. Consequently, seeing that it is a
        greater perfection to know the truth than to be ignorant of it, even when it
        is to our disadvantage, I must conclude that it is better to be less cheerful
        and possess more knowledge. So it is not always the most cheerful person
        who has the most satisfied mind; on the contrary, great joys are commonly
        sober and serious, and only slight and passing joys are accompanied by
        laughter. So I cannot approve of trying to deceive oneself by feeding on
        false imaginations; for the resulting pleasure can touch only the surface of
306   the soul, leaving it to feel inner bitterness when it perceives their falsehood.
        It could indeed happen that the soul was so continually diverted that it
        never perceived this; but that would not amount to the enjoyment of the
        happiness we are discussing, since the latter must depend on our conduct,
        whereas the former could come only from fortune.
            But the case is different when we can turn our minds to different
        considerations which are equally true, some leading to contentment and
        others preventing it. In such a case it seems to me that prudence demands
        that we dwell primarily on those which give us satisfaction. Indeed, since
        almost everything in the world can be looked at from one point of view
        which makes it appear good, and from another which brings out its
        defects, I think that the primary way in which we should display skill is in
        looking at things from the point of view which makes them seem most to
        our advantage, provided this does not involve self-deception.
            So, when Your Highness considers the circumstances which have given
        her more leisure to cultivate her reason than many others of her age, if she
        will please also consider how much more she has profited from them than
        others, I am sure that she will have reason to be contented. And I do not see
        why she should prefer to compare herself to other women in a matter
307   which gives her cause for regret than in a matter which could give her
        satisfaction. Our nature is so constituted that our mind needs much

relaxation if it is to be able to spend usefully a few moments in the search for truth. Too great application to study does not refine the mind, but wears it down. Consequently, we should not reckon the time which we could have spent on instructing ourselves by comparison with the number of hours we have had at our disposition but rather, I think, by comparison with what we see commonly happens to others, as an indication of the normal scope of the human mind.

I think also that there is nothing to repent of when we have done what we judged best at the time when we had to decide to act, even though later, thinking it over at our leisure, we judge that we made a mistake. There would be more ground for repentance if we had acted against our conscience, even though we realized afterwards that we had done better than we thought. For we are responsible only for our thoughts, and it does not belong to human nature to be omniscient, or always to judge as well on the spur of the moment as when there is plenty of time to deliberate.

Besides, the vanity which makes a man think better of himself than he deserves is a vice which only weak and base souls display; but this does not mean that the strongest and most noble souls have a duty to despise themselves. We must do ourselves justice, and recognize our perfections as well as our faults. Propriety forbids us to boast of our good qualities, but it   308
does not forbid us to be aware of them.

Finally, it is true that we lack the infinite knowledge which would be necessary for a perfect acquaintance with all the goods between which we have to choose in the various situations of our lives. We must, I think, be contented with a modest knowledge of the most necessary truths such as those I listed in my last letter.[1]

In that letter I have already given my opinion on Your Highness's question whether it is more correct to see everything in relation to oneself or to put oneself to great anxiety for others. If we thought only of ourselves, we could enjoy only the goods which are peculiar to ourselves; whereas, if we consider ourselves as parts of some other body, we share also in the goods which are common to its members, without losing any of those which belong only to ourselves. With evils, the case is not the same, because philosophy teaches that evil is nothing real, but only a privation. When we are sad on account of some evil which has happened to our friends, we do not share in the defect in which this evil consists; and whatever sadness or distress we feel on such occasions cannot be as great as the inner satisfaction which always accompanies good actions, and   309
especially actions which proceed from a pure affection for others which

---

1 The letter of 15 September 1645, p. 265 above.

has no reference to oneself, that is, from the Christian virtue called charity. In this way it is possible, even while weeping and deeply distressed, to have more pleasure than while laughing and at one's ease.

It is easy to show that the pleasure of the soul which constitutes happiness is not inseparable from cheerfulness and bodily comfort. This is proved by tragedies, which please us more the sadder they make us, and by bodily exercises like hunting and tennis which are pleasant in spite of being arduous – indeed we see that often the fatigue and exertion involved increase the pleasure. The soul derives contentment from such exercise because in the process it is made aware of the strength, or skill, or some other perfection of the body to which it is joined; but the contentment which it finds in weeping at some pitiable and tragic episode in the theatre arises chiefly from its impression that it is performing a virtuous action in having compassion for the afflicted. Indeed in general the soul is pleased to feel passions arise in itself no matter what they are, provided it remains in control of them.

310   But I must examine these passions in more detail so as to be able to define them. It will be easier for me to do so in this letter than if I were writing to anyone else, because Your Highness has taken the trouble to read the treatise which I once drafted on the nature of animals.[1] You know already how I think various impressions are formed in their brain: some by the external objects which act upon the senses, and others by the internal dispositions of the body, either by the traces of previous impressions left in the memory, or by the agitation of the spirits which come from the heart. In man the brain is also acted on by the soul, which has some power to change cerebral impressions, just as these impressions in their turn have the power to arouse thoughts in the soul which do not depend on the will. Consequently, the term 'passion' can be applied in general to all the thoughts which are thus aroused in the soul by cerebral impressions alone, without the concurrence of its will, and therefore without any action of the soul itself; for whatever is not an action is a passion. Commonly, however, the term is restricted to thoughts which are caused by some special agitation of the spirits. For thoughts that come from external objects, or from internal dispositions of the body – such as the perception of colours,

311   sounds, smells, hunger, thirst, pain, and the like – are called external or internal sensations. Those that depend solely on the traces left by previous impressions in the memory and the ordinary movement of the spirits are dreams, whether they are real dreams in sleep or daydreams in waking life

---

1 Descartes is probably referring to a treatise on animal physiology which he drafted in 1629–31, and not to writings prepared after the publication of the *Principles of Philosophy*.

when the soul does not determine itself to anything of its own accord, but idly follows the impressions that happen to be in the brain. But when the soul uses the will to determine itself to some thought which is not just intelligible but also imaginable, this thought makes a new impression in the brain; this is not a passion within the soul, but an action – and this is what is properly called imagination. Finally, when the normal flow of the spirits is such that it commonly arouses sad or cheerful thoughts or the like, this is not attributed to passion, but to the nature or humour of the person in whom they are aroused; and so we say that one person has a sad nature, another is of a cheerful humour, and so on. So there remain only the thoughts that come from some special agitation of the spirits, whose effects are felt as in the soul itself. It is these that are passions properly so called.

Of course almost all our thoughts depend on more than one of the causes I have just listed; but each thought is called after its chief cause or   312
the cause with which we are chiefly concerned. This makes many people confuse the sensation of pain with the passion of sadness, and pleasurable sensation with the passion of joy, which they also call enjoyment or delight. People also confuse the sensations of thirst and hunger with the desires to drink and eat, which are passions. This is because the causes that give rise to pain commonly also agitate the spirits in such a way as to arouse sadness, and those that produce a pleasurable sensation agitate them in such a way as to arouse joy, and likewise in other cases.

Sometimes also people confuse the inclinations or habits which dispose to a certain passion with the passion itself, though the two are easy to distinguish. For instance, when it is announced in a town that enemies are coming to besiege it, the inhabitants at once make a judgement about the evil which may result to them: this judgement is an action of their soul and not a passion. And though this judgement is to be found in many alike, they are not all equally affected by it; some are more affected than others in proportion to the greater or less habit or inclination they have towards fear. Their souls can receive the emotion that constitutes the passion only after they have made the judgement, or else at least conceived the danger without making a judgement, and then imprinted an image of it in the brain, by another action, namely imagining. When a soul does this it acts upon the spirits which travel from the brain through the nerves into the   313
muscles, and makes them enter the muscles whose function is to close the openings of the heart. This retards the circulation of the blood so that the whole body becomes pale, cold and trembling, and the fresh spirits returning from the heart to the brain are agitated in such a way that they are useless for forming any images except those which excite in the soul the passion of fear. All these things happen so quickly one after the other that

the whole thing seems like a single operation. Similarly, in all the other passions there occurs some special agitation in the spirits leaving the heart.

That is what I was going to write to Your Highness a week ago, and I was planning to add a detailed explanation of all the passions. But I found it difficult to list them, and so I had to let the postman leave without my letter. Having in the meantime received the one Your Highness was kind enough to write me, I now have more points to answer, and so I must postpone the examination of the passions.[1]

314   I must say at once that all the reasons that prove that God exists and is the first and immutable cause of all effects that do not depend on human free will prove similarly, I think, that he is also the cause of all the effects that do so depend. For the only way to prove that he exists is to consider him as a supremely perfect being; and he would not be supremely perfect if anything could happen in the world without coming entirely from him. It is true that faith alone tells us about the nature of the grace by which God raises us to a supernatural bliss; but philosophy by itself is able to discover that the slightest thought could not enter into a person's mind without God's willing, and having willed from all eternity, that it should so enter. The scholastic distinction between universal and particular causes is out of place here. The sun, although the universal cause of all flowers, is not the cause of the difference between tulips and roses; but that is because their production depends also on some other particular causes which are not subordinated to the sun. But God is the universal cause of everything in such a way as to be also the total cause of everything; and so nothing can happen without his will.

It is true also that knowledge of the immortality of the soul, and of the
315   felicity of which it will be capable after this life, might give occasion to those who are tired of this life to leave it, if they were certain that they would afterwards enjoy all that felicity. But no reason guarantees this, and there is nothing to show that the present life is bad except the false philosophy of Hegesias (whose book was banned by Ptolemy because many of its readers killed themselves).[2] True philosophy, on the contrary, teaches that even amid the saddest disasters and most bitter pains we can always be content, provided that we know how to use our reason.

As for the extent of the universe, I do not see how the consideration of it

---

1 In Elizabeth's reply to Descartes' letter of 15 September, she made the points that resignation to God's will does not reconcile one to the ill-will of men; that belief in immortality might make one seek death; and that consideration of the vast extent of the universe might make us doubt of God's providence (AT v 301).
2 Hegesias, a Greek philosopher of the third century B.C. who advocated suicide. See Cicero, *Tusculana*, I, 34.

tempts one to separate particular providence from the idea we have of God. God is quite different from finite powers. They can be used up; so when we see that they are employed in many great effects, we have reason to judge it unlikely that they also extend to lesser ones. But the greater we deem the works of God to be, the better we observe the infinity of his power; and the better known this infinity is to us, the more certain we are that it extends even to the most particular actions of human beings.

When Your Highness speaks of the particular providence of God as being the foundation of theology, I do not think that you have in mind   316
some change in God's decrees occasioned by actions that depend on our free will. No such change is theologically tenable; and when we are told to pray to God, that is not so that we should inform him of our needs, or that we should try to get him to change anything in the order established from all eternity by his providence – either of these aims would be blameworthy – but simply to obtain whatever he has, from all eternity, willed to be obtained by our prayers. I believe that all theologians agree on this, including the Arminians, who seem the most jealous of the rights of free will.[1]

I agree that it is difficult to determine exactly how far reason ordains that we should devote ourselves to the community. However, it is not a matter on which it is necessary to be very precise; it is enough to satisfy one's conscience, and in doing so one can leave a lot of room for one's inclination. For God has so established the order of things, and has joined men together in so close a community, that even if everyone were to relate everything to himself and had no charity for others, he would still commonly work for them as much as was in his power, provided he exercised prudence, and especially if he lived in an age in which morals were not   317
corrupted. Moreover, as it is a nobler and more glorious thing to do good to others than to oneself, it is the noblest souls who have the greatest inclination thereto and who make least account of the goods they possess. Only weak and base souls value themselves more than they ought, and are like small vessels that a few drops of water can fill. I know that Your Highness is not at all like that. Base souls cannot be persuaded to take trouble for others unless you can show them that they will reap some profit for themselves; but in order to persuade Your Highness to look after her health, it is necessary to point out to her that she cannot long be useful to those she loves if she neglects herself.

---

1 Followers of the Dutch theologian Jakob Hermans (1560–1609), who opposed the Calvinist doctrine of predestination.

AT IV   TO [THE MARQUESS OF NEWCASTLE], OCTOBER 1645

(326)   . . . The treatise on animals, on which I began work more than fifteen years ago, cannot be finished until I have made many observations which are essential for its completion, and which I have not yet had the opportunity to make (nor do I know when I shall have it). Consequently I dare not promise to publish it for a long time yet. Nevertheless, I will obey you in all you may command me, and I regard it as a very great favour that you take pleasure in learning my opinions on a number of philosophical problems.

I am convinced that hunger and thirst are felt in the same manner as colours, sound, smells, and in general all the objects of the external senses, that is, by means of nerves stretched like fine threads from the brain to all the other parts of the body. They are so disposed that whenever one of these parts is moved, the place in the brain where the nerves originate moves also, and its movement arouses in the soul the sensation attributed to that part. I have tried to explain this at length in my *Optics*.[1] I said there that the different movements of the optic nerve make the soul aware of all

327   the diversities of colours and light; and similarly, I believe that the sensation of hunger is caused by a movement of the nerves which go to the base of the stomach and that the sensation of thirst is caused by a different movement of the same nerves and of the nerves which go to the throat. To explain what causes these nerves to move in this way, I observe that just as one's mouth waters when one has a good appetite and sees food on the table, so normally a great quantity of water comes into the stomach in the same circumstances. It is carried thither by the arteries, whose ends have narrow openings of such a shape as to permit the passage of this liquid but not of the other parts of the blood. It is like a kind of acid which mingles with the small particles of the food one has eaten and dissolves them into chyle, and then returns with them through the veins into the blood. But if this liquid finds no food to dissolve when it enters the stomach, it exerts its force on the wall of the stomach and stimulates the nerves attached to it in such a way as to make the soul have the sensation of hunger. And so if there is no food in the stomach, one cannot but have that sensation, unless there are obstructions preventing the liquid from entering, or cold and sticky humours to weaken its force, or unless the blood is in poor condition so that the liquid which it sends into the stomach is in some way unusual. (It is always one of these causes which takes away the appetite in sickness.)

328   Another possibility is that the blood, though not in poor condition, may contain little or none of that liquid: I think this is what happens to those

1 AT VI 130–47; CSM I 167–75.

who have gone a long time without eating. It is said that after some days they stop being hungry. The reason for this is that during that time all the liquid may have left the pure blood and been exhaled in sweat, or lost by insensible transpiration or urination. This is confirmed by the story of a man who is said to have survived three weeks underground without eating, simply by drinking his urine. Since he was shut up underground, his blood did not diminish so much by insensible transpiration as it would have done in the open air.

Moreover, I think thirst is caused in the following manner. The blood serum which usually goes through the arteries to the stomach and the throat in liquid form and thus wets them sometimes travels thither in the form of vapour which dries them up and thus agitates their nerves in the manner needed to arouse in the soul the desire to drink. Thus there is no more difference between this vapour which gives rise to thirst and the liquid which causes hunger than there is between sweat and what is exhaled from the whole body through insensible transpiration.

I think the only general cause of all the movements in the world is God. At the first instant of his creation of matter, he began to move its various parts in different ways; and now, by the same action by which he keeps matter in existence, he also preserves as much movement as he then put into it. I have tried to explain this in Part Two of my *Principles*.[1] And in 329 Part Three I have described in detail the matter of which I take the sun to be composed,[2] and in Part Four I described the nature of fire.[3] And so I could not add anything now which would not be less readily understood than what I then wrote. I also said expressly in article 18 of Part Two that I think the existence of a vacuum involves a contradiction, because we have the same idea of matter as we have of space.[4] Because this idea represents a real thing to us, we would contradict ourselves, and assert the contrary of what we think, if we said that that space was void, that is, that something we conceive as a real thing is not real.

The preservation of health has always been the principal end of my studies, and I do not doubt that it is possible to acquire much information about medicine which has hitherto been unknown. But the treatise on animals which I plan and which I have not yet been able to complete is only a prolegomenon to the acquisition of this information, and so I am careful not to boast that I already possess it. All I can say at present is that I share the opinion of Tiberius, who was inclined to think everyone over thirty had enough experience of what was harmful or beneficial to be his own 330

1 *Principles*, Part II, art. 36: AT VIIIA 61; CSM I 240.
2 *Principles*, Part II, art. 54: AT VIIIA 107.
3 *Principles*, Part II, art. 80: AT VIIIA 249.
4 AT VIIIA 50; CSM I 230.

doctor.¹ Indeed it seems to me that anybody who has any intelligence, and who is willing to pay a little attention to his health, can better observe what is beneficial to it than the most learned doctors. I pray God with all my heart for the preservation of yours, and that of your brother.²

AT IV   TO PRINCESS ELIZABETH, 3 NOVEMBER 1645

330   So seldom do good arguments come my way, not only in the conversations I have in this isolated place³ but also in the books I consult, that I cannot read those which occur in Your Highness's letters without feeling an extraordinary joy. What is more, I find your arguments so strong that I would rather confess I am overwhelmed by them than attempt to rebut

331   them. For, although the comparison which Your Highness refuses to make to her advantage⁴ could be adequately confirmed by experience, yet the virtue of judging others favourably is so praiseworthy, and it fits so well with the generosity that prevents you from wishing to measure the scope of the human mind by the example of the average person, that I am bound to hold both these virtues of yours in very high esteem.

Nor would I venture to contradict what Your Highness writes about repentance. For this is a Christian virtue which serves to make us correct our faults – not only those committed voluntarily, but also those done through ignorance, when some passion has prevented us from knowing the truth.

I agree that the sadness of tragedies would not please as it does if we feared that it might become so excessive as to make us uncomfortable. But when I said that there are passions which are the more useful the more they tend to excess, I only meant to speak of those which are altogether good; as I indicated when I added that they should be subject to reason. There are, indeed, two kinds of excess. There is one which changes the nature of a thing, and turns it from good to bad, and prevents it from remaining subject to reason; and there is another which only increases its quantity,

332   and turns it from good to better. Thus excess of courage is recklessness

---

1 Suetonius, *Life of Tiberius*, art. 69.
2 Sir Charles Cavendish.
3 Egmond–Binnen.
4 In her letter of 28 October, Elizabeth had written: 'You have shown that it is better to know truths which are disadvantageous to us than to be deceived in an agreeable fashion, and that it is only matters allowing different considerations which are equally true which ought to oblige us to dwell upon those which bring us more happiness. Your arguments for these views are so good that I am astonished that you want me to compare myself with others of my age in respect of something which I do not know about, rather than something of which I cannot be ignorant, even though the latter is more advantageous to me' (AT IV 321: see also the letter to Elizabeth, 6 October 1645, p. 268 above).

only when the courage passes the limits of reason; but while remaining within those limits, it can have another kind of excess, which consists in the absence of irresolution and fear.

These last few days I have been thinking about the number and order of all the passions, in order to examine their nature in detail. But I have not yet sufficiently digested my opinions on this topic to dare to tell them to Your Highness. I shall not fail to do so as soon as I can.

As for free will, I agree that if we think only of ourselves we cannot help regarding ourselves as independent; but when we think of the infinite power of God, we cannot help believing that all things depend on him, and hence that our free will is not exempt from this dependence. For it involves a contradiction to say that God has created human beings of such a nature that the actions of their will do not depend on his. It is the same as saying that his power is both finite and infinite: finite, since there is something which does not depend on it; infinite, since he was able to create that independent thing. But just as the knowledge of the existence of God should not take away our certainty of the free will which we experience and feel in ourselves, so also the knowledge of our free will should not 333 make us doubt the existence of God. The independence which we experience and feel in ourselves, and which suffices to make our actions praiseworthy or blameworthy, is not incompatible with a dependence of quite another kind, whereby all things are subject to God.

As for the state of the soul after this life, I am not so well informed as M. Digby.[1] Leaving aside what faith tells us, I agree that by natural reason alone we can make many favourable conjectures and have fine hopes, but we cannot have any certainty. The same natural reason teaches us also that we have always more good than evil in this life, and that we should never leave what is certain for what is uncertain. Consequently, in my opinion, it teaches that though we should not seriously fear death, we should equally never seek it.

I do not need to reply to the objection which theologians may make about the vast extent which I have attributed to the universe, since Your Highness has already replied on my behalf. I will add only that if such a vast extent could make the mysteries of our Faith less credible, the same is true of the vast extent that the astronomers have always attributed to the heavens. They have always thought them so large as to make the earth, by 334 comparison, only a point; yet the objection is never made against them.

If prudence were mistress of events, I do not doubt that Your Highness would succeed in everything she undertakes; but all men would have to be perfectly wise before one could infer from what they ought to do what they

1 See above, p. 251.

will in fact do. At least it would be necessary to know in detail the humour of all those with whom one was to have any dealings. Even that would not be enough, because they have in addition their own free will, whose movements are known only to God. Our judgements about the actions of others are normally based on what we would wish to do ourselves if we were in their place. And so it often happens that ordinary and mediocre minds, being similar to those which they have to deal with, see into their purposes with greater penetration and enable them to succeed in their undertakings more easily than more refined minds do; for the latter, dealing only with those who are inferior in knowledge and prudence, make judgements about matters in an utterly different way. Your Highness should be consoled by this fact when fortune is opposed to your plans.

AT IV

TO MESLAND, 1645 OR 1646

345   I have read with much emotion the last farewell that I found in the letter which you took the trouble to write me.[1] It would have affected me even more if I had not been living in a country where every day I meet people who have returned from the Antipodes. These commonplace occurrences prevent me from losing all hope that I shall see you again some day in Europe. Your aim of converting the savages is very noble and saintly. Nevertheless, because I imagine that its execution requires only a great deal of zeal and patience, and not much intelligence and knowledge, it seems to me that the talents which God has given you could be applied

346   more usefully in converting our own atheists, who pride themselves on their intellect and are prepared to give way only to the evidence of reason. This makes me hope that after you have made an expedition to the places where you are going, and conquered many thousand souls for God, the same spirit which leads you there will bring you back. I desire this with all my heart.

You will find enclosed some brief replies to the objections which you so kindly sent me regarding my *Principles*.[2] I would have made them longer except that I am quite confident that most of the difficulties which occurred to you initially, when you began reading the book, will vanish of their own accord when you have finished it.

The difficulty which you find in the explanation of the Blessed Sacrament can also, I think, be resolved easily. For, in the first place, it is quite true to say that I have the same body now as I had ten years ago, although

---

1 A note in the margin of a manuscript copy of this letter says: 'This Father was banished to Canada, where he died, because of his close relations with M. Descartes. He made some learned remarks and commentaries on the Meditations of M. Descartes.'
2 Probably the comments in the following letter.

the matter of which it is composed has changed, because the numerical identity of the body of a man does not depend on its matter, but on its form, which is the soul. In the same way, the words of our Lord are still quite true: 'This is my body, which is given for you.' I do not see in what other way he could have spoken, in order to signify transubstantiation in the sense in which I have explained it.

Next, regarding the way in which the body of Jesus Christ was in the host which was consecrated at the time of his death, I do not know whether the Church has settled anything about this. We must, I think, take care to distinguish the views determined by the Church from those commonly accepted by the learned, which are based on a shaky physics. Nevertheless, even if the Church had determined that the soul of Jesus Christ was not united to his body in the host which was consecrated at the time of his death, in saying that the matter of the host would then have been as much disposed to be united to the soul of Jesus Christ as the matter of his body which was in the sepulchre, we would say enough to ensure that this matter was truly his body. For the matter in the sepulchre was called the body of Jesus Christ only because of the dispositions which it had to receive his soul. And to say that the matter (of the host or)[1] of the bread would have had the dispositions of the body without the blood, and the matter of the wine the dispositions of the blood without the flesh, is enough to convince us that the body alone, without the blood, would then have been in the host, and the blood alone in the chalice. Likewise, when one says that it is only by concomitance that the body of Jesus Christ is in the chalice: this can readily be understood if you think that although the soul of Jesus Christ is united to the matter contained in the chalice, just as to a whole human body, and consequently that this matter is truly the whole body of Jesus Christ, nevertheless it is united to this matter solely in virtue of the dispositions which the blood has to be united with a human soul, and not in virtue of those belonging to the flesh. Thus I do not see any shadow of a difficulty in all this. None the less, I willingly abide, like you, by the words of the Council[2] that he is there †with that form of existence which we can scarcely express in words†.

347

348

TO ***, 1645 OR 1646

AT IV

I do not remember where I spoke of the distinction between essence and existence.[3] However, I make a distinction †between modes, strictly so

348

---

1 The parentheses and the word 'or' were added by Clerselier to the MS copy of this letter.
2 The Council of Trent (1545–63). See Fourth Replies: AT VII 252; CSM II 175 and the letter to Mesland, 9 February 1645, p. 241 above.
3 See Med. V: AT VII 68–9; CSM II 47.

349 called, and attributes, without which the things whose attributes they are cannot be; or between the modes of things themselves and the modes of thinking.† (Forgive me if I here change into another language to express myself better.) †Thus shape and motion are modes, in the strict sense, of corporeal substance; because the same body can exist at one time with one shape and at another with another, now in motion and now at rest; whereas, conversely, neither this shape nor this motion can exist without this body. Thus love, hatred, affirmation, doubt, and so on are true modes in the mind. But existence, duration, size, number and all universals are not, it seems to me, modes in the strict sense; nor in this sense are justice, mercy, and so on modes in God. They are referred to by a broader term and called attributes, or modes of thinking, because we do indeed understand the essence of a thing in one way when we consider it in abstraction from whether it exists or not, and in a different way when we consider it as existing; but the thing itself cannot be outside our thought without its existence, or without its duration or size, and so on. Accordingly I say that shape and other similar modes are strictly speaking modally distinct from the substance whose modes they are; but there is a lesser distinction between the other attributes. This latter can be called modal – as I did at the end of my Replies to the First Objections – but only in a broad sense of the term, and it is perhaps better called formal. But to avoid confusion, in article 60 of Part One of my *Principles of Philosophy*[1] where I discuss it explicitly, I call it a conceptual distinction – that is, a distinction made by reason *ratiocinatae*. I do not recognize any distinction made by reason *ratiocinantis* – that is, one which has no foundation in reality – because we cannot have any thought without a foundation; and consequently in that

350 article, I did not add the term *ratiocinatae*.[2] It seems to me that the only thing which causes difficulty in this area is the fact that we do not sufficiently distinguish between things existing outside our thought and the ideas of things, which are in our thought. Thus, when I think of the essence of a triangle, and of the existence of the same triangle, these two thoughts, as thoughts, even taken objectively[3] differ modally in the strict sense of the term 'mode'; but the case is not the same with the triangle existing outside thought, in which it seems to me manifest that essence and existence are in no way distinct. The same is the case with all universals. Thus, when I say Peter is a man, the thought by which I think of Peter differs modally from the thought by which I think of man, but in Peter

---

1 AT VIIIA 28; CSM I 213.
2 In scholastic philosophy a distinction made by reason is *ratiocinatae* if it has a foundation in reality, and *ratiocinantis* if it has no foundation in reality.
3 I.e. even in respect of their representational content.

himself being a man is nothing other than being Peter. So, then, I postulate three kinds of distinction: first, real distinction between two substances; and then modal and formal distinctions, which are distinctions of reason *ratiocinatae*. All these three can be called real in contrast to the distinction of reason *ratiocinantis*; and in this sense it can be said that essence is really distinct from existence. Again, if by essence we understand a thing as it is objectively in the intellect,[1] and by existence the same thing in so far as it is outside the intellect, it is manifest that the two are really distinct.[†]

Thus, almost all the controversies of philosophy arise only from misunderstandings between philosophers. Forgive me if this discussion is too confused; the postman is about to leave, and I have only time to add here that I am very obliged to you for your remembrance of me, and that I am, etc.

TO PRINCESS ELIZABETH, JANUARY 1646

AT IV

I cannot deny that I was not surprised to learn that Your Highness was annoyed, to the point where her health was affected, by an event which most people will consider to be good, and which the rest may overlook for several strong reasons.[2] In fact, all those who share my religion – which is undoubtedly the majority of people in Europe – are obliged to approve it, even though they might see in it some circumstances and apparent motives which could be condemned; for we believe that God employs various means of drawing souls to him, and that someone who enters a monastery for bad reasons may thereafter lead a life of great holiness. As for those of a different faith, if they speak badly of such a person, we may challenge their judgement; for in all affairs where there are different sides, it is impossible to please one without displeasing the other. If they recall that they would not belong to the church to which they belong if they, or their fathers, or their grandfathers had not left the Church of Rome, then they will have no reason to ridicule those who leave their church, or to accuse them of inconstancy.

As regards the wisdom of the times, it is true that those who have Fortune as a house guest are right to stay close to her, and to join forces in order to prevent her from escaping; whereas I think that those whose home she has fled do well to agree to follow various different paths, so that at

351

352

---

1 See First Replies: AT VII 102; CSM II 75.
2 In November 1645 Princess Elizabeth's brother, Prince Edward, became a Catholic in order to marry the Princess of Mantua. Elizabeth wrote to Descartes expressing her distress at his conversion (AT IV 335).

least one of them may meet her, even if not all can find her. At the same time, because each of them is thought to have many resources, including friends in various places, this makes them more powerful than if they all followed the same path. This makes it impossible for me to imagine that the authors of this advice wanted to harm your House. But I do not suppose that my arguments could prevent Your Highness from feeling the resentment she does; I hope only that time will have weakened the feeling before this letter reaches you, and I fear that I would reawaken it if I were to discuss this topic at greater length.

353   I turn to Your Highness's problem about free will. I will try to give an illustration to explain how this is both dependent and free. Suppose that a king has forbidden duels, and knows with certainty that two gentlemen of his kingdom who live in different towns have a quarrel, and are so hostile to each other that if they meet, nothing will stop them from fighting. If this king orders one of them to go on a certain day to the town where the other lives, and orders the other to go on the same day to the place where the first is, he knows with certainty that they will meet, and fight, and thus disobey his prohibition; but he does not thereby compel them, and his knowledge, and even his will to determine their course of action in the way he did, does not prevent their fighting when they meet from being as voluntary and as free as if they had met on some other occasion and he had known nothing about it. And they can be no less justly punished for disobeying the prohibition. Now what a king can do in such a case, concerning certain free actions of his subjects, God with his infinite foresight and power does infallibly in regard to all the free actions of all men. Before he sent us into the world he knew exactly what all the inclinations of our will would be; it is he who gave us them, it is he who has arranged all the other things

354   outside us so that such and such objects would present themselves to our senses at such and such times, on the occasion of which he knew that our free will would determine us to such or such an action; and he so willed, but he did not thereby will that our will should be constrained to the choice in question. In the king of my story it is possible to distinguish two different types of volition, one according to which he willed that these gentlemen should fight, since he caused them to meet; and the other according to which he did not so will, since he forbade duels. In the same way the theologians make a distinction in God's willing: he has an absolute and independent will, according to which he wills all things to come about as they do, and another relative will which concerns the merit and demerit of men, according to which he wants them to obey his laws.

I must also make a distinction between two sorts of goods, in order to defend what I wrote earlier – namely that in this life we have always more good things than evil – against Your Highness's objection concerning all the inconveniences of life.[1] When we consider the idea of goodness as a rule for our actions, we take the goodness to consist in all of the perfection that can exist in the thing we are calling 'good', and we compare the perfection with a straight line, which is unique among the infinite number of curves, with which we compare evils. This is the sense in which philosophers commonly say that †the good comes from the cause whole and entire; the evil from any defect whatsoever.† But when we consider the good and evil which may exist in a single thing, in order to discover what value to put on it, as I did when I spoke of the value we should put on this life, we must take the good to consist in whatever may be advantageous to us, and the evil to consist in whatever may be disadvantageous; the other defects which the thing may have are not taken into account. Thus, if a man is offered a post, he considers as goods the honour and profit he may expect from it, and as evils the trouble, the danger, the loss of time, and other such things. Having compared the evils and the goods, he accepts or declines according as he finds the latter greater or less than the former. It was in this latter sense that I said that there are always more good things than evil in this life; and I said this because I think we should take little account of all the things outside us that do not depend on our free will in comparison with those that do depend on it. Provided we know how to use our will well, we can make everything which depends on it good and thus prevent the evils that come from elsewhere, however great they may be, from penetrating any further into our souls than the sadness which actors arouse in it when they enact before us some tragic history. But I agree that to reach such a point we have to be very philosophical indeed. Nevertheless, I think that even those who most give rein to their passions really judge deep down, even if they do not themselves perceive it, that there are more good things than evil in this life. Sometimes they may call upon death to help them when they feel great pain, but it is only to help them bear their burden, as in the fable, and for all that they do not want to lose their life. And if there are some who do want to lose it, and who kill themselves, it is due to an intellectual error and not to a well-reasoned judgement, or to an opinion imprinted on them by nature, like the one which makes a man prefer the goods of this life to its evils. . . .

355

356

TO CLERSELIER, 2 MARCH 1646

AT IV

It is only a week since I had the honour of writing to you. But today I received your last letter, and it gives me a new reason to thank you – for

372

1 'Human beings', Elizabeth had written, 'have more occasions for distress than delight, and there are a thousand errors for one truth' (AT IV 337).

taking the trouble to receive the letters from my sister,[1] who addressed them previously to Father Mersenne. I write to her only two or three times a year, and so I hope you will not be inconvenienced too much by doing this.

As for the difficulty you mention, concerning the Blessed Sacrament, I have no reply except that if God puts one purely corporeal substance in place of another such substance, like a piece of gold in place of a piece of bread, or one piece of bread in place of another, he changes only the numerical unity of their matter by bringing it about that †numerically† the same matter, which was gold, takes on the accidents of the bread; or rather, that †numerically† the same matter, which was the bread A, takes on the accidents of the bread B – that is to say, this matter is placed under the same dimensions, and the matter of bread B is removed from these dimensions. But there is something more in the Blessed Sacrament. For besides the matter of the body of Jesus Christ, which is placed under the dimensions of the bread, the soul of Jesus Christ, which informs[2] this matter, is present there as well.

373

I sent you the copy of the licence to publish,[3] along with my opinion regarding the Fifth Objections, a week ago.

AT IV

TO***, [MARCH 1646][4]

374   As for the difficulty you speak of, I do not see that it applies any differently to my philosophy than to the philosophy of the Schools. For there are two principal questions about this mystery. One is how it can

375   come about that all the accidents of the bread remain in a place where the bread is no longer present, and where another body is taking its place. The other is how the body of Jesus Christ can exist within the same dimensions where the bread was.

My reply to the first difficulty had to differ from that given by the scholastic philosophers, because I have a different view about the nature of accidents. As for the second difficulty, however, I do not need to look for any new explanation; and even if I could find one, I would not wish to divulge it, because in these matters the most common opinions are the best. Thus one may put the following question not just to me, but to all

---

1 Anne, Descartes' younger sister.

2 Fr. *informe*. Descartes sometimes uses the standard scholastic term, though he rejects the Aristotelian account of the soul as the 'form' of the body (see also p. 244 above).

3 The licence to publish granted to Descartes from the King of France in 1637 covered not only the *Discourse* and *Essays*, but all Descartes' works, including the French translations of the *Meditations* and the *Principles*, which were published at the beginning of 1647.

4 In the manuscript containing the letter to Clerselier (p. 283 above), this extract comes immediately afterwards. The addressee is unknown and the date is uncertain.

theologians: 'When one corporeal substance is changed into another and all the accidents of the former remain, what is it that has changed?' And they must reply, as I do, that there is no change in anything that falls under the senses, and hence none in anything underlying the different names we have given to these substances. For it is certain that this difference in the names arises solely from our having observed different perceptible properties in the substances.

TO MERSENNE, 20 APRIL 1646

AT IV

... Finally, it is a most absurd suggestion that in all the particles of the matter of the universe there resides some property in virtue of which they are mutually drawn towards and attract each other; and that in each particle of terrestrial matter in particular there is a similar property in respect of other terrestrial particles which does not interfere with the former property. For in order to make sense of this, one has to suppose not only that each particle of matter has a soul, and indeed several different souls, which do not impede each other, but also that these souls are capable of thought, and indeed divine, to enable them to know without any intermediary what was happening in those distant places, and to exercise their powers there...

(401)

TO PRINCESS ELIZABETH, MAY 1646

AT IV

I discover by experience that I was right to include pride among the passions; for when I see the favourable judgement which Your Highness has made of my little treatise about them,[1] I cannot prevent myself from feeling proud. I am not at all surprised that you have also noticed faults in it, since I had no doubt there must be many. It is a topic that I have never before studied, and I have only made a sketch without adding the colours and embellishments which would be needed for it to be presented to eyes less perceptive than those of Your Highness.

407

Moreover, I did not mention all the principles of physics which I used to work out the particular movements of blood accompanying each passion. This was because I could not properly prove them without explaining the formation of all the parts of the human body; and that is something so difficult that I would not yet dare to undertake it, though I am more or less convinced in my own mind of the truth of the principles presupposed in the treatise. The chief ones are as follows. The function of the liver and the

---

1 A first draft of the *Passions of the Soul* which Descartes had sent to Elizabeth earlier in the year.

spleen is to contain reserve blood, less purified than the blood in the veins; and the fire in the heart needs constantly to be fed either by the juices of food coming directly from the stomach, or in their absence by this reserve

408   blood (since the other blood in the veins expands too easily). Our soul and our body are so linked that the thoughts which have accompanied some movements of our body since our life began still accompany them at present; so that if the same movements are excited afresh by some external cause, they arouse in the soul the same thoughts; and conversely, if we have the same thoughts they produce the same movements. Finally, the machine of our body is constructed in such a way that a single thought of joy or love or the like is sufficient to send the animal spirits through the nerves into all the muscles needed to cause the different movements of the blood which, as I said, accompany the passions. It is true that I found difficulty in working out the movements peculiar to each passion, because the passions never occur singly; nevertheless, since they occur in different combinations, I tried to discover the changes that occur in the body when they change company. Thus, for instance, if love were always joined with joy, I could not know which of the two was responsible for the heat and swelling that they make us feel around the heart; but since love is some-times also joined with sadness, and in that case the heat is still felt but not the swelling, I decided that the heat belongs to the love and the swelling to the joy. Again, although desire almost always goes with love, they are not

409   always together in the same degree, for when there is no hope we may have much love and little desire. In such a case we do not have the diligence and alertness we would have if our desire were greater, and consequently it can be deduced that these characteristics arise from desire and not from love.

I quite believe that sadness takes away many people's appetite; but because I have always found in my own case that it increases it, I have based my account on that. I think that the difference between people in this matter arises thus: for some people the first thing that made them sad as babies was their not getting enough food, while for others it was that the food they received was bad for them. In the latter case, the movement of animal spirits which takes away the appetite has ever afterwards remained joined with the passion of sadness. We see also that the movements which accompany other passions differ slightly from person to person, and this can be attributed to some similar cause.

It is true that wonder has its origin in the brain, and cannot be caused solely by the condition of the blood, as joy and sadness can. Yet by means of the impression it makes in the brain, it can act on the body just like any other passion, and in a way more effectively because the surprise which it involves causes the promptest of all movements. We can move our hands

or our feet more or less at the same instant as the thought of moving them   410
occurs, because the idea of this movement formed in the brain sends the
spirits into the muscles appropriate for this result. In the same way the idea
of a pleasant thing, if it takes the mind by surprise, immediately sends the
spirits into the nerves that open the orifices of the heart. By the surprise it
involves, wonder simply increases the force of the movement which gives
rise to joy. The effect of this is that, the orifices of the heart being suddenly
dilated, the blood flows into the heart from the vena cava and out again via
the arterial vein, thus causing the lungs suddenly to inflate.

The same external signs that usually accompany the passions may
indeed sometimes be produced by other causes. Thus, a red face is not
always the result of shame; it may come from the heat of a fire or from
exercise. A sardonic grin may be due to a convulsion of the nerves of the
face. Similarly one may sigh sometimes out of habit, or out of sickness, but
this does not mean that sighs are not external signs of sadness and desire
when they are in fact caused by these passions. I have never heard or
noticed that sighs may also be caused by a full stomach; but when that
happens I think it is a movement which nature uses to make the alimentary
juices pass more rapidly through the heart, thus speeding up the emptying
of the stomach. For sighs, by exercising the lungs, make the blood they
contain descend more quickly through the venous artery into the left side   411
of the heart. This facilitates the reception into the lungs of the new blood,
made up of alimentary juices, which comes up from the stomach through
the liver and the heart.

I agree that the remedies against excessive passions are difficult to
practise, and also that they are insufficient to prevent bodily disorders; but
they may suffice to prevent the soul being troubled by them and losing its
free judgement. For this purpose I do not consider it necessary to have an
exact knowledge of the truth on every topic, or even to have foreseen in
detail all possible eventualities, which would doubtless be impossible. It is
enough in general to have imagined circumstances more distressing than
one's own and to be prepared to bear them. Moreover, I do not think that
one can sin by excess in desiring the necessities of life; it is only desires for
evil or superfluous things that need controlling. As for those which tend
only to good, it seems to me that the stronger they are, the better. To
palliate my own faults I listed a certain irresolution as an excusable
passion, but nevertheless I esteem much more highly the diligence of those
who are swift and ardent in performing what they conceive to be their duty
even when they do not expect much profit from it.

I lead such a retired life, and have always been so far from the conduct of   412
affairs, that I would be no less impudent than the philosopher who wished
to lecture on the duties of a general in the presence of Hannibal if I took it

on me to enumerate here the maxims one should observe in a life of public service. I do not doubt that Your Highness's maxim is the best of all, namely that it is better to be guided by experience in these matters than by reason. It is rarely that we have to do with people who are as perfectly reasonable as everyone ought to be, so that one can judge what they will do simply by considering what they ought to do; and often the soundest advice is not the most successful. That is why one has to take risks and put oneself in the power of fortune, which I hope will always be as obedient to your desires as I am.

AT IV

TO PRINCESS ELIZABETH, MAY 1646

414　　The opportunity to give this letter to M. de Beclin, a very close friend of mine whom I trust as much as I do myself, has led me to take the liberty of confessing that I made a glaring mistake in my treatise on the passions. In order to palliate my own diffidence, I counted as one of the emotions of the soul which are excusable a sort of irresolution which sometimes prevents us from performing actions that have been approved by our judgement.[1] And what has given me the most concern here is my recollection that Your Highess commented on this passage in particular, as showing that I do not disapprove of acting on this emotion in matters where I can see its utility. I admit indeed that we are quite right to take time to deliberate before undertaking tasks of any importance. But once a project is begun and we are agreed upon the main aims, I do not see that we have anything to gain by delaying matters in arguing about the details. For if the project succeeds

415　despite this, then all the minor benefits we may have gained in this way are entirely offset by the harmful effects of the disgust that such delays ordinarily cause. And if it does not succeed, then all this does is to show the world that we had plans which failed. In addition, when we delay undertaking a project, it often happens – more often in the case of good projects than in the case of bad ones – that the opportunity is lost. This is why I am convinced that resolution and dispatch are virtues which are very necessary for projects already begun. And we have no reason to fear what we have no knowledge of. For often the things we most dreaded before coming to know them turn out to be better than those we desired. Thus it is best in these matters to trust in divine providence, and to let oneself be guided by it. I am certain that Your Highness understands my thought very well, even though I explain it very badly; and that she will pardon the ardour which obliges me to write this.

---

1 See *Passions of the Soul*, art. 170: AT XI 459; CSM I 390.

TO CHANUT, 15 JUNE 1646

AT IV

I was very glad to learn from the letter you did me the honour of writing   440
that Sweden is not so far from here that one cannot have news from it in a
few weeks. So I shall sometimes have the happiness of corresponding with
you and sharing in the results of the studies which I see you are planning to   441
make. Since you are good enough to look at my *Principles* and examine
them, I am sure that you will notice in them many obscurities and faults. It
will be very valuable for me to discover them, and I know no one who can
inform me of them better than you. I only fear that you will soon grow
tired of reading the book, since what I have written is only distantly
connected with moral philosophy, which you have chosen as your principal study.

Of course, I agree with you entirely that the safest way to find out how
we should live is to discover first what we are, what kind of world we live
in, and who is the creator of this world, or the master of the house we live
in. But I cannot at all claim or promise that all I have written is true, and
besides there is a very great distance between the general notion of heaven
and earth, which I have tried to convey in my *Principles*, and the detailed
knowledge of the nature of man, which I have not yet discussed. However,
I do not want you to think I wish to divert you from your plan, and so I
must say in confidence that what little knowledge of physics I have tried to
acquire has been a great help to me in establishing sure foundations in
moral philosophy. Indeed I have found it easier to reach satisfactory
conclusions on this topic than on many others concerning medicine, on
which I have spent much more time. So instead of finding ways to preserve   442
life, I have found another, much easier and surer way, which is not to fear
death. But this does not depress me, as it commonly depresses those whose
wisdom is drawn entirely from the teaching of others, and rests on
foundations which depend only on human prudence and authority.

I will say, moreover, that while I am waiting for the plants to grow in my
garden which I need for some experiments to continue my physics, I am
spending some time also in thinking about particular problems in ethics.
Last winter, for instance, I sketched a little treatise on the nature of the
passions of the soul, without any idea of publication; and I would now feel
inclined to write something more on the topic, if I were not made indolent
by seeing how depressingly few people condescend to read what I write.
But in your service I will never be indolent.

TO CLERSELIER, JUNE OR JULY 1646

AT IV

My hope of soon being in Paris makes me lazy about writing to those   443
whom I hope to have the honour to see there. So it is already some time

since I received the letter which you were kind enough to write; but I thought that you could not be very anxious for an answer to your question as to what should be taken as the *first principle*, since you replied to it yourself in the same letter better than I could do.

444

I will only add that the word 'principle' can be taken in several senses. It is one thing to look for a *common notion* so clear and so general that it can serve as a principle for proving the existence of all the beings, or entities, to be discovered later; and another thing to look for a *being* whose existence is known to us better than that of any other, so that it can serve as a *principle* for discovering them.

In the first sense, it can be said that 'It is impossible for the same thing both to be and not to be at the same time' is a principle which can serve in general, not properly speaking to make known the existence of anything, but simply to confirm its truth once known, by the following reasoning: 'It is impossible that that which is, is not; I know that such a thing is; so I know that it is impossible that it is not.' This is of very little importance, and makes us no better informed.

In the second sense, the first principle is *that our soul exists*, because there is nothing whose existence is better known to us.

I will also add that one should not require the first principle to be such that all other propositions can be reduced to it and proved by it. It is enough if it is useful for the discovery of many, and if there is no other

445 proposition on which it depends, and none which is easier to discover. For it may be that there is no principle at all to which alone all things can be reduced. They do indeed reduce other propositions to the principle 'It is impossible for the same thing both to be and not to be at the same time', but their procedure is superfluous and useless. On the other hand it is very useful indeed to convince oneself first of *the existence of God*, and then of the existence of all creatures, *through the consideration of one's own existence*.

Father Mersenne had told me that M. le Conte[1] has taken the trouble to compose some objections against my philosophy; but I have not yet seen them. Please assure him that I am waiting for them and that I take it as an honour that he has taken the trouble to write them.

The Achilles of Zeno is not difficult to solve if you bear in mind what follows. If you add to the tenth part of a certain quantity the tenth of that tenth, which is a hundredth, and then the tenth of this latter, which is a thousandth of the first, and so on *ad infinitum*, all these tenths, though

---

1 Antoine le Conte, adviser to the King and friend of Chanut; the objections concern Parts III and IV of the *Principles of Philosophy*, and were sent to Descartes by Clerselier in July 1646 (AT IV 454–71).

supposed to be really infinite, add up only to a finite quantity, namely a ninth of the first quantity, as can easily be demonstrated. For example, if from line AB you take away the tenth part of the side towards A, namely

```
                G
A───────────────────────────────────────────────B
        C E F      D
```

AC, and at the same time you take away eight times as much from the   446
other side, namely BD, there will remain between them only CD which is equal to AC; then in turn if you take away from CD the tenth on the side towards A, that is CE, and eight times as much from the other side, that is DF, there will remain between them only EF which is the tenth of the whole CD; and if you continue indefinitely to take away from the side marked A a tenth of what you took away beforehand, and eight times as much from the other side, you will always find that there will remain, between the two last lines that you have taken away, a tenth of the whole line from which they have been taken away; and from that tenth you will always be able to take away further lines in the same way. But if you suppose that this has been done an actually infinite number of times, then nothing at all will remain between the two last lines which have thus been taken away; and from each side you will have arrived exactly at point G, supposing that AG is a ninth of the whole AB, and consequently that BG is eight times AG. For since what you have taken away from the side towards B will always have been eight times what you took away from the side towards A, it follows that the aggregate or total of all these lines taken away from the side towards B, which together make up line BG, will also be eight times AG, which is the aggregate of all those which have been taken away from the side of A. Consequently, if to line AC you add CE, which is a tenth of it, and then a tenth of that tenth, and so on *ad infinitum*, all these lines together will only make up line AG, which is a ninth of the   447
whole AB, which is what I set out to prove.

Once we realize this, we have an answer to anyone who says that a tortoise which has ten leagues' start can never be overtaken by a horse which goes ten times as fast as it, because while the horse travels these ten leagues, the tortoise travels one more, and while the horse travels the league, the tortoise goes ahead another tenth of a league, and so on for ever. The answer is that it is true that the horse will never overtake it while travelling that league and that tenth of a league and that hundredth and thousandth and so on of a league; but it does not follow from this that it will never overtake it, because the tenth and hundredth and thousandth only add up to a ninth of a league, at the end of which the horse will start to be in the lead. The catch is that people imagine this ninth of a league to be an infinite quantity, because they divide it in their imagination into infinite parts. I am infinitely, etc.

AT IV   TO PRINCESS ELIZABETH, SEPTEMBER 1646

486   I have read the book[1] which Your Highness commanded me to discuss, and I find in it many maxims which seem excellent: for instance, in chapters 19 and 20, that a prince should always avoid the hatred and contempt of his subjects, and that the love of the people is worth more than fortresses. But there are also many others which I cannot approve. I think that the author's greatest fault is that he does not sufficiently distinguish between princes who have come to power by just means and those who have usurped it by illegitimate methods; and that he recommends indiscriminately maxims that are suitable only for the latter. If you are building a house on foundations insufficient to support high thick walls, the walls will have to be low and insubstantial; and similarly, those who have gained power by crime are usually compelled to continue their course of crime, and would be unable to remain in power if they took to virtue.

It is of such princes that what he says in chapter 3 is true: that they cannot help being hated by many, and that it is often more advantageous for them to do great harm than to do slight harm because slight offences merely arouse a desire for revenge, whereas great ones take away the power to exact it. And similarly in chapter 15 he says that if they decided to be good they could not but be ruined, being in the midst of the great
487   number of wicked people throughout the world. And in chapter 19 he says that one can be hated for good actions no less than for bad ones.

On these foundations he erects some very tyrannical maxims: for instance, he urges princes to be willing to ruin a whole country in order to remain master of it; to use great cruelty, provided it is soon over and done with; to try to appear good rather than to be good in reality; to keep their word only as long as it is useful; to dissimulate and to betray. Finally, he says that in order to rule one must strip oneself of all humanity and become as ferocious as any animal.

It is a sorry thing to make a book full of maxims which at the end of the day cannot even give any security to those to whom they are offered. He agrees himself that princes cannot protect themselves from the first fellow who is willing to risk his own life to take revenge on them.

It seems to me that quite contrary maxims should be proposed for the

1 *The Prince* (1513), by Niccolò Machiavelli (1469–1527).

instruction of good princes, however newly they may have come to power; and it should be presupposed that the means which they have used to gain power have been just. Almost always, I think, they are just, provided the princes who use them think them to be; for justice between sovereigns does not have the same bounds as justice between individuals. It seems to me that in this instance God gives the right to those to whom he gives power. But of course the most just actions become unjust when those who do them think them so.

A distinction must also be made between subjects, friends or allies, and enemies. With regard to these last, one has a virtual licence to do anything, provided that some advantage to oneself or one's subjects ensues; and I do not think it wrong in such a case to join the fox with the lion and use artifice as well as force. And I include among enemies all those who are neither friends nor allies, because one has a right to make war on such people when it is to one's advantage and when their power is increasing in a suspicious and alarming manner. But I rule out one type of deception which is so directly hostile to society that I do not think it is ever permissible to use it, although our author approves it in several places; and that is pretending to be a friend of those one wishes to destroy, in order to take them by surprise. Friendship is too sacred a thing to be abused in this way; and someone who has once feigned love for someone in order to betray him deserves to be disbelieved and hated by those whom he afterwards genuinely wishes to love.

As for allies, a prince should keep his word to them strictly, even when it is to his own disadvantage; for no disadvantage can outweight the utility of a reputation for keeping one's promises; and a prince can acquire this reputation only on occasions when it involves him in some loss. But in situations where he would be altogether ruined, the law of nations dispenses him from his promise. It is necessary to use much circumspection in promising if one is to be able always to keep faith. It is a good thing to be on friendly terms with the majority of one's neighbours, but I think it best not to have strict alliances except with sovereigns less powerful than oneself. For however loyal one intends to be oneself, one should not expect the same from others; one should count on being betrayed whenever one's allies find it to their advantage. Those who are more powerful may find it to their advantage to do so whenever they wish; not so those who are less powerful.

As for subjects, there are two kinds: great people and common people. I mean by the expression 'great people' all those who can form parties against the prince. Of their fidelity he must be very certain; if he is not, he should employ all his efforts to bring them low, and if they show any tendency to rock the ship of state, he should treat them as he would his

488

489

enemies. On this all politicians agree. As for his other subjects, he should above all avoid their hatred and contempt. This, I think, he can always do provided he dispenses justice strictly according to their custom – that is, in accordance with the laws with which they are familiar – without excessive rigour in punishment or excessive indulgence in pardoning.

The prince must not hand over everything to his ministers; he should leave them to pronounce the most odious condemnations, and he should display his own concern with everything else. He should also guard his dignity; he should not waive a jot of the honour and deference the people think due to him, but should not ask for more. He should perform in public 490 only important or universally commendable actions, taking his pleasures in private and never at anyone else's expense. Finally he should be immovable and inflexible. I do not mean that he should hold fast to his own first designs; he cannot have his eye everywhere and so he must ask for advice, and hear many people's reasons, before coming to a decision. But once he has announced his decision, he must be inflexible in holding to it even if this does him harm; for it can hardly be as harmful to him as the reputation of being irresolute and inconstant.

Consequently, I disapprove of the maxim of chapter 15, that 'since the world is very corrupt, a man who tries always to be good is bound to come off badly', and that 'a prince, if he is to remain in power, must learn to be wicked when the occasion demands'. Unless, by a good man, he means a superstitious and simple man who would not dare to give battle on the sabbath, and whose conscience could never rest unless he changed the religion of his people. But if we consider that a good man is one who does all that true reason tells him, it is certain that the best thing is to try always to be good.

Again, I do not believe what is said in chapter 19, that one may be hated for good actions as much as for bad ones. It is true that envy is a kind of hatred, but that is not what the author means; princes are not commonly envied by the majority of their subjects but only by great people or by their 491 neighbours, among whom the same virtues which cause envy cause fear. Hence no prince should ever abstain from doing good in order to avoid that sort of hatred; and the only kind which can harm him is hatred arising from the injustice or arrogance which the people judge him to have. For we see that even people condemned to death do not commonly hate their judges, if they think they have deserved the sentence; and even undeserved evils are borne if it is thought that the prince from whom they come is in some way forced to inflict them and does so with regret; for it is thought to be just that he should prefer the general good to that of individuals. The only difficulty is when there are two parties to be satisfied who make different judgements about what is just, as when the Roman emperors had to satisfy both citizens and soldiers. In such a case it is reasonable to grant something to both sides without trying to bring instantly to reason people unaccustomed to listen to it. They must be gradually made acquainted with it by the publication of pamphlets or the preaching of sermons or other means. Altogether, the common people will put up with whatever they can be persuaded is just, and they are offended by whatever they imagine to be unjust. The arrogance of princes – that is, the usurpation of some authority or rights or honours thought undue – is odious to the common people only because it is regarded as a kind of injustice.

Moreover, I do not share the opinion which this author expresses in his 492 preface, namely that just as a man who wants to sketch mountains must be in the plain if he is to see their shape, so also one must be a private citizen in order to discover the office of a prince. For the pencil represents only what is seen from afar; but the chief motives of the actions of princes often depend on circumstances so special that one cannot imagine them if one is not oneself a prince or has not been long privy to a prince's secrets.

For this reason I would be ridiculous if I thought I could teach anything to Your Highness on this topic. That is not my purpose: I only wish my letters to provide some sort of diversion which will be different from those which I imagine she will have on her journey.[1] And I pray that this journey will be a perfectly happy one, as doubtless it will be if Your Highness resolves to follow the maxims that each person's felicity depends on himself and that one must not let oneself be ruled by Fortune. We must take every advantage that Fortune offers, but we must not be unhappy over those she refuses. In all the affairs of the world there are many reasons *pro* and many reasons *contra*; and so we must dwell principally on those which make us approve what we cannot avoid. The most unavoidable evils, I think, are the diseases of the body, from which I pray God preserve you.

TO MERSENNE, 5 OCTOBER 1646   AT IV

... A few days ago I saw a book which will make me henceforth much less (510) free in communicating my thoughts than I have been hitherto; it is a book by a professor at Utrecht, Regius, entitled *Foundations of Physics*.[2] In it he repeats most of the things I put in my *Principles of Philosophy*, my *Optics* and my *Meteorology*, and piles up whatever he has had from me in private, and even things he could only have had by indirect routes and which I did not want him to be told. Moreover he retails all this in such a confused

1 Elizabeth's family were moving from The Hague to Berlin.
2 *Fundamenta Physices* (1646), by Henri le Roy (Regius).

manner, and provides so few arguments, that his book can only make my opinions look ridiculous, and give a handle to my critics in two ways. Those who know that he hitherto made great profession of friendship with me, and followed blindly all my opinions, will blame all his faults on me. And if I ever decide to publish the views I have not yet published, it will be said that I have borrowed them from him, since they will have some resemblance to what he has written. But the worst is that while in matters of physics he has followed closely whatever he thought to be in accordance with my views (though in some places he has made serious mistakes even about this), he has done just the opposite in matters of metaphysics; and in four or five places where he treats of them, he takes exactly the opposite position to the one in my *Meditations*. I wanted to warn you of this so that if the book should fall into your hands, you will know my opinion of it, and know that it has been published against my wishes and without my knowledge, and that I do not regard its compiler as my friend. If you have not yet got it, you can save the price of it . . .

511

AT IV   TO PRINCESS ELIZABETH, OCTOBER OR NOVEMBER 1646

528   It was a great favour of Your Highness to write informing me that her voyage was successful and that she has arrived happily in a place where, enjoying the esteem and devotion of all around her, it seems to me that she possesses as many goods as may reasonably be desired in this life. For in view of the condition of human affairs, our demands upon Fortune would be excessive if we expected so many favours from her that we could find no cause for complaint even by exercising our imagination. When there are no objects present which offend the senses, or any indisposition which troubles the body, it is easy for a mind that follows true reason to be contented. For that, we do not need to forget or neglect objects which are not present: it is enough that we try to be dispassionate about those which may cause us distress. This does not go against charity, for we can often more readily find remedies for evils which we examine dispassionately than for those which afflict us sorely. But bodily health and the presence of agreeable objects greatly aid the mind by chasing from it all the passions which partake of sadness and making way for those which partake of joy. So too, conversely, when the mind is full of joy, this helps greatly to cause the body to enjoy better health and to make the objects which are present appear more agreeable.

529

Indeed I even venture to think that an inner joy has some secret power to make Fortune more favourable. I would not care to say this to persons who possess a weak mind, for fear that it would lead them into some superstition. So far as Your Highness is concerned, however, my only fear is that she will mock me for becoming so credulous. Nevertheless, I have countless experiences, and even the authority of Socrates, to confirm my opinion. The experiences consist in my frequent observation that the things I have done with a cheerful heart and without any inner reluctance have usually brought me success. Even in games of chance, where Fortune alone rules, I have always enjoyed better luck when I had reasons for joy   530 than when I was sad. And what is commonly called the 'inner voice' of Socrates was undoubtedly nothing other than his being accustomed to follow his inner inclinations, and his believing that an undertaking would have a happy outcome when he entered upon it with a secret feeling of cheerfulness, but an unhappy outcome when he was sad. Admittedly, it would be very superstitious to believe as strongly in this as it is said he did. For Plato reports that Socrates would even stay at home whenever his conscience advised him not to go out.[1] But with regard to the important actions of life, when their outcome is so doubtful that prudence cannot tell us what we ought to do, I think it is quite right for us to follow the advice of 'the voice within'. Moreover, it is beneficial to have a strong conviction that we will not fail to succeed in those undertakings that we enter upon without reluctance and with the freedom that ordinarily accompanies joy.

Since Your Highness is now in a place where she is surrounded by objects that give her nothing but satisfaction, I venture to urge her to make her own contribution to the endeavour to achieve happiness. She can do this easily, I think, by fixing her mind solely on the things before her and thinking about affairs of state only at times when the messenger is ready to leave. I judge it fortunate that Your Highness's books could not be brought   531 to her as soon as she expected; for reading them is not so apt to foster gaiety as to engender sadness. This is true especially of the book of that Physician of Princes[2] who depicts solely the difficulties which princes face in order to stay in power and the cruel or treacherous actions which he advises them to perform, and so causes private citizens who read his book to have more reason to pity the condition of princes than to envy it.

Your Highness has noted his faults – and mine – perfectly. For it is true that it was his plan to laud Cesare Borgia that led him to lay down general maxims in order to justify particular actions which may be difficult to excuse. I have recently read his discourse on Livy,[3] and found nothing bad in it. His main precept, to eliminate one's enemies completely or else make them into one's friends, without ever taking the middle way, is undoubt-

---

1 See Plato, *The Apology of Socrates*, 31 d.
2 Machiavelli, author of *The Prince* (1513).
3 *Discourses on the First Decade of Titus Livius* (1513).

edly always the safest. But when one has no reason to be fearful, this is not the most generous way to proceed.

Your Highness has also noted very clearly the secret of the miraculous spring.[1] There are many wretched people who broadcast its virtues, and are perhaps hired by those who hope to make a profit from it. For it is certain that there is no cure for all ills; but many people have made use of this spring, and those who have benefited from it speak well of it, while no one mentions the others. However that may be, the purgative quality in one of the springs, and the white colour, softness and refreshing quality of the other, make me think that they pass through deposits of antimony or mercury, which are both bad drugs, especially mercury. That is why I would advise no one to drink from them. The acid and iron in the waters of Spa are much less to be feared; and because they diminish the spleen and chase away melancholy, I value them both.

If Your Highness will allow me, I shall finish this letter in the way I began it, by wishing her above all peace of mind and joy. These are not only the fruits which we hope to gain from all other goods, but also often a means of increasing the opportunities we have been granted of attaining them. Although I am incapable of contributing in any way to your service except through my wishes, yet I dare to assure you that I am, more perfectly than any other person on earth, etc.

TO CHANUT, 1 NOVEMBER 1646

If I did not place a singularly high value on your knowledge and did not have an extreme desire to increase mine, I would not have been so importunate in urging you to look at my writings. I am not in the habit of begging people to do this, and indeed I have published them before they were ready and before they had any of the embellishments that may attract the gaze of the public. For I wanted my writings not to be seen by those who attend only to external things, but to be considered only by certain people of good sense, who would take the trouble to examine them with care, so that I could learn something from them. Although you have not yet done me this favour, yet you have not failed to oblige me greatly in other ways. In particular, as I have learnt on good authority, you have spoken favourably about me to many people. Indeed, M. Clerselier has written that you are expecting to receive from him the French version of my *Meditations* in order to present it to the Queen of the country where you are living.[2] I have never been so ambitious as to desire that persons of that

1 At Hornhausen, a village about 180 km south of Berlin.
2 Queen Christina of Sweden.

rank should know my name. Indeed if only I had been as wise as the savages are said to believe monkeys are, I would never have been known at all as a writer of books. For the savages are said to believe that monkeys could speak if they wished to, but they abstain from doing so in order to avoid being forced to work. Because I have not taken the same care to abstain from writing, I do not have as much leisure or peace as I would if I had had the wit to keep quiet. But since the error has already been committed and I am known by countless Schoolmen, who look askance at my writings and try from every angle to find in them the means of harming me, I have good reason to wish to be known by persons of greater distinction, whose power and virtue might protect me.

Moreover, I have heard that this Queen is held in such high esteem that, although I have often complained about those who wished to introduce me to some grand person, I cannot forbear thanking you for having spoken so kindly to her about me. I have seen M. de la Thuillerie[1] since his return from Sweden, and he has given such a glowing description of her qualities 536 as to make me think that being a queen is one of the least of them. I would not have ventured to believe half of what he said had I not seen at first hand, in the Princess[2] to whom I dedicated my *Principles of Philosophy*, that persons of high birth, whether men or women, do not need to be very old in order to be able to go far beyond other people in learning and virtue. But I am afraid that my published writings are not worthy of being read by her, and that accordingly she will not be grateful to you for having recommended them to her.

Had I dealt with moral philosophy, then perhaps I would have reason to hope that she might find my writings more agreeable; but this is a subject which I must not get involved in writing about. The Regents[3] are so worked up against me because of the harmless principles of physics they have seen, and they are so angry at finding no pretext in them for slandering me, that if I dealt with morality after all that, they would never give me any peace. A certain Father Bourdin thought he had good reason to accuse me of being a sceptic, because I refuted the sceptics; and a certain minister[4] tried to argue that I was an atheist, without giving any reason other than the fact that I tried to prove the existence of God. So what would they not say if I undertook to examine the right value of all the 537 things we can desire or fear, the state of the soul after death, how far we ought to love life, and how we ought to live in order to have no reason to fear losing our life? It would be pointless for me to have only those

1 Gaspard Coignet de la Thuillerie (1596–1653), French Ambassador to Sweden.
2 Princess Elizabeth.
3 Of the University of Utrecht.
4 Voetius.

opinions which agree as closely as possible with religion and which are as beneficial as possible for the state: for my critics would still try to convince people that I had opinions which are opposed to both. And so the best thing I can do henceforth is to abstain from writing books. Having taken for my motto

> Him doth a painful death await
> Who, known too well by all, too late
> To know himself doth meet his fate[1]

I shall pursue my studies only for my own instruction, and communicate my thoughts only to those with whom I can converse privately. I would count myself extremely fortunate, I assure you, if I could do this with you; but I do not think I shall ever go to the places where you are, or that you will retire to this place. All I can hope for is that perhaps after some years you will do me the favour of stopping at my retreat on your way back to France, and that I shall then have the opportunity to entertain you with an open heart. Many things can be said in a short time, and I find that long associations are not necessary for establishing close friendships, when these are based upon virtue. From the moment I had the honour of meeting 538 you, I felt entirely at one with you, and as I have presumed since then to count on your goodwill, so I beg you to believe that I could not be more attached to you than if I had spent all my life with you.

For the rest, you seem to conclude from the fact that I have studied the passions that I must no longer have any. But let me tell you, on the contrary, that in examining the passions I have found almost all of them to be good, and to be so useful in this life that our soul would have no reason to wish to remain joined to its body for even one minute if it could not feel them. Anger is indeed one of the passions which I judge one must guard against, in so far as its object is an insult that one has received. To do this we must try to elevate our mind so high that we are simply untouched by the insults of others. In place of anger, however, I believe it is right to feel indignation, which I confess I have often felt at the ignorance of those who wish to be taken as learned, when I see this ignorance joined with malice. But I can assure you that the passions I feel regarding you are admiration for your virtue and a very special devotion, etc.

AT IV   TO MERSENNE, 23 NOVEMBER 1646

565   The news you sent me of our friends' illness upset me, but I am nevertheless grateful to you for telling me. Although I am quite unable to

---

1 Seneca, *Thyestes*, 400.

offer them any comfort, I think that sharing in the ills of those we are fond of is one of the duties of friendship. M. Picot[1] had already told me of the trouble with his eyes, but since he did not make a big fuss about it, I was hoping that it would have improved by now. I found M. Clerselier's illness more of a shock; but it is a common enough malady, and in the light of your description I would judge that it is certainly not either life-threatening or incurable. My only fear is that the ignorance of the doctors may lead to treatments that do more harm than good. They were right to prescribe bleeding to begin with, and I am sure that this will have lessened the force and frequency of the fits; but they are great ones for bleeding in Paris, and I am afraid that when they see the benefits of one blood-letting, they will keep on with the treatment, which will greatly weaken the brain without improving his bodily health. You tell me that his illness began with a kind of gout in the toe. If it is still not better, and he continues to have epileptic fits, I think it would be beneficial to make an incision right to the bone in the part of the toe where the trouble began, especially if he is known to have been injured in that area; there may be some infection still present which is the cause of the trouble, and it needs to be driven out before a cure can be effected. But I should be most embarrassed were it known that I was interfering with medical consultations, especially concerning an illness on which I have only limited information. So if you think it right to pass on my suggestion to one of his doctors, please make sure that he is quite unaware that it comes from me.

566

You are right in supposing that I do not share Regius' opinion that [†]the mind is a corporeal principle[†], or indeed his view that [†]we know nothing except by appearance[†]; for in my writings I have said exactly the opposite.[2] As for his way of explaining the movement of the muscles, although this comes from me, and has pleased him so much that he has twice repeated it word for word, it is nevertheless quite worthless, since he has not understood what I wrote and has forgotten the main point. Moreover, he has not seen my diagram, and has drawn his own very badly, in such a way as to contradict the laws of mechanics. It is now twelve or thirteen years since I described all the functions of the human or animal body; but the manuscript is in such a mess that I would be hard put to it to read it myself. Nevertheless, four or five years ago I could not avoid lending it to a close friend, who made a copy which was then recopied by two more people, with my permission but without my rereading or correcting the transcripts. I begged those concerned not to show it to anyone; and I never wanted Regius to see it. Knowing his character, and

567

1 See footnote 1, p. 302 below.
2 For Regius see above, pp. 295ff.

thinking I might publish my views, I did not want anyone else detracting from their novelty. But despite my efforts Regius got hold of a copy – though I cannot imagine how – and he extracted from it his splendid account of the movement of the muscles. He could have lifted much else besides so as to fill out his book, but I am told that he only got hold of my manuscript when the printing of his own work had almost been completed...

AT IV   TO THE MARQUESS OF NEWCASTLE, 23 NOVEMBER 1646

(569)   ... I agree entirely with your Lordship's judgement about the chemists. I
570   think they use words in an uncommon sense only in order to make it seem that they know what in fact they do not know. I think also that what they say about reviving flowers with their salts is only an idle fancy, and that the powers of their extracts are quite different from the virtues of the plants from which they are taken. This is clear empirically because wine, vinegar and brandy, three extracts made from the same grapes, have quite different tastes and powers. In my view, the chemists' salt, sulphur and mercury are no more different from each other than the four elements of the philosophers, and not much more different from each other than water is from ice, foam and snow. I think that all these bodies are made of the same matter, and that the only thing which makes a difference between them is that the tiny parts of this matter which constitute some of them do not have the same shape or arrangement as the parts which constitute the others. I hope that your Lordship will soon be able to see this explained at some length in my *Principles of Philosophy*, which is about to be printed in French[1]...

(573)   I cannot share the opinion of Montaigne[2] and others who attribute understanding or thought to animals. I am not worried that people say that human beings have absolute dominion over all the other animals; for I agree that some of them are stronger than us, and I believe that there may also be some animals which have a natural cunning capable of deceiving the shrewdest human beings. But I consider that they imitate or surpass us only in those of our actions which are not guided by our thought. It often happens that we walk or eat without thinking at all about what we are doing; and similarly, without using our reason, we reject things which are harmful for us, and parry the blows aimed at us. Indeed, even if we expressly willed not to put our hands in front of our head when we fall, we

---

1   The French version of the *Principles*, by Claude Picot (*c.* 1601–68), was published in Paris in 1647.
2   Michel de Montaigne (1533–92), author of the famous *Essays*, in which he maintains that all human virtues can be found in non-human animals.

could not prevent ourselves. I consider also that if we had no thought then we would walk, as the animals do, without having learnt to; and it is said that those who walk in their sleep sometimes swim across streams in which they would drown if they were awake. As for the movements of our passions, even though in us they are accompanied by thought because we have the faculty of thinking, it is nevertheless very clear that they do not depend on thought, because they often occur in spite of us. Consequently   574
they can also occur in animals, even more violently than they do in human beings, without our being able to conclude from that that animals have thoughts.

In fact, none of our external actions can show anyone who examines them that our body is not just a self-moving machine but contains a soul with thoughts, with the exception of spoken words, or other signs that have reference to particular topics without expressing any passion. I say 'spoken words or other signs', because deaf-mutes use signs as we use spoken words; and I say that these signs must have reference, to exclude the speech of parrots, without excluding the speech of madmen, which has reference to particular topics even though it does not follow reason. I add also that these words or signs must not express any passion, to rule out not only cries of joy or sadness and the like, but also whatever can be taught by training to animals. If you teach a magpie to say good-day to its mistress when it sees her approach, this can only be by making the utterance of this word the expression of one of its passions. For instance it will be an expression of the hope of eating, if it has always been given a titbit when it says it. Similarly, all the things which dogs, horses and monkeys are taught to perform are only expressions of their fear, their hope or their joy; and consequently they can be performed without any thought. Now it seems to   575
me very striking that the use of words, so defined, is something peculiar to human beings. Montaigne and Charron[1] may have said that there is a greater difference between one human being and another than between a human being and an animal; yet there has never been known an animal so perfect as to use a sign to make other animals understand something which bore no relation to its passions; and there is no human being so imperfect as not to do so, since even deaf-mutes invent special signs to express their thoughts. This seems to me a very strong argument to prove that the reason why animals do not speak as we do is not that they lack the organs but that they have no thoughts. It cannot be said that they speak to each other but we cannot understand them; for since dogs and some other animals express their passions to us, they would express their thoughts also if they had any.

1 Pierre Charron (1541–1603), theologian and moralist.

I know that animals do many things better than we do, but this does not surprise me. It can even be used to prove that they act naturally and mechanically, like a clock which tells the time better than our judgement does. Doubtless when the swallows come in spring, they operate like clocks. The actions of honeybees are of the same nature; so also is the discipline of cranes in flight, and of apes in fighting, if it is true that they keep discipline. Their instinct to bury their dead is no stranger than that of dogs and cats which scratch the earth for the purpose of burying their excrement; they hardly ever actually bury it, which shows that they act only by instinct and without thinking. The most that one can say is that though the animals do not perform any action which shows us that they think, still, since the organs of their bodies are not very different from ours, it may be conjectured that there is attached to these organs some thought such as we experience in ourselves, but of a very much less perfect kind. To this I have nothing to reply except that if they thought as we do, they would have an immortal soul like us. This is unlikely, because there is no reason to believe it of some animals without believing it of all, and many of them such as oysters and sponges are too imperfect for this to be credible. But I am afraid of boring you with this discussion, and my only desire is to show you that I am, etc.

AT IV   TO PRINCESS ELIZABETH, DECEMBER 1646

589   Never have I found such good news in any of the letters I have been honoured to receive from Your Highness as I found in that of 29 November. For it leads me to think that you now enjoy better health and greater happiness than previously; and I believe that these are the two chief goods that one can possess in this life – leaving aside virtue, which you have never lacked. I am not taking any account of that slight illness which the doctors claimed would give them employment;[1] for although it is sometimes a little uncomfortable, I come from a country where it is so common among young people, who are otherwise quite healthy, that I do not consider it an illness so much as a sign of health and a means of warding off other illnesses. Through practical experience our doctors have learnt certain remedies for it, though they advise against trying to get rid of it in any season other than spring, when the pores are more open and so the cause can be eliminated more readily. Thus Your Highness has very good reason for not wanting to try a remedy for this illness, especially at the beginning of winter, which is the most dangerous time. And if the discom-

1 In her letter of 29 November 1646, Elizabeth had mentioned a swelling in her hands, for which her doctors had prescribed various remedies.

fort persists till the spring, it will be easy to drive it away by taking some   590
gentle purgatives or refreshing broths which contain nothing but known
kitchen-herbs, and by not eating food that is too salty or spicy. Being bled
may also be quite useful; but since there is some danger in this remedy, and
its frequent use shortens one's life, I advise Your Highness against it unless
she is accustomed to it. For when one has been bled in the same season for
three or four years in succession, one is almost forced to do the same each
year thereafter. Your Highness also is quite right not to want to try any
chemical remedies. It is useless having long experience of their power, for if
you make the slightest change in preparing them, even when you think you
are doing your best, you can wholly change their qualities, and make them
into poisons rather than medicines.

It is almost the same with science, when it is in the hands of those who
try to apply it without knowing it well. For whenever they believe they are
correcting or adding something to what they have learnt, they change it
into error. The proof of this can, I think, be seen in the book of Regius,[1]
which has finally seen the light of day. I would make some comments
about it here, if I thought he had sent a copy to Your Highness. But it is so
far from here to Berlin that I believe he will await your return before
presenting it to you; and I shall also wait before telling you my views about
it.

I am not surprised that in the country where you are[2] Your Highness   591
finds that all the learned people she meets are wholy preoccupied with
scholastic views. For I observe that even in Paris and the rest of Europe
there are few other learned people, and if I had known this beforehand I
would perhaps never have had anything published. Nevertheless I am
consoled by the fact that no one has entered the lists against me, although I
am certain that many people have not lacked the will to attack me. Indeed I
receive compliments from the Jesuit fathers, who I have always believed
would have the greatest interest in the publication of a new philosophy and
would be least likely to pardon me if they thought they could reasonably
find any fault in it . . .

TO CHANUT, 1 FEBRUARY 1647   AT IV

I cannot rest until I have replied to the most welcome letter I have just   600
received from you. The problems you set would be difficult for wiser men   601
than I to discuss in a short time, and I know that however long I spent I
could not solve them fully. Consequently, I prefer to write at once what my

1 Regius' book *Fundamenta Physices* was published in 1646.
2 Princess Elizabeth had recently moved to Berlin.

enthusiasm dictates rather than to take longer thought and after all write nothing any better.

You ask my opinion about three things.[1] 1. What is love? 2. Does the natural light by itself teach us to love God? 3. Which is worse if immoderate and abused, love or hatred?

In answer to the first question, I make a distinction between the love which is purely intellectual or rational and the love which is a passion. The first, in my view, consists simply in the fact that when our soul perceives some present or absent good, which it judges to be fitting for itself, it joins itself to it willingly,[2] that is to say, it considers itself and the good in question as forming two parts of a single whole. Then, if on the one hand the good is present – that is, if the soul possesses it, or is possessed by it, or is joined to it not only by its will but also in fact and reality in the appropriate manner – in that case, the movement of the will which accompanies the knowledge that this is good for it is joy; if on the other hand the good is absent, then the movement of the will which accompanies the knowledge of its lack is sadness; while the movement which accompa-

602 nies the knowledge that it would be a good thing to acquire it is desire. All these movements of the will which constitute love, joy, sadness and desire, in so far as they are rational thoughts and not passions, could exist in our soul even if it had no body. For instance, if the soul perceived that there are many very fine things to be known about nature, its will would be infallibly impelled to love the knowledge of those things, that is, to consider it as belonging to itself. And if it was aware of having that knowledge, it would have joy; if it observed that it lacked the knowledge, it would have sadness; and if it thought it would be a good thing to acquire it, it would have desire. There is nothing in all these movements of its will which would be obscure to it, or anything of which it could fail to be perfectly aware, provided it reflected on its own thoughts.

But while our soul is joined to the body, this rational love is commonly accompanied by the other kind of love, which can be called sensual or sensuous. This (as I said briefly of all passions, appetites and sensations on page 461 of the French edition of my *Principles*[3]) is nothing but a confused

603 thought, aroused in the soul by some motion of the nerves, which makes it disposed to have the other, clearer, thought which constitutes rational love. Just as in thirst the sensation of the dryness of the throat is a confused thought which disposes the soul to desire to drink, but is not identical with

---

1 Chanut had asked the questions on behalf of Queen Christina.
2 Fr. *de volonté*. By this phrase Descartes means 'the assent by which we consider ourselves as joined with what we love in such a manner that we imagine a whole, of which we take ourselves to be only a part' (*Passions*, art. 80:AT XI 387; CSM I 356).
3 AT VIIIA 321; CSM I 284.

that desire, so in love a mysterious heat is felt around the heart, and a great abundance of blood in the lungs, which makes us open our arms as if to embrace something, and this inclines the soul to join to itself willingly the object presented to it. But the thought by which the soul feels the heat is different from the thought which joins it to the object; and sometimes it happens that the feeling of love occurs in us without our will being impelled to love anything, because we do not come across any object we think worthy of it. It can also happen, on the other hand, that we are aware of a most worthwhile good, and join ourselves to it willingly, without having any corresponding passion, because the body is not appropriately disposed.

Commonly, however, these two loves occur together; for the two are so linked that when the soul judges an object to be worthy of it, this immediately makes the heart disposed to the motions which excite the passion of love; and when the heart is similarly disposed by other causes, that makes the soul imagine lovable qualities in objects in which, at another time, it would see nothing but faults. There is no reason to be surprised that certain motions of the heart should be naturally connected in this way with certain thoughts, which they in no way resemble. The soul's natural capacity for union with a body brings with it the possibility of an association between each of its thoughts and certain motions or conditions of this body so that when the same conditions recur in the body, they induce the soul to have the same thought; and conversely when the same thought recurs, it disposes the body to return to the same condition. In the same way when we learn a language, we connect the letters or the pronunciation of certain words, which are material things, with their meanings, which are thoughts, so that when we later hear the same words, we conceive the same things, and when we conceive the same things, we remember the same words.

But there is no doubt that the bodily conditions that were the first to accompany our thoughts when we came into the world must have become more closely connected with them than those which accompany them later. This will help to explain the origin of the heat felt around the heart, and the other bodily conditions that accompany love. I consider it probable that the soul felt joy at the first moment of its union with the body, and immediately after it felt love, then perhaps also hatred, and sadness; and that the same bodily conditions which then caused those passions have ever since naturally accompanied the corresponding thoughts. I think that the soul's first passion was joy, because it is not credible that the soul was put into the body at a time when the body was not in a good condition; and a good condition of the body naturally gives us joy. I say that love followed because the matter of our body is in a perpetual flux like the water in a

604

605

stream, and there is always need for new matter to take its place, so that it is scarcely likely that the body would have been in a good condition unless there were nearby some matter suitable for food. The soul, uniting itself willingly to that new matter, felt love for it; and later, if the food happened to be lacking, it felt sadness. And if its place was taken by some other matter unsuitable as food for the body, it felt hatred.

Those four passions, I believe, were the first we had, and the only ones we had before our birth. I think they were then only sensations or very confused thoughts, because the soul was so attached to matter that it could not yet do anything else except receive various impressions from it. Some years later it began to have other joys and other loves besides those which depend only on the body's being in a good condition and suitably nourished, but nevertheless the intellectual element in its joys or loves has always been accompanied by the first sensations which it had of them, and even the motions or natural functions which then occurred in the body. Before birth, love was caused only by suitable nourishment which, entering in abundance into the liver, heart and lungs, produced an increase of heat: this is the reason why similar heat still always accompanies love, even though it comes from other very different causes. If I were not afraid of boring you, I could show in detail how all the other bodily conditions which at the beginning of our life occurred with these four passions still accompany them. But I will only say that it is because of these confused sensations of our childhood, which remain joined with the rational thoughts by which we love what we judge worthy of love, that the nature of love is difficult for us to understand. And I may add that many other passions, such as joy, sadness, desire, fear and hope, etc., mingle in various ways with love and thus prevent us from discovering exactly what constitutes it. This is particularly noticeable in the case of desire, which is so commonly taken for love that people have distinguished two sorts of love: one called 'benevolent love', in which desire is less apparent, and the other called 'concupiscent love', which is simply a very strong desire, founded on a love which is often weak.

To treat fully of this passion would take a large volume, and though its nature is to make one very communicative, so that it incites me to try to tell you more than I know, I must restrain myself for fear that this letter may become tediously long. So I pass to your second question, whether the natural light by itself teaches us to love God, and whether one can love him by the power of that light alone.

I see two strong reasons for doubting that one can. The first is that the attributes of God most commonly considered are so high above us that we do not see at all how they can be fitting for us, and so we do not join ourselves to them willingly. The second is that nothing about God can be visualized by the imagination, which makes it seem that although one might have an intellectual love for him, one could not have any sensuous love, because it would have to pass through the imagination if it were to reach the senses by way of the intellect. Consequently I am not surprised that some philosophers are convinced that the only thing which makes us capable of loving God is the Christian religion, which teaches the mystery of the Incarnation in which God so humbled himself as to make himself like us. They say too that those who appear to have had a passion for some divinity without knowing about the mystery of the Incarnation have not loved the true God, but only some idols to which they gave his name; just as, so the poets tell us, Ixion embraced a cloud by mistake for the Queen of the Gods. Nevertheless, I have no doubt at all that we can truly love God 608 by the sole power of our nature. I do not assert that this love is meritorious without grace – I leave the theologians to unravel that – but I make bold to say that with regard to the present life it is the most delightful and useful passion possible; and it can even be the strongest, though only if we meditate very attentively, since we are continually distracted by the presence of other objects.

In my view, the way to reach the love of God is to consider that he is a mind, or a thing that thinks; and that our soul's nature resembles his sufficiently for us to believe that it is an emanation of his supreme intelligence, a 'breath of divine spirit'.[1] Our knowledge seems to be able to grow by degrees to infinity, and since God's knowledge is infinite, it is at the point towards which ours strives; and if we considered nothing more than this, we might arrive at the absurdity of wishing to be gods, and thus make the disastrous mistake of loving divinity instead of loving God. But we must also take account of the infinity of his power, by which he has created so many things of which we are only a tiny part; and of the extent of his providence, which makes him see with a single thought all that has been, all that is, all that will be and all that could be; and of the infallibility of his decrees, which are altogether immutable even though they respect our free will. Finally, we must weigh our smallness against the greatness of 609 the created universe, observing how all created things depend on God, and regarding them in a manner proper to his omnipotence instead of enclosing them in a ball as do the people who insist that the world is finite. If a man meditates on these things and understands them properly, he is filled with extreme joy. Far from being so injurious and ungrateful to God as to want to take his place, he thinks that the knowledge with which God has honoured him is enough by itself to make his life worth while. Joining himself willingly entirely to God, he loves him so perfectly that he desires

1 Horace, *Satires*, II, ii, 79.

nothing at all except that his will should be done. Henceforth, because he knows that nothing can befall him which God has not decreed, he no longer fears death, pain or disgrace. He so loves this divine decree, deems it so just and so necessary, and knows that he must be so completely subject to it that even when he expects it to bring death or some other evil, he would not will to change it even if, *per impossibile*, he could do so. He does not shun evils and afflictions, because they come to him from divine providence; still less does he eschew the permissible goods or pleasures he may enjoy in this life, since they too come from God. He accepts them with joy, without any fear of evils, and his love makes him perfectly happy.

It is true that the soul must be very detached from the traffic of the senses if it is to represent to itself the truths which arouse such a love. That is why it appears that it cannot communicate this love to the imaginative faculty so as to make it a passion. Nevertheless I have no doubt that it does do this. For although we cannot imagine anything in God, who is the object of our love, we can imagine our love itself, which consists in our wanting to unite ourselves to some object. That is, we can consider ourselves in relation to God as a minute part of all the immensity of the created universe. Since objects differ from each other, there are different ways of uniting oneself to them or joining them to oneself; and the idea of such a union by itself is sufficient to produce heat around the heart and cause a violent passion.

It is true that the custom of our speech and the courtesy of good manners does not allow us to tell those whose condition is far above ours that we love them; we may say only that we respect, honour, esteem them, and that we have zeal and devotion for their service. I think that the reason for this is that friendship between human beings makes those in whom it is reciprocated in some way equal to each other, and so if, while trying to make oneself loved by some great person, one said that one loved him, he might think that one was treating him as an equal and so doing him wrong. But philosophers are not accustomed to give different names to things which share the same definition, and I know no other definition of love save that it is a passion which makes us join ourselves willingly to some object, no matter whether the object is equal to or greater or less than us. So it seems to me that if I am to speak philosophically, I must say that it is possible to love God.

And if I asked you frankly whether you love that great Queen at whose Court you now are, it would be useless for you to say that you had only respect, veneration and admiration for her; I would judge none the less that you have also a very ardent affection for her. You write so fluently when you speak of her that although I believe all that you say, because I know that you are very truthful and I have also heard others speak of her,

610

611

still I do not in the least believe that you could describe her as you do if you did not feel great devotion for her, and I do not think you could be in the presence of so great a light without being somewhat warmed by it as well.

It is not at all the case that the love which we have for objects above us is less than that which we have for other objects. I think that by nature such love is more perfect, and makes one embrace with greater ardour the interests of that which one loves. It is the nature of love to make one consider oneself and the object loved as a single whole of which one is but a part; and to transfer the care one previously took of oneself to the preservation of this whole. One keeps for oneself only a part of one's care, a part which is great or little in proportion to whether one thinks oneself a 612 larger or smaller part of the whole to which one has given one's affection. So if we are joined willingly to an object which we regard as less than ourselves — for instance, if we love a flower, a bird, a building or some such thing — the highest perfection which this love can properly reach cannot make us put our life at any risk for the preservation of such things. For they are not among the nobler parts of the whole which we and they constitute any more than our nails or our hair are among the nobler parts of our body; and it would be preposterous to risk the whole body for the preservation of our hair. But when two human beings love each other, charity requires that each of the two should value his friend above himself; and so their friendship is not perfect unless each is ready to say in favour of the other: 'It is I who did the deed, I am here, turn your swords against me.'[1] Similarly, when an individual is joined willingly to his prince or his country, if his love is perfect he should regard himself as only a tiny part of the whole which he and they constitute. He should be no more afraid to go to certain death for their service than one is afraid to draw a little blood from one's arm to improve the health of the rest of the body. Every day we see examples of this love, even in persons of low condition, who give their lives cheerfully for the good of their country or for the defence of some great person they are fond of. From all this it is obvious that our love for God should be, beyond comparison, the greatest and most perfect of all 613 our loves.

I have no fear that these metaphysical thoughts hold any difficulty for your mind, for I know that nothing is beyond its capacity; but I must confess that my mind is easily tired by them and that the presence of sensible objects does not allow me to dwell on such thoughts for long. So I pass to your third question, whether love or hatred is worse if immoderate. I find it more difficult to answer this than the other two, since you have

1 Virgil, *Aeneid*, IX, 427.

explained less clearly what you mean. The question can be understood in different senses, which I think should be examined separately. One passion might be called worse than another because it makes us less virtuous; or because it is more of an obstacle to our happiness; or because it carries us to greater excesses, and disposes us to do more harm to other people.

The first point I find doubtful. If I attend to the definitions of the two passions, I consider that love for an undeserving object can make us worse than hatred for an object we should love, because there is more danger in being joined to a thing which is bad, and in being as it were transformed into this thing, than there is in being separated willingly from a thing which is good. But if I pay attention to the inclinations or habits which arise from these passions, I change my mind. Love, however immoderate, always has the good for its object, and so it seems to me that it cannot corrupt our morals as much as hatred, whose only object is evil. We see by experience that the best people, if they are obliged to hate someone, become malicious by degrees; for even if their hatred is just, they so often call to mind the evils they receive from their enemy, and the evils they wish him, that they become gradually accustomed to malice. By contrast, those who abandon themselves to love, even if their love is immoderate and frivolous, often become more decent and virtuous than they would if they turned their mind to other thoughts.

I do not find any difficulty in the second point. Hatred is always accompanied by sadness and grief; and if some people take pleasure in doing harm to others, I think their delight is like that of the demons, who, according to our religion, are no less damned even though they continually imagine themselves to be revenged on God by tormenting human beings in hell. Love, on the contrary, however immoderate it may be, gives pleasure; and though the poets often complain of it in their verses, I think that men would naturally give up loving if they did not find it more sweet than bitter. All the afflictions which are blamed on love come solely from the other passions which accompany it – that is, from rash desires and ill-founded hopes.

But if I am asked which of the two passions carries us to greater excesses, and makes us capable of doing more harm to other people, I think I must say that it is love. It has by nature much more power and strength than hatred; and often affection for an unimportant object causes incomparably more evils than the hatred of a more valuable one could ever do. I can show that hatred has less vigour than love by considering the origin of each. As I said earlier, our first feelings of love arose because our heart was receiving suitable food in abundance, whereas our first feelings of hatred were caused by harmful nourishment reaching the heart, and the same motions still accompany the same passions. If this is so, it is evident that when we love, all the purest blood in our veins flows in abundance towards the heart, which sends a great quantity of animal spirits to the brain, and so gives us more power, more strength and more courage; by contrast, if we feel hatred, the bitterness of gall and the sourness of the spleen mixes with our blood and diminishes and weakens the spirits going to the brain, and so we become feebler, colder and more timid. Experience confirms what I say, for heroes like Hercules and Roland love more ardently than other men, whereas people who are weak and cowardly are more inclined to 616 hatred. Anger can indeed make people bold, but it borrows its strength from the love of self which is always its foundation, and not from the hatred which is merely an accompaniment. Despair also calls forth great efforts of courage, and fear can lead to great cruelties; but there is a difference between these passions and hatred.

I still have to show that love for an unimportant object, if immoderate, can cause more evil than hatred for another more valuable. My argument for this is that the evil arising from hatred extends only to the hated object, whereas immoderate love spares nothing but its object, which is commonly very slight in comparison with all the other things which it is ready to abandon and destroy to serve as seasoning for its immoderate passion. It might perhaps be said that hatred is the proximate cause of the evils attributed to love, because if we love something, at the same time we hate whatever is contrary to it. But even so, love is more to blame than hatred for the evils which come about in this way, because it is the first cause, and the love of a single object can give rise in this way to hatred for many others. Moreover, the greatest evils of love are not those which are committed through the intermediary of hatred; the chief and most dangerous are those which are done or permitted for the sole pleasure of the loved object or for oneself. I remember an outburst of Théophile, which could be 617 used as an instance of this: he makes a person mad with love say:

> How fine, ye Gods, the deed of his desire
> How fair his victim's fame,
> When noble Paris put all Troy to fire
> To quench his own heart's flame.[1]

This shows that even the greatest and most tragic disasters can be, as I have said, seasoning for an immoderate love, and make it more delicious the

1 Théophile de Viau, *Stances pour Mademoiselle de M.*

more they raise its price. I do not know if my thoughts on this will accord with yours; but I assure you that they accord in this – that as you have promised me great goodwill, so I am with a very ardent passion, etc.

AT IV   TO PRINCESS ELIZABETH, MARCH 1647

624   Learning of the contentment which Your Highness enjoys at the place[1] where she is now, I do not dare to desire her return; and yet I find it difficult to prevent myself from having this desire, especially at the present time, when I am in The Hague. And because I notice from your letter of 21 February that we cannot expect to see you here before the end of summer. I intend to make a trip to France to deal with my personal affairs there, and to return here towards the winter. I shall not leave for two months, so that I may have the honour of receiving the commands of Your Highness, these always having more power over me than any other thing on earth.

625   I praise God that you now enjoy perfect health. But I beg you to pardon me if I venture to contradict your opinion about not using remedies because the illness that afflicted your hands has cleared up. For it is to be feared that, in the case of Your Highness as well as your sister, the humours which are purged in this way have been stopped by the cold of the season, and that in the spring they will bring back the same illness, or will put you at risk of some other malady, unless you cure it by means of a good diet – that is, by consuming only food and drinks which restore the blood and purge without any effort. As for drugs, either of apothecaries or of empirics, I have such a low opinion of them that I would never venture to advise anyone to use them.

    I do not know what I can have written to Your Highness about Regius' book, which makes you wish to have my observations on it – perhaps that I would not express any opinion about it so as not to prejudice your judgement, in case you already had the book. But now that I know you do not yet have it, I shall tell you frankly that I do not think it worth Your Highness taking the trouble to read it. It contains nothing on physics except for my assertions in a jumbled order and without their true proofs. As a consequence they appear paradoxical, and what comes at the beginning can be proved only by what comes towards the end. He has put in it

626 almost nothing of his own, and few things that I have not published. But he has still failed to fulfil his obligation to me. For he professed friendship with me, and he knew full well my desire that what I had written about the description of animals should not be made public (indeed I had not wanted

1 Berlin.

to show these writings to him, on the grounds that he would not be able to keep from telling his pupils about them once he had seen them). Despite all this he did not hesitate to borrow several things from them, and without my knowledge he arranged to have them copied, transcribing in particular the whole section where, dealing with the movement of the muscles, I take as an example two of those that move the eye. So fond was he of this passage that twice in his book he repeats, word for word, two or three pages from this section. And yet he has not understood what he wrote, for he has omitted the main point, namely that the animal spirits which flow from the brain to the muscles cannot return by the same passages through which they came. Without this observation, everything he writes is worthless, and because he did not have my diagram, he produced one that clearly shows his ignorance. They tell me that he now has another book on medicine in the press,[1] in which I expect he will have put all the rest of my book, or as much as he could assimilate. No doubt he would have taken much else besides, but I learnt that he had got a copy only when his own book was printed. But just as he follows blindly what he believes to be my views regarding physics and medicine, even though he does not understand them, so he blindly contradicts me on all metaphysical questions. I had begged him not to write on these topics, because they are not relevant to his subject, and I was certain that he could not write anything about them which would not be bad. But all I got from him was the reply that, not intending to satisfy me in this regard, he had no scruples about offending me in other ways as well.

I shall not fail to take a copy of his book to Princess Sophie tomorrow. Its title is *The Foundations of Physics*, by Henricus Regius. I shall also take another little book, by my friend M. de Hogelande.[2] He does just the opposite of Regius, in that everything Regius writes is borrowed from me, and yet manages to contradict my views, whereas everything Hogelande writes is quite alien to my own views (indeed I think he has never even read my books properly) and yet he is always on my side, in that he has followed the same principles. I shall ask the Princess to include these two books, which are not large, in the first packages that she sends to Hamburg. And I shall add to this the French version of my *Meditations*, if I can get a copy before leaving here. For it is quite a while since I heard that the printers have finished it.

627

628

---

1 *Ultrajectini Fundamenta Medica*, published in 1647.
2 The work of Hogelande, dedicated to Descartes and published in 1646, was entitled *Cogitationes, quibus Dei existentia, item animae spiritalitas, et possibilis cum corpore unio, demonstrantur (Thoughts by which it is demonstrated that God exists, that the soul is spiritual, and that the soul may be united with the body)*.

AT V   TO THE CURATORS OF LEIDEN UNIVERSITY, 4 MAY
1647

(7)   ... I have been told that at the disputation, when the opponent[1] asked
the respondent and the chairman from what passage in my writings they
could prove that I hold God to be a deceiver, the first passage which they
8   cited and kept on bringing up was the following from page 13 of my
Meditations: 'I will suppose therefore, that not God, who is supremely
good and the source of truth, but some malicious demon of the utmost
power and cunning has employed all his energies in order to deceive me.'[2]
Immediately the opponent showed that in that passage I expressly distinguished between the supremely good God, the source of truth, on the
one hand, and the malicious demon on the other. He denied that I wanted
to hold (there was here no question of that) or even suppose the supremely
good God to be a deceiver, and said that I had made this supposition
instead about the evil demon. I could not do otherwise, he said, since I had
added that God is the *source of truth*, displaying an attribute of his that is
incompatible with deception. They replied that I had called the deceiver
supremely powerful, and that no one was supremely powerful except the
true God. At this reply I could exclaim that by the same token they must
hold all the demons, all the idols, all the gods of the heathen to be the true
God or gods, because in the description of any one of them there will be
found some attribute which in reality belongs only to God. And I could
rightly add that this is a 'horrible and impious blasphemy', especially as it
is no mere supposition but an assertion scandalously taught in a public
lecture hall in support of a calumny. But I will merely say that since I knew
that 'good needs a faultless cause while evil follows any defect', and since
the context demanded the supposition of an extremely powerful deceiver, I
made a distinction between the good God and the evil demon, and taught
that if *per impossibile* there were such an extremely powerful deceiver, he
9   would not be the good God, since he would have the defect entailed by
deceitfulness, and could only be regarded as some malicious demon. My
use of this supposition cannot be criticized on the grounds that 'evils are
not to be done that good may come'; for such a supposition has no moral
evil or goodness in it except in virtue of the purpose it serves, because it is
an act of the intellect and not of the will, and shows all the more that we
neither believe it nor want it believed. Now my purpose was excellent,
because I was using the supposition only for the better overthrow of

---

1   In this letter Descartes is protesting about a public disputation, held in the theological
college at Leiden, to the effect that Descartes' doctrines were atheistic. The opponent is the
person whose function in the disputation was to attack the theses and defend Descartes.
2   Med. 1: AT VII 22; CSM II 15.

scepticism and atheism, and to prove that God is no deceiver, and to establish that as the foundation of all human certitude. Indeed I dare to boast that there is no single mortal who can less justly and less plausibly be accused of holding God as a deceiver than I myself; because nobody before me whose writings have survived has so expressly, so earnestly and so carefully demonstrated that the true God is no deceiver . . .

TO PRINCESS ELIZABETH, 10 MAY 1647   AT V

Although I may find urgent reasons for remaining in France when I am   15
there, no reason will be strong enough to keep me from returning here before winter, so long as I still have my life and health. For the letter I have had the honour of receiving from Your Highness leads me to hope that you will return to The Hague towards the end of the summer. Indeed I may say that this is the chief reason why I would rather live in this country than in any other. As for the peace I had previously sought here, I foresee that henceforth I may not get as much of that as I would like. For I have not yet   16
received all the satisfaction that is due to me for the insults I suffered at Utrecht, and I see that further insults are on the way. A troop of theologians, followers of scholastic philosophy, seem to have formed a league in an attempt to crush me by their slanders. They are scheming to their utmost to try to harm me, and if I did not keep up my guard, they would find it easy to injure me in various ways.

As proof of this scheming, three or four months ago a certain professor at the College of Theologians in Leiden, named Revius,[1] raised objections against me in four different theses. He did so in order to distort the meaning of my *Meditations* and make people believe that I said some things in it which are quite absurd and are contrary to the glory of God – for example, that we must doubt that there is a God. He would even have it that I want people to deny absolutely for a while that there is a God, and things of that sort. But this man is not clever, and most of his own students make fun of his slanders. For this reason my friends in Leiden saw fit merely to warn me of his actions. But then some other theses were published by Triglandius,[2] their leading professor of theology, in which he included these words: 'It is blasphemy to regard God as a deceiver, as Descartes mischievously does.' At this, my friends – even those who are themselves theologians – recognized that what these people intended, by accusing me of such a serious crime as blasphemy, was nothing less than to   17
get my views condemned as utterly wicked. In the first instance they would

1 Jacobus Revius (1586–1658).
2 Jacques Trigland (1583–1654).

have this done by a Synod where they are very influential; and then they would try to get the magistrates, who are their allies, to attack me. My friends decided that in order to prevent this I would have to oppose their schemes. That is why I wrote a long letter last week to the Curators of the Academy of Leiden, in which I requested legal protection against the slanders of these two theologians.[1] I cannot say how they will reply to this letter. From what I know about the temperament of the people of this country, however, I do not expect anything but some soothing words which will leave untouched the cause of the injury, and will serve only to exacerbate it. For I know that what these people revere in theologians is not their honesty and virtue so much as their distinguished beards and sonorous voices and grave expressions. Here, as in all democratic states, those who complain the loudest when they are insulted have the greatest power, even if they have the least reason for their complaints. For my part, I think I am obliged to do my best to get full satisfaction for these insults and also, by the same token, for those of Utrecht. If I cannot obtain justice – which I foresee it will be very difficult for me to do – I shall find myself obliged to leave these provinces straightaway. But since everything is done so slowly here, I am sure it will take more than a year for this to happen.

18   I would not take the liberty of discussing these trivial matters with Your Highness if you had not expressed a wish to read what M. Hogelande and Regius said about me in their books.[2] This made me think that you would not be displeased to have a first-hand account of my activities. Quite apart from that, the duty and respect which I owe to you puts me under an obligation to provide such an account.

I praise God that the physician to whom Your Highness lent a copy of my *Principles* has taken so long to return the book. For this shows that no one is ill at the Court of the Electress,[3] and we seem to enjoy more nearly perfect health when we are living where there is generally good health than when we are surrounded by sick people. This doctor will have had that much more leisure to read the book which it pleased Your Highness to lend him, and you will be better able to tell me his opinion of it.

Just as I was writing this, I received letters from The Hague and from Leiden telling me that the assembly of Curators has been postponed, so that they have not yet received my letter. I see that they are turning a minor disagreement into a major dispute. It is said that the theologians want to act as judges in this affair – that is to say, they want to subject me to an inquisition more severe than the Spanish one, and turn me into an oppo-

---

1 See above, p. 316.
2 See above, p. 315.
3 The Dowager Electress of Brandenburg, at whose Court Elizabeth was staying.

nent of their religion. People tell me that if this happens I should make use 19
of the good offices of the Ambassador of France and the authority of the
Prince of Orange not merely to obtain justice, but to intercede and prevent
my enemies from doing worse things. But I do not think I shall follow this
advice[1]: I shall simply seek justice, and if I cannot obtain it then I believe
the best course of action will be for me to prepare for a gentle retreat. But
whatever I may think or do, and wherever in the world I may go, I will
never hold anything more dear than to obey your commands.

TO CHANUT, 6 JUNE 1647 AT V

As I was passing through this place[2] on my way to France, I learnt from 50
M. Brasset[3] that he had sent your letters for me to Egmond. Although my
journey was urgent, I decided to wait for them; but as they reached my
house three hours after I had left, they were sent on to me immediately. I
read them with avidity, and discovered in them great proofs of your
friendship and your tact. I was alarmed when I read in the first pages that
M. du Rier had spoken to the Queen[4] of one of my letters and that she had
asked to see it. Later, when I reached the place where you say that she
heard it with some satisfaction, I was greatly relieved. I do not know
whether I was more overcome with admiration at her so easily understand- 51
ing what the most learned men find obscure, or with joy that she did not
find it displeasing. But my admiration doubled when I saw the force and
weight of the objections which Her Majesty made regarding the size I
attributed to the universe. I wish that your letter had found me in my
normal abode, because the problem is so difficult and so judiciously posed
that I would perhaps have unravelled it better in a place where I could
collect my thoughts than in the room of an inn. But I do not want to use this
as an excuse, and I will try to write all I can say on this topic, provided I
may be allowed to think that it is to you alone that I am writing, so that my
imagination may not be too clouded by veneration and respect.

In the first place I recollect that the Cardinal of Cusa[5] and many other
Doctors have supposed the world to be infinite without ever being censured by the Church; on the contrary, to represent God's works as very
great is thought to be a way of doing him honour. And my opinion is not so

1 In fact, Descartes did follow the advice: on 12 May 1647 he wrote to Servien, the acting
Ambassador of France, requesting him to get the Prince of Orange to intercede on his
behalf (AT v 24).
2 The Hague.
3 French chargé d'affaires in The Hague.
4 Queen Christina of Sweden; du Rier was physician to the Queen.
5 Nicholas of Cusa (1401–44), who stressed the incomplete nature of man's knowledge of
God and of the universe.

difficult to accept as theirs, because I do not say that the world is *infinite*, but only that it is *indefinite*. There is quite a notable difference between the two: for we cannot say that something is infinite without a reason to prove this such as we can give only in the case of God; but we can say that a thing is indefinite simply if we have no reason which proves that it has bounds. Now it seems to me that it is impossible to prove or even to conceive that there are bounds in the matter of which the world is composed. For when I examine the nature of this matter I find it to consist merely in its having extension in length, breadth and depth, so that whatever has these three dimensions is a part of this matter; and there cannot be any completely empty space, that is, space containing no matter, because we cannot conceive such a space without conceiving in it these three dimensions and consequently matter. Now if we suppose the world to be finite, we are imagining that beyond its bounds there are some spaces which are three-dimensional and so not purely imaginary, as the philosophers' jargon has it. These spaces contain matter; and this matter cannot be anywhere but in the world, and this shows that the world extends beyond the bounds we had tried to assign to it. Having then no argument to prove, and not even being able to conceive, that the world has bounds, I call it *indefinite*. But I cannot deny on that account that there may be some reasons which are known to God though incomprehensible to me; that is why I do not say outright that it is *infinite*.

If we consider the extension of the world in this way and then compare it with its duration, it seems to me that the only thought it occasions is that there is no imaginable time before the creation of the world in which God could not have created it if he had so willed. I do not think that we have any grounds for concluding that he really did create it an indefinitely long time ago. For the actual or real existence of the world during these last five or six thousand years is not necessarily connected with the possible or imaginary existence which it might have had before then, in the way that the actual existence of the spaces conceived as surrounding a globe (i.e. surrounding the world as supposed *finite*) is connected with the actual existence of the same globe. Moreover, if we could infer the eternal past duration of the world from its indefinite extension, we could infer it even better from its eternal future duration. Faith teaches us that although heaven and earth will pass away – that is, will change their appearance – yet the world – that is to say, the matter of which they are composed – will never pass away. This is clear from the promise of eternal life for our bodies, and consequently for the world in which they will exist, after the Resurrection. But no one infers from the infinite duration which the world must have in the future that it must have been created from all eternity; because every moment of its duration is independent of every other.

The prerogatives which religion attributes to human beings need some explanation, since they seem difficult to believe in, if the extension of the universe is supposed indefinite. We may say that all created things are made for us in the sense that we may derive some utility from them; but I do not know that we are obliged to believe that man is the end of creation. On the contrary, it is said that †all things are made for his (God's) sake,† 54 and that God alone is the final as well as the efficient cause of the universe. And in so far as created beings are of service to each other, any of them may ascribe to itself a privileged position and consider that all those useful to it are made for its sake.

The six days of the creation are indeed described in Genesis in such a way as to make man appear its principal object; but it could be said that the story in Genesis was written for man, and so it is chiefly the things which concern him that the Holy Spirit wished particularly to narrate, and that indeed he did not speak of anything except in its relationship to man. Preachers, whose concern is to spur us on to the love of God, commonly lay before us the various benefits we derive from other creatures and say that God made them for us. They do not bring to our attention the other ends for which he might be said to have made them, because this would be irrelevant to their purpose. This makes us very inclined to believe that God made all these things for us alone. But preachers go even further: they say that each person in particular owes gratitude to Jesus Christ for all the blood which he shed on the cross, just as if he had died merely for a single person. What they say is indeed true; but it does not mean that he did not redeem with the same blood a very large number of other people. In the same way I do not see that the mystery of the Incarnation, and all the other favours God has done to man, rule out his having done countless other 55 great favours to an infinity of other creatures.

I do not on that account infer that there are intelligent creatures in the stars or elsewhere, but I do not see either that there is any argument to prove that there are not. I always leave questions of this kind undecided, rather than deny or assert anything about them. The only difficulty, I think, which remains is that we have long believed that man has great advantages over other creatures, and it looks as if we lose them all when we change our opinion. But I distinguish between those of our goods which can be lessened through others possessing the like, and those which cannot be so lessened. A man who has only a thousand pistoles would be very rich if there were no one else in the world who had as much; and the same man would be very poor if everyone else had much more. Similarly, all praise-worthy qualities give so much more glory to those who have them, the fewer the people who share them; that is why we commonly envy the glory and riches of others. But virtue, knowledge, health, and in general all other goods considered in themselves without regard to glory are not in any way lessened in us through being found in many others; and so we have no grounds for being distressed because they are shared by others.

Now the goods which could belong to all the intelligent creatures in an
56 indefinite world belong to this class; they do not diminish those we possess. On the contrary, when we love God and through him unite ourselves willingly[1] to all the things he has created, then the more great, noble and perfect we reckon them, the more highly we esteem ourselves as being parts of a more perfect whole, and the more grounds we have for praising God on account of the immensity of his works. When Holy Scripture speaks in many places of the innumerable multitude of angels, it entirely confirms this view; for we regard the least of the angels as incomparably more perfect than human beings. This is also confirmed by the astronomers when they measure the size of the stars and find them very much bigger than the earth. For if the indefinite extension of the universe gives ground for inferring that there must be inhabitants of places other than the earth, so does the extension which all the astronomers attribute to it; for every one of them judges that the earth is smaller in comparison with the entire heavens than a grain of sand in comparison with a mountain.

I now pass to your question about the reasons which often impel us to love one person rather than another before we know their worth. I can discover two, one belonging to the mind and one to the body. The one in the mind presupposes too many things concerning the nature of our souls which I would not dare to try to explain in a letter; so I will speak only of
57 the one in the body. It consists in the arrangement of the parts of our brain which is produced by objects of the senses or by some other cause. The objects which strike our senses move parts of our brain by means of the nerves, and there make as it were folds, which undo themselves when the object ceases to operate; but afterwards the place where they were made has a tendency to be folded again in the same manner by another object resembling even incompletely the original object. For instance, when I was a child I loved a little girl of my own age who had a slight squint. The impression made by sight in my brain when I looked at her cross-eyes became so closely connected to the simultaneous impression which aroused in me the passion of love that for a long time afterwards when I saw persons with a squint I felt a special inclination to love them simply because they had that defect. At that time I did not know that was the reason for my love; and indeed as soon as I reflected on it and recognized that it was a defect, I was no longer affected by it. So, when we are inclined to love someone without knowing the reason, we may believe that this is

1 See footnote 2, p. 306 above.

because he has some similarity to something in an earlier object of our love, though we may not be able to identify it. Though it is more commonly a perfection than a defect which thus attracts our love, yet since it can sometimes be a defect as in the example I quoted, a wise man will not 58 altogether yield to such a passion without having considered the worth of the person to whom he thus feels drawn. But because we cannot love equally all those in whom we observe equal worth, I think that our only obligation is to esteem them equally; and since the chief good of life is friendship, we are right to prefer those to whom we are joined by secret inclinations, provided we also see worth in them. Moreover, when these secret inclinations are aroused by something in the mind and not by something in the body, I think they should always be followed. The principal criterion by which they can be known is that those which come from the mind are reciprocated, which is often not the case in the others. But the proofs which I have of your affection give me such assurance that my inclination towards you is reciprocated that I would have to be entirely ungrateful and disobedient to all the rules of friendship if I were not with great devotion, etc.

TO PRINCESS ELIZABETH, 6 JUNE 1647   AT V

As I was passing through The Hague en route to France, it occurred to 59 me that I ought to write and assure Your Highness that my ardour and devotion will not alter even though I am changing my place of abode. For while I am there I shall be unable to have the honour of being at your command and of paying my respects to you. Two days ago I received a letter from the French resident in Sweden, who put to me a question which the Queen had raised (I became known to her when the resident showed her my reply to an earlier letter he had written to me). From the way he describes this Queen, and the reports he gives of her talk, I have formed a high opinion of her – so high, indeed, that I think you would be worthy partners of each other in conversation. I think too that there are so few in the world who would be worthy of this that it would not be difficult for 60 Your Highness to forge a strong friendship with her. Over and above the intellectual satisfaction such a friendship would give you, it could be desirable for other reasons. In replying to a previous letter from my friend the resident in which he had spoken of the Queen, I had written that I did not find what he told me at all unbelievable, because I had the honour of knowing Your Highness, and this had taught me how far persons of high birth are able to surpass others.[1] But I do not know whether I said this in

1 See above, p. 299.

the letter he showed to her, or in an earlier one. It is likely that from now on he will show her all the letters he receives from me, and so I shall always try to put in them something which gives her a reason to desire the friendship of Your Highness – unless you forbid me to do this.

The theologians who were trying to harm me have been silenced, but this was done by means of flattery and by taking all possible care not to offend them. They said that this came about because of the temper of the times, but I fear that these times will last for ever, and the theologians will be allowed to gain so much power that they will be intolerable.

The printing of the French version of my *Principles* has been completed. Because the dedicatory letter will be printed last, I am enclosing a copy of it. Should there be anything in it which does not please Your Highness, and which you believe ought to be expressed differently, please be so good as to convey this fact to me.

AT V　　　　TO QUEEN CHRISTINA, 20 NOVEMBER 1647

81　　　I learn from M. Chanut that it pleases Your Majesty that I should have the honour to expound to her my view of the supreme good understood in
82　　the sense of the ancient philosophers. I count this command such a great favour that my desire to obey it turns away all other thoughts; so without making excuses for my inadequacy I will put in a few words all that I have been able to discover on the topic.

The goodness of each thing can be considered in itself without reference to anything else, and in this sense it is evident that God is the supreme good, since he is incomparably more perfect than any creature. But goodness can also be considered in relation to ourselves, and in this sense I do not see anything which we can deem good unless it somehow belongs to us and our having it is a perfection. Thus the ancient philosophers, unenlightened by the light of faith and knowing nothing about supernatural beatitude, considered only the goods we can possess in this life; and what they were trying to discover was which of these is the supreme, that is, the chief and greatest good.

In trying to decide this question, my first observation is that we should not consider anything as good, in relation to ourselves, unless we either possess it or have the power to acquire it. Once this is agreed, it seems to me that the supreme good of all men together is the total or aggregate of all the goods – those of the soul as well as those of the body and of fortune – which can belong to any human being; but that the supreme good of each individual is quite a different thing, and consists only in a firm will to do well and the contentment which this produces. My reason for saying this is
83　　that I can discover no other good which seems so great or so entirely within

each man's power. For the goods of the body and of fortune do not depend absolutely upon us; and those of the soul can all be reduced to two heads, the one being to know, and the other to will, what is good. But knowledge is often beyond our powers; and so there remains only our will, which is absolutely within our disposal. And I do not see that it is possible to dispose it better than by a firm and constant resolution to carry out to the letter all the things which one judges to be best, and to employ all the powers of one's mind in finding out what these are. This by itself constitutes all the virtues; this alone really deserves praise and glory; this alone, finally, produces the greatest and most solid contentment in life. So I conclude that it is this which constitutes the supreme good.

In this way I think I can reconcile the two most opposed and most famous opinions of the ancient philosophers – that of Zeno, who thought virtue or honour the supreme good, and that of Epicurus, who thought the supreme good was contentment, to which he gave the name of pleasure.[1] Just as all vices arise simply from the uncertainty and weakness that come from ignorance and lead to regret, so virtue consists only in the resolution and vigour with which we are inclined to do the things we think good – this vigour, of course, must not stem from stubbornness, but from the knowledge that we have examined the matter as well as we are morally able. 84 What we do after such examination may be bad, but none the less we can be sure of having done our duty; whereas, if we do a virtuous action thinking we are doing wrong, or take no trouble to find out whether we are doing right or wrong, we are not acting like a virtuous person. As for honour and praise, these are often awarded to the other goods of fortune; but because I am sure that Your Majesty values virtue more than her crown, I shall not hesitate to express my opinion that nothing except virtue really deserves praise. All other goods deserve only to be esteemed and not to be honoured or praised, except in so far as they are supposed to have been acquired or obtained from God by the good use of free will. For honour and praise is a kind of reward, and only what depends on the will provides grounds for reward or punishment.

I still have to prove that the good use of free will is what produces the greatest and most solid contentment in life. This does not seem difficult if we consider carefully what constitutes pleasure, or delight, and in general all the sorts of contentment we can have. I observe first that all of them are entirely within the soul, though many of them depend on the body; just as it is the soul that sees, though by means of the eyes. Next I observe that there is nothing that can make the soul content except its belief that it 85 possesses some good, and that often this belief is only a very confused

1 See above, p. 261.

representation in the soul. Moreover, the soul's union with the body causes it commonly to represent certain goods to itself as being incomparably greater than they are; but if it knew distinctly their just value, its contentment would always be in proportion to the greatness of the good from which it proceeded. I observe also that the greatness of a good, in relation to us, should not be measured only by the value of the thing which constitutes it but principally also by the manner in which it is related to us. Now free will is in itself the noblest thing we can have, since it makes us in a way equal to God and seems to exempt us from being his subjects; and so its correct use is the greatest of all the goods we possess; indeed there is nothing that is more our own or that matters more to us. From all this it follows that nothing but free will can produce our greatest happiness. Moreover, the peace of mind and inner satisfaction felt by those who know they always do their best to discover what is good and to acquire it is, we see, a pleasure incomparably sweeter, more lasting and more solid than all those which come from elsewhere.

I omit here many other things, because when I call to mind how much business is involved in ruling a great kingdom, and how much of it Your Majesty attends to personally, I do not dare to ask for a longer audience. But I am sending to M. Chanut some papers in which I have expressed my sentiments on the matter at greater length.[1] If it pleases Your Majesty to look at them, he will oblige me by presenting them to her, which will help to show how much zeal and devotion belongs, Madame, to Your Majesty's most humble and obedient servant, DESCARTES.

AT V

86

TO CHANUT, 20 NOVEMBER 1647

86
87
It is true that normally I refuse to write down my thoughts concerning morality. I have two reasons for this. One is that there is no other subject in which malicious people can so readily find pretexts for vilifying me; and the other is that I believe only sovereigns, or those authorized by them, have the right to concern themselves with regulating the morals of other people. But these two reasons are nullified by the honour which you have bestowed upon me by writing, on behalf of the incomparable Queen in whose presence you reside, that she will be pleased if I write down for her my views on the sovereign good. This command provides sufficient authorization, but I hope that what I write will be seen only by her and by you. I desire so ardently to obey her that, far from holding back, I would like to be able to encompass in one letter everything that I have ever thought about this subject. In fact, I have tried to put so much into the letter[2] I have

1 See footnote 2, p. 327 below.
2 See above, p. 324.

ventured to write her that I am afraid I have not explained anything sufficiently well. In order to make up for this fault, however, I am sending you a collection of some other letters in which I have explained these matters at greater length. And I have included also a little treatise on the passions, which forms the larger part of the collection.[1] For above all we must seek acquaintance with the passions if we are to attain the sovereign good as I have described it. If I had been so bold as to include the replies that I had the honour of receiving from the Princess to whom these letters are addressed, the collection would have been more complete – and I could   88
have added another two or three of my letters, which are not intelligible without hers. But I would have had to seek her permission, and she is now quite far from here.

Moreover, I ask you not to present this collection to the Queen straight away, for I fear that by sending letters I have written to another person, instead of writing to Her Majesty what I judge she will find agreeable, I would not be showing the respect and veneration which I owe to her. If you judge it proper to speak to her about them, however, you may say that I sent them to you, and if she then wants to look at them, my hesitation on this score will be removed. I am convinced that she will perhaps find it more agreeable to look at what I have written for someone else than at something addressed to her; for she may then feel assured that I have not changed anything or concealed anything for her sake. But I beg you, if possible, to see that these writings do not fall into other hands.

TO MERSENNE, 13 DECEMBER 1647   AT V

It is already some time since M. de Zuylichem sent me the publication by   98
M. Pascal[2] (for which I must thank the author, since it was sent to me at his request). In it he seems to want to oppose my subtle matter, and I wish him well in this endeavour; but I beg him not to forget to advance all his best arguments on this subject, and not to be upset if in due course I defend myself by explaining all the points which I believe to be relevant.

You ask me to write something on the experiments with mercury, and yet you neglect to inform me about them, as if I were to guess what they are. But I must not take the risk of doing that, for if I hit upon the truth,   99

---

1 Descartes sent to Queen Christina copies of the letters to Elizabeth dated 21 July, 4 August, 18 August, 1 September and 15 September 1645, and a copy of the first half of the letter dated 6 October 1645. The 'little treatise', a forerunner to the *Passions of the Soul*, was written for Elizabeth in 1646.
2 M. de Zuylichem is Constantijn Huygens. Blaise Pascal (1623–92) brought out his *Expériences nouvelles touchant le vide* (*New Observations on the Vacuum*) in October 1647.

people might think that I had done the experiment here, and if I failed to do so, people would have a poorer opinion of me. But I shall be obliged to you if you would please give me a straightforward account of everything you have observed; and if it turns out that I use these observations, I shall not forget to say where I got them.

I had advised M. Pascal to do an experiment to see whether the mercury rises as high on the top of a mountain as at the foot, and I do not know whether he has done it.[1] But to enable us to know also whether a change in the weather or place has any effect on the result, I am sending you a piece of paper 2½ feet long, on which the third and fourth inch beyond 2 feet are divided into lines; and I am keeping an exactly similar piece here so that we might see if our observations agree. I ask you, then, to try to observe the point on this scale to which the mercury rises when the weather is cold and when it is hot, and when the wind blows from the north and when it blows from the south. To enable you to know if there is any difference, and to encourage you to inform me plainly what you observe, I shall tell you that last Monday the height of the mercury was exactly 2 feet 3 inches on this scale, and yesterday, which was Thursday, it was a bit above 2 feet 4 inches; but today it was three or four lines lower. In order to make these observations I keep a tube attached in the same place day and night. I believe there is no need to report them right away: it would be better to wait till M. Pascal's book is published.

I would also like you to try to light a fire in your vacuum, and observe whether the smoke goes up or down and what shape the flame is. You can do this experiment by suspending a bit of sulphur or camphor at the end of a string in the vacuum, and lighting it through the glass with a mirror or a burning glass. I cannot do that here, because the sun is not hot enough, and I have not yet been able to adjust the tube and the bottle.

I am surprised that you have kept this experiment secret for four years, as has the afore-mentioned M. Pascal, without ever reporting anything about it to me or telling me that you had begun it before this summer. For as soon as you told me about it, I reckoned that it was important, and that it could strongly verify what I have written on physics.

AT V   TO PRINCESS ELIZABETH, 31 JANUARY 1648

111   I received the letter from Your Highness dated 23 December almost at the same time as the earlier letter. I confess that I am in a quandary as to

---

1 Descartes met Pascal in Paris on 23 and 24 September 1647, and it was probably at the second meeting that he gave the advice. In a letter of 15 November 1647 Pascal asked his brother-in-law, Florin Périer, to perform the famous experiment, which he duly did on 19 September 1648 on the Puy-de-Dôme. See also below, p. 380.

how I ought to reply to the latter. In it Your Highness expresses a wish that I should write the treatise on learning which I once had the honour of telling her about.[1] Now there is nothing I desire more ardently than to obey your commands; but I will tell you the reasons why I dropped the plan of writing this treatise; and if they do not satisfy Your Highness, then   112
I shall not fail to take it up again.

The first is that I could not put in it all the truths that ought to be there without arousing the opposition of the scholastics, and in my present state I do not think I could treat their hatred with complete contempt. The second is that I have already touched upon some of the points which I had wanted to put in this treatise, in a preface to the French translation of my *Principles* (which I believe Your Highness has now received). The third is that I am now working on another manuscript, which I hope Your Highness may find more agreeable.[2] This is a description of the functions of animals and of man. The draft I made about twelve or thirteen years ago (which Your Highness has seen) fell into the hands of some people who transcribed it badly, and I thought I ought to put it in order – that is to say, rewrite it. Just in the last eight or ten days I have even ventured to try to explain the manner in which animals develop from the very beginning of their existence. I say 'animals' in general, for I would not be so bold as to undertake such a thing in the particular case of man, because I simply do not have a sufficient number of observations for such an undertaking.

Moreover, what makes me prefer to spend my time on this work instead of some other requiring less concentration is that I believe the remainder of this winter will be perhaps the most tranquil time I shall enjoy in my life.   113
What makes me fear that I shall have less leisure after the winter is that I am obliged to return to France next summer and to spend the following winter there. My domestic affairs and several other matters force me to do this. Also, I have been honoured by being offered a pension by the King, without my having asked for one. This will not bind me, though much can happen in a year. In any case nothing could possibly happen that might prevent me from preferring the happiness of living in the place where Your Highness lives, if I had the chance to do so, to that of living in my own country or in any other place at all.

My letter[3] about the sovereign good was held up in Amsterdam for almost a month, through the fault of the person I had sent it to for

1 In her letter of 5 December 1647, Elizabeth urges Descartes to write 'the *Treatise on Learning* which you once wished to produce' (AT v 97).
2 This work is the unfinished *Description of the Human Body* which was published posthumously in 1664 (AT XI 223; CSM I 313).
3 The letter to Queen Christina of 20 November 1647 (above, p. 324), which was not sent to Stockholm until 20 December 1647.

forwarding. So I do not expect a reply for some time. As soon as I have any news about this letter, I shall certainly let Your Highness know. It did not contain anything new which was worth sending to you. In the mean time I have received some letters from that country, in which I am advised that
114 they are waiting for my letters. From what they tell me about this Princess, she must be strongly inclined to virtue and capable of judging things well. I am told that she will be presented with the French version of my *Principles*, and I am assured that she will read the first part with satisfaction and that she would be quite capable of reading the rest, if affairs of state allowed her the leisure to do so.

With this letter I am sending a booklet of slight importance.[1] I am not enclosing it in the same package, since the book is not worth the cost of sending it. I was compelled to write it by the insults of M. Regius. It has been published sooner than I wished, and they have even added to it some verses and a preface of which I disapprove. (The verses are by M. Heydanus, but he did not dare to put his name to them – as indeed he was entitled not to.)

AT V   TO [SILHON], MARCH OR APRIL 1648

(135)   ... First, then, I must tell you that I hold that there is a certain quantity of motion in the whole of created matter, which never increases or diminishes; and thus, when one body makes another body move, it loses as much of its own motion as it gives to the other. Thus, when a stone falls to earth from above, if it stops and does not rebound, I think that this is because it moves the earth, and thus transfers to it its motion. But if the
136 earth which it moves contains a thousand times more matter, when it transfers its motion it gives it only a thousandth of its speed. So if two unequal bodies receive the same amount of motion as each other, this same quantity of motion does not give as much speed to the larger as it does to the smaller; and so it can be said in this sense that the more matter a body contains, the more natural inertia it has. To this one may add that a large body can transfer its motion more easily to other bodies than a small one can, and can less easily be moved by them. So there is one sort of inertia which depends on the quantity of the matter, and another which depends upon the area of the surfaces.

You have yourself, it seems to me, given a good answer to your other question about the nature of our knowledge of God in the beatific vision: you distinguish it from our present knowledge of God in virtue of its being

---

1 The *Comments on a Certain Broadsheet*, which was published in Amsterdam early in 1648 (AT VIIIB 341; CSM I 293).

intuitive. If this term does not satisfy you, and if you think that this intuitive knowledge of God will be similar to ours or different only in extent and not in the manner of knowing, that is where, in my opinion, you go wrong. Intuitive knowledge is an illumination of the mind, by which it sees in the light of God whatever it pleases him to show it by a direct impress of the divine clarity on our understanding, which in this is not considered as an agent but simply as a receiver of the rays of divinity. Whatever we can know of God in this life, short of a miracle, is the result of reasoning and discursive inquiry. It is deduced from the principles of faith, which is obscure, or it comes from the natural ideas and notions we have, which even at their clearest are only gross and confused on so sublime a topic. Consequently, whatever knowledge we have or acquire by way of reason is as dark as the principles from which it is derived, and is moreover infected with the uncertainty we find in all our reasonings. 137

Now compare these two kinds of knowledge to see if there is any similarity between such a troubled and doubtful perception (which costs us much labour and which is enjoyed only momentarily once acquired) and a pure, constant, clear, certain, effortless and ever-present light.

Can you doubt that our mind, when it is detached from the body, or has a glorified body which will no longer hinder it, can receive such direct illumination and knowledge? Why, even in this body the senses give it such knowledge of corporeal and sensible things, and our soul has already some direct knowledge of the beneficence of its creator without which it would not be capable of reasoning. I agree that such knowledge is somewhat obscured by the soul's mingling with the body; but still it gives us a primary, unearned and certain awareness which we touch with our mind with more confidence than we give to the testimony of our eyes. You will surely admit that you are less certain of the presence of the objects you see than of the truth of the proposition 'I am thinking, therefore I exist.' Now this knowledge is not the work of your reasoning or information passed on to you by teachers; it is something that your mind sees, feels and handles; and although your imagination insistently mixes itself up with your thoughts and lessens the clarity of this knowledge by trying to clothe it with shapes, it is nevertheless a proof of the capacity of our soul for receiving intuitive knowledge from God. 138

I think that I can see that what makes you doubtful is your view that an intuitive knowledge of God is one in which we know God by himself. On this foundation you have built the following argument. 'I know that God is unique, because I know that he is a necessary being; this form of knowledge uses nothing but God himself; so I know by God himself that God is unique; and consequently I know intuitively that God is unique.'

I do not think it takes a long examination to show that this argument will not do. You see, to know God by himself, that is to say, by an immediate light cast by the Godhead on our mind, which is what is meant by the expression 'intuitive knowledge', is quite different from using God himself in order to make an induction[1] from one attribute to another; or, to speak more accurately, using the natural (and consequently compara-

139 tively rather obscure) knowledge of one attribute of God, to construct an argument leading to another attribute of God. So you must admit that in this life you do not see, in God and by his light, that he is unique; but you deduce it from a proposition you have made about him, and you draw the conclusion by the power of argument, which is a machine which often breaks down. You see what power you have over me, since you make me go beyond the limits I have set for my philosophizing, to show you how much I am, etc.

AT V   CONVERSATION WITH BURMAN, 16 APRIL 1648[2]

146 'Whatever I have up till now accepted as true I have acquired either from the senses or through the senses.'[3]

From the senses: i.e. from sight, by which I have perceived colours, shapes, and such like. Leaving aside sight, however, I have acquired everything else through the senses, i.e. through hearing; for this is how I acquired and gleaned what I know, from my parents, teachers, and others.

The objection cannot be made here that this leaves out the common principles and ideas of God and of ourselves, which were never in the senses ... For, firstly, I acquired these in the same way, through the senses, that is to say, through hearing. Secondly, the author is considering at this point the man who is only just beginning to philosophize and who is paying attention only to what he knows he is aware of. As regards the common principles and axioms, for example 'It is impossible that one and the same thing should both be and not be', men who are creatures of the senses, as we all are at a pre-philosophical level, do not think about these or pay attention to them. On the contrary, since they are at present in us from birth with such clarity, and since we experience them within our-selves, we neglect them and think about them only in a confused manner, and never in the abstract, or apart from material things and particular

1 See *Regulae*, Rule 7: AT x 388f.; CSM I 25f.
2 For details of the Conversation with Burman, see Introduction, p. x above. The work consists of a string of quotations from Descartes' works, each of which is followed either by Descartes' reported comments or by a reported dialogue between Descartes and Burman. Where dialogue occurs, the names of the speakers have been inserted in square brackets for the reader's convenience.
3 Med. 1: AT VII 18; CSM II 12.

instances. Indeed, if people were to think about these principles in the abstract, no one would have any doubt about them; and if the sceptics had done this, no one would ever have been a sceptic; for they cannot be denied by anyone who carefully focuses his attention on them. Thirdly, here we are dealing primarily with the question of whether anything has real existence.

'I will suppose therefore that ... some malicious demon of the utmost   147
power has employed all his energies in order to deceive me.'[1]

The author is here making us as doubtful as he can and casting us into as many doubts as possible. This is why he raises not only the customary difficulties of the sceptics but every difficulty that can possibly be raised; the aim is in this way to demolish completely every single doubt. And this is the purpose behind the introduction of the demon, which some might criticize as a superfluous addition.

'. . . of the utmost power'

What the author says here is contradictory, since malice is incompatible with supreme power.

'When we become aware that we are thinking beings, this is a primary notion, which is not derived by means of any syllogism.'[2]

[Burman] But is not the opposite asserted at *Principles* I, 10?

[Descartes] Before this inference, 'I am thinking, therefore I exist', the major 'whatever thinks exists' can be known; for it is in reality prior to my inference, and my inference depends on it. That is why the author says in the *Principles*[3] that the major premiss comes first, namely because implicitly it is always presupposed and prior. But it does not follow that I am always expressly and explicitly aware of its priority, or that I know it before my inference. This is because I am attending only to what I experience within myself – for example 'I am thinking, therefore I exist'. I do not pay attention in the same way to the general notion 'whatever thinks exists'. As I have explained before, we do not separate out these general propositions from the particular instances; rather, it is in the particular instances that we think of them. This, then, is the sense in which the words cited here should be taken.

1 Med. 1: AT VII 22; CSM II 15.
2 Second Replies: AT VII 140; CSM II 100.
3 AT VIIIA 8; CSM I 195f.

'As for the assertion that it is self-contradictory that men should be deceived by God, this is clearly demonstrated from the fact that the form of deception is non-being, towards which the supreme being cannot incline.'[1]

[Descartes] As far as we are concerned, since we are composed partly of nothingness and partly of being, we incline partly towards being and partly towards nothingness. As for God, on the other hand, he cannot incline to nothingness, since he is supreme and pure being. This consideration is a metaphysical one and is perfectly clear to all those who give their mind to it. Hence, inasmuch as I have my faculty of perception from God, and in so far as I use it correctly, by assenting only to what I clearly perceive, I cannot be deceived or tricked by it; if I were, God would have to incline to nothingness. For this would be a case of God's deceiving me and so tending to non-being.

148

[Burman] Someone, however, may still raise the following objection: after I have proved that God exists and is not a deceiver, then I can say that my mind certainly does not deceive me, since a reliable mind was God's gift to me; but my memory may still deceive me since I may think I remember something which I do not in fact remember. This is because of the weakness of memory.

[Descartes] I have nothing to say on the subject of memory. Everyone should test himself to see whether he is good at remembering. If he has any doubts on that score, then he should make use of written notes and so forth to help him.

'I was not guilty of circularity when I said that the only reason we have for being sure that what we clearly and distinctly perceive is true is the fact that God exists, but that we are sure that God exists only because we perceive this clearly.'[2]

[Burman] It seems there is a circle. For in the Third Meditation the author uses axioms to prove the existence of God, even though he is not yet certain of not being deceived about these.

[Descartes] He does use such axioms in the proof, but he knows that he is not deceived with regard to them, since he is actually paying attention to them. And for as long as he does pay attention to them, he is certain that he is not being deceived, and he is compelled to give his assent to them.

[Burman] But our mind can think of only one thing at a time, whereas the proof in question is a fairly long one involving several axioms. Then again, every thought occurs instantaneously, and there are many thoughts

1 Sixth Replies: AT VII 428; CSM II 289.
2 Fourth Replies: AT VII 245; CSM II 171.

which come to mind in the proof. So one will not be able to keep the attention on all the axioms, since any one thought will get in the way of another.

[Descartes] Firstly, it is just not true that the mind can think of only one thing at a time. It is true that it cannot think of a large number of things at the same time, but it can still think of more than one thing. For example, I am now aware and have the thought that I am talking and that I am eating; and both these thoughts occur at the same time. Then, secondly, it is false that thought occurs instantaneously; for all my acts take up time, and I can be said to be continuing and carrying on with the same thought during a period of time.

[Burman] But on that showing, our thought will be extended and divisible.

[Descartes] Not at all. Thought will indeed be extended and divisible with respect to its duration, since its duration can be divided into parts. But it is not extended and divisible with respect to its nature, since its nature remains unextended. It is just the same with God: we can divide his duration into an infinite number of parts, even though God himself is not therefore divisible ... Accordingly, since our thought is able to grasp more   (149) than one item in this way, and since it does not occur instantaneously, it is clear that we are able to grasp the proof of God's existence in its entirety. As long as we are engaged in this process, we are certain that we are not being deceived, and every difficulty is thus removed.

'The fact that there can be nothing in the mind, in so far as it is a thinking thing, of which it is not aware, seems to me to be self-evident.'[1]

[Burman] But how can it be aware, since to be aware is itself to think? In order to have the thought that you are aware, you must move on to another thought; but if you do this, you can no longer be thinking of the thing you were thinking of a moment ago. It follows that you cannot be aware that you *are* thinking, but only that you *were* thinking.

[Descartes] It is correct that to be aware is both to think and to reflect on one's thought. But it is false that this reflection cannot occur while the previous thought is still there. This is because, as we have already seen, the soul is capable of thinking of more than one thing at the same time, and of continuing with a particular thought which it has. It has the power to reflect on its thoughts as often as it likes, and to be aware of its thought in this way ...

---

1 Fourth Replies: AT VII 246; CSM II 171.

'In view of this I do not doubt that the mind begins to think as soon as it is implanted in the body of an infant.'[1]

[Burman] The author of these objections conjectured that it would follow from this that the mind must always be thinking, even in the case of infants.

[Descartes] The author agreed.

[Burman] But since we have an innate idea of God and of ourselves, would not the mind of an infant therefore have an actual idea of God?

[Descartes] It would be rash to maintain that, since we have no evidence relevant to the point. It does not, however, seem probable that this is so. For in infancy the mind is so swamped inside the body that the only thoughts it has are those which result from the way the body is affected.

[Burman] But the mind can think of more than one thing at once.

[Descartes] It can, provided that one thought does not obstruct another, which is what happens in this case. The body has an obstructive effect on the soul. We are aware of this phenomenon in ourselves, when we prick ourselves with a needle or some sharp instrument: the effect is such that we cannot think of anything else. It is the same with people who are half asleep: they can scarcely think of more than one thing. In infancy, therefore, the mind was so swamped inside the body that it could think only of bodily matters. The body is always a hindrance to the mind in its thinking, and this was especially true in youth.

As to the fact that we have no memory of the thoughts we had in infancy, this is because no traces of these thoughts have been imprinted on the brain ... By the same token, there are many thoughts we had yesterday, etc., which we cannot now remember. But the mind cannot ever be without thought; it can of course be without this or that thought, but it cannot be without *some* thought. In the same way, the body cannot, even for a moment, be without extension.

[Burman] But even if traces are not imprinted on the brain, so that there is no bodily memory, there still exists an intellectual memory, as is undoubtedly the case with angels or disembodied souls, for example. And this intellectual memory ought to enable the mind to remember its thoughts.

[Descartes] I do not refuse to admit intellectual memory: it does exist. When, for example, on hearing that the word 'k-i-n-g' signifies supreme power, I commit this to my memory and then subsequently recall the meaning by means of my memory, it must be the intellectual memory that makes this possible. For there is certainly no relationship between the four letters (k-i-n-g) and their meaning, which would enable me to derive the

1 *Ibid.*

meaning from the letters. It is the intellectual memory that enables me to recall what the letters stand for. However, this intellectual memory has universals rather than particulars as its objects, and so it cannot enable us to recall every single thing we have done...

'Of course, if I considered just the ideas themselves simply as modes of my (152) thought, without referring them to anything else, they could scarcely give me any material for error.'[1]

[Burman] But since all error concerning ideas comes from their relation and application to external things, there seems to be no subject-matter for error whatsoever if they are not referred to externals.

[Descartes] Even if I do not refer my ideas to anything outside myself, there is still subject-matter for error, since I can make a mistake with regard to the actual nature of the ideas. For example, I may consider the idea of colour, and say that it is a thing or a quality; or rather I may say that the colour itself, which is represented by this idea, is something of the kind. For example, I may say whiteness is a quality; and even if I do not refer this idea to anything outside myself – even if I do not say or suppose that there is any white thing – I may still make a mistake in the abstract, with regard to whiteness itself and its nature or the idea I have of it...

'But if no such idea can be found in me, I shall simply have no argument to convince me of the existence of anything apart from myself. For despite a most careful and comprehensive survey, this is the only argument I have so far been able to find.'[2]

[Burman] But is there not another argument later on in the Fifth Meditation?

[Descartes] At this point the author is speaking of the sort of argument 153 that can take some effect of God as a premiss from which the existence of a supreme cause, namely God, can subsequently be inferred. In fact, however, he discovered no such effect: after a most careful survey of all the effects, he found none which would serve to prove God's existence except for the idea of God. By contrast, the other argument in the Fifth Meditation proceeds *a priori* and does not start from some effect. In the *Meditations* that argument comes later than the one here; the fact that it comes later, while the proof in this Meditation comes first, is the result of the order in which the author discovered the two proofs. In the *Principles*,

1 Med. iii: AT vii 37; CSM ii 26.
2 Med. iii: AT vii 42; CSM ii 29.

however, he reverses the order; for the method and order of discovery is one thing, and that of exposition another. In the *Principles* his purpose is exposition, and his procedure is synthetic.

'And since there can be no ideas which are not as it were of things...'[1]

[Burman] But we have an idea of nothing, and this is not an idea of a thing.

[Descartes] That idea is purely negative, and can hardly be called an idea. In this passage the author is taking the word 'idea' in its strict and narrow sense. We do also have ideas of common notions, which are not, strictly speaking, ideas of things. But this is a rather extended use of the word 'idea'.

'How could I understand that I doubted and desired – that is, lacked something – or that I was not wholly perfect, unless there were in me some idea of a more perfect being, which enabled me to recognize my own defects by comparison?'[2]

[Burman] But in the *Discourse*[3] the author says he has seen most clearly that knowledge is a greater sign of perfection than doubt. He must, then, have known this without reference to the perfect being; and so it is not the case that his knowledge of God was prior to the knowledge of himself.

[Descartes] In that part of the *Discourse* you have a summary of these *Meditations*, and its meaning must be explicated by reference to the *Meditations* themselves. In that part of the *Discourse*, then, the author recognized his own imperfection by recognizing the perfection of God. He did this implicitly if not explicitly. Explicitly, we are able to recognize our own imperfection before we recognize the perfection of God. This is because we are able to direct our attention to ourselves before we direct our attention to God. Thus we can infer our own finiteness before we arrive at his infiniteness. Despite this, however, the knowledge of God and his perfection must implicitly always come before the knowledge of ourselves and our imperfections. For in reality the infinite perfection of God is prior to our imperfection, since our imperfection is a defect and negation of the perfection of God. And every defect and negation pre-supposes that of which it falls short and which it negates.

[Burman] But in that case nothingness would have to presuppose being, would it not?

---

1 Med. III: AT VII 44; CSM II 30.
2 Med. III: AT VII 45; CSM II 31.
3 AT VI 33; CSM I 127f.

[Descartes] In metaphysics our understanding of nothingness derives from that of being...

'If I had derived my existence from myself ... I should certainly not have (154) denied myself the knowledge in question, which is something much easier to acquire, or indeed, any of the attributes which I perceive to be contained in the idea of God; for none of them seem any harder to achieve.'[1]

Now here one must carefully distinguish between understanding, conception and imagination — a distinction of great value. Take, for example, the perfections of God. We do not imagine these, or conceive of them, but we understand them: the way in which God understands all things in a single mental act, or the way in which his decrees are identical with himself, are things which we understand, but we do not conceive of, since we cannot, so to speak, represent them to ourselves. Thus, we understand the perfections and attributes of God, but we do not conceive of them — or, rather, in order to conceive of them, we conceive of them as indefinite. Now, if it were I who had given myself my nature and make-up, I would have given myself all the perfections of God. I think I would have given myself these perfections in accordance with my indefinite conception of them. For example, I would have given myself greater knowledge than I now possess; and when I had that greater knowledge, I would then have given myself greater knowledge still, and so on. Now when indefinites are multiplied in this way they become infinite; or rather they become the infinite, since the infinite is the same as the indefinite multiplied in this way. As I increased my knowledge more and more in this way, I would by the same token have increased my other attributes (I do not think these would prove any harder than knowledge, since it is by means of knowledge that they are to be attained), and I would end up as God. As it is, however, I know by experience that I cannot do this and am unable to increase my knowledge as I should like to. It follows that I do not derive my existence from myself, etc....

'But the mere fact that God created me is a very strong basis for believing (156) that I am somehow made in his image and likeness.'[2]

[Burman] But why do you say that? Surely God could have created you without creating you in his image?

[Descartes] No. It is a common axiom and a true one that the effect is

---

1 Med. III: A T VII 48; CSM II 33.
2 Med. III: A T VII 51; CSM II 35. See also Fifth Replies: A T VII 373; CSM II 257.

like the cause. Now God is the cause of me, and I am an effect of him, so it follows that I am like him.

[Burman] But a builder is the cause of a house, yet for all that the house is not like him.

[Descartes] He is not the cause of the house, in the sense in which we are taking the word here. He merely applies active forces to what is passive, and so there is no need for the product to be like the man. In this passage, however, we are talking about the total cause, the cause of being itself. Anything produced by this cause must necessarily be like it. For since the cause is itself being and substance, and it brings something into being, i.e. out of nothing (a method of production which is the prerogative of God), what is produced must at the very least be being and substance. To this extent at least, it will be like God and bear his image.

[Burman] But in that case even stones and suchlike are going to be in God's image.

[Descartes] Even these things do have the image and likeness of God, but it is very remote, minute and indistinct. As for me, on the other hand, God's creation has endowed me with a greater number of attributes, and so his image is in me to a greater extent. I am not, however, taking 'image' here in the ordinary sense of an effigy or picture of something, but in the broader sense of something having some resemblance to something else. The reason I used these particular words in the *Meditations* was that throughout the Scriptures we are said to be created in the image of God . . .

157 'It follows . . . that I have the power of conceiving that there is a thinkable number which is larger than any number that I can think of, and hence that this power is something which I have received not from myself but from some other being which is more perfect than I am.'[1]

This argument could not have any force for an atheist, who would not allow himself to be convinced by it. Indeed, it is not suitable for this purpose, and the author does not wish it to be understood in this way. It must rather be conjoined with other arguments concerning God, since it presupposes such arguments, and takes God's existence as already proved by them. Thus, the author had already proved the existence of God from the idea of God in this part of the *Replies*, so the sense of this passage should accordingly be as follows: 'I know God exists and have proved it. And at the same time, I notice that when I count I can never reach a highest number, but there is always a number that can be thought of which is greater than any number that I can think of. It follows that the power of

---

1 Second Replies: AT VII 139; CSM II 100.

conceiving of this is something I do not derive from myself, but must have received from some entity more perfect than myself. And this entity is God, whose existence I have proved by means of the arguments already adduced' ...

'And for this reason alone I consider the customary search for final causes   158
to be totally useless in physics.'[1]

This rule – that we must never argue from ends – should be carefully heeded. For, firstly, the knowledge of a thing's purpose never leads us to knowledge of the thing itself; its nature remains just as obscure to us. Indeed, this constant practice of arguing from ends is Aristotle's greatest fault. Secondly, all the purposes of God are hidden from us, and it is rash to want to plunge into them. I am not speaking here of purposes which are known through revelation; it is purely as a philosopher that I am considering them. It is here that we go completely astray. We think of God as a sort of superman, who thinks up such-and-such a scheme, and tries to realize it by such-and-such a means. This is clearly quite unworthy of God ...

'For although God's will is incomparably greater than mine, both in virtue of the knowledge and power that accompany it ... and also in virtue of its object, in that it ranges over a greater number of items, nevertheless it does not seem any greater than mine when considered as will in the essential and strict sense.'[2]

[Burman] But when considered in this abstract way, understanding is understanding, and so our understanding too is not going to differ from that of God, even though God's understanding ranges over a greater number of objects.

[Descartes] But understanding depends on its object and cannot be separated from it; so it is not the case that 'understanding is understanding'. Moreover, it is not just that our understanding ranges over fewer objects than that of God: rather, it is extremely imperfect in itself, being obscure, mingled with ignorance, and so on.

[Burman] But in that case our will too is imperfect. We will one moment, and not the next; one moment we have a volition, the next – when our will is imperfect – merely a slight inclination.

[Descartes] That simply shows that there is a lack of constancy in our volition, not that there is any imperfection in our will. Each act of the will

1 Med. IV: AT VII 55; CSM II 39. See also Fifth Replies: AT VII 373; CSM II 258.
2 Med. IV: AT VII 57; CSM II 40.

is as perfect as the next: the fluctuation you speak of has its origin in judgement, and is due to the fact that our judgement is faulty.

[Burman] But judgement itself is an operation of the will.

159   [Descartes] It is indeed an operation of the will, and as such it is perfect. Every imperfection under which the judgement labours comes from intellectual ignorance. If this were removed, the fluctuation would disappear too, and our judgement would be stable and perfect. But there is no point in arguing like this on these matters. Let everyone just go down deep into himself and find out whether or not he has a perfect and absolute will, and whether he can conceive of anything which surpasses him in freedom of the will. I am sure everyone will find that it is as I say. It is in this, then, that the will is greater and more godlike than the intellect.

'Even if I have no power to avoid error in the first way . . . which requires a clear perception of everything I have to deliberate on, I can avoid error in the second way, which depends merely on my remembering to withhold judgement on any occasion when the truth of the matter is not clear.'[1]

[Burman] But in that case why should I not also have this ability with regard to the pursuit of good and evil, or again with regard to supernatural matters, since these things too depend on the will, and the will is always autonomous and indifferent?

[Descartes] We must leave the latter point for the theologians to explain. For the philosopher, it is enough to study man as he is now in his natural condition. I have written my philosophy in such a way as to make it acceptable anywhere – even among the Turks – and to avoid giving the slightest offence to anyone. Now we have inner consciousness of our freedom, and we know that we can withhold our assent when we wish. In the pursuit of good and evil, however, when the will is indifferent with respect to each of the two, it is already at fault, since it ought to seek after the good alone without any indifference, in contrast to the situation in theoretical matters. With regard to supernatural matters, the theologians teach that this is an area where we are corrupted through original sin: we need grace to enable us to recognize and pursue the good in this sphere. Indeed, almost all sins have their source in ignorance, since no one can pursue evil *qua* evil. So it is through his grace that God has promised us eternal life – something no one would have thought of or ever aspired to – in return for those good works of ours which in any case we were bound to perform. But it can be said that our will is corrupted by the emotions.

1 Med. IV: AT VII 62; CSM II 43.

'For it is impossible to imagine that anything is thought of in the divine intellect as good or true, or worthy of belief or action or omission, prior to the decision of the divine will to make it so.'[1]

[Burman] But what then of God's ideas of possible things? Surely these are prior to his will.

[Descartes] These too depend on God, like everything else. His will is the cause not only of what is actual and to come, but also of what is possible and of the simple natures. There is nothing we can think of or ought to think of that should not be said to depend on God.

[Burman] But does it follow from this that God could have commanded a creature to hate him, and thereby made this a good thing to do?

[Descartes] God could not now do this: but we simply do not know what he could have done. In any case, why should he not have been able to give this command to one of his creatures?

'When, for example, I imagine a triangle, even if perhaps no such figure exists, or has ever existed, anywhere outside my thought, there is still a determinate nature or essence or form of the triangle which is immutable and eternal and not invented by me or dependent on my mind. This is clear from the fact that various properties can be demonstrated of the triangle.'[2]

[Burman] But since I can demonstrate various properties of a chimera, on your view not even a chimera is going to be a fictitious entity.

[Descartes] Everything in a chimera that can be clearly and distinctly conceived is a true entity. It is not fictitious, since it has a true and immutable essence, and this essence comes from God just as much as the actual essence of other things. An entity is said to be 'fictitious', on the other hand, when it is merely our supposition that it exists. Thus, all the demonstrations of mathematicians deal with true entities and objects, and the complete and entire object of mathematics and everything it deals with is a true and real entity. This object has a true and real nature, just as much as the object of physics itself. The only difference is that physics considers its object not just as a true and real entity, but also as something actually and specifically existing. Mathematics, on the other hand, considers its object merely as possible, i.e. as something which does not actually exist in space but is capable of so doing. It must be stressed at this point that we are talking of clear perception, not of imagination. Even though we can with the utmost clarity imagine the head of a lion joined to the body of a goat, or some such thing, it does not therefore follow that they exist, since we do

1 Sixth Replies: AT VII 432; CSM II 291.
2 Med. IV: AT VII 64; CSM II 44f.

not clearly perceive the link, so to speak, which joins the parts together. For example, I may clearly see Peter standing, but I do not clearly see that standing is contained in and conjoined with Peter. Now if we are accustomed to clear perceptions, we will never have a false conception. As to whether our perceptions are clear or not, this is something we know perfectly well from our own inner awareness. This is the point of all the explanations which the author went through in Book One of the *Principles*, and it is of very great benefit to be acquainted with them...

(161)   'When we examine through a magnifying glass those lines which appear most straight, we find they are irregular and always form wavy curves. Hence, when in childhood we first happened to see a triangular figure drawn on paper, it cannot have been this figure that showed us how we should conceive of the true triangle studied by geometers.'[1]

[Burman] But it is from the imperfect triangle that you frame in your mind the perfect triangle.

162   [Descartes] But why then does the imperfect triangle provide me with the idea of a perfect triangle rather than an idea of itself?

[Burman] It provides you with both: firstly itself, and then, from that, the perfect triangle. For you deduce the perfect triangle from the imperfect.

[Descartes] That cannot be. I could not conceive of an imperfect triangle unless there were in me the idea of a perfect one, since the former is the negation of the latter. Thus, when I see a triangle, I have a conception of a perfect triangle, and it is by comparison with this that I subsequently realize that what I am seeing is imperfect...

'If there exists some body to which the mind is so joined that it can apply itself to contemplate it, as it were, whenever it pleases, then it may possibly be this very body that enables me to imagine corporeal things.'[2]

[Burman] What does 'to contemplate it' mean? Does it mean the same as 'to understand it'? If so, why do you use a different expression? If not, then the mind is more than an understanding or thinking thing, and even before it has a body it has this ability to contemplate a body. Or is this ability of the mind an effect of its union with the body?

[Descartes] It is a special mode of thinking, which occurs as follows. When external objects act on my senses, they print on them an idea, or rather a figure, of themselves; and when the mind attends to these images imprinted on the gland in this way, it is said to have sensory perception. When, on the other hand, the images on the gland are not imprinted by

1 Fifth Replies: AT VII 381; CSM II 262.
2 Med. VI: AT VII 73; CSM II 51.

external objects but by the mind itself, which fashions and shapes them in the brain in the absence of external objects, then we have imagination. The difference between sense-perception and imagination is thus really just this, that in sense-perception the images are imprinted by external objects which are actually present, whilst in imagination the images are imprinted by the mind without any external objects, and with the windows shut, as it were. This makes it quite clear why I can imagine a triangle, pentagon, and suchlike, but not, for example, a chiliagon. Since my mind can easily form and depict three lines in the brain, it can easily go on to contemplate them, and thus imagine a triangle, pentagon, etc. It cannot, however, trace out and form a thousand lines in the brain except in a confused manner, and this is why it does not imagine a chiliagon distinctly, but only in a confused manner. This limitation is so great that it is only with the greatest difficulty that we can imagine even a heptagon or an octagon. The author, who is a fairly imaginative man and has trained his mind in this field for some time, can imagine these figures reasonably distinctly; but others lack this ability. This now also makes it clear why we see the lines as if they were present in front of us, and it further explains the surprising mental concentration we need for imagining, and for contemplating, the body in this way. All this is clear from what has been said.

163

'I know that everything which I clearly and distinctly understand is capable of being created by God so as to correspond exactly with my understanding of it. Hence the fact that I can clearly and distinctly understand one thing apart from another is enough to make me certain that the two things are distinct.'[1]

You cannot ask whether the mind is a substance or, instead, a mode; nor can you say that it can be both these, since that is a contradiction; if it is one, it is not the other. You can, however, pose the following question: since thinking or thought is an attribute, to what substance does it belong? To corporeal substance? Or rather to incorporeal and spiritual substance? The answer to this is clear. You have a clear conception of corporeal substance, and you also have a clear conception of thinking substance as distinct from, and incompatible with, corporeal substance, just as corporeal substance is incompatible with thinking substance. In view of this, you would be going against your own powers of reasoning in the most absurd fashion if you said the two were one and the same substance. For you have a clear conception of them as two substances which not only do not entail one another but are actually incompatible. 'Nature also teaches me by

1 Med. VI: AT VII 78; CSM II 54.

these sensations of pain, hunger, thirst, and so on, that I am not merely present in my body as a sailor is present in a ship, but that I am very closely joined and, as it were, intermingled with it.'[1]

[Burman] But how can this be, and how can the soul be affected by the body and vice versa, when their natures are completely different?

[Descartes] This is very difficult to explain; but here our experience is sufficient, since it is so clear on this point that it just cannot be gainsaid. This is evident in the case of the passions, and so on.

'Again, dryness of the throat may sometimes arise not, as it normally does, from the fact that a drink is necessary to the health of the body, but from some quite opposite cause, as happens in the case of the man with dropsy. Yet it is much better that it should mislead on this occasion than that it should always mislead when the body is in good health.'[2]

[Burman] But if this is the way our senses are naturally constituted, why did God not make up for this defect by giving the soul awareness of the errors of the senses, so that it could be on its guard against them?

[Descartes] God made our body like a machine, and he wanted it to function like a universal instrument which would always operate in the same manner in accordance with its own laws. Accordingly, when the body is in good health, it gives the soul a correct awareness; but when it is ill, it still affects the soul in accordance with its own laws, and the necessary result of this is a state of awareness whereby the soul will be deceived. If the body did not induce this misleading state, it would not be behaving uniformly and in accordance with its universal laws; and then there would be a defect in God's constancy, since he would not be permitting the body to behave uniformly, despite the existence of uniform laws and modes of behaviour . . .

(165)   A point to note is that one should not devote so much effort to the *Meditations* and to metaphysical questions, or give them elaborate treatment in commentaries and the like. Still less should one do what some try to do, and dig more deeply into these questions than the author did; he has dealt with them quite deeply enough. It is sufficient to have grasped them once in a general way, and then to remember the conclusion. Otherwise, they draw the mind too far away from physical and observable things, and make it unfit to study them. Yet it is just these physical studies that it is most desirable for people to pursue, since they would yield abundant

1 Med. VI: AT VII 81; CSM II 56.
2 Med. VI: AT VII 89; CSM II 61.

benefits for life. The author did follow up metaphysical questions fairly thoroughly in the *Meditations*, and established their certainty against the sceptics, and so on; so everyone does not have to tackle the job for himself, or need to spend time and trouble meditating on these things. It is sufficient to know the first book of the *Principles*, since this includes those parts of metaphysics which need to be known for physics, and so forth.

[Burman] In the *Comments on a Certain Broadsheet* the author says that no ideas of things, in the form in which we think of them, are provided by the senses, but that they are all innate.[1] Does it then follow that the mystery of the Trinity, for example, is innate?

[Descartes] The author does not say that all ideas are innate in him. He says there are also some which are adventitious, for example the idea he has of the town of Leiden or Alkmaar. Secondly, even though the idea of the Trinity is not innate in us to the extent of giving us an express representation of the Trinity, none the less the elements and rudiments of the idea are innate in us, as we have an innate idea of God, the number 3, and so on. It is from these rudiments, supplemented by revelation from the Scriptures, that we easily form a full idea of the mystery of the Trinity. This is how the conception we have of it is formed.

'There is always a single identical and perfectly simple act by means of which God simultaneously understands, wills and accomplishes everything.'[2]

[Descartes] We cannot conceive of how this happens, only understand it. Any different conception we may have arises from the fact that we think of God as a man who accomplishes all things as we would – by means of many different acts. If, however, we pay careful attention to the nature of God, we shall see that we can only understand him as accomplishing all things by means of a single act.

[Burman] It seems that this cannot be, since there are some of God's decrees which we can conceive of as not having been enacted and as 166 alterable. These decrees, then, do not come about by means of the single act which is identical with God, since they can be separated from him, or at least could have been. One example of this, among others, is the decree concerning the creation of the world, with respect to which God was quite indifferent.

1 AT viiib 358; CSM i 303f.
2 *Principles*, Part i, art. 23: AT viiia 14; CSM i 201.

[Descartes] Whatever is in God is not in reality separate from God himself; rather it is identical with God himself. Concerning the decrees of God which have already been enacted, it is clear that God is unalterable with regard to these, and, from the metaphysical point of view, it is impossible to conceive of the matter otherwise.

Concerning ethics and religion, on the other hand, the opinion has prevailed that God can be altered, because of the prayers of mankind; for no one would have prayed to God if he knew, or had convinced himself, that God was unalterable. In order to remove this difficulty and reconcile the immutability of God with the prayers of men, we have to say that God is indeed quite unalterable, and that he has decreed from eternity either to grant me a particular request or not to grant it. Coupled with this decree, however, he has made a simultaneous decree that the granting of my request shall be in virtue of my prayers, and at a time when, in addition, I am leading an upright life; the effect of which is that I must pray and live uprightly if I wish to obtain anything from God. This then is the situation from the point of view of ethics; and here, after weighing the truth of the matter, the author finds himself in agreement with the Gomarists, rather than the Arminians or even, amongst his brethren, the Jesuits.[1]

From the metaphysical point of view, however, it is quite unintelligible that God should be anything but completely unalterable. It is irrelevant that the decrees could have been separated from God; indeed, this should not really be asserted. For although God is completely indifferent with respect to all things, he necessarily made the decrees he did, since he necessarily willed what was best, even though it was of his own will that he did what was best. We should not make a separation here between the necessity and the indifference that apply to God's decrees; although his actions were completely indifferent, they were also completely necessary. Then again, although we may conceive that the decrees could have been separated from God, this is merely a token procedure of our own reasoning: the distinction thus introduced between God himself and his decrees is a mental, not a real one. In reality the decrees could not have been separated from God: he is not prior to them or distinct from them, nor could he have existed without them. So it is clear enough how God accomplishes all things in a single act. But these matters are not to be grasped by our powers of reasoning, and we must never allow ourselves the indulgence of trying to subject the nature and operations of God to our reasoning...

---

1 In the fierce controversy following the death of Calvin, Francis Gomar (1563–1641) had adhered to strict predestinarianism, while Jacobus Arminius (1560–1609) held that the sovereignty of God was compatible with a measure of human freedom.

'And it would be the height of presumption if we were to imagine that all   (168)
things were created by God for our benefit alone.'[1]

Nevertheless, it is a common habit of men to suppose they themselves
are the dearest of God's creatures, and that all things are therefore made
for their benefit. They think their own dwelling place, the earth, is of
supreme importance, that it contains everything that exists, and that for its
sake everything was created. But what do we know of what God may have
created outside the earth, on the stars, and so on? How do we know that he
has not placed on the stars other species of creature, other lives and other
'men' – or at least beings analogous to men? Maybe souls separated from
bodies, or other creatures whose nature escapes us, are able to live there.
And how do we know that God has not produced an infinite number of
kinds of creatures, and thus as it were, poured forth his power in the
creation of things? All these matters are surely quite hidden from us, since
God's purposes are hidden from us; and this is why we ought not to have
so high an opinion of ourselves as to think that everything in the universe is
to be found here on earth, or exists for our benefit. For an infinite number
of other creatures far superior to us may exist elsewhere.

'For there is no doubt that the world was created right from the start with
all the perfection which it now has.'[2]

The author could give an adequate explanation of the creation of the
world based on his philosophical system, without departing from the
description in Genesis. (Incidentally, if anyone can provide an explanation   169
of this book, the author will regard him as a 'mighty Apollo', and the same
goes for the Song of Solomon and the Revelation.) The author did at one
time attempt such an explanation of the creation, but he abandoned the
task because he preferred to leave it to the theologians rather than provide
the explanation himself. As far as Genesis is concerned, however, the story
of the creation to be found there is perhaps metaphorical, and so ought to
be left to the theologians. In that case, the creation should not be taken as
divided into six days, but the division into days should be taken as
intended purely for the sake of our way of conceiving of things; this was
the way Augustine proceeded when he made the divisions by means of the
thoughts of angels. Why, for example, is the darkness said to precede the
light? With regard to the waters of the flood, they were undoubtedly
supernatural and miraculous. The statement about the cataracts of the
deep is metaphorical, but the metaphor eludes us. Some say they came

1 *Principles*, Part III, art. 2: AT VIIIA 81; CSM I 248.
2 *Principles*, Part III, art. 45: AT VIIIA 99; CSM I 256.

down from heaven, and argue that this was where the waters were originally placed at the creation, on the grounds that God is said to have placed the waters above *ha shamayim*. But this word is also very commonly used in Hebrew to denote the air, and I think that it is out of a prejudice of ours that we regard this as 'heaven'. Accordingly, the waters placed above the air are clouds...

(175) 'I observed with regard to logic that syllogisms and most of its other techniques are of less use for learning things than for explaining to others the things one already knows, or ... for speaking without judgement about matters of which one is ignorant.'[1]

   This really applies not so much to logic, which provides demonstrative proofs on all subjects, but to dialectic, which teaches us how to hold forth on all subjects. In this way it undermines good sense, rather than building on it. For in diverting our attention and making us digress into the stock arguments and headings, which are irrelevant to the thing under discussion, it diverts us from the actual nature of the thing itself. Professor Voetius[2] is a past master at this: throughout his books he simply presents his opinions, lays down the law – declaring 'this is how it is' – and then lumps together a lot of authorities.

176   'Those long chains composed of very simple and easy reasonings which geometers customarily use ... had given me occasion to suppose that all the things which fall within the scope of human knowledge are interconnected in the same way.'[3]

   [Burman] But is it not the case that in theology too all the items are mutually related in the same sort of sequence and chain of reasoning?

   [Descartes] Undoubtedly they are. But these are truths which depend on revelation, and so we cannot follow or understand their mutual connection in the same way. And certainly theology must not be subjected to our human reasoning, which we use for mathematics and for other truths, since it is something we cannot fully grasp; and the simpler we keep it, the better theology we shall have. If the author thought anyone would abuse his philosophy by taking arguments from it and applying them to theology, he would regret all the trouble he had taken. However, we can and should prove that the truths of theology are not inconsistent with those of philosophy, but we must not in any way subject them to critical examin-

1 *Discourse*: AT vi 17; CSM i 119.
2 See footnote 3, p. 220 above.
3 *Discourse*: AT vi 19; CSM i 120.

ation. This is how the monks have opened the way to all the sects and heresies – I mean, through scholastic theology, which is something that should above all else have been stamped out. Why do we need to spend all this effort on theology, when we see that simple country folk have just as much chance as we have of getting to heaven? This should certainly be a warning to us that it is much more satisfactory to have a theology as simple as that of country folk than one which is plagued with countless controversies. This is how we corrupt theology and open the way for disputes, quarrels, wars and suchlike. Indeed, the theologians have made such a habit of foisting every kind of doctrine on to the theologians of the opposing school and then denigrating it that they have completely mastered the art of denigration, and can scarcely do anything but denigrate, even when they do not mean to.

'From this [mathematics] . . . I hoped . . . to accustom my mind to nourish itself on truths, and not to be satisfied with bad reasoning.'[1]

This benefit cannot be derived from mathematics as it is commonly taught. For this consists almost entirely in the history or explanation of terms, and the like, all of which can easily be learnt by memorization. All this develops the memory, but not the intelligence. To enable the intelligence to be developed, you need mathematical knowledge, and this is something which is not to be gleaned from books, but rather from actual practice and skill. The author had to teach himself the subject this way, since he had no books with him, and the results he obtained were very happy.

However, not everyone has this aptitude for mathematics: one needs a mathematical mind which must be polished by actual practice. Now this mathematical knowledge must be acquired from algebra; but this is a 177 subject in which we cannot do ourselves much good without the aid of a teacher – unless, that is, we are willing to follow step by step the lead which the author has given us in the *Geometry*, so as to end up with the ability to solve problems and discover truths whatever they may be . . .

A study of mathematics, then, is a prerequisite for making new discoveries, both in mathematics itself and in philosophy. You do not, however, need mathematics in order to understand the author's philosophical writings, with the possible exception of a few mathematical points in the *Optics*. The topics on which the author wants us to exercise our minds are very simple ones, such as the nature and properties of the triangle, and so on; these must be thought about and pondered on. Mathematics accus-

1 *Ibid.*

toms the mind to recognizing the truth, because it is in mathematics that examples of correct reasoning, which you will find nowhere else, are to be found. Accordingly, the man who has once accustomed his mind to mathematical reasoning will have a mind that is well equipped for the investigation of other truths, since reasoning is exactly the same in every subject. The fact that there are some people who are clever at mathematics but less successful in subjects like physics is not due to any defect in their powers of reasoning, but is the result of their having done mathematics not by reasoning but by imagining – everything they have accomplished has been by means of imagination. Now, in physics there is no place for imagination, and this explains their signal lack of success in the subject.

Then again, mathematics accustoms the mind to distinguishing arguments which are true and valid from those which are probable and false. For, in mathematics, anyone who relies solely on probable arguments will be misled and driven to absurd conclusions; this will make him see that a demonstrative proof does not proceed from probable premisses, which in this respect are equivalent to false ones, but only from those which are certain. It is because philosophers have not followed this advice that they can never distinguish proofs from probable arguments in philosophy and physics; moreover, they nearly always try to argue in terms of probabilities, since they do not believe that there can be a place for demonstrative proofs in the sciences which deal with reality. And this is why the sceptics and others have believed that the existence of God cannot be proved, and why many still think that it is unprovable; whereas in fact it is conclusively provable and, like all metaphysical truths, is capable of a more solid proof than the proofs of mathematics. For if you were to go to the mathematicians and cast doubt on all the things the author cast doubt on in his metaphysical inquiries, then absolutely no mathematical proof could be given with certainty; whereas the author went on to give metaphysical proofs in spite of the doubt. So the proofs in metaphysics are more certain than those in mathematics. And at every point, the author tried to provide 'mathematical' proofs, as they are commonly called, in his philosophy; though these cannot be grasped as such by those who are unfamiliar with mathematics.

178 'I formed for myself a provisional moral code consisting of just three or four maxims, which I should like to tell you about.'[1]

The author does not like writing on ethics, but he was compelled to include these rules because of people like the Schoolmen; otherwise, they

1 *Discourse*: AT VI 22; CSM I 122.

would have said that he was a man without any religion or faith and that he intended to use his method to subvert them.

'But if we did not know that everything real and true within us comes from a perfect and infinite being, then however clear and distinct our ideas were, we would have no reason to be sure that they had the perfection of being true.'[1]

If we did not know that all truth has its origin in God, then however clear our ideas were, we would not know that they were true, or that we were not mistaken – I mean, of course, when we were not paying attention to them, and when we merely remembered that we had clearly and distinctly perceived them. For on other occasions, when we do pay attention to the truths themselves, even though we may not know God exists, we cannot be in any doubt about them. Otherwise, we could not prove that God exists.

'We might free ourselves from innumerable diseases . . . and perhaps even from the infirmity of old age, if we had sufficient knowledge of their causes...'[2]

[Descartes] Whether man was immortal before the Fall, and if so how, is not a question for the philosopher, but must be left to the theologians. And as to how men before the Flood could achieve such an advanced age, this is something which defeats the philosopher: and it may be that God brought this about miraculously, by means of supernatural causes, and without recourse to physical causes. Or then again, it could have been that the structure of the natural world was different before the Flood, and that it then deteriorated as a result of the Flood. The philosopher studies nature, as he does man, simply as it is now; he does not investigate its causes at any more profound level, since this is beyond him. However, it should not be doubted that human life could be prolonged, if we knew the appropriate art. For since our knowledge of the appropriate art enables us to increase and prolong the life of plants and suchlike, why should it not be the same with man? But the best way of prolonging life, and the best method of keeping to a healthy diet, is to live and eat like animals, i.e. eat as much as we enjoy and relish, but no more.

[Burman] This might work out all right in sound and healthy bodies,   179
where the appetite is working properly for the body; but it will not work for those who are sick.

1 *Discourse*: AT VI 39; CSM I 130.
2 *Discourse*: AT VI 62; CSM I 143.

[Descartes] Nonsense. Even when we are ill, nature still remains the same. What is more, it seems that nature plunges us into illnesses, so that we can emerge all the stronger, and makes light of any obstacles in her way, provided we obey her. And perhaps if doctors would only allow people the food and drink they frequently desire when they are ill, they would often be restored to health far more satisfactorily than they are by means of all those unpleasant medicines. Indeed, experience confirms this. In such cases nature herself works to effect her own recovery; with her perfect internal awareness of herself, she knows better than the doctor who is on the outside.

[Burman] But there is such an infinite number of foods, etc.; so what choice should we make among them, and what order should we take them in, and so on?

[Descartes] This is something our own experience teaches us. We always know whether a food has agreed with us or not, and hence we can always learn for the future whether or not we should have the same food again, and whether we should eat it in the same way and in the same order. So, as Tiberius Caesar said[1] ... no one who has reached the age of thirty should need a doctor, since at that age he is quite able to know for himself through experience what is good or bad for him, and so be his own doctor.

AT V   FOR [ARNAULD], 4 JUNE 1648

192   The author of the objections which reached me yesterday has chosen to conceal his person and his name: but the better part of him, his mind, cannot remain unknown. This I find to be acute and learned, so that I shall not be ashamed to be worsted in argument or to learn from him. But because he says that he is moved by desire to discover the truth, and not by zeal for disputation, I shall reply to him here only briefly, and save some things for discussion face to face. I find it safer to treat with argumentative people by letter, but pleasanter to treat with seekers of truth by word of mouth.

I agree with you that there are two different powers of memory; but I am convinced that in the mind of an infant there have never been any pure acts of understanding, but only confused sensations. Although these confused sensations leave some traces in the brain, which remain there for life, that does not suffice to enable us to remember them. For that we would have to observe that the sensations which come to us as adults are like those which
193   we had in our mother's womb; and that in turn would require a certain reflective act of the intellect, or intellectual memory, which was not in use

1. See footnote 1, p. 276 above.

in the womb. Nevertheless it seems necessary that the mind should always be actually engaged in thinking; because thought constitutes its essence, just as extension constitutes the essence of a body. Thought is not conceived as an attribute which can be present or absent like the division of parts, or motion, in a body.

What is said about duration and time rests on the scholastic opinion, with which I strongly disagree, that the duration of motion is of a different kind from that of things which are motionless.[1] I have explained this in article 47 of Part One of the *Principles*.[2] Even if no bodies existed, it could still not be said that the duration of the human mind was entirely simultaneous like the duration of God; because our thoughts display a successiveness which cannot be found in the divine thoughts. We clearly understand that it is possible for me to exist at this moment, while I am thinking of one thing, and yet not to exist at the very next moment, when, if I do exist, I may think of something quite different.

The axiom 'What can do the greater can do the lesser' seems to be self-evident in the case of first causes that are not otherwise limited; but in the case of a cause determined to a particular effect, it is commonly said that it is a greater thing for it to produce some effect other than that to which it is determined and adapted. In that sense it is a greater thing for a man to move the earth from its place than to perform an act of understanding. It is also a greater thing to preserve oneself in existence than to give oneself some of the perfections one perceives oneself to lack; and this is enough to validate the argument, although it may well be less than to give oneself   194 omnipotence and the other divine perfections all together.

Since the Council of Trent itself was unwilling to explain how the body of Christ is in the Eucharist, and wrote that it was there 'in a manner of existing which we can scarcely express in words', I should fear the accusation of rashness if I dared to come to any conclusion on the matter; and such conjectures as I make I would prefer to communicate by word of mouth rather than in writing.

Finally, I have hardly anything to say about the vacuum, which is not already to be found somewhere or other in my *Principles of Philosophy*.[3] What you call the hollowness of a barrel seems to me to be a body with three dimensions, not to be identified with the sides of the barrel.[4]

---

1 Against Descartes' treatment of the duration of the soul in the Third Meditation (AT VII 49; CSM II 33), Arnauld had objected that the duration of a spiritual being was non-successive.

2 AT VIIIA 27; CSM I 212.

3 See *Principles*, Part II, art. 16–18: AT VIIIA 49f; CSM I 229f.

4 Arnauld had suggested that God could destroy the wine in a barrel and leave behind only the hollowness of the barrel without introducing any other substance (AT V 190).

But all these things can be more easily discussed at a meeting, which I would gladly arrange, being the most respectful servant of all men who love honesty and truth.

FOR [ARNAULD], 29 JULY 1648

219 Recently I was given some objections which appeared to come from an inhabitant of this city.[1] I answered them very briefly, thinking that any omission could easily be remedied in conversation. But now that I realize the writer lives elsewhere,[2] I hasten to reply to his second most courteous letter. Since he conceals his name, I will dispense with any exordium, for fear I commit some solecism in addressing him.

1. It seems to me very true that, as long as the mind is united to the body, it cannot withdraw itself from the senses whenever it is stimulated with great force by external or internal objects. I concede further that it cannot withdraw itself whenever it is attached to a brain which is too soft or damp, as in children, or otherwise in poor condition, as in those who are lethargic, apoplectic or frenetic, or as in all of us when we are deeply asleep – for whenever we have a dream that we afterwards remember, that means we are sleeping only lightly.

220 2. If we are to remember something, it is not sufficient that the thing should previously have been before our mind and have left some traces in the brain which give occasion for it to occur in our thought again; it is necessary in addition that we should recognize, when it occurs the second time, that this is happening because it has already been perceived by us earlier. Thus verses often occur to poets which they do not remember ever having read in other authors, but which would not have occurred to them unless they had read them elsewhere.

From this it is clear that it is not sufficient for memory that there should be traces left in the brain by preceding thoughts. The traces have to be of such a kind that the mind recognizes that they have not always been present in us, but were at some time newly impressed. Now for the mind to recognize this, I think that when these traces were first made it must have made use of pure intellect to notice that the thing which was then presented to it was new and had not been presented before; for there cannot be any corporeal trace of this novelty. Consequently, if ever I wrote that the thoughts of children leave no traces in their brain, I meant traces sufficient for memory, that is, traces which at the time of their impression are observed by pure intellect to be new. In a similar way we say that there are

1 Paris, which Descartes visited in May–August 1648.
2 Arnauld had been banished from Paris to Port-Royal des Champs.

no human tracks in the sand if we cannot find any impressions shaped like a human foot, though perhaps there may be many unevennesses made by human feet, which can therefore in another sense be called human tracks. Finally, we make a distinction between direct and reflective thoughts corresponding to the distinction we make between direct and reflective vision, one depending on the first impact of the rays and the other on the second. I call the first and simple thoughts of infants *direct* and not reflective – for instance the pain they feel when some wind distends their intestines, or the pleasure they feel when nourished by sweet blood. But when an adult feels something, and simultaneously perceives that he has not felt it before, I call this second perception *reflection*, and attribute it to the intellect alone, in spite of its being so linked to sensation that the two occur together and appear to be indistinguishable from each other. 221

3. I tried to remove the ambiguity of the word 'thought' in articles 63 and 64 of Part One of the *Principles*.[1] Just as extension, which constitutes the nature of body, differs greatly from the various shapes or modes of extension which it assumes, so thought, or a thinking nature, which I think constitutes the essence of the human mind, is very different from any particular act of thinking. It depends on the mind itself whether it produces this or that particular act of thinking, but not that it is a thinking thing; just as it depends on a flame, as an efficient cause, whether it turns to this side or that, but not that it is an extended thing. So by 'thought' I do not mean some universal which includes all modes of thinking, but a particular nature, which takes on those modes, just as extension is a nature which takes on all shapes.

4. Being conscious of our thoughts at the time when we are thinking is not the same as remembering them afterwards. Thus, we do not have any thoughts in sleep without being conscious of them at the moment they occur; though commonly we forget them immediately. But it is true that we are not conscious of the manner in which our mind sends the animal 222 spirits into particular nerves; for that depends not on the mind alone but on the union of the mind with the body. We are conscious, however, of every action by which the mind moves the nerves, in so far as such action is in the mind, where it is simply the inclination of the will towards a particular movement. The inflow of the spirits into the nerves, and everything else necessary for this movement, follows upon this inclination of the will. This happens because of the appropriate way the body is constructed, of which the mind may not be aware, and because of the union of the mind with the body, of which the mind is certainly conscious. Otherwise it would not incline its will to move the limbs.

1 AT VIIIA 31; CSM I 215.

That the mind, which is incorporeal, can set the body in motion is something which is shown to us not by any reasoning or comparison with other matters, but by the surest and plainest everyday experience. It is one of those self-evident things which we only make obscure when we try to explain them in terms of other things. Nevertheless, I will use a simile. Most philosophers, who think that the heaviness of a stone is a real quality distinct from the stone, think they understand clearly enough how this quality can impel the stone towards the centre of the earth, because they think that they have a manifest experience of such an occurrence. I, however, am convinced that there is no such quality in nature, and that consequently there is no real idea of it in the human intellect; and I think that in order to represent this heaviness to themselves they are using the idea they have within them of an incorporeal substance. So it is no harder for us to understand how the mind moves the body than it is for them to understand how such heaviness moves a stone downwards. Of course they deny that heaviness is a substance, but that makes no difference, because they conceive it in fact as a substance since they think that it is real and that it is possible by some power (namely divine power) for it to exist without the stone. Again it makes no difference that they think it is corporeal. For if we count as corporeal whatever belongs to a body, even though not of the same nature as body, then even the mind can be called corporeal, in so far as it is made to be united to the body; on the other hand, if we regard as corporeal only what has the nature of body, then this heaviness is no more corporeal than the human mind is.[1]

5. I understand the successive duration of things in motion, and of the motion itself, no differently from that of things that are not in motion; for earlier and later in any duration are known to me by the earlier and later of the successive duration which I detect in my own thought, with which the other things co-exist.

6. The difficulty in recognizing the impossibility of a vacuum seems to arise primarily because we do not sufficiently consider that nothing can have no properties; otherwise, seeing that there is true extension in the space we call empty, and consequently all the properties necessary for the nature of body, we would not say that it was wholly empty, that is, mere nothingness. Secondly, it arises because we have recourse to the divine power: knowing this to be infinite, we attribute to it an effect without noticing that the effect involves a contradictory conception, that is, is inconceivable by us. But I do not think that we should ever say of anything that it cannot be brought about by God. For since every basis of truth and goodness depends on his omnipotence, I would not dare to say that God

223

224

1 On this topic see above, p. 219.

cannot make a mountain without a valley, or bring it about that 1 and 2 are not 3. I merely say that he has given me such a mind that I cannot conceive a mountain without a valley, or a sum of 1 and 2 which is not 3; such things involve a contradiction in my conception. I think the same should be said of a space which is wholly empty, or of an extended piece of nothing, or of a limited universe; because no limit to the world can be imagined without its being understood that there is extension beyond it; and no barrel can be conceived to be so empty as to have inside it no extension, and therefore no body; for wherever extension is, there, of necessity, is body also.

TO [POLLOT], 1648   AT V

I am very glad you were not displeased that I took the liberty of giving 556
you my opinion; and I am obliged to you for indicating that you mean to 557
follow it, even though you have, I admit, very strong reasons for not doing so. For I do not doubt that your mind could provide you with better things to occupy you than the worries of everyday life. Through custom and example people have come to regard the profession of arms as the most noble of all; for myself, however, considering the matter as a philosopher, I accord it only the value it deserves. Indeed I find it difficult to give it a place among the honourable professions, seeing that idleness and debauchery are nowadays the main motives that lead most men to take it up. For this reason I would be exceedingly sorry if things turned out badly for you. In any case, I acknowledge that a man with an illness ought to regard himself as older than other men, and it is better to retire when one is winning than when one is losing. In the game under consideration, however, I do not think there is any question of losing, but only of winning or not winning. For this reason I think it is time enough to retire from the game when one is no longer winning. I have often met old men who told me that in their youth they were less healthy than other men who had died before them. So it seems to me that whatever weakness or bodily indisposition we may suffer, we ought to live our lives and perform our tasks just as if we were certain to reach a ripe old age. But on the other hand, however energetic or healthy we may be, we ought also to be prepared to meet death without regret when it comes, because it may come at any time, and any action we 558 perform may cause it. If we eat a piece of bread, it may be poisoned; as we walk down the street we may be hit by a falling roof-tile; and so on. Accordingly, since we are surrounded by so many unavoidable hazards, it seems to me that wisdom does not forbid us to expose ourselves to the hazards of war when obliged by a fine and just cause – provided we do so without fear and we do not refuse to put our arms to the test so far as we

can. In fact, I believe that the occupations we choose for ourselves, however agreeable they may be, do not keep us from thinking about our infirmities so well as the occupations we are obliged to undertake by some duty. I think too that our body becomes so well accustomed to the style of life we lead that when we change this style, then, more often than not, our health worsens rather than improves, especially when the change is too sudden. That is why I think it best to pass from one extreme to another only by degrees. In my case, for instance, before coming to this country in search of solitude I spent a winter in France, in that part of the country where I received my early education. And if I were leading a style of life which my indisposition did not allow me to continue for a long time, I would not try to hide this indisposition; instead I would try to make it seem

559   greater than it was, thus enabling me honestly to avoid any action which might make it worse. And so, by increasing my leisure-time little by little, I would gradually achieve complete freedom.

AT V   TO MORE, 5 FEBRUARY 1649

267   The praises which you heap on me are proof rather of your kindness than of any merit of mine, which could never equal them. Such generosity,

268   however, based on the mere reading of my writings, displays so clearly the candour and nobility of your mind that though unacquainted with you hitherto, I have been completely captivated. So I will answer very willingly the queries which you put to me.

1. The first question was why I defined body as extended substance, rather than perceptible, tangible or impenetrable substance. It is clear that if body is called perceptible substance, it is defined by its relation to our senses, and thus we explain only a certain property of it, rather than its whole nature. This nature certainly does not depend upon our senses, since it could exist even though there were no men, and so I do not see why you say that it is altogether necessary that all matter should be perceptible by the senses. Just the opposite is the case: all matter is completely imperceptible if it is divided into parts much smaller than the particles of our nerves and the individual parts are given a sufficiently rapid movement.

The argument of mine which you call 'cunning and almost sophistical' I used only to refute the opinion of those who, like you, think that every body is perceptible by the senses.[1] I think it does give a clear and definitive refutation of that view. For a body can retain its whole bodily nature without being soft or hard or cold or hot to the senses – indeed without having any perceptible quality.

1 See *Principles*, Part II, art. 4: AT VIIIA 42; CSM I 224.

You make a comparison with some wax, which although it can be not square and not round, cannot be completely without shape. But since according to my principles, all perceptible qualities consist solely in the   269 fact that the particles of a body are in motion or at rest in a certain manner, in order to fall into the error which you seem to attribute to me here, I would have had to conclude that a body could exist without any of its particles being either at motion or at rest. But this is something which never entered my mind. Body, therefore, is not rightly defined as perceptible substance.

Let us see next whether body is more appropriately called 'impenetrable or tangible substance', in the sense which you explained. Now tangibility or impenetrability in body is something like the ability to laugh in man; according to the common rules of logic it is a 'property of the fourth kind', and not a true and essential differentia such as I claim extension to be. Consequently, just as man is defined not as an animal capable of laughter, but as a rational animal, so body should be defined not by impenetrability but by extension. This is confirmed by the fact that tangibility and impenetrability involve a reference to parts and presuppose the concept of division or limitation; whereas we can conceive a continuous body of indeterminate size, or an indefinite body in which there is nothing to consider except extension.

'But', you say, 'God, or an angel, or any other self-subsistent thing is extended, and so your definition is too broad.' It is not my custom to argue about words, and so if someone wants to say that God is in a sense extended, since he is everywhere, I have no objection. But I deny that true extension as commonly conceived is to be found in God or in angels or in our mind or in any substance which is not a body. Commonly when people   270 talk of an extended being, they mean something imaginable. In this being – I leave on one side the question whether it is conceptual or real – they can distinguish by the imagination various parts of determinate size and shape, each non-identical with the others. Some of these parts can be imagined as transferred to the place of others, but no two can be imagined simultaneously in one and the same place. Nothing of this kind can be said about God or about our mind; they cannot be apprehended by the imagination, but only by the intellect; nor can they be distinguished into parts, and certainly not into parts which have determinate sizes and shapes. Again, we easily understand that the human mind and God and several angels can all be at the same time in one and the same place. So we clearly conclude that no incorporeal substances are in any strict sense extended. I conceive them as sorts of powers or forces, which although they can act upon extended things, are not themselves extended – just as fire is in white-hot iron without itself being iron. Some people indeed do confuse the notion of substance with that of extended thing. This is because of the false preconceived opinion which makes them believe that nothing can exist or be intelligible without being also imaginable, and because it is indeed true that nothing falls within the scope of the imagination without being in some way extended. Now just as we can say that health belongs only to human beings, though by analogy medicine and a temperate climate and many other things also are called healthy, so too I call extended only what is imaginable as having parts within parts, each of determinate size and shape – although other things may also be called extended by analogy.

271   2. I pass to your second difficulty. If we examine what is this extended being which I described, we will find that it is no different from the space which is popularly regarded sometimes as full and sometimes as empty, sometimes as real and sometimes as imaginary. For in a space – even an imaginary and empty space – everyone readily imagines various parts of determinate size and shape; and some of the parts can be transferred in imagination to the place of others, but no two of them can in any way be conceived as compenetrating each other at the same time in one and the same place, since it is contradictory for this to happen without some part of space being removed. Now since I consider that such real properties can exist only in a real body, I dared to assert that there can be no completely empty space, and that every extended being is a genuine body. On this topic I did not hesitate to disagree with great men such as Epicurus, Democritus and Lucretius, for I saw that they were guided by no solid reason, but only by the false preconception with which we have all been imbued from our earliest years. As I warned in article 3 of Part Two,[1] our senses do not always show us external bodies exactly as they are, but only in so far as they are related to us and can benefit or harm us. Despite this, we all decided when we were still children that there is nothing in the world besides what the senses show us, and hence there are no bodies which are not perceivable by the senses, and all places in which we do not perceive anything are empty. Since Epicurus, Democritus and Lucretius never overcame this preoccupation, I have no obligation to follow their authority.

272   I am surprised that a man otherwise so perspicacious, having seen that he cannot deny that there is some substance in every space, since all the properties of extension are truly found in it, should nevertheless prefer to say that the divine extension fills up the space in which there are no bodies, rather than admit that there can be no space without body. For as I said earlier, the alleged extension of God cannot be the subject of the true properties which we perceive very distinctly in all space. For God is not

1 *Principles*: AT VIIIA 41; CSM I 224.

imaginable or distinguishable into parts that are measurable and have shape.

But you are quite ready to admit that in the natural course of events there is no vacuum: you are concerned about God's power, which you think can take away the contents of a container while preventing its sides from meeting. For my part, I know that my intellect is finite and God's power is infinite, and so I set no limits to it; I consider only what I am capable of perceiving, and what not, and I take great pains that my judgement should accord with my perception. And so I boldly assert that God can do everything which I perceive to be possible, but I am not so bold as to assert the converse, namely that he cannot do what conflicts with my conception of things – I merely say that it involves a contradiction. And so, since I see that it conflicts with my way of conceiving things for all body to be taken out of a container and for there to remain an extension which I conceive in no way differently than I previously conceived the body contained in it, I say that it involves a contradiction that such an extension should remain there after the body has been taken away. I conclude that the sides of the container must come together. This is altogether in accord with my other opinions. For I say elsewhere[1] that all motion is in a manner 273 circular; from which it follows that it cannot be distinctly understood that God should remove some body from a container unless we understand at the same time that another body, or the sides of the container, should move into its place by a circular motion.

3. In the same way I say that it involves a contradiction that there should be any atoms which are conceived as extended and at the same time indivisible.[2] Though God might make them such that they could not be divided by any creature, we certainly cannot understand that he might deprive himself of the power of dividing them. Your comparison with things which have been done and cannot be undone is not to the point. For we do not take it as a mark of impotence when someone cannot do something which we do not understand to be possible, but only when he cannot do something which we distinctly perceive to be possible. Now we certainly perceive it to be possible for an atom to be divided, since we suppose it to be extended; and so, if we judge that it cannot be divided by God, we shall judge that God cannot do one of the things which we perceive to be possible. But we do not in the same way perceive it to be possible for what is done to be undone – on the contrary, we perceive it to be altogether impossible, and so it is no defect of power in God not to do it.

1 Cf. *Principles*, Part II, art. 34: AT VIIIA 59; CSM I 239.
2 Cf. *Principles*, Part II, art. 20: AT VIIIA 51; CSM I 231.

The case is different with the divisibility of matter; for though I cannot count all the parts into which it is divisible (and which I say are on that account indefinite in number), yet I cannot assert that their division by God could never be completed, because I know that God can do more things than I can encompass within my thought. Indeed I agreed in article 34[1] that such indefinite division of certain parts of matter sometimes actually takes place.

4. In my view it is not a matter of affected modesty, but of necessary caution, to say that some things are indefinite rather than infinite. God is the only thing I positively understand to be infinite. As to other things like the extension of the world and the number of parts into which matter is divisible, I confess I do not know whether they are absolutely infinite; I merely know that I know no end to them, and so, looking at them from my own point of view, I call them indefinite. True, our mind is not the measure of reality or of truth; but certainly it should be the measure of what we assert or deny. What is more rash or absurd than to want to make judgements about matters which we admit our mind cannot perceive? I am surprised that you seem to wish to do this when you say 'if extension is infinite only in relation to us, then it will in fact be finite'. Not only this, but you also imagine some divine extension which goes further than the extension of bodies; and thus you suppose that God has parts within parts and is divisible, and even attribute to him all the essence of a corporeal thing.

To remove all difficulties here, I should explain that I call the extension of matter indefinite in the hope that this will prevent anyone imagining a place outside it into which the particles of my vortices might escape,[2] for on my view, wherever such a place may be conceived, there is some matter. When I say that matter is indefinitely extended, I am saying that it extends further than anything a human being can conceive. Nevertheless, I think there is a very great difference between the vastness of this bodily extension and the vastness of the divine substance or essence (I do not say 'divine extension', because strictly speaking, there is none); and so I call the latter simply 'infinite', and the former 'indefinite'.

Moreover, I do not agree with what you very generously concede, namely that the rest of my opinions could stand even if what I have written about the extension of matter were refuted. For it is one of the most important, and I believe the most certain, foundations of my physics; and I confess that no reasons satisfy me even in physics unless they involve that

1 *Principles*: AT VIIIA 59; CSM I 239.
2 On vortices, see *Principles*, Part III, art. 65: AT VIIIA 116.

necessity which you call logical or analytic,[1] provided you except things which can be known by experience alone, such as that there is only one sun and only one moon around the earth, and so on. Since in other matters you are well disposed to my views, I hope that you will come to agree with these too, if you reflect that it is a preconceived opinion which makes many people think that an extended being in which there is nothing to affect the senses is not a true corporeal substance but merely an empty space, and that there are no bodies which are not perceivable by the senses, and no substance which does not fall within the scope of the imagination and is consequently extended.

5. But there is no preconceived opinion to which we are all more accustomed from our earliest years than the belief that dumb animals   276
think. Our only reason for this belief is the fact that we see that many of the organs of animals are not very different from ours in shape and movements. Since we believe that there is a single principle within us which causes these movements – namely the soul, which both moves the body and thinks – we do not doubt that some such soul is to be found in animals also. I came to realize, however, that there are two different principles causing our movements. The first is purely mechanical and corporeal, and depends solely on the force of the spirits and the structure of our organs, and can be called the corporeal soul. The other, an incorporeal principle, is the mind or that soul which I have defined as a thinking substance. Thereupon I investigated very carefully whether the movements of animals originated from both these principles or from one only. I soon perceived clearly that they could all originate from the corporeal and mechanical principle, and I regarded it as certain and demonstrated that we cannot at all p.. ⁓ the presence of a thinking soul in animals. I am not disturbed by the astuteness and cunning of dogs and foxes, or by all the things which animals do for the sake of food, sex and fear; I claim that I can easily explain all of them as originating from the structure of their bodily parts.

But though I regard it as established that we cannot prove there is any thought in animals, I do not think it can be proved that there is none, since the human mind does not reach into their hearts. But when I investigate   277
what is most probable in this matter, I see no argument for animals having thoughts except this one: since they have eyes, ears, tongues and other sense-organs like ours, it seems likely that they have sensation like us; and since thought is included in our mode of sensation, similar thought seems to be attributable to them. This argument, which is very obvious, has taken possession of the minds of all men from their earliest age. But there are

1 Lat. *contradictoria*, i.e. that whose denial involves a contradiction.

other arguments, stronger and more numerous, but not so obvious to everyone, which strongly urge the opposite. One is that it is more probable that worms, flies, caterpillars and other animals move like machines than that they all have immortal souls.

In the first place, it is certain that in the bodies of animals, as in ours, there are bones, nerves, muscles, animal spirits and other organs so arranged that they can by themselves, without any thought, give rise to all the movements we observe in animals. This is very clear in convulsions, when the mechanism of the body moves despite the mind, and often moves more violently and in a more varied manner than usually happens when it is moved by the will.

Second, since art copies nature, and people can make various automatons which move without thought, it seems reasonable that nature should even produce its own automatons, which are much more splendid than artificial ones – namely the animals. This is especially likely since we know no reason why thought should always accompany the sort of arrangement of organs that we find in animals. It is much more wonderful that a mind should be found in every human body than that one should be lacking in every animal.

But in my opinion the main reason for holding that animals lack thought is the following. Within a single species some of them are more perfect than others, as humans are too. This can be seen in horses and dogs, some of which learn what they are taught much better than others; and all animals easily communicate to us, by voice or bodily movement, their natural impulses of anger, fear, hunger, and so on. Yet in spite of all these facts, it has never been observed that any brute animal has attained the perfection of using real speech, that is to say, of indicating by word or sign something relating to thought alone and not to natural impulse. Such speech is the only certain sign of thought hidden in a body. All human beings use it, however stupid and insane they may be, even though they may have no tongue and organs of voice; but no animals do. Consequently this can be taken as a real specific difference between humans and animals.

For brevity's sake I here omit the other reasons for denying thought to animals. Please note that I am speaking of thought, and not of life or sensation. I do not deny life to animals, since I regard it as consisting simply in the heat of the heart; and I do not even deny sensation, in so far as it depends on a bodily organ. Thus my opinion is not so much cruel to animals as indulgent to human beings – at least to those who are not given to the superstitions of Pythagoras – since it absolves them from the suspicion of crime when they eat or kill animals.

Perhaps I have written at greater length than the sharpness of your intelligence requires; but I wished to show you that very few people have yet sent me objections which were as agreeable as yours. Your kindness and candour have made you a friend of that most respectful admirer of all who seek true wisdom.

TO PRINCESS ELIZABETH, 22 FEBRUARY 1649   AT V

Several pieces of distressing news have come to me recently from various quarters, but it was the news of Your Highness's illness which affected me most deeply. And even though I have also learnt of your recovery, I still feel some remaining traces of sadness, which will not readily go away. The inclination to compose verses, which Your Highness felt during her illness, reminds me of Socrates, for according to Plato he had a similar desire while he was in prison. I believe that this desire results from a strong agitation of the animal spirits, which may completely disorient the imagination of those who lack a well-balanced mind, but which merely stimulates the imagination of those having a more stable mind, and makes them inclined to compose poetry. I take this tendency to be the mark of a mind which is stronger and more refined than usual.

If I did not know your mind to have this quality, I would fear that you would have been extremely grieved on learning the fatal conclusion of the tragedies of England.[1] But I am certain that Your Highness, being accustomed to the adversities of fortune and finding her own life in great danger recently, would be less surprised and distressed to learn of the death of a close relation than if she had not herself previously suffered other afflictions. And although such a violent death seems more horrible than the death that comes in one's bed, yet properly regarded it is more glorious, happier and sweeter, and so the features of it which especially distress the common run of people should provide consolation for Your Highness. For there is great glory in dying for a reason which ensures that one is universally pitied, praised and missed by everyone with any human feeling. It is certain that without this ordeal, the clemency and other virtues of the late King would not be so well noticed or so highly esteemed as they are and will be in the future by those who read his history. I am certain also that the satisfaction he felt in his conscience during the last moments of his life was greater than the unhappiness caused by the resentment which is said to be the only melancholy passion that afflicted him. As for pain, I do not take that into account at all. For it is so short-lived that if murderers could employ fevers or any of the other illnesses which nature commonly uses to remove men from this world, we would have reason to think them crueller than those who kill with the blow of an axe. But I do not care to

281

282

---

1 Princess Elizabeth's uncle, Charles I, was executed in London on 9 February 1649.

283   dwell any longer on such a morbid subject. I would add only that it is much better to be entirely free from a false hope than to be futilely tied to it.

As I was writing these lines I received letters from a place which I had not heard from for seven or eight months. One of the letters was from the person[1] to whom I sent the treatise on the passions a year ago: she wrote in her own hand to thank me for it. That she remembers a man as unimportant as I after so much time makes me think that she will not forget to reply to the letters from Your Highness, although she has delayed doing so for four months. I am told that she has asked some of her attendants to study my *Principles*, in order to help her to read it. But I do not think she will have enough leisure to apply herself to it, even though she seems to be willing to do so. She thanks me, in very express terms, for the treatise on the passions, but she makes no mention of the letters which accompanied it.[2] Nor do I hear anything at all from that country on matters that concern Your Highness. From this I can guess only that since the conditions of the peace in Germany are not so favourable to your House as they might have been, those who have contributed to it are in doubt as to whether you think

284   badly of them and for this reason are reluctant to show friendship to you . . .

AT V   TO CHANUT, 26 FEBRUARY 1649

(290)   . . . I received as an altogether undeserved favour the letter which that matchless Princess[3] condescended to write to me. I am surprised that she should take the trouble to do so; but I am not so surprised that she took the trouble to read my *Principles*, because I am convinced that it contains many truths which are difficult to find elsewhere. It might be said that they are only unimportant truths about physics, which appear to have nothing in common with the things a queen ought to know. But because her mind is universal in its capacity, and because these truths of physics are part of the

291   foundations of the highest and most perfect morality, I dare to hope that she will derive satisfaction from learning them. I should be glad to learn that she had chosen you, in addition to Freinshemius[4], to lighten the study for her; and I would be most grateful to you if you would take the trouble to notify me of the places where I have not explained myself sufficiently. I would be careful always to reply to you the same day as I received your letters. But this would serve only for my own information, because it is so far from here to Stockholm, and the letters go through so many hands

1 Queen Christina; the other letter was from Chanut (AT v 251, 252).
2 See above, p. 327.
3 Queen Christina; the letter is dated 12 December 1648 (AT v 251).
4 Johannes Freinsheim (1608–60), a German scholar who was librarian to Queen Christina in 1647.

before arriving there, that you would have solved the difficulties for yourselves before you could have had the solution from here.

I will merely observe at this point two or three things which experience has taught me about the *Principles*. The first is that though the first part is only an abridgement of what I wrote in my *Meditations*, there is no need to take time off to read my *Meditations* in order to understand them; many people find the *Meditations* much more difficult, and I would be afraid that Her Majesty might become bored. The second is that there is no reason to spend a lot of time examining the rules of motion in articles 46 and following of Part Two;[1] they are not needed in order to understand the rest. The last is that it must be remembered, while reading this book, that although I consider nothing in bodies except the sizes, shapes and motions   292 of their parts, I claim none the less to explain the nature of light and heat and all other qualities that are perceivable by the senses; for I presuppose that these qualities are only in our senses, like pleasure and pain, and not in the objects which we perceive by the senses, in which there are only certain shapes and motions which cause the sensations we call light, heat, etc. This I did not explain and prove until the end of Part Four;[2] nevertheless it is useful to know and observe it from the beginning of the book, so as to understand it better . . .

TO QUEEN CHRISTINA, 26 FEBRUARY 1649   AT V

If a letter was sent to me from heaven and I saw it descending from the   294 clouds, I would not be more surprised than I was to receive the letter which Your Highness so graciously wrote me; and I could not receive such a letter with more respect and veneration than I feel on receiving your letter. But I know myself to be so unworthy of the compliments contained in it that I can accept them only as a grace and favour, for which my indebtedness is so great that I do not know how I shall ever be able to repay it. When M. Chanut, on behalf of Your Majesty, asked me about the sovereign good, I received an honour which more than amply paid me for the answer I gave him. And when he reported that this answer had been favourably received, I found myself under an obligation which was so strong that I could not expect or desire anything greater for something so slight – especially from a Princess whom God has elevated to such a high place, who is beset by so many important issues to which she gives her personal attention, and whose slightest actions have such consequences for the general well-being of the whole earth that all who love virtue must consider themselves

1 AT VIIIA 68–9.
2 AT VIIIA 315ff; CSM I 279ff.

fortunate whenever they have an opportunity to render a service to her. Since I make a special point of being one of these persons, I venture to swear to Your Majesty that she could not command me to do anything so difficult that I would not always be ready to do everything possible in order to accomplish it.

AT V

TO CHANUT, 31 MARCH 1649

326   I shall give you, if I may, the trouble of reading two of my letters on this occasion. For I assume that you will want to show the other to the Queen of Sweden, and I have saved something for this one which I thought she need not see – namely that I am having much more difficulty deciding about this visit than I had imagined I would have.[1] It is not that I do not have a great desire to serve this Princess. My confidence in your words, and my great admiration and esteem for the character and mind which you

327   ascribe to her, are such that I would wish to undertake an even longer and more arduous journey than one to Sweden in order to have thee honour to offer whatever I may contribute towards the satisfaction of her wishes. I would do so even if she did not occupy such an exalted place, and had only a common birth, if I dared to hope that the journey would be useful to her. But experience has taught me that very few people, even if they have an excellent mind and a great desire for knowledge, can take the time to enter into my thoughts; so that I have no grounds for hoping as much of a Queen who has countless other occupations. Experience has also taught me that although my views are found surprising at first, because they are so different from received opinions, nevertheless once they are understood they appear so simple and so conformable to common sense that they are no longer objects of wonder or regarded as important; for human nature is such that people value only things which they wonder at and do not completely possess. Health is the greatest of all the goods which concern our bodies, but it is the one we least reflect upon and savour. The knowledge of truth is like the health of the soul: once a man possesses it, he thinks no more of it. Although my greatest desire is to communicate openly and freely to everyone all the little I think I know, I meet hardly anyone who condescends to learn it. But I see that those who boast of possessing secrets, in chemistry or judicial astrology, however ignorant and impudent they may be, never fail to find curious people who buy their impostures at a high price.

1 In a letter of 27 February 1649 (AT v 295). Chanut told Descartes of Queen Christina's desire for him to visit Stockholm and give her instruction in his philosophy. In the letter to Chanut of 31 March 1649 which was to be shown to Queen Christina (AT v 323), Descartes declares himself ready without hesitation to make the visit.

For the rest, I have never wished to expect anything of Fortune, and I 328 have tried to conduct my life in such a way that she has never had any power over me. This has, it seems, made Fortune jealous of me, for she never fails to disappoint me whenever she has any chance to do so. I have experienced this in all three of the visits I have made to France since retiring to this country, but especially on the last one, which I had been commanded to make as it were by the King. To get me to make the journey, they sent me letters on parchment, sealed very elegantly, which contained a eulogy more extravagant than I deserve and the offer of a rather handsome pension. And those who sent these letters from the King also wrote and promised me much more as soon as I arrived there. But when I got there unexpected difficulties brought it about that, instead of seeing any sign of what had been promised, I found that one of my friends had had to pay for the letters to be sent to me, and I was obliged to pay him back. So it seems that I went to Paris merely in order to buy a parchment – the most expensive and most useless that I have ever held in my hands. But I do not mind that very much, for I would have regarded it simply as one of those unfortunate things that happen in public affairs, and I would still have been satisfied if I had found that my visit could have some use for those who had summoned me. What most disgusted me, however, is that none of them showed any sign of wishing to know any part of me other than my 329 face. So I came to think that they wanted to have me in France as they would wish to have an elephant or a panther – that is, as a rare specimen and not as something that could be useful.

I do not imagine that anything similar will happen in the place where you are. But my lack of success in all the visits I have made for the last twenty years makes me fear that on this one I shall simply find myself waylaid by highwaymen who will rob me, or involved in a shipwreck which will cost me my life. Nevertheless this will not deter me, if you believe that this incomparable Queen still desires to examine my views, and that she can find the time to do so. If that is so, then I shall be delighted to be so fortunate as to be able to serve her. But if it is not so, and she merely had some curiosity about my views which has now passed, then I beg and urge you to arrange it so that, without displeasing her, I may be excused from making this voyage.

TO MORE, 15 APRIL 1649   AT V

I have received your welcome letter of 5 March at a time when I am 340 distracted by so much other business that I must either write in haste this 341 very minute, or put off replying for many weeks. I have decided on haste: I prefer to seem lacking in skill rather than in courtesy.

Reply to the First Counter-Objections

'Some properties are prior to others.'[1]

Being perceivable by the senses seems to be merely an extraneous description of perceptible things. Nor is it even an adequate description of the things in question; for if it refers to our senses, then it does not apply to the smallest particles of matter; if it refers to other senses such as we might imagine God to construct, it might well apply also to angels and souls. For sensory nerves so fine that they could be moved by the smallest particles of matter are no more intelligible to me than a faculty enabling our mind to sense or perceive other minds directly. Although in extension we easily understand the relation of parts to each other, yet I seem to perceive extension perfectly well without thinking of the relation of these parts to each other. You should admit this even more readily than I, since you conceive extension in such a way that it applies to God; and yet you deny any parts in him.

'It has not been shown that tangibility or impenetrability are essential properties of extended substance.'

If you conceive extension by the relation of the parts to each other, it seems that you cannot deny that each of its parts touches the other 342 adjacent parts. This tangibility is a real property, intrinsic to a thing, unlike the tangibility which is named after the sense of touch. Moreover, it is impossible to conceive of one part of an extended thing penetrating another equal part without thereby understanding that half the total extension is taken away or annihilated; but what is annihilated does not penetrate anything else; and so, in my opinion, it is established that impenetrability belongs to the essence of extension and not to that of anything else.

'I say that there is another, equally genuine, extension.'[2]

At last we are in substantial agreement; there only remains a question of terms, whether this second sort of extension is to be called equally genuine. For my part, in God and angels and in our mind I understand there to be no extension of substance, but only extension of power. An angel can exercise power now on a greater and now on a lesser part of corporeal substance; but if there were no bodies, I could not conceive of any space with which an angel or God would be co-extensive. But to attribute to a substance an

---

1 Here and below the quoted phrases are from More's letter of 5 March (AT v 298). More had argued that body should be defined in terms of perceptibility rather than extension.
2 More had admitted that God and angels were not extended in the sense of being tangible and impenetrable, but maintained they were still genuinely extended.

extension which is only an extension of power is an effect of the preconceived opinion which regards every substance, including God himself, as
imaginable.

Reply to the Second Counter-Objections

'Some parts of empty space would absorb others.'[1]
I repeat here that if they are absorbed, then half the space is destroyed
and ceases to be; but what ceases to be does not penetrate anything else; so
impenetrability must be admitted in every space.

'This interval between worlds would have its own duration.'[2]   343
I think it involves a contradiction to conceive of any duration interven-
ing between the destruction of an earlier world and the creation of a new
one. To relate this duration to a succession of divine thoughts or something similar would simply be an intellectual error, not a genuine perception of anything.
I have already replied to what follows by observing that the extension
which is attributed to incorporeal things is an extension of power and not
of substance. Such a power, being only a mode in the thing to which it is
applied, could not be understood to be extended once the extended thing
corresponding to it is taken away.

Reply to the Penultimate Counter-Objections

'God is positively infinite, that is, exists everywhere.'
I do not agree with this 'everywhere'. You seem here to make God's
infinity consist in his existing everywhere, which is an opinion I cannot
agree with. I think that God is everywhere in virtue of his power; yet in
virtue of his essence he has no relation to place at all. But since in God there
is no distinction between essence and power, I think it is better to argue in
such cases about our own mind or about angels, which are more on the
scale of our own perception, rather than to argue about God.
The difficulties that follow all seem to me to arise from the preconceived
opinion which makes us too accustomed to imagine as extended all
substances including those that we deny to be bodies, and which makes us
too accustomed to philosophize intemperately about conceptual entities,

---

1 More had said that he could not conceive parts of extension changing places unless some
  parts of empty space absorbed others.
2 More wrote 'If God destroyed this world and much later created a new one out of nothing,
  the interval without a world would have its own duration which could be measured in
  days, years, and centuries' (see AT v 302).

attributing to *non-beings* the properties of a *being* or a *thing*. It is import-
344 ant to remember that non-being can have no true attributes, nor can it be
understood in any way in terms of *part and whole, subject, attribute,* etc.
And so you are perfectly right when you conclude that when the mind
considers logical fictions it is 'playing with its own shadows'.

'A certain and finite number of states would be enough.'[1]

It conflicts with my conception to attribute any limit to the world; and I
have no measure of what I should affirm or deny except my own perception. The reason why I say that the world is indeterminate, or indefinite, is
that I can discover no limits in it; but I would not dare to call it infinite,
because I perceive that God is greater than the world, not in extension (for
I have often said I do not think he is strictly speaking extended) but in
perfection.

Reply to the Final Counter-Objections

'If you do this.'[2]

I am not certain that the continuation of my *Philosophy* will ever see the
light of day, because it depends on many experiments which I may never
have the opportunity to do. But I hope to publish this summer a small
treatise on the passions, in which it will be seen how I think that even in us
all the motions of our limbs which accompany our passions are caused not
by the soul but simply by the machinery of the body. The wagging of a
dog's tail is only a movement accompanying a passion, and so is to be
345 sharply distinguished, in my view, from speech, which alone shows the
thought hidden in the body.

'You could say the like about infants.'

Infants are in a different case from animals: I should not judge that
infants were endowed with minds unless I saw that they were of the same
nature as adults; but animals never develop to a point where any certain
sign of thought can be detected in them.

Reply to the Questions

1. It conflicts with my conception, or, what is the same, I think it
involves a contradiction, that the world should be finite or bounded;

---

1 More had claimed that a universe of determinate dimensions would suffice for Cartesian
physics.
2 An allusion to Descartes' hope of explaining animals' behaviour by the construction of
their organs, which More expected would appear in Parts v and vi of the *Principles.*

because I cannot but conceive a space beyond whatever bounds you assign to the universe; and on my view such a space is a genuine body. I do not care if others call this space imaginary and thus regard the world as finite; for I know what are the preconceived opinions that gave rise to this error.

2. When you imagine a sword going through the limits of the universe, you show that you too do not conceive the world as finite; for in reality you conceive every place the sword reaches as a part of the world, though you give the name 'vacuum' to what you conceive . . .

6. I have tried to explain most of what you here ask in my treatise on the (347) passions. I will add only that I have not yet met anything connected with the nature of material things for which I could not very easily think up a mechanical explanation. It is no disgrace for a philosopher to believe that God can move a body, even though he does not regard God as corporeal; so it is no more of a disgrace for him to think much the same of other incorporeal substances. Of course I do not think that any mode of action belongs univocally to both God and his creatures, but I must confess that the only idea I can find in my mind to represent the way in which God or an angel can move matter is the one which shows me the way in which I am conscious I can move my own body by my own thought.

Moreover, my mind cannot be more or less extended or concentrated in relation to place, in virtue of its substance, but only in virtue of its power, which it can apply to larger or smaller bodies . . .

TO [BRASSET], 23 APRIL 1649   AT V

No one has found it strange that Ulysses left the enchanted isles of   349
Calypso and Circe, where he could enjoy every imaginable pleasure, and that he scorned the song of the sirens, in order to go and live in a rocky and infertile country. For this was his birthplace. But consider a man who, born in the gardens of Touraine, now resides in a country where there is conceivably more milk, if not so much honey, as in the land which God promised to the Israelites. Such a man, I confess, cannot find it so easy to decide to leave this land in order to live in a land of bears, rocks and ice. But this country is also inhabited by human beings, and governed by a Queen who possesses in herself more knowledge, intelligence and reason than all   350 the learned churchmen and academics spawned by the fertile lands where I have resided. And so I am convinced that the beauty of a place is not necessary for wisdom, and that human beings are not like trees, which are never seen to grow so well when they are transplanted in soil less rich than the soil in which they had been sown. You will say that in return for the important and genuine news which you so kindly imparted to me, I am giving you only fictions and fables. But at present my solitude cannot yield

any better fruits. Moreover, my delight upon learning that France has avoided being shipwrecked in a very great storm has so carried me away that I cannot say anything serious here, except that I am, etc.[1]

AT V   TO CLERSELIER, 23 APRIL 1649

353   I will not spend long in thanking you for all the care and precautions you have taken to ensure that the letters which I have been honoured to receive from that northern country should reach me;[2] for I am already so obliged to you, and have so many other proofs of your friendship, that it is nothing new to me. I will only say that none have gone astray, and that I am resolved to make the journey to which the latest letters invite me, though I was at first more reluctant than perhaps you can imagine. My journey to Paris last summer disheartened me; and I can assure you that the extraordinary esteem in which I hold M. Chanut, and the certainty I have of his friendship, are not the least important reasons which have made me decide to go.

354   I do not expect that the treatise on the passions will be printed before I arrive in Sweden; for I have been indolent in revising it and adding the things you thought lacking, which will increase its length by a third. It will contain three parts, of which the first will deal with the passions in general, and incidentally the nature of the soul, the second with the six primitive passions, and the third with all the others.

        As for the difficulties which you kindly put to me, I answer the first as follows. My purpose[3] was to base a proof of the existence of God on the idea or thought which we have of him, and so I thought that I was obliged first of all to distinguish all our thoughts into certain classes, so as to observe which are those that can deceive. By showing that not even chimeras contain falsehood in themselves, I hoped to forestall those who might reject my reasoning on the grounds that our idea of God belongs to the class of chimeras. I was also obliged to distinguish the ideas which are born with us from those which come from elsewhere, or are made by us, in order to forestall those who might say that the idea of God is made by us or acquired by hearing others speak of him. Moreover, the reason why I insisted on our lack of certainty concerning the convictions that arise from all the ideas which we think come from outside was in order to show that

1 The 'storm' was the threat of civil war, which was averted by the signing of a peace treaty by the Court and the deputies of Parliament.
2 Descartes is referring to letters of 12 December 1648 from Queen Christina and Chanut, and of 27 February 1649 from Chanut, which had been sent to Descartes in Paris, and were forwarded to Holland by Clerselier.
3 In the Third Meditation.

there is no single idea which gives such certain knowledge as the one we have of God. Finally, I could not have said 'there is another way'[1] if I had not first rejected all the others and thus prepared my readers to understand what I was about to write. 355

2. To the second I reply that I think I see very clearly that there cannot be an infinite regress in the ideas I possess, because I feel myself to be finite, and in the place where I wrote that,[2] I am acknowledging in myself nothing except what I know to be there. Later, when I say that I dare not exclude an infinite regress, I am referring to the works of God, whom I know to be infinite; and so it is not for me to set any limits to his works.[3]

3. To the words 'substance', 'duration', 'number',[4] etc. I could have added, 'truth', 'perfection', 'order' and many others of a class which is not easy to delimit. In each case there might be room for discussion whether or not they should be distinguished from the first which I mentioned; for †there is no distinction between truth and the thing or substance that is true, nor between perfection and the thing that is perfect†, etc. That is why I merely said 'and anything else of this kind'.

4. †By 'infinite substance' I mean a substance which has actually infinite and immense, true and real perfections. This is not an accident added to the notion of substance, but the very essence of substance taken absolutely and bounded by no defects; these defects, in respect of substance, are accidents; but infinity or infinitude is not.† It should be observed that I never use the word 'infinite' to signify the mere lack of limits (which is something negative, for which I have used the term 'indefinite') but to signify a real thing, which is incomparably greater than all those which are in some way limited. 356

5. I say[5] that the notion I have of the infinite is in me before that of the finite because, by the mere fact that I conceive being, or that which is, without thinking whether it is finite or infinite, what I conceive is infinite being; but in order to conceive a finite being, I have to take away something from this general notion of being, which must accordingly be there first.

6. 'This idea, I say, is true in the highest degree.'[6] Truth consists in *being*, and falsehood only in *non-being*, so that the idea of the infinite, which includes all being, includes all that there is of truth in things, and

1 Med. III: AT VII 40; CSM II 27.
2 Med. III: AT VII 42; CSM II 29.
3 Med. III: AT VII 50; CSM II 34.
4 Med. III: AT VII 44; CSM II 30.
5 Med. III: AT VII 45; CSM II 31.
6 Med. III: AT VII 46; CSM II 31.

cannot contain anything false; and this is so even if you want to suppose it untrue that that infinite being exists.

7. 'It is enough that I understand the infinite.'[1] [†]I mean, that it is sufficient for me to understand *the fact that God is not grasped by me* in order to understand God in very truth and as he is, provided I judge also that there are in him all perfections which I clearly understand, and also many more which I cannot grasp.[†]

357　　8. 'As regards my parents, even if . . .'[2] That is to say, even though everything we are accustomed to believe of them is perhaps true, that is, that they begat our bodies, still I cannot imagine that they made me, in so far as I consider myself only as a thing which thinks, because I see no relation between the physical act by which I am accustomed to believe they begat me, and the production of a substance which thinks.

[†]That every deception depends on some defect is manifest to me by the natural light; for a being in which there is no imperfection cannot tend to non-being, that is, cannot have non-being, or non-good, or non-true as its end or purpose, since these three things are the same. It is manifest that in every deception there is falsehood, and that falsehood is something non-true and therefore non-being and non-good.[†] Forgive me for having interlarded this letter with Latin; the brief time I have had to write it has not allowed me to think of words, and I only want to assure you that I am, etc.

AT V　　　　　TO PRINCESS ELIZABETH, JUNE 1649

359　　Since Your Highness wishes to know what I have decided about the visit to Sweden, I can tell you that I still intend to go there provided the Queen

360　indicates that she still wishes me to. A week ago M. Chanut, our resident in that country, passed through here on his way to France. He spoke so glowingly of this marvellous Queen that the voyage no longer seems so long and arduous as it did previously. But I shall depart only after getting further news from this country; and I shall try to await the return of M. Chanut in order to make the voyage with him (for I hope they will send him back to Sweden). For the rest, I would count myself extremely fortunate if I could be of service to Your Highness while I am there. I shall certainly look for opportunities to do so, and I shall not hesitate to write and tell you quite openly whatever I may do or think on this matter. For I am incapable of having any intention which would be detrimental to those whom I am obliged to respect, and I observe the maxim that the most useful and sure

1 Med. III: AT VII 47; CSM II 32.
2 Med. III: AT VII 50; CSM II 35.

ways are those which are just and honest. So even if my letters are seen, I trust that they will not be interpreted badly, or fall into the hands of people who are so unjust that they think badly of me for doing my duty and for openly professing that I am, etc.

TO FREINSHEMIUS, JUNE 1649

AT V

... I have one more favour to ask you. I am being urged by a friend[1] to (363) give him the little treatise on the passions which I had the honour of offering to Her Majesty some time ago. I know that he plans to have it printed with a preface of his own, but I have not yet dared to send it to him, because I do not know whether Her Majesty will approve of something which was presented to her in private being published without a dedication to her. But because this treatise is too small to deserve to bear the name of so great a Princess, to whom, if this sort of homage is not 364 unpleasing to her, I might some day be able to offer a more important work, I thought that perhaps she would not object to my granting this friend's request. That is what I ask you most humbly to tell me, because my chief concern is to try to obey and please her ...

TO CARCAVI, 11 JUNE 1649

AT V

I am greatly obliged to you for your kind offer to enter into correspon- 365 dence with me concerning scholarly matters: I accept this offer as a favour which I shall try to deserve by serving you in every way that I can. During the life of the good Father Mersenne,[2] I enjoyed the advantage of always being informed, in painstaking detail, about everything that was going on in the learned world, even though I never made any inquiries about such matters. In this way, if I ever raised any questions, he freely gave me the answers, and advised me about all the observations that he and others had made, all the curious devices that people had discovered or were seeking, all the new books which enjoyed any favour and all the controversies which the learned were engaged upon.

I fear I would be tiresome if I requested all these things from you. But I hope you will not be displeased if I ask you to inform me about the success of an experiment[3] which M. Pascal is said to have done or to have had done

---

1 The identity of this friend is unknown. Baillet identifies him as Clerselier, but Adam suggests Picot. The friend's letters and Descartes' replies were printed as a preface to the *Passions of the Soul*, which appeared in November 1649 with a dedication to Queen Christina (cf. AT XI 322ff; CSM I 326f).
2 Father Mersenne had died in September 1648.
3 See above, p. 328.

in the mountains of Auvergne, in order to discover whether mercury rises higher in a tube at the base of a mountain, and how much higher it is than on the top of the mountain. I should rightly expect to hear about this from him rather than from you, since it was I who advised him to do this experiment two years ago, and who assured him that I did not doubt it would be successful even though I had not done it myself . . .

AT V   TO CARCAVI, 17 AUGUST 1649

391   I am greatly obliged to you for the trouble you have taken to write and tell me about the success of M. Pascal's experiment with mercury,[1] showing that it rises less in a tube on a mountain-top than in one lower down. I had some interest in learning this because it was I who had asked him to try the experiment two years ago, and I had assured him of its success, as it agrees completely with my principles; without these principles he would not even have thought of it, since he was of the opposite opinion. Previously he sent me a brief publication in which he described his first experiments on the vacuum, and undertook to refute my subtle matter, and if you see him I would be glad if you will let him know that I am still waiting for this refutation, and that I shall receive it in good part, as I
392   have always received objections made against me that are not mere vilifications . . .

AT V   TO MORE, AUGUST 1649

402   When I received your letter of 23 July I was just on the point of sailing to Sweden.[2]
          1. 'Do angels have sense-perception in the strict sense, and are they corporeal or not?'[3]
          I reply that the human mind separated from the body does not have sense-perception strictly so called; but it is not clear by natural reason alone whether angels are created like minds distinct from bodies, or like minds united to bodies. I never decide about questions on which I have no certain reasons, and I never allow room for conjectures. I agree that we should not think of God except as being what all good people would wish there to be if he did not exist.
          Your counter-objection concerning the acceleration of motion, to prove that the same substance can occupy a larger or smaller place at different

---

1 See above, p. 328.
2 In April 1649 a Swedish admiral was sent to Descartes, and Chanut visited him in June to persuade him to accept the invitation to Sweden. Descartes left on 31 August.
3 A quotation from More's letter of 23 July 1649 (AT v 377).

times, is ingenious,[1] but there is a great disparity, in that motion is not a substance but a mode, and a mode of such a kind that we can inwardly conceive how it can diminish or increase in the same place. For each type of being there are appropriate notions, and in judging about any being we must use these notions instead of comparisons with other beings. Thus 403 what is appropriate to shape is not what is appropriate to motion; and neither of these is what is appropriate to an extended thing. Remember that nothing has no properties, and that what is commonly called empty space is not nothing, but a real body deprived of all its accidents (i.e. all the things which can be present or absent without their possessor ceasing to be). Anyone who has fully realized this, and who has observed how each part of this space or body differs from all others and is impenetrable, will easily see that no other thing can have the same divisibility, tangibility and impenetrability.

I said that God is extended in virtue of his power, because that power manifests itself, or can manifest itself, in extended being. It is certain that God's essence must be present everywhere for his power to be able to manifest itself everywhere; but I deny that it is there in the manner of extended being, that is, in the way in which I just described an extended thing . . .

The transfer which I call 'motion' is no less something existent than shape is: it is a mode in a body.[2] The power causing motion may be the power of God himself preserving the same amount of transfer in matter as 404 he put in it in the first moment of creation; or it may be the power of a created substance, like our mind, or of any other such thing to which he gave the power to move a body. In a created substance this power is a mode, but it is not a mode in God. Since this is not easy for everyone to understand, I did not want to discuss it in my writings. I was afraid of seeming inclined to favour the view of those who consider God as a world-soul united to matter.

I agree that 'if matter is left to itself and receives no impulse from anywhere' it will remain entirely still. But it receives an impulse from God, who preserves the same amount of motion or transfer in it as he placed in it at the beginning. And this transfer is no more violent for matter than rest is: the term 'violent' refers only to our will, which is said to suffer violence when something happens which goes against it. In nature, however, nothing is violent: it is equally natural for bodies to collide with each other, and perhaps to disintegrate, as it is for them to be still. I think that what

1 More had argued 'numerically the same motion can occupy now a larger body, now a smaller one, on your own principles'.
2 See *Principles*, Part II, art. 25: AT VIIIA 53; CSM I 233.

causes you difficulty in this matter is that you conceive of a certain force in a quiescent body, by which it resists motion, as being something positive, namely as a certain action distinct from the body's being at rest; whereas in fact the force is nothing but a modal entity.

You observe correctly that 'motion, being a mode of body, cannot pass from one body to another'. But that is not what I wrote; indeed I think that motion, considered as such a mode, continually changes. For there is one
405 mode in the first point of a body A in that it is separated from the first point of a body B; and another mode in that it is separated from the second point; and another mode in that it is separated from the third point; and so on. But when I said that the same amount of motion always remains in matter, I meant this about the force which impels its parts, which is applied at different times to different parts of matter in accordance with the laws set out in articles 45 and following of Part Two.[1] So there is no need for you to worry about the transmigration of rest from one object to another, since not even motion, considered as a mode which is the contrary to rest, transmigrates in that fashion.

You add that body seems to you to be 'alive with a stupid and drunken life'. This, I take it, is just a fine phrase; but I must tell you once for all, with the candour which you permit me, that nothing takes us further from the discovery of truth so much as setting up as true something of which we are convinced by no positive reason, but only by our own will. That is what happens when we have invented or imagined something and afterwards take pleasure in our fictions, as you do in your corporeal angels, your shadow of the divine essence, and the rest. No one should entertain any such thoughts, because to do so is to bar the road to truth against oneself.

AT V   TO PRINCESS ELIZABETH, 9 OCTOBER 1649

429   Having arrived in Stockholm four or five days ago, I believe that one of my first duties is to renew the offers of my very humble service to Your Highness, so that you might know that the change of air and of country cannot change or diminish my devotion in any way. So far I have had the honour of seeing the Queen only twice; but already I think I know her well enough to venture to say that she has as much merit and more virtue than she is reputed to possess. Together with the generosity and majesty that shine forth in all her actions, one sees in her such sweetness and goodness that all who love virtue and have the honour of approaching her have no choice but to be utterly devoted to serving her. One of the first things she asked me was whether I had any news of you, and I did not hesitate to tell

1 *Principles*: AT VIIIA 67; CSM I 244.

her at once what I thought of Your Highness; for, observing the strength of
her mind, I did not fear that this would make her jealous, just as I am   430
certain that Your Highness will not be jealous if I write frankly my
opinions of the Queen. She is strongly drawn to scholarly pursuits; but
because I do not know that she has ever read any philosophy, I cannot
judge her tastes in this subject, or whether she will have time for it, and
consequently whether I shall be capable of giving her any satisfaction or of
being in any way useful to her. Her great passion for scholarly knowledge
is driving her at the present time to learn Greek and to collect many ancient
books; but perhaps this will pass. And while it goes on, the virtue I observe
in this Princess will oblige me always to prefer the utility of serving her to
the desire of pleasing her. Thus it will not prevent me from honestly telling
her my opinions; and if they fail to please her, which I do not think will
happen, I shall at least have the satisfaction of having done my duty, and
this will give me an opportunity to return that much sooner to my solitude,
away from which it is difficult for me to make any advances in the search
for truth; for this is where my chief good in this life lies. M. Freinshemius
has secured Her Majesty's approval for my going to the castle only at the
times when it pleases her to give me the honour of speaking with her. Thus
it will not be hard for me to perform my courtly duties, and that suits my
temperament very well. In the end, however, although I have a great   431
veneration for Her Majesty, I do not think that anything is capable of
keeping me in this country longer than next summer; but I cannot completely guarantee the future. I can only assure you that I shall be for all my
life, etc.

TO BREGY, 15 JANUARY 1650   AT V

I take it as a great compliment that you have gone to the trouble of   460
writing to me from Hamburg, and I wish I had some news worth sending
you. But since I had the pleasure of last writing, I have seen the Queen only
four or five times, always in the morning in her library, in the company of
M. Freinshemius. So I have had no opportunity to speak about any matter
that concerns you. A fortnight ago she went to Uppsala. I did not go with
her, nor have I seen her since she returned on Thursday evening. I know
also that our ambassador saw her only once before her visit to Uppsala,
apart from his first audience at which I was present.[1] I have not made any   467
other visits, nor have I heard about any. This makes me think that during
the winter men's thoughts are frozen here, like the water. But for all that,

1 Chanut became French ambassador in September 1649, and the mentioned audience took
  place on 23 December 1649.

my desire to be of service to you can never grow cold. I am greatly obliged to you for having spoken so well about me to M. Salvius. I fear only that if I am still here when he comes, he will find me to be so different from the man you described that he will be able to see my faults more easily. But I swear to you that my desire to return to my solitude grows stronger with each passing day, and indeed I do not know whether I can wait here until you return. It is not that I do not still fervently wish to serve the Queen, or that she does not show me as much goodwill as I may reasonably hope for. But I am not in my element here. I desire only peace and quiet, which are benefits that the most powerful kings on earth cannot give to those who are unable to acquire them for themselves. I pray God that you are granted the good things which you desire, and I beg you to be assured that I am, Sir, your must humble and obedient servant, DESCARTES.

Notes on Descartes' correspondents

Arnauld, Antoine (1612–94), French theologian and philosopher. After studying theology at the Sorbonne, Arnauld was ordained as a Roman Catholic priest in 1641. A relentless critic of the Jesuits and fearless supporter of the unorthodox theology of the Jansenists, he was expelled from the Sorbonne in 1656, and persecuted on and off for the rest of his life. After a period of exile in Holland, he settled in Belgium, where he remained until his death. At the invitation of his friend Mersenne (*q.v.*), Arnauld wrote a set of objections to the *Meditations* which were included in the first and subsequent editions as the Fourth Objections. Along with Pierre Nicole he wrote the influential *Logic or the Art of Thinking* (1662).

Balzac, Jean-Louis Guez de (1597–1654), French man of letters and patron of the arts. After spending some time as a student in Leiden and Rome, Balzac hoped to pursue a career in politics; but when his hopes failed, he retired to his house in the country and devoted the rest of his life to literature. His *Letters* (brief essays on moral and literary themes) which appeared first in 1624, were enormously popular, and had a considerable influence on the development of modern French prose.

Beeckman, Isaac (1588–1637), Dutch physician and scholar. After their first meeting in Holland in 1618 Beeckman became Descartes' mentor, introducing him to all that was new in science and mathematics. Descartes' first work, the *Compendium of Music*, was written at Beeckman's request. The friendship between the two men cooled between 1628 and 1631, but was renewed, if less warmly, thereafter. Beeckman graduated in medicine from the University of Caen in 1618, when he began his career as an academic teacher. He became Rector of the University of Utrecht, where he remained until his death.

Brasset, Henri (1591–1654), French diplomat. Brasset spent some time in the French embassies in Brussels and The Hague, and later became secretary to various members of the French government. He was French resident in The Hague from 1648 to 1654.

Brégy, Vicomte de Flécelles (1615–89), French diplomat. In the autumn of 1649 Brégy, at the time French Ambassador to Poland, he was in Stockholm on a diplomatic mission. There he met Descartes, who had himself recently arrived, and soon became his friend.

Buitendijk, one of the curators of the University of Dordrecht, about whom little is known.

Burman, Frans (1628–79), a Dutch scholar who, as a young man of twenty, visited Descartes at his home in Egmond Binnen in order to discuss Descartes' philosophy with him. Burman's detailed record of his interview, the *Conversation with Burman*, throws light on some vexed questions in the interpretation of Descartes' philosophy.

Carcavi, Pierre de (*c.* 1600–84), French government officer. After Mersenne's (*q.v.*) death in 1648 Carcavi offered to take his place as Descartes' informant on all that was happening in the world of science. Descartes willingly accepted the offer, though Carcavi turned out to be a disappointment, being a poor mathematician.

Chanut, Hector-Pierre (1601–62), French diplomat. Descartes got to know Chanut, one of his best friends, through Chanut's brother-in-law Clerselier (*q.v.*). It was Chanut who, as French resident in Stockholm (1645–9), persuaded Descartes to accept Queen Christina's invitation to Sweden in 1649; he was also the friend from whom Descartes caught his fatal respiratory infection in February 1650. Appointed French Ambassador to Sweden in 1649, Chanut was later Ambassador to Holland (1653–5).

Charlet, Etienne (1570–1652), Jesuit priest and theologian. Charlet was a teacher at the College of la Flèche, where Descartes had been his pupil (1606–14). He went on to become head of the Jesuits in Paris and assistant to the head of the Jesuits in Rome. He appears to have been of some help in smoothing the way for Descartes' philosophy in the Catholic Church. Descartes' warm affection for him remained undiminished.

Christina, Queen of Sweden (1626–89). Daughter of King Gustav II, Adolph (killed at the battle of Lützen when she was six) and Maria Eleonora of Brandenburg, Christina was crowned when she came of age in 1644. Within a few years she made her Court in Stockholm a cultural centre of dazzling brilliance. After her conversion to Roman Catholicism (proscribed in Sweden), she abdicated from the throne in 1654, departing for Rome on the day of her abdication. In 1647, hearing through his friend Chanut (*q.v.*) that the Queen was interested in his philosophy, Descartes sent her a copy of his correspondence with Princess Elizabeth (*q.v.*) and a 'little treatise' on the passions, an early draft of his last book *The Passions of the Soul* which was dedicated to the Queen and published in November 1649. After several overtures, Descartes accepted the Queen's invitation to Stockholm, where he arrived early in September 1649. The last work Descartes composed was verses for a ballet in celebration of the Queen's birthday.

Clerselier, Claude (1614–84), French government officer. A close friend of Descartes, Clerselier was the first editor of his writings. He may have been the anonymous friend who brought out *The Passions of the Soul* in 1649. He produced three volumes of Descartes' letters (1657, 1659, 1667), the *Treatise on Man* (1664), *The World* (1677), and other works.

Colvius, Andreas (1594–1676), Dutch Protestant minister and amateur scientist. A native of Dordrecht, where he spent most of his life, Colvius was a friend of Beeckman (*q.v.*).

Debeaune, Florimond (1601–52), French mathematician and student of astronomy and astrology. A keen supporter of Descartes, Debeaune produced a short commentary on the *Geometry*, which was included in the 1649 edition of that work.

Delaunay, the Abbé, perhaps Jean de Launay (1603–78), a French theologian, about whom not much is known.

Elizabeth, Princess of Bohemia (1618–80), daughter of Frederick IV of Bohemia and Elizabeth Stuart (daughter of James VI of Scotland and I of England). After the defeat of Bohemia by the Austrians in 1620 Princess Elizabeth's family went into exile in The Hague, under the protection of the Prince of Orange. Hearing in October 1642 that Princess Elizabeth had read the *Meditations* with enthusiasm, Descartes wrote to her offering to elucidate any difficulties, thus beginning a remarkable correspondence which lasted until his death in 1650. He dedicated *The Principles of Philosophy* (1644) to the Princess, and his last book, *The Passions of the Soul* (1649), began as a little treatise on the subject that he wrote for her in 1646.

Freinshemius (Johannes Freinsheim, 1608–60), German classical scholar. Freinshemius became Professor of Rhetoric at Uppsala University in 1642 and Librarian to Queen Christina (*q.v.*) in 1647. He was responsible for arranging Descartes' activities at the Swedish Court in 1649. He left Sweden in 1651 and became a professor in Heidelberg.

Fromondus (Libert Froidmont, 1587–1653), Belgian theologian. Fromondus succeeded the controversial theologian Cornelius Jansen (1585–1638) in the Chair of Holy Scripture in the University of Louvain in 1639, which he held until his death. A very conservative thinker, he supported the doctrine of the immobility of the earth.

Gibieuf, Guillaume (1591–1650), French Catholic priest and theologian. A member of the Sorbonne and the religious order of the Oratory in Paris, Gibieuf took a keen, but critical, interest in Descartes' philosophy. His favourite topic was the freedom of the will, on which he published a book, *De Libertate Dei et Creaturae* (1631).

Golius (Jacob Gool, 1596–1667), Dutch mathematician. Golius succeeded Wilebrord van Snel (1580–1626) in the Chair of Mathematics at Leiden University in 1626. He met Descartes when the philosopher was a student of mathematics at Leiden in 1630. It was through Golius that Descartes got to know Constantijn Huygens (*q.v.*), one of his principal correspondents. Golius became Professor of Oriental Languages at Leiden in 1641.

Grandamy, Jacques (1588–1672), French Jesuit priest. A physicist and astronomer, Grandamy taught philosophy at various Jesuit colleges in France. In his book *Nova Demonstratio Immobilitatis Terrae* (1645), he tried to demonstrate the doctrine of the immobility of the earth.

Hobbes, Thomas (1588–1679), the most gifted English philosopher of his time. After graduating from Oxford University in 1608 Hobbes became private tutor to William Cavendish, thus beginning a lifelong association with the Cavendish family. A prominent royalist, he fled to France as a political refugee in 1640. There he joined Mersenne's (*q.v.*) circle, and wrote, at Mersenne's invitation, the Third Objections to the *Meditations*. During his exile in France, Hobbes wrote some of his most important books, including *De Cive* (1642), *De Corpore* (1655), *De Homine* (1658), and his masterpiece, *Leviathan* (1651). Making his peace with the Commonwealth regime, he returned to England in 1651, and regained favour at the Restoration of Charles II in 1660. He retained the full vigour of his intellect till the end of his long and eventful life.

Hogelande, Cornelis van (1590–1662), Dutch physician. Hogelande was a good friend of Descartes, who entrusted him with the safekeeping of a chest of papers on his departure for Sweden in August 1649.

Huygens, Constantijn (1596–1687), Dutch diplomat and amateur scientist. Huygens was an enthusiastic supporter of Descartes and one of his principal correspondents. A versatile and learned man of the world, he was introduced to Descartes by Golius (*q.v.*) in 1632, and the two men became good friends. Not himself an original thinker, he was the father of the famous mathematician and physicist Christian Huygens (1629–95).

Mersenne, Marin (1588–1648), Catholic priest, theologian, physicist and polymath. A man of inexhaustible curiosity and energy, Mersenne conducted a vast correspondence with most of the great thinkers of his age, acting as a sort of clearing-house of ideas and information. Like Descartes he was educated at the College of La Flèche. Their friendship dates from about 1625 or earlier. From the beginning of their correspondence in 1629 until the end of 1647 Mersenne kept Descartes constantly supplied with questions and news 'in painstaking detail about everything that was going on in the learned world', as Descartes himself said. Mersenne was closely involved in the publication of both the *Discourse on the Method* and the *Meditations*, and he put together the seven sets of Objections and Replies to the latter work. He was a member of the monastic order of Minims in Paris. He died on 1 September 1648, shortly after his last meeting with Descartes in Paris.

Mesland, Denis (1616–72), Jesuit priest. An enthusiastic supporter of Descartes, Mesland produced an abstract of the *Meditations*. He went to North America as a missionary in 1645, and was to remain there until his death. His intellectual gifts, Descartes thought, would have been better spent converting the heathens at home.

Meysonnier, Lazare (1602–72), French physician and student of astrology and alchemy. Honorary physician to Louis XIV, he wrote numerous books on medicine. Descartes thought more highly of his medical than his alchemical talents.

More, Henry (1614–87), English philosopher and poet. One of the Cambridge Platonists, More was respectfully critical of Descartes' theory of the relation between the mind and the body. He published their correspondence on this topic under the title *The Immortality of the Soul* in 1659. His own philosophical writings include *Enchiridion Metaphysicum* (1671).

Morin, Jean-Baptiste (1583–1656), French mathematician, physician and astrologer. Morin was Professor of Mathematics at the Collège de France from 1629 until his death. A very conservative thinker, he supported the doctrine of the immobility of the earth in his book *Pro Telluris Quiete* (1634).

Newcastle, Marquess of (William Cavendish, 1593–1676), patron of letters. A prominent royalist, Newcastle was governor of the future Charles II, and was a commander in the Civil War. He fled to the Continent in 1644, living as a political refugee in France and Holland. He returned to England on the Restoration of Charles II in 1660, and was made a Duke in 1665. In 1647 (or 1648) he gave a dinner in Paris at which Descartes was reconciled with his old critics Pierre Gassendi and Thomas Hobbes (*q.v.*).

Noël, Etienne (1581–1660), Jesuit priest and physicist. A friend of Descartes, Noël was rector of various Jesuit colleges in France. His special interest was the vacuum and the weight of the air.

Plempius (Vopiscus-Fortunatus Plemp, 1601–61), Dutch physician and philosopher. Plempius studied philosophy under Fromondus (*q.v.*) at Louvain and medicine at Leiden, Padua and Bologna. After practising medicine in Amsterdam he became Professor of Medicine at Louvain in 1633, and Rector in 1637. A friend of Descartes from about 1629, he became more and more critical of Descartes' philosophy in his later years. His *Fundamenta Medicinae* was published in 1638.

Pollot, Alphonse (1602–68), French soldier and courtier. Pollot was gentleman-in-waiting to the Prince of Orange. His friendship with Descartes dates from early 1638, when he sent the philosopher, through Reneri (*q.v.*), some objections to the *Discourse on the Method* and *Essays*.

Regius (Henri le Roy, 1598–1679), Dutch physician. His teaching of Descartes' ideas on physics and physiology led to his appointment to the Chair of Medicine at the University of Utrecht in 1638. Partly because of his brash style, there was an intense reaction against him led by the Professor of Theology, Voetius (*q.v.*), who attempted, unsuccessfully, to have him removed from his Chair. For several years Regius enjoyed an amicable pupil–teacher relationship with Descartes, who supported him in his battles with Voetius; but relations between the two men deteriorated after Regius published his *Fundamenta Physices* in 1646. Regius, Descartes complained, had not only borrowed his ideas but had also seriously distorted them and denied their metaphysical foundations. Descartes repudiated the book in the preface to the French edition of *The Principles of Philosophy*

(1647). Regius responded by bringing out an anonymous broadsheet which set out all the points where he disagreed with Descartes. Descartes counter-attacked with his *Comments on a Certain Broadsheet* (1648).

Reneri (Henri Regnier, 1593–1639), French philosopher. A pupil of Fromondus (*q.v.*) at Louvain, Reneri became a Protestant, and was disowned by his staunchly Catholic parents. In 1634 he was appointed as the first Professor of Philosophy at the newly founded University of Utrecht, which became the first university to teach Descartes' ideas. He was a good friend of Descartes until his death.

Silhon, Jean de (*c.* 1600–67), French government secretary and amateur theologian. Silhon was a good friend of Balzac (*q.v.*) and a founding member of the French Academy. He was instrumental in the award of a royal pension to Descartes in 1647 (which he never drew). His book *The Two Verities: God and the Immortality of the Soul* was published in 1626.

Vatier, Antoine (1596–1659), French Jesuit priest and theologian. A sympathetic friend of Descartes among the Jesuits, Vatier was a teacher at Descartes' old school, the College of la Flèche, where he had himself been a pupil.

Ville-Bressieu, Etienne de, French physician, chemist and engineer to the King of France. A good friend of Descartes, whom he had known from about 1626.

Voetius (Gisbert Voët, 1589–1676), Dutch theologian. Voetius was Professor of Theology, and later Rector, at the University of Utrecht. He waged a relentless campaign against the Professor of Medicine, Regius (*q.v.*), who was somewhat brashly propagating Descartes' philosophy in the University. In 1641 Voetius tried, unsuccessfully, to have Regius removed from his Chair; in 1642 he succeeded in getting the Senate of the University to issue a public condemnation of Descartes' philosophy and to forbid Regius to teach anything but medicine. A talented polemicist himself, Descartes gave an account of this controversy in the *Letter to Father Dinet* which was included in the second edition of the *Meditations* in 1642. Voetius' complaint was that the Cartesian philosophy controverted traditional doctrines in philosophy and theology. He persuaded his pupil Martin Schook to publish an attack on Descartes' philosophy; and Descartes counter-attacked with the highly inflammatory *Letter to Voetius*, for which he would have been sued for libel had it not been for the intervention of the French Ambassador and the Prince of Orange.

Vorstius (Adolph Vorster, 1597–1663), Dutch physician. Vorstius became Professor of Medicine at the University of Utrecht in 1625, and was later Rector.

Table of citations of Descartes' works

AT VII 111; CSM II 80: 166
AT VII 112; CSM II 71: 165
AT VII 114; CSM II 82: 166
AT VII 118; CSM II 84: 187
AT VII 119; CSM II 85: 174
AT VII 120; CSM II 86: 201

Second Set of Objections and Replies (Mersenne)
AT VII 138; CSM II 99: 230
AT VII 139; CSM II 100: 340
AT VII 140; CSM II 100: 333
AT VII 144; CSM II 103: 230
AT VII 148; CSM II 105: 191

Fourth Set of Objections and Replies (Arnauld)
AT VII 208; CSM II 146: 176
AT VII 209; CSM II 147: 176
AT VII 213; CSM II 150: 176
AT VII 233; CSM II 163: 230
AT VII 235ff; CSM II 165ff: 213
AT VII 245; CSM II 171: 197, 334
AT VII 246; CSM II 171: 335, 336
AT VII 248–55; CSM II 173–9: 28, 210
AT VII 251; CSM II 174: 241
AT VII 252; CSM II 175: 235, 242, 279
AT VII 253–6; CSM II 176–8: 199, 213

Fifth Set of Objections and Replies (Gassendi)
AT VII 351; CSM II 243: 189n
AT VII 354; CSM II 245: 189n
AT VII 357; CSM II 247: 191
AT VII 367; CSM II 253: 193
AT VII 369; CSM II 254: 192, 193
AT VII 370; CSM II 255: 192
AT VII 373; CSM II 257: 339
AT VII 373; CSM II 257: 341
AT VII 374; CSM II 257: 194
AT VII 381; CSM II 262: 344
AT VII 383; CSM II 263: 196
AT VII 384; CSM II 263: 196

Sixth Set of Objections and Replies
AT VII 413; CSM II 278: 180
AT VII 415; CSM II 279: 179
AT VII 417; CSM II 281: 179
AT VII 425; CSM II 287: 194

Index